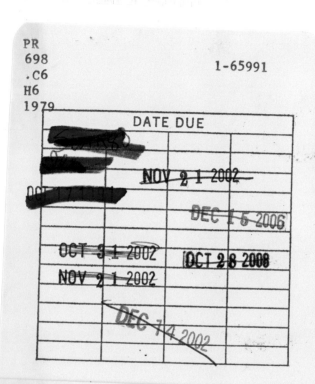

m/w

# The ornament of action

*Text and Performance in Restoration Comedy*

Thomas Betterton

# The ornament of action
## Text and Performance in Restoration Comedy

PETER HOLLAND

*Fellow and Director of Studies in English*
*Trinity Hall, Cambridge*

CAMBRIDGE UNIVERSITY PRESS

CAMBRIDGE

LONDON · NEW YORK · MELBOURNE

Published by the Syndics of the Cambridge University Press
The Pitt Building, Trumpington Street, Cambridge CB2 1RP
Bentley House, 200 Euston Road, London NW1 2DB
32 East 57th Street, New York, NY 10022, USA
296 Beaconsfield Parade, Middle Park, Melbourne 3206, Australia

First published 1979

Photoset and printed in Malta
by Interprint (Malta) Ltd

*Library of Congress cataloguing in Publication Data*

Holland, Peter, 1951–
The ornament of action

Bibliography: p. 274
Includes index.
1. English drama – Restoration, 1660–1700 – History and
criticism.   2. English drama (Comedy) – History and
criticism.   3. Theatre – Great Britain – History – 17th
century.   I. Title.
PR698.C6H6   1979        822'.052        78–1157

ISBN 0 521 22048 3

FOR ADAM

*Stage-director* No; the Art of the Theatre is neither acting nor the play, it is not scene nor dance, but it consists of all the elements of which these things are composed: action, which is the very spirit of acting; words, which are the body of the play; line and colour, which are the very heart of the scene; rhythm, which is the very essence of dance . . . A dramatic poem is to be read. A drama is not to be read, but to be seen upon the stage . . . And now, just as you must not confound the dramatic poem with the drama, neither must you confound the dramatic poet with the dramatist. The first writes for the reader, or listener, the second writes for the audience of a theatre.

E. G. Craig, *On the Art of the Theatre* (1911)

# Contents

*List of illustrations*                                              viii
*Preface*                                                             ix
*Note on references*                                                 xiii

1  The text and the audience                                          1
2  Performance: theatres and scenery                                 19
3  Performance: actors and the cast                                  55
4  Performance and the published text                                99
5  Text and performance (1): the comedies, 1691 to 1693             138
6  Text and performance (2): Wycherley's *The Plain-Dealer*         170
7  Text and performance (3): the comedies of Congreve               204
   Appendix A  Restoration promptbooks                               244
   Appendix B  The casts for comedies, 1691 to 1693                  246
   Appendix C  The casts of Congreve's comedies                      249

   *Notes*                                                           250
   *Select bibliography*                                            274
   *Index*                                                          280

# Illustrations

Thomas Betterton (*National Portrait Gallery*)      *frontispiece*

1   Inigo Jones: ground-plan and elevation of the      22
Cockpit-in-Court Theatre (*The Provost and
Fellows of Worcester College, Oxford*)

2   Inigo Jones and John Webb: a theatre project      25
(*The Provost and Fellows of Worcester College,
Oxford*)

3   Wren: a sketch for a theatre (*The Warden and*      27
*Fellows of All Souls College, Oxford*)

4   Wren: design for Theatre Royal, Drury Lane      30
(*The Warden and Fellows of All Souls College,
Oxford*)

# Preface

| | |
|---|---|
| *To the Bearer* | Hold, are you mad? you damn'd confounded Dog, |
| | I am to rise, and speak the Epilogue. |
| *To the Audience* | I come, kind Gentlemen, strange news to tell ye, |
| | I am the Ghost of poor departed *Nelly*. |
| | Sweet Ladies, be not frighted, I'le be civil, |
| | I'm what I was, a little harmless Devil. |

. . .

As for my Epitaph when I am gone,
I'll trust no Poet, but will write my own.
*Here* Nelly *lies, who, though she liv'd a Slater'n,*
*Yet died a Princess, acting in S.* Cathar'n.[1]

Dryden's extraordinary epilogue to *Tyrannic Love* (1670) is much more than a joke. Once the audience is reminded that the virtuous Valeria is really Nell Gwyn the whole fabric of the play's morality crumbles into fantasy. Without the epilogue, it would be a very different play, much more bombastic and more than a little hysterical. With the epilogue, the play is revealed as pure pretence and we can never take it quite as seriously again. The epilogue is of course inseparable from the personality of Nell Gwyn: she is genuinely both slattern (the Protestant whore) and princess (as Charles's mistress). Yet Dryden combines that reality with the play's fiction; Nell is a princess when an actress. The unreal moral world of tragedy is fractured irreversibly; it is simply a performance.

How do we understand the meaning of such a moment? For someone like François Hédelin the answer is simple: we can't. Hédelin sets limits to the text that are far too constrained to admit the identity of the actors themselves. He distinguishes between the 'Truth of Theatral Action' and the 'Representation':

But that *Floridor* or *Beauchasteau* act the part of *Cinna*, that they are good or ill Actors, well or ill dress'd, that they are separated from the people by a Stage, which is adorn'd with painted cloth, representing Palaces and Gardens, . . . that an Actor goes behind the Stage, when he says he goes into

the Kings Closet, and speaks to his Wife, instead of speaking to a Queen, . . .
all these things are, and do depend on the Representation.[2]

Not only are they classed as 'Representation' but they are therefore
not to be considered by the reader or spectator. French neo-classic-
ism could not admit to the double reality of the stage, the reality of
the performance itself as well as that of the action represented. For
Hédelin, there is no essential difference between the aspects of the
stage representation I have already quoted and such matters as
whether the spectators are 'silent or make a noise, that there are
quarrels in the Pit or none'.[3] Hédelin excludes them from the meaning of the play.

This book argues that most of these attributes of the representation – though not the quarrels in the pit – can be an essential part of
the play's communication of its meaning and that to exclude them
from the study of the play is to remove many of the means by which
the meaning of the play is understood. In making this statement I
have not specified a historical time or place. There is not a great
difference between Molière's frequent use of the audience's knowledge
of the personnel of his company and Shakespeare's of his at the
Globe or William Gaskill's of his at the Royal Court in the 1960s.
I have chosen to investigate the relationship of performance to play
and of performance to published text, in terms of the physical conditions of the English theatre between 1660 and about 1705 and the
force of those conditions on comedy. This field of study I un-
ashamedly call 'Restoration Comedy', not because it is an unchanging monolithic category – far from it – but because around 1700
comedy does begin to change radically and because the conventional
use of the word 'Restoration' seems adequate.[4]

The first step must be to examine the nature of performance in the
Restoration. To find out how the audience understood the play that
they watched, a study of Thomas Betterton is as important as one
of John Dryden. Chapters 2 and 3 examine the relevant evidence
about acting and staging. They also provide some examples of the
way in which applying this information to the conventional notion
of text produces new modes of understanding how the meaning of
a play is realised by performance. The physical shape of the
theatres, the use of scenery, the casting of the actors and other such
details of playhouse activities are the basis from which a concept of
a larger 'text', a text that has performance as part of its own meaning, rather than as a necessary evil, can be understood. It is not that
any such understanding of the plays is necessarily radically different

from the conventional readings, though it frequently is, but that without this information the text occupies a limbo that denies the force of historical circumstance.

For Hédelin, the experience of reading the text is an imaginative reconstruction of the 'theatral action', not the representation:

A Play may be regarded two ways; it is made to be acted by persons, who are to do every thing, as if they were the true persons represented; and likewise Plays are made to be read by people, who without seeing them acted, can by their imagination, and the strength of the impressions the Poet gives, make those persons as it were present to their Idea. Now whether a Play be acted or read, it must be understood by the Spectators, and by the Reader; it cannot be known to the Spectators, but just as the Actors shall make it so; and the Reader can understand no more of it, than the Verses or Expressions do inform him . . .[5]

Since the experience of the audience in the theatre was geared to a comprehension of the significance of the representational elements in the performance, Hédelin's view would divorce the reader's experience totally from that theatrical experience. But the difference between reading and seeing a play is not necessarily as Hédelin describes it. Chapter 4 explores the relation of the conventional form of play publication to the manner of performance.

The last part of the book moves on to examine three particular examples of the interconnection of text and performance: chapter 5 analyses the relationship between the theatre and the comedies produced in two theatre seasons between 1691 and 1693; chapter 6 examines *The Plain-Dealer* by William Wycherley; chapter 7 looks at the four comedies of Congreve.

Restoration Comedy does not consist only of eleven plays, three by Etherege, and four each by Wycherley and Congreve. Even to study these plays in performance means setting them in the company of the Restoration hacks, the fifth-rate playwrights who also made use of the talents of Betterton, Hart and the other actors. The raw material for this study is then the whole corpus of plays. A particular use of scenery or a particular piece of casting can only be seen as a substantial alteration from the tradition if that tradition has been traced through a mass of undistinguished plays. For the Restoration, the publication of the first part of *The London Stage 1660–1800* (Carbondale, 1965), edited by E. L. Avery, W. van Lennep and others, made information on casts and performances relatively easily accessible. Even though it is not entirely trustworthy, *The London*

*Stage* is a brilliant coasting-map to the territory. It is now accompanied by the first volumes of the *Biographical Dictionary*, edited by Professor Highfill and others, which gives a summary of information about all actresses, actors and others connected with the theatre. But these works do not establish the conventions themselves, only an abstract of some sources of information that point to them. It is now customary for critics writing on Restoration drama to genuflect in the direction of the theatre and mention, in a passing footnote, some piece of casting. I believe that performances and theatrical practice deserve much better than this from critics. If we are to understand the full complexity of the experience of watching a play, one in particular or any play at all, we *must* look at the actors and their careers, at the shape of the theatres, at the use of scenery and at a host of other matters in detail. The text grows into performance; it is not a being apart.

Without the help of many people this study would not have been completed. I would especially like to thank the following: the Master and Fellows of Trinity Hall, for a research fellowship which enabled me to complete the work; the staff of numerous libraries, particularly the British Library, the National Library of Ireland, the Public Record Office, Nottingham University Library, many of the Cambridge college libraries, especially King's, Trinity, and the Pepys Library at Magdalene, and most of all David McKitterick and the long-suffering staff of the Rare Books Room of the University Library, Cambridge; the Cambridge Group for the History of Population and Social Structure; Don McKenzie, whose 1976 Sandars Lectures brilliantly argued a very different view of Congreve's text from the one I argue here; Peter Blayney, for an endless supply of help in all things bibliographical; Jonathan Culler and Richard Luckett, who both, in widely differing ways, helped me to understand just how complicated the process of watching a play is; Michael Black, for a mass of helpful notes on an earlier stage of the manuscript; Michael Cordner, for happy hours of chatting about the comedies; Anne Barton, who, as my supervisor when this study was a Cambridge thesis, struggled with my style and my wilder flights of fancy with greater patience and good-humour than any supervisor ought to possess, all the time demonstrating in her own approach to the plays the right way of going about things; and my wife, not least for inventing the names of some 'newly rediscovered' Restoration comedies.

# Note on references

Unless otherwise stated, all quotations from plays are from the first published edition. Plays are dated according to that edition, since the fragmentary nature of our knowledge of performance dates would make any other date too often hypothetical. I have not scrupled to ignore italicisation where necessary. For unpaginated texts, page-references are to the gatherings: hence, 'π 2a' means 'unsigned preliminary gatherings, leaf 2 recto'; 'A4b' means 'gathering A, leaf 4 verso'. The following books are referred to so frequently that the reference is abbreviated in the notes:

| | |
|---|---|
| *Apology* | C. Cibber, *An Apology for the life of Mr Colley Cibber* ed. R. W. Lowe (1889). |
| *Critical Works* | J. Dennis, *Critical Works* ed. E. N. Hooker (Baltimore, 1939–43). |
| Downes | J. Downes, *Roscius Anglicanus* ed. M. Summers (1928). |
| Dryden, *Essays* | J. Dryden, *Of Dramatic Poesy and Other Critical Essays* ed. G. Watson (1962). |
| Dryden, *Works* | J. Dryden, *Works* ed. E. N. Hooker *et al.* (Berkeley, 1956– ). |
| Farquhar, *Works* | G. Farquhar, *Works* ed. C. Stonehill (1930). |
| Jonson, *Works* | B. Jonson, *Works* ed. C. H. Herford and P. and E. Simpson (Oxford, 1925–52). |
| Otway, *Works* | T. Otway, *Works* ed. J. C. Ghosh (Oxford, 1932). |

# 1

# The text and the audience

When Furness introduced his New Variorum edition of *Hamlet* in 1877, describing it as providing 'some facilities to the study of this great *poem*',[1] he implied that, for him, the stage was an unnecessary encumbrance. Too little criticism of plays in the century since Furness has troubled itself with what happens on stage. Locked off into a separate compartment, 'Theatre History' (information about the manner of performance, the form of the stage, the style of acting and so on) is kept hygienically apart from the 'text' itself. Critics, with a few brilliant exceptions, have not been concerned with the specific context for which the plays were written and within which they were first seen or read. Conditions of performance affect both the author and the audience. By focusing on that moment of performance, we can rediscover the contact between playwright and audience. My emphasis is then primarily on the ways that an audience understands a play as it watches it or reads the published text.

Most of this opening chapter will be concerned with the nature of that theatre audience for whom Restoration comedies were written and performed. But I must first briefly sketch the 'theatre history', that is the history of the theatre companies, the ground on which my later work is built.[2]

For all the fragmentary records of occasional performances during the Interregnum, it was only with the return of Charles II in 1660 that regular professional theatre returned openly to London. There is something monarchic and autocratic about the way in which Thomas Killigrew and Sir William Davenant established a theatrical monopoly in the capital under licence from the King. Within a few months, they had stamped out all opposition to their control, gained patents to make any rivals illegal, formed two companies and fitted out theatres to play in.[3]

On 8 November 1660, Killigrew's company, known as the King's, opened in a theatre converted from Gibbon's Tennis Court in Vere Street. The theatre was little different from the pre-Restoration stages of the private theatres; it had no scenery and was quickly found to be old-fashioned. Killigrew managed to form his company around a nucleus of experienced actors who had worked before the Civil War. His principal actors were Charles Hart, Edward Kynaston and Michael Mohun with other experienced men like Cartwright, Shaterall and Wintersell and the brilliant comedian John Lacy. To them, Killigrew added actresses, now appearing on the professional stage for the first time, women like Katherine Corey, Margaret Rutter, Nell Gwyn, Anne Marshall and the first great tragedienne of the London stage, Rebecca Marshall.[4]

Davenant took longer to establish his company, the Duke's, in a permanent home but, at the end of June 1661, he opened a new theatre in Lincoln's Inn Fields, the first public theatre in the country to be equipped with facilities for movable scenery. By comparison with Killigrew, Davenant had to make do with inexperienced actors. Thomas Betterton quickly proved to be his greatest star but there were others who would show their brilliance, actors like Henry Harris, Samuel Sandford, the comedians James Nokes and Cave Underhill and actresses like Mary Saunderson, later Mrs Betterton. But this inexperience was no disadvantage; for some time, Davenant needed no other attraction than the scenery to bring in the audience. Pepys commented on visiting the King's company on 4 July 1661, 'strange to see this house, that used to be so thronged, now empty since the Opera [Davenant's theatre] begun – and so will continue for a while I believe'.

By May 1663, when Killigrew moved into the newly-constructed Theatre Royal in Bridges Street, his company's prospects were brighter. From the start Killigrew had one advantage over Davenant, the major counterbalance to the attractions of the scenery: Killigrew had secured sole right to perform a massive list of pre-Restoration plays. In the short term it left Davenant with an acute shortage of plays to put on; he had to innovate to survive – hence the emphasis on scenic display. But that innovation proved to be the strength of the company.

For nearly two years the plague and its aftermath kept the theatres closed. When the companies began to act again in October 1666, the rivalry between the companies was at its height. Killigrew scored spectacularly with the triumphant success of Nell Gwyn and Charles Hart in a stream of comedies. In April 1668 Davenant died and the effective management of the Duke's company passed to Betterton and Harris, even after Davenant's son Charles assumed his patrimony in 1673. Harris was succeeded by William Smith in 1677, and Betterton and he ran the company with great success until 1682. Following the guidelines already established by Davenant, the company opened a magnificent new theatre, the Duke's Theatre in Dorset Garden, in November 1671. Dorset Garden was the grandest of the Restoration theatres, an ornate structure fully equipped with the very latest stage machinery, much of it based on Betterton's reports on the Paris playhouses. Not surprisingly, the nature of this theatre to a large extent determined that the company continued with the type of repertoire which Davenant had earlier produced, particularly spectacular tragedy and opera. The Duke's company was marked by conspicuously successful management in its diagnosis of popular taste, as well as by harmonious relations inside the company.

By contrast, the history of the King's company at this time is a sad one, for all the brilliance of its actors. Troubles with the King, troubles with the actors, troubles with the scene-painters and playwrights were as nothing compared to the disastrous fire which burnt down the theatre with all its scenery and costumes in January 1672. Conveniently, the Duke's company had just left Lincoln's Inn Fields for Dorset Garden and Killigrew's men moved in for two years while money was raised for the construction of a new theatre. In March 1674, the Theatre Royal, Drury Lane, designed by Wren, allowed the company to work once more in an up-to-date theatre. But it was too late. The company was already in a disastrous state. Killigrew's complete lack of business sense and inability to manage his actors resulted in litigation in 1677 that forced Killigrew to give up in favour of his son, aided by the senior actors of the company. Even this did not halt the decline: props and costumes were stolen by the actors; some of the best young actors ran off to Edinburgh in despair to set up on their own and were only persuaded to return with difficulty. Again and again the Lord Chamberlain had to step in to arbitrate on disputes or simply to close the theatre down. In such a state, the company could not match the successes of the Duke's company and were reduced to parodying the operas at Dorset Garden. Successive attempts to revive the company failed and in the end the remnant of the King's company were absorbed into the Duke's in a manoeuvre that was dignified by the title of the Union of the companies.[5]

The articles of Union were signed in May 1682 and from then until 1695 there was only one company in London. The company had at its disposal two theatres, using Dorset Garden only for opera and spectacle and using Drury Lane for comedy and less extravagant tragedies. Many of the older actors retired at the Union but the company found new stars, actors like William Mountfort, Tony Leigh and Thomas Jevon, actresses like Elizabeth Barry, Anne Bracegirdle and Susanna Mountfort. Throughout the political crises of the 1680s the theatre suffered from the inevitable perils of performing partisan satire. But it was only a matter of time before mismanagement and internal dispute again led to trouble. Sharp practices of all sorts in the administration of the company culminated in the flight of Alexander Davenant with embezzled funds and the control of the company by one of the great villains of theatrical management, Christopher Rich. Eventually, the actors petitioned for redress of their grievances and, dissatisfied with the patentees' reply, Betterton led the senior actors in a secession that split the Union in 1695. The younger actors tended to stay with Rich, in the hope of promotion, but nearly every actor of note went with Betterton. The secessionists were granted licence to act and established themselves in Lincoln's Inn Fields, empty for over twenty years. The theatres began a new period of acrimonious competition with each other and, after Jeremy Collier's attack on the immorality of the stage in 1698, with the new forces of morality. Rich's company benefited from the rise to stardom of George Powell, John Verbruggen, Colley Cibber, Robert Wilks and Anne Oldfield. Rich's tyranny proved more successful than Betterton's and, after much subtle dealing, the companies reunited in 1708. As in the years before the 1682 Union, the aging stars had no answer to the newer talents of their rivals. The other battle, with Collier-ism, leads in a complex way towards the sentimental drama of the eighteenth century.

But who went to the theatre in this half-century? Only in recent years has the myth of the Restoration audience as a court coterie at last been exploded;[6] there is no excuse now for seeing the theatre audience as the extension of a debauched and immoral court. E. L. Avery, in particular, has demonstrated how many and how various were the people who attended the theatres. Of course there is a risk of going too far in the opposite direction: the audience of the Restoration theatre is not made up of the same sort of people in the same sort of proportions as would have filled the Globe sixty years earlier. Instead we find an analogous cross-section of society in the Elizabethan and Jacobean private theatres like the Blackfriars, just as those theatres mark a major tradition behind the Restoration theatre in stage design and performance style. Everything we know about theatre-goers at Blackfriars seems remarkably similar to the list of those who attended the Restoration theatres.[7] But a simple list of those who went to the theatre is not enough. What has been lacking is an analysis of how often the members of the audience attended, how they considered a visit to the theatre and of what sort of place drama occupied in Restoration society.

Theatre-going was not an occasional rare practice for a lordly few. It was an habitual part of day-to-day living in London or visiting it. Nathaniel Wanley, vicar of Holy Trinity Church, Coventry, beseeches a friend in town for news of London life,

are all the coffee houses downe? Are the Temple & Grayes Inne walkes all depopulated? Are the playe houses blowne up; If none of these; let mee entreate you for the future not to stick your words in a paper at the distance of cloves in a gammon of Bacon . . . [8]

In June 1689, Rowland Davies, the Dean of Ross, noted in his diary a few days after his arrival in England from the Irish troubles,

After dinner I went with Mr. N. Lysaght and W. Jephson to see Circe acted at the Queen's Theatre, which was done to admiration, with better scenes than I could imagine.[9]

That final phrase seems to me to smack of the discriminating eye of a knowledgeable theatre-goer.

John Ward, later vicar of Stratford-on-Avon, went to see Jonson's *The Alchemist*, while he was in London in 1662, and praises the acting, even though his visit was probably caused by his obsession with all things medical.[10]

But amongst most professional people and certainly gentlemen of leisure, theatre-going is too much of a habit to be noted in any but the fullest of diaries. Thomas Bruce, Earl of Ailesbury, casually notes one particular visit, to Betterton's secessionist company in Lincoln's Inn Fields around June 1695, because 'it being before five . . . I discoursed with Mr Bettertin [sic] until the curtain was drawn up'.[11] There is no surprise in his casually chatting with Betterton before the performance, but it was worth noting. Henry Savile notes one visit in a letter, only because he found the play so distasteful.[12] Peregrine Bertie wrote to the Countess of Rutland because there had been a disturbance at the playhouse that stopped the play.[13] Only the exceptions to the rule of regular peaceful theatre-going seemed worth mentioning.

Even the scientist Robert Hooke, much as he disliked immoral and satirical plays – particularly when, like Shadwell's *The Virtuoso* (1676), they were aimed at himself – attended fairly often. Apart from his visits, he took a scientist's interest in the working of special effects at the theatre: 'I told them of the way of making lightning in the playhouse and Sir Christopher [Wren] of the way of thunder . . .'[14] In addition Hooke bought copies of plays. On 1 January 1674, for instance, he lent his 'housekeeper' Nell his copy of Shadwell's *The Sullen Lovers*.[15] Hooke records theatre-visits by other members of the Royal Society, including John Hoskins, Abraham Hill, Sir Jonas More and Flamsteed, the great astronomer. In addition men like Newton and Locke included many plays in their libraries and probably went to the theatre. The strong connection between play-going and play-buying seems to me to be probable but there is, of course, little direct evidence for it. Nonetheless the evidence of library and sale catalogues indicates the presence of plays in the hands of precisely those sorts of people whom we know to have been in the theatre audience. Some of the evidence is examined in chapter 4.[16]

Those concerned with the moral welfare of the young might be expected to have a different attitude to play-going. But in 1686, Edmund Verney, a fairly puritanical man, wrote to his son at Oxford that 'I heard that the players are gon down to Oxford, but I am unwilling that you should go to see them act', not, as one might expect, out of a moral objection, but 'for fear on your coming out of the hot play house in to the cold ayer, you should catch harm'.[17]

When one looks at the formal educational and courtesy literature, the interdiction on play-going is nothing like so absolute as one has been led to believe. In many of them the question of drama is avoided completely. Henry Peacham's *The Compleat Gentleman* (1622), one of the most important pre-Restoration examples, provides a detailed curriculum for poetry but no mention of English dramatists. Significantly, the explicit warning against drama, where given, is far more common in educational tracts than in courtesy books. Obadiah Walker attacks romances for their portrayal of false honour, lust and imaginary worlds; the most dangerous are enticements from seriousness and virtue, to vanity and filthiness: *Comedies* I mean, which who with delight frequenteth, returns with the passions and humors there *represented*, shall I say? or *recommended*. The design of them is sensuall delight and pleasure (to say no worse) which a good serious man looks upon as his greatest enemy.[18]

William Freke makes the same link between plays, romances and illusions: 'there are some men so weak as to look for Morality even in Plays and Romances; but alass! they but flatter themselves, and seek but for the Colours of Vertue'.[19] Frequently plays are allowed grudgingly as part of a necessary relaxation from business.[20]

The most interesting and extended discussions of plays are in those works which are aware of the theoretic advantages of plays and acting but are also conscious of what they consider to be the immorality of contemporary practice. The nonjuror Francis Brokesby admires any play which 'recommends virtuous actions and insinuates a love thereof into the Readers minds'.[21] He fully accepts the argument that acting in schools can help in giving boys 'carriage . . . vigour and generosity'.[22] He will not 'deny the use of a thing which is of advantage, for some abuses which may easily be severed from it' which includes the 'Lightness of too many Comedies, the intermixture of Oaths . . . together with the abuses and inconveniences . . . which have been occasioned by the Acting of them'.[23] Yet he is genuinely terrified that his approval might lead to an acceptance of the contemporary drama and advises reading Collier and that 'Instructions should be given them concerning the Nature and Ends of Dramatic Poetry, *viz*. To represent the odious nature of and wretched Consequents of Improbity, and the loveliness and Excellent fruits of true Virtue'.[24]

As the title implies, Gailhard's *The Compleat Gentleman, or Directions for the Education of Youth* (1678) stands midway between the educational and the courtesy literature. Gailhard, who announces himself on the title-page as 'Tutor Abroad to several of the Nobility and Gentry', is caught by the same doubt as Brokesby and, in spite of his otherwise liberal attitude towards education, he sums up by saying 'a good use may be made of Plays, though generally none but a bad one be made of them'.[25]

Significantly, Gailhard attacks 'the life of Actors and Actrices, their gestures, actions, carriage . . . joyned to the bad inclinations of the generality of spectators';[26] the emphasis on stage movement implies that he had seen performances himself.

The nearer one approaches to gentlemanly discussion of the problem, the more the practice of play-going is seen as a normal pleasure for a sensible man in town, neither frivolous nor immoral. At the opposite extreme, Caleb Trenchfield's *A Cap of Gray Hairs for a Green Head* (1671), a work directed at apprentices, lauds hard work and industry and attacks plays 'where the design is laid, rather to corrupt Youth, then to inform it'.[27]

*The Country Gentleman's Vade Mecum* (1699) complains that some modern plays are immoral and also 'profoundly dull and flat' (p. 46) but the author's critical theory of the proper purpose of drama does not exclude contemporary practice:

the true Design of the *Stage*, is ... to expose and detect Rebellion and Faction, and Vice in general; and to exalt and commend Loyalty, Honour and Vertue; and truly, there's hardly any Play (if you take it right) that's acted at either of the Houses in *London*, but makes some kind of advances towards one of these Ends. (p. 51)

The author finishes his analysis of the theatre by advising 'you may pass away an hour or two at the *Play-house*, once in a Month, but no oftner, without any great matter of Hazard, and with some kind of Advantage' (p. 52).

Plays are recommended reading in William Ramesey's *The Gentleman's Companion* (1672), especially Jonson, Shakespeare, Fletcher and Dryden – the last surprising in view of the early date. Richard Blome's magnificent volume *The Gentleman's Recreation* includes, in the second edition (1710), a lengthy discussion of drama in which Restoration drama is considered the pinnacle of achievement: 'For who is there in *Tragedy* to match our *Otway*? Our *Etheridge*, *Wicherley*, *Congreve*, *Vanbrugh* in *Comedy*? ... and for all sorts of Versification, our Immortal *Dryden* ...' (p. 22). Samuel Vincent mocks the foolishness of young would-be gallants in the theatres in his updated version of Dekker's *The Guls Horne-booke*, *The Young Gallant's Academy* (1674), a brilliant mocking inversion of the courtesy books. But in giving the 'Character of A True, Noble, Liberal, and Stayed Gentleman', a section not taken from Dekker, Vincent does not reject plays as immoral; on the contrary, his concern is purely with the right way of attending the playhouse, that is, by concentrating on the play:

His pleasures and pastimes are sometimes Reading History, sometimes Hunting, Hawking, Fowling and Fishing, & sometimes to see a Play ... the true-bred Gentleman sits the Play out patiently ... where if he observes any thing that is good or ingenious, he turns it into practice; and after the

Play is done, home he goes to his Lodging, and can there laugh at the
Fopperies of some Persons that were presented. (pp. 95–7)

Vincent's emphasis here is precisely the one I am concerned with.
The shift from evaluating the plays themselves to evaluating the
right relationship of play to spectator shows clearly that the theatre is
accepted. Vincent has no need to write apologetics for the stage;
instead his work is designed to exist in a social and cultural milieu
where play-going is frequent, unremarkable and enjoyable. In
addition, Vincent sees play-going as a serious, responsible and
profitable action.

In one of the most important discussions of the problem, Clarendon, standing back from the debate, presents his concept of the place
of drama in society in a dialogue of old men, thereby locating the
different strands of the debate in different social attitudes.[28] The old
lawyer complains that the theatre is a corruption and a waste of
money. He emphasises, surprisingly, how many poor citizens attend:

for I cannot but think it a great Unthriftiness . . . when an ordinary Citizen,
who is to maintain his Family by his Industry, will spend a Shilling to see
a Play, when he hath not gotten so much that Day to support his Wife and
Children. (p. 343)

The old alderman praises the theatre as a great relaxation, especially for bookish intellectuals:

there is no Sort of Men resort more greedily to Plays, than they who are
most intent upon their Books, the Noise of the Stage giving great Life to
the Silence of the Study. (p. 344)

For the old courtier, the theatre is an innocent relaxation from the
troubles of politics, while, for the old soldier, play-going is educative
as well as relaxing:

I have thought myself often the wiser for having been there, and, it may be,
the honester for the Discourses I have heard there, which make greater
Impressions by the seasonable Application of good Rules to proper Occasions, than the same Things pronounced more dogmatically in more
serious Assemblies. (p. 346)

When John Dennis traced the decline in the quality of the drama
to, amongst other causes, the declining standards of the audience,
it was precisely the decline of such serious-minded play-going of
which he complained: the modern gentlemen of business 'come to a
Playhouse full of some business which they have been solliciting

... so that they meerly come to unbend, and are utterly incapable of duly attending'.[29] James Brydges, the future Duke of Chandos, for instance, rarely seems to have stayed more than one act at the theatre in his restless rushing around London. He recorded in his diary (1697–1702) whom he met or saw, not what play he might have watched. On 27 February 1697, for instance, he records,

I went to ye Dean of Peterborough's, but he being at church I went to ye playhouse in Lincolns inn fields, where I met Dr. Davenant & Ld. Rumny after which I came home[30]

He does not bother to note that the play was Congreve's *The Mourning Bride*, a spectacular success.

Perhaps there is not much to choose between Brydges and those fops who, throughout the period, came to the theatre more to be seen than to see. But parts of Dennis's analysis of that changing audience after 1700 indicate a radical change in the audience's expectations from the theatrical performance. The audience contains new groups, like a rising class of wealth made up of men still 'in Love with their old sports', that is 'Tumbling and Vaulting' and such like, who 'encourage these noble Pastimes still upon the stage'.[31] This change, the addition of a variety of unconnected entertainments to the main play, starts with the furious competition and desperate finances of the rival companies after 1700. Before then the programme at the theatre consisted of a single play, performed with a dance but no other extraneous additions; the audience expected nothing else. Even more infuriating for Dennis was:

a 3d sort of People, who may be said to have had no education at all in relation to us and our Plays ... that considerable number of Foreigners ... some of whom not being acquainted with our Language, and consequently with the sense of our Plays, and others disgusted with our extravagant, exorbitant Rambles, have been Instrumental in introducing Sound and Show, where the business of the Theatre does not require it ... [32]

Of course Dennis is biased against tourists and Samuel Pepys' interests in the theatre were not solely dramatic. But the evidence of Pepys' diary is of a different world from the frenetic activity of Brydges' social round. Not that Pepys was not busy, but he does seem to have been genuinely interested in plays and so too do his friends. The diary records not only his own habitual and almost obsessive play-going but also the consistency of the visits made by his friends.

It is worth examining one section of the diary in detail as an example. By January 1668 Pepys' financial well-being had enabled him to conquer his puritanical scruples and innate thriftiness and he was able to go to the theatre as frequently as he wished. Between 1 January and 31 August, eight months in all, he visited the theatres 73 times. Apart from 4 visits to the training theatre, the Nursery (on one of which there was no performance), he visited the Theatre Royal, Bridges Street 43 times and Lincoln's Inn Fields Theatre 27 times.[33] But it is not Pepys' own frequent visits that is significant so much as the frequent visits of his wife and friends. Of the 73 visits, 26 were made by Pepys alone.[34] But that figure disguises the fact that 21 of those lonely afternoons were during April and May. On 1 April Mrs Pepys left for the countryside and did not return until 18 June – Pepys holidayed with her between 5 and 17 June. In that two month period Pepys made 33 visits to the theatre, the other 12 including 4 with Lord Brouncker, 2 with Creed and 4 with Mary Mercer and her friends. But while Mrs Pepys was in London, she usually accompanied Pepys to the theatre. Of the 40 possible visits, Mrs Pepys came with her husband on 32 occasions, 13 of those just accompanied by her maid Deb Willet and 10 more with Deb and Mary Mercer. Deb Willet, a lady's maid, thus went to the theatre over 23 times in the eight months. On 7 January, for instance, Pepys went to the Nursery to meet his wife and her maids as arranged but, the Nursery not acting, he looked for them at the other two theatres. They had seen *Henry IV Part I* at the Bridges Street theatre 'and saw me, but I could [not] see them'. On 18 February, Pepys went with Penn to the theatre but he did not enjoy the play, 'I being out of humour, being at a play without my wife and she ill at home'. In June, when Mrs Pepys returned from her trip, she was rather cross at Pepys' gallivanting in her absence and was not 'willing to go to a play, though a new one' (18 June). They were reconciled and the following day Mrs Pepys and Deb went to the Theatre Royal at Bridges Street 'thinking to spy me there' since there was a new play by Dryden, *An Evening's Love*. It was not just suspicions over Pepys' behaviour that led Mrs Pepys to go; she appears to have been interested in new plays, telling Pepys that Dryden's play 'is wholly . . . taken out of the *Illustr. Bassa*' (20 June) and reading to him the extracts from Mme de Scudéry's novel on 21 June after dinner. The ease with which Mrs Pepys went to the theatre on her own, with no moral comment from Pepys, finally belies the old myth that all unattached women in the Restoration theatre were whores or aristocrats or both.

On 20 June, Pepys went with his wife to see the 'new play my wife saw yesterday'. On 29 June, Pepys took his wife to see Sedley's *The Mulberry Garden*, because 'she had not seen' it – Pepys had seen it twice while she was away. For Mrs Pepys as well as her husband, theatre-going was a habit.

But there were others who went regularly with Pepys or whom he meets there in this period: Lord Brouncker, Penn, Creed and others from the office, Mrs Pierce, Mrs Corbet and other friends. On 15 April Pepys, on his own at *The Maid's Tragedy*, saw Creed come in, 'dropping presently here'. When Pepys went to *The Man's the Master* on 26 March he met his wife, Deb, Mrs Pierce, Mrs Corbet and Betty Turner, all of whom 'my wife carried with her' and later they met Mr Pierce as well. On 7 February, Pepys' theatre-party, including Sir William Penn, Lord Brouncker and Sir Arnold Breames, met Penn's son there by chance. This habit of running into friends and relatives indicates the extent to which we may in fact need to talk of a coterie audience but a coterie made up of regular theatre-goers.

It is not only Pepys' well-known friendship with Mrs Knep and other players that makes it possible for him to chat easily with Etherege after the first night of *She Would If She Could* on 6 February 1668 (at the rival playhouse) or with Thomas Killigrew and Henry Harris so frequently throughout the diary period. The impression is that the companies up to the Union in 1682 and probably beyond had a regular theatre audience of whom Pepys was an unremarkable example.

In spite of Clarendon's old lawyer, for most of the audience that mattered (to both playwrights and actors), the cost of theatre-going was not great. Pepys frequently appears to have spent more on coaches than on his seat at the play.[35] Gregory King, the pioneer demographer, recorded fully his annual expenditure for his family (wife, clerk, maid and boy) around 1695. Out of a total of £152, King spent £5 on 'Plays, Shews, gifts & Charities' (£3 for himself; £1 10s. 0d. for his wife; 8s. for his clerk; 1s. 6d. for his maid and 6d. for the boy), the same sum as he spent on 'Books and Papers' (£4 for himself and £1 for his clerk) and half that spent on 'Tavern and Ale ho. & Coffee ho.'.[36]

The audience was not a single coherent unit. Different groups sat in different areas. It seems to have been true that the pit-and-boxes audience preferred a 'higher' form of drama than those in the middle and upper galleries. Lacy, in the prologue to *The Old Troop*

(1672), appeals on behalf of his farce,

> Defend me, O my friends, of th' upper Region,
> From the hard censure of this lower Legion.   (B1b)

The division of the audience between the various parts of the theatre
was as much economic as social. Pepys was surprised and annoyed
to see so many apprentices in the pit on 1 January 1668 but it was
a holiday when the city contingent might well have spent more than
normal,

Here a mighty company of citizens, prentices and others; and it makes
me observe that when I began first to be able to bestow a play on myself, I
do not remember that I saw so many by half of the ordinary prentices and
mean people in the pit, at 2s–6d apiece, as now . . .

But Pepys' other occasional comments about citizens in the audience
are worth examining further for their implications about the rivalry
of the two theatre companies up to the Union. On 27 December
1662, Pepys the snob was 'not so well pleased with the company at
the house today, which was full of Citizens, there hardly being a
gentleman or woman in the house'. Five days later, Pepys was cross
again because the 'house was full of Citizens' (1 January 1663). On 12
September 1667, he saw Cooke's *Tu Quoque*, disliked it but was sure
'it will please the citizens'. Except for the last, all the references are
at holiday time, but more significantly, all four references are to
performances at Davenant's theatre in Lincoln's Inn Fields.

The deduction is obvious: Davenant's spectacular use of scenery
and his inclination to farcical comedy led to his theatre being patro-
nised by a more bourgeois and less intellectually critical and demanding audience. Dryden's prologue to *Marriage A-la-Mode* (1673)
indicates this separation of the two theatres into scenes and sense,
as well as indicating a geographical reason for the distinction,

> Our City Friends so far will hardly come,
> They can take up with Pleasures nearer home;
> And see gay Shows, and gawdy Scenes elsewhere:
> For we presume they seldom come to hear.   (a1b)

The prologue by Sedley to Shadwell's *Epsom Wells* (1673) a Duke's
company play, shows that Davenant's company were content with
the easily-pleased citizen audience rather than the over-scrupulous,
never-satisfied gallants against whom the prologue is directed,

> Let easie Citts be pleas'd with all they hear,

> Go home and to their Neighbours praise our Ware.
> They with good stomachs come, and fain wou'd eat,
> You nothing like, and make them loath their meat.   (A3a)

That this is more than prologue rhetoric is proved by the drama-
tists' practice. Dryden, for instance, even while under contract to the
King's company, wrote *Sir Martin Mar-all* (1668), by far his most
farcical play to date, for the Duke's company. If one compares
*Secret Love* (1668), *An Evening's Love* (performed 1668) and *Marriage
A-la-Mode* (all plays for Killigrew at the King's company) with
*Limberham* (1680) and *The Spanish Friar* (1681) (both, like *Sir Martin*,
Duke's company plays), this differentiation of the theatres is clear.

With the Union of the companies this distinction vanished and
there is no significant evidence that it re-emerged with the division
after Betterton's secession in 1695. But the geographical argument
continued. Dryden's epilogue at the opening of the Theatre Royal,
Drury Lane emphasises satirically that a journey there was less of
a foray into the wilderness than one to Dorset Garden,

> Our House relieves the Ladies from the frights
> Of ill pav'd Streets and long dark Winter Nights;
> The *Flanders* Horses from a cold bleak Road,
> Where Bears in Furs dare scarcely look abroad . . . [37]

Similar arguments were used by Cibber over the opening of the
Haymarket in 1705:

for at that time it had not the Advantage of almost a large City, which
has since been built in its Neighbourhood . . . [the streets] were then
all but so many green Fields of Pasture, from whence they could draw
little or no Sustenance, unless it were that of a Milk-Diet. The City, the
Inns of Court, and the middle Part of the Town, which were the most
constant Support of a Theatre, and chiefly to be relied on, were now
too far out of the Reach of an easy Walk, and Coach-hire is often too hard
a Tax upon the Pit and Gallery.[38]

The Inns of Court had always been an important part of the audience
but Cibber's emphasis on the city audience would seem to mark a
significant change from the traditional picture.

However, as I have indicated, to some extent at least the city
audience was always present. If one examines the analysis of the
social composition of the theatre audience given in *The Country
Gentleman's Vade Mecum* (1699), the picture is not radically different
from one built up from Pepys' and others' comments on the audience

of the 1660s and 1670s. The author divides the house into four
sections. There was an upper gallery full of servants. Next came the
boxes, 'one peculiar to the King and Royal Family, and the rest for
the Persons of Quality . . . unless some Fools . . . crowd in among
'em' (p. 39). The Pit is reserved for '*Judges*, *Wits* and *Censurers* . . .
in common with these sit the *Squires*, *Sharpers*, *Beaus*, *Bullies* and
*Whores*, and here and there an extravagant *Male* and *Female Cit*.'[39]
Finally there was the middle gallery, 'where the Citizens Wives and
Daughters, together with the *Abigails*, Serving-men, Journey-men
and Apprentices commonly take their Places; and now and then
some disponding Mistresses and superannuated Poets' (p. 39). This
pattern is one that seems then to have remained constant for the
would expect, must have sat in the pit.[40] As in Pepys' dairy, the
to indicate where someone sat but Jeffrey Boys, a Gray's Inn student
and young would-be gallant, paid 2*s*. 6*d*. and therefore, as one
would expect, must have sat in the pit.[40] As in Pepys' diary, the
strict division of classes is marked as being broken by those extravagant with their money. The line from Pepys' audience to Dennis's
does not seem to be a change of balance so much as a change in
power. It was the control of the theatre by the gentlemen, not their
presence that Dennis saw as weakened. Clearly, though, any significant power among the merchants and citizens was only won after
1700. As Dennis saw it, the change came about not only because of
the presence of three new groups – younger brothers, merchants
and foreigners – but more particularly because the gentlemen themselves were now too busy: 'a great part of the Gentlemen have not
leisure, because want throws them upon employments, and there
are ten times more Gentlemen now in business, than there were in
King *Charles* his Reign.'[41] Dennis is complaining of inattention and
a lack of concern with the intellectual pleasure of the play itself,
rather than the changing social composition of the audience.

There is one group which has been often indicated as a major
cause of the alteration of comic form, the 'ladies'. John Harrington
Smith's claims for their power in the 1680s[42] are well-argued but he
is mistaken to assume that the group first appeared at this time.
The ladies had no compunction about attacking bawdiness from
the beginning. As early as January 1667, for instance, we find Richard
Legh, writing to his wife about London plays, commenting that 'there
is a new one at the King's House as they say . . . calld *The Custome
o' th' Country* . . . which is so dam'd bawdy that the Ladyes flung theire
peares and fruites att the Actors'.[43] In fact appeals to the ladies for

favour appeared in the 1670s, even if the cabal-like power they exerted later was absent or at least unrecorded. Thus, for instance, Ravenscroft's epilogue to *The Citizen Turn'd Gentleman* (1672) announces 'Ladies, our Author trusts in you' (A4a). The ladies' cabal was derived from a group made up of play-goers as habitual in their visits as the gallants whose taste for bawdy plays the 'Ladies' sought to change.

How large was the theatre audience? In the next chapter I shall be examining the shape of the theatres, but their capacity is virtually impossible to measure accurately. The only viable method is based on the figures for theatre income. Downes recorded that Shadwell's *The Squire of Alsatia* was a gigantic success: '*Note*, The Poet receiv'd for his third Day in the House in *Drury-Lane* at single Prizes 130l. which was the greatest Receipt they ever had at that House at single Prizes.'[44] We can assume that the figure is accurate and represents the maximum receipts for the Theatre Royal full to capacity. The prices of admission were constant throughout almost the whole period: 4s. for boxes, 2s. 6d. for the pit and the first gallery, 1s. 6d. for the middle gallery and 1s. for the upper gallery. W. J. Lawrence estimated that for a theatre holding 1000 people, the proportions were probably 140 in the boxes,[45] 140 in the middle gallery, 170 in the upper gallery and 550 in the pit and first gallery.[46] This produces a house worth £115 15s. 0d. The difference may have been made up by, for instance, another row of boxes or by seats on the stage. Other estimates of capacity are based on complicated and dubious systems of measurement and calculation from theatre plans and reconstructions.[47] Only with the survival of certain sets of receipts after 1700 can any precise estimates be made. Thus Sawyer calculates that the enlarged Lincoln's Inn Fields theatre of 1727 held up to 1400.[48] Some details for the Queen's Theatre in the Haymarket, built in 1705, can be deduced from receipts for three performances in 1710 and 1711.[49]

The theatres were rarely full to capacity; the average audience numbered nearer 500. The litigation over the shares in the United company show that the company took, between 1682 and 1692, about £10,400 a year, which means that in an acting season of around 200 performances the takings were about £50 a night.[50] There is one reported document for the Restoration period giving receipts at Drury Lane for *All for Love* on 12 December 1677 and *The Rival Queens* on 26 December 1677.[51] The document is of dubious validity, supposedly found 'among some waste-paper',[52] but there is little enough else to work from and the conclusions from the document are close to what one would expect. The figures for *All for Love* show the audience to have consisted of 36 in boxes, 117 in the pit, 63 in the middle gallery and 33 in the upper gallery, 249 in all. The receipts were £28 4s. 0d. For *The Rival Queens*, the audience was much larger. The King's box was used – not necessarily by the King – and cost £1 10s. 0d; there were 53 in the boxes, 191 in the pit, 144 in the middle gallery and 119 in the upper gallery, a total of 507 plus the King's box party, earning the company £52 14s. 0d. This size seems to represent a holiday audience – the size of the gallery audience is a significantly higher proportion than for *All for Love*. On a normal day, the proportion of the audience in the pit must have been higher. With two theatres operating, the average audience could not have been much more than 300 at each a night.

However I cannot show how this audience compares with the size of the whole population of London. Gregory King computed the population at 527,600 in 1695 and recent demographic studies have not altered the figure significantly.[53] But socio-economic analysis of that total has been limited. King analysed a few parishes but realised the problems of attempting to extrapolate from them. Thus St Bennet Paul's Wharf had 133 people who were surtaxed in assessments out of a total population of 562 but 'This great Number of Persons of quality is by reason of Doctors Comons and yᵉ Heralds Office'.[54] Recent studies by D. V. Glass have been based on the lists of London inhabitants 'within the walls' made in 1695 for the Marriage Tax Act (1694)[55] but this represents only 60,000 individuals in the city itself and again one cannot extrapolate for the more fashionable outparishes. Nonetheless, it is clear that an average pit-and-box audience represents a significant proportion of the wealthy population of London.

Given Dryden's and Cibber's comments on the reluctance of the audience to stir very far, the probable size of London's population and the size of the theatres, any play that ran for more than four or five nights must have been playing to an audience many of whom were seeing it for the second or third time. Pepys' repeated visits were nearer the norm than we usually believe.

Allardyce Nicoll's description of the Restoration theatre audience sums up the traditional picture:

The spectators, then, for whom the poets wrote and the actors played were the courtiers and their satellites. The noblemen in the pit and

boxes, the fops and beaux and wits or would-be-wits who hung on
to their society, the women of the court, depraved and licentious as
the men, the courtesans with whom these women of quality moved
and conversed as on equal terms, made up at least four-fifths of the
entire audience.[56]

Nicoll's view, it should be clear by now, is of an audience that never
existed. The real audience was 'informed', made up of regular
visitors to the playhouse, an audience that would recognise the
changes that a playwright might make in an established mode. When
they entered the theatre, they had a set of preconceptions, of patterns, of predictions that the playwrights could fulfil or frustrate.
The form of the theatres that the audience filled is the subject of
the next chapter.

# 2

## Performance: theatres and scenery

In an article on costume in the theatre, Roland Barthes demanded that it 'must find that kind of rare balance which allows it to help the reading of the theatrical act, without hindering it with a parasitical value'. The costume is to be noticeable but inseparable from the rest of the event: 'on doit le voir mais non le regarder'.[1]

The nature of theatrical perception requires that the entire dramatic *gestalt* should be interpretable as part of the text. Every fragment of the event potentially carries meaning. The information offered by each segment can be read both in terms of the momentary theatrical event and as a series of signs, a system that helps the comprehension of the structure of the whole play text. A semiotics of scenery would allow the double attraction of scenery to text, not only pulled towards the moment but also towards its own separable system, embodying a meaning that could be contrary to the information offered by the other codes of the text. The possibility of this second system is partially dependent on the ease with which the audience can perceive the scenery as part of a system. Clearly, the connection of scene to moment is even discernible within the emphatic realistic stage of the late nineteenth century.[2] But the peculiarities of staging comedy on the Restoration stage allowed the audience to 'read' the scenery, not just absorb it. Barthes' formulation of the twin acts, seeing and observing, should be turned into an acceptance of the equal importance of the two types of regarding. The scenery is not only 'transparent',[3] by not being parasitical, but also opaque, its opacity defined by the fullness of the specific information that it offers to the audience.

Scenery, as sign, offers a series of separable functions: it can be read as index of place, as commentary on the action, and also as its own structure. To take an example, in Shadwell's *The Squire of Alsatia* (1688), 'Enter ... Mrs *Termagant*, in her fine Lodgings' (p. 68) is an index to the place of the action, where the scene occurs. The lodgings are 'fine', indicating precisely Mrs Termagant's status in society and helping to define the nature of the action of the scene. In turn, the set is part of the system of scenery in the play; it is compared directly with the sleaziness of Whitefriars, with the formal elegance of the set of Sir Edward's house and with all the other sets of the play. This system, almost independent within the action of the play, is a visible structure for the play's argument for a morality of restraint. In this chapter I want to investigate how this system of scenery operated and how it affected the audience's understanding of Restoration comedy.

### The form of the theatres

The disposition of the constituent parts of the theatre space (stage, set and audience) is indicative of a particular interrelationship of actor and audience, scenery and spectators. This implicit statement of the theoretic basis of that drama reflects in particular its attitude towards the significance of visual mimetic realism. In the mid-nineteenth-century theatre, for instance, the overwhelming emphasis on the proscenium arch signifies the divide between audience and performance, between reality and stage illusion. Within such a theatre the applicability of the moral claims of the drama to the life outside the theatre, or even just on the other side of the pro-scenium, is difficult to maintain. Only by placing disproportionate emphasis on the fracture of the preconceptions of decorum that that theatre embodied could a socially responsible drama, like Ibsen's, exist. As a sweeping generalisation I would suggest that the greater the proportion of acting within the scenic stage, the greater the emphasis on theatrical illusion, on a drama of idealistic purity. The moral power of English Renaissance drama is closely bound up with, perhaps dependent on, the intimate relationship of actors to audience. When Brecht seeks to combine distance and dispassion, it is achieved by breaking the illusion brought about through distance, by utilising devices like song and aside.

In the particular theatres newly built or adapted from existing buildings after 1660, the oscillation of importance of forestage and scenic stage, the areas either side of the proscenium divide, works in a subtle interchange with the ways in which the plays used the stage-space. In this context, the transition from pre-Civil War practice will show how the characteristics altered.

The notorious De Witt sketch of the Swan shows the tiring-house (the 'mimorum aedes') as set *within* the frame of the auditorium. The play space is confined *within* the internal form of the audience area: De Witt's 'sedilia' allows many spectators to be behind the stage even if they are to be excluded from the gallery over the stage. This form is fundamental to the Elizabethan playhouse. As Glynne Wickham puts it, 'Square, rectangular, octagonal, or circular as the frame might be, this relationship between *platea* and *plegstow* or *pleghus*, between acting area and auditorium, remained unchanged.'[4]

The basis of this drama as a communal act is typified by the demands made on the audience as auditors to define locality and is dependent on this inclusion of the actors in the audience area. Even within the Elizabethan private theatres the play-space is still part of the fundamental structure of the theatre as a Great Hall, with the elaborate wall of the tiring-house marking off the effective limits to this area, like a hall-screen. This is not the place to undertake the detailed examination of the structure of private theatres, such as the second Blackfriars Theatre used by Shakespeare's company. These theatres obviously provided a major early source for Restoration theatre design, simply by virtue of being roofed, but it is with the next stage of development that I am particularly concerned.

Frances Yates suggests that the relationship of square stage to circular building in the Elizabethan public theatres symbolised the relationship of man to universe.[5] I am disinclined to accept that the influence of classical architecture was expressed so strongly in the form and meaning of the sixteenth-century English playhouse. But the theatre designs of Inigo Jones used continental classical models in an attempt to solve the problem posed by the dominating tiring-house wall in the private theatres: how was that structure to incorporate a stage equipped with scenery?

The particular Renaissance relationship of the two areas, acting-space and audience-space, was carried over into Inigo Jones's designs for the Cockpit-in-Court Theatre (plate 1).[6] In spite of the need to pivot the theatre around the throne, the relationship of stage to audience is the same as it always had been. The basic form of the theatre is two concentric octagons. The stage-area is half the inner octagon and the noble audience, ambivalently seated so as to half-face both stage and King, take up the other half of the inner structure. But the stage is surrounded by the outer octagon and its audience is seated around the forestage and up to the proscenium line. There were occasional performances of plays with scenery in

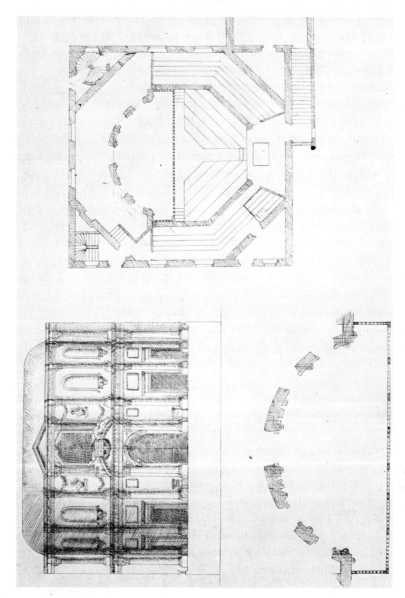

Inigo Jones: ground-plan and elevation of the Cockpit-in-Court Theatre

this theatre even before the Civil War,[7] with the scenery placed behind the central arch. This is the first example of the basic form for one aspect of the Restoration theatre up to the 1690s, the use of scenery as an extra, separate decoration, divorced from the acting-area and hence from the basic theatre structure but here placed in consonance with the King's throne as the best place from which to appreciate the perspective. The Palladian theatre is designed to allow all spectators a good view of the scenery and acting. It was precisely this democratic nature of Palladio's Teatro Olimpico at Vicenza, as opposed to the monarchic structure of perspective in the masque, that Inigo Jones felt it necessary to note in his copy of Palladio while at 'Vicensa. Mundaie y$^e$ 23 of September 1613 ... the cheaf artifice was that whear so euer you satt you sawe on of thes Prospectes ...'[8] The practice at the Cockpit-in-Court of using only the central arch for scenery thus contradicts the Palladian design of the *frons scenae*, the facade dividing stage from scenery. The *frons* has five openings along its arc and these are not all visible as 'Prospectes' from the throne. There is at least a possibility that the openings were as much entrances for actors as scenic perspectives and that this theatre thus marks only a small step from the private theatres. Unlike the permanent set of the Teatro Olimpico, the perspective scenery in England was not yet fundamental to the theatre form: at the Cockpit-in-Court, the *frons scenae* frequently fronted nothing.

In the stage design developed for the court masque, the elaborate scenic stage is used for the visual embodiment of the emblematic meaning. Scenery is used here not just as decoration but as the Hieroglyph to the truth, to pure meaning. But the area in front of the scenic stage, the dancing area, fractures the rigidity of the perspective stage which focused on the central isolated position of the King. This destroys the status of the distanced emblem on stage as an illusion, primarily through the rapprochement with the audience, that great moment in the masque when masquers and audience are combined in the dance. Then the emblem becomes real. The masque-stage keeps its two component parts separate for two distinct functions and makes the transition part of its central meaning, the 'making true' of the emblem. The masque-stage does not need a forestage; in fact, it cannot have one since the dancing area must be on the level with the audience.[9]

The problem in theatre design was then to combine the stage

with scenery and the stage for acting, both somehow to relate to that inclusive structure of the Elizabethan theatre. It was this combination that was proving so difficult to achieve. One possibility was to develop a stage dominated by scenery, with virtually no forestage acting area at all (in effect the rear half of the masque-stage). This solution is best seen in John Webb's brilliant design for the staging of Davenant's *The Siege of Rhodes* at Rutland House in 1656 – an event to which I shall return, to analyse the significance of the scenery. In 1658 Davenant transferred *The Siege of Rhodes* into the Cockpit Theatre in Drury Lane, a private theatre built in 1616 and not to be confused with the Cockpit-in-Court. John Orrell has brilliantly argued that a design by Inigo Jones represents this theatre.[10] Before the Civil War, scenery could havé been used at the Cockpit in much the same way as at the Cockpit-in-Court. But if the Rutland House stage is placed into Jones's theatre, then the audience would have confronted the action without in any way surrounding the acting. When the theatre was used by the combined company of Davenant and Killigrew for one month in October 1660, I suspect the earlier style of scenery would have been used. Significantly, the exigencies of the site forced on Jones a semicircular design for the seating, placing this theatre firmly in the tradition which I am investigating.

The other possible solution to the problem of accommodating the scenery was to diminish the importance of the scenery-stage as acting-area, thus reversing the masque tradition, but without making the scenery as insignificant and occasional as it was at the Cockpit-in-Court and in the Cockpit in Drury Lane. The most important example of this was an unrealised theatre project of Inigo Jones and John Webb (plate 2).[11] This design is strongly influenced both by Palladio's Teatro Olimpico and by Serlio's design for a stage in Book II of his *Architettura* (Paris, 1545).[12] This project reduces the multiple perspectives and five entries of the Cockpit into a single major perspective. But the scenery is still separated from the main form of the auditorium. The acting-area is the rectangular space surrounded by the *frons scenae*, behind the semicircular orchestra, with the audience benches curved around it. The scenic stage cannot be used as an acting-space without gross distortion of the perspective. In fact, for his theatre, Serlio suggested that groups of figures, cut from cardboard, should be pulled across the scenic perspective at appropriate moments.[13] The Jones/Webb project includes that distinctive combination of actor and audience within a structure which makes acting with scenery more nearly practicable.

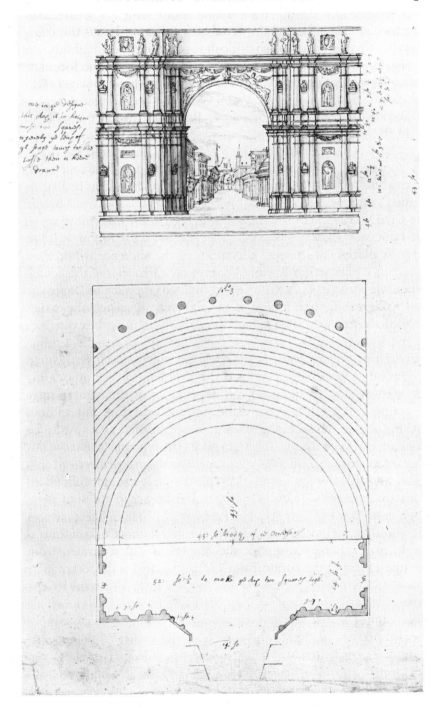

Inigo Jones and John Webb: a theatre project

If it was indeed a design for a public theatre then it indicates a new balance between the novelty of scenery and that embracing shape, even before the Civil War.

The line of descent of theatre designs related to the concepts of the Jones/Webb drawing is extremely significant. The closest parallel is the Wren sketch often taken as the plan for the Theatre Royal, Bridges Street (opened on 7 May 1663 and burnt down on 25 January 1672) (plate 3).[14] The sketch shows the same pattern of including the audience in a circular form (here built without orchestra) but again using an acting-area with the scenery excluded and placed behind. It could almost be the earlier design with a new *frons* and with the auditorium altered to accommodate more spectators, a theatre-manager's response to a successful theatre. In spite of showing the influence of a drama where scenery is more important (Wren's proscenium arch is significantly wider than the Jones/Webb one), the drawings are remarkably similar. The Bridges Street theatre certainly was constructed on a circular form: Magalotti described the theatre in 1669 and emphasised that 'this theatre is nearly of a circular form, surrounded, in the inside, by boxes'.[15] But the evidence to connect the Wren sketch with this theatre is slim. Both theatres have domes, but the Wren sketch has no boxes surrounding the pit and the isolated square on the circumference of the centre circle on the Wren sketch is more probably a throne than an entrance, hence implying that the design was not for a public theatre. The throne in the Cockpit-in-Court was in an analogous position. The Wren sketch seems to have fallen victim to the manic urge on the part of all theatre historians to fit any available sketch to some theatre or other,[16] just as the Jones/Webb design has been ascribed to such theatres as Davenant's projected Fleet Street Theatre of 1639 and Salisbury Court. Nonetheless, insofar as the design does relate to a concept of a theatre for plays, it is still significant in the theory of theatre architecture in the Restoration.

While the link of these two important drawings shows that a native tradition of the theatre with a semicircular audience form extended across the Interregnum, this concept is also oddly preserved as a classical echo in contemporary dictionaries. Blount in *Glossographia* (1656) defines an amphitheater as a place that 'differs from a Theater as the Full Moon from the half: this was but half-circled, that round, and composed as it were of two Theaters, and is thereof so called'.

The third part of the same line of descent that took in the Wren

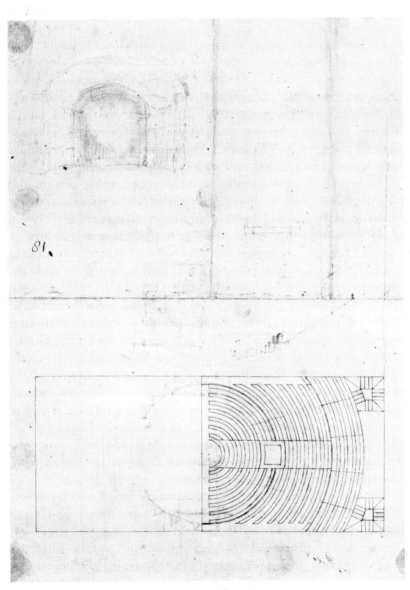

Wren: a sketch for a theatre

sketch is Vanbrugh's Queen's Theatre in the Haymarket opened in
1705. Vanbrugh's design like the other two was insistently semicircular in the arrangement of seats for the audience. A contemporary wit commented:

> When I their Boxes, Pit, and Stage, did see,
> Their Musick Room, and middle Gallery,
> In *Semi-circles* all of them to be;
> I well perceiv'd they took peculiar Care
> Nothing to make, or do, upon the *Square*.[17]

The auditorium form is again remarkably close to the pattern.[18]
Although originally constructed with one door opening on to the
forestage and one stage-box on each side, the theatre was altered in
1707 and the proscenium door was replaced by another stage-box
on each side. All entrances and exits onto this stage after 1707 therefore had to be made within the scenic area behind the proscenium
arch, even though the audience surrounded the forestage. As Cibber
pointed out about Drury Lane, after alterations there in 1696, 'from
the additional Interposition of those Stage-Boxes, the Actors (in
respect to the Spectators that fill them) are kept so much more backward from the main Audience than they us'd to be'.[19] That the proscenium doors could be eliminated at all – that is, that the traditional
manner for making nearly all moves on or off the stage could be
stopped – is an indication of the degree to which the forestage
was losing its significance. In effect, Vanbrugh's design inherits the
characteristics of a stage with emphasis on an acting-area (the
Elizabethan *and* Palladian traditions) and, in combining it with the
present requirements of acting within the scene indicates the use-
lessness and obsolescence of the previous style. Vanbrugh's theatre
was of course principally used as an opera house.

The tradition of acting within the scenic area begins for the
Restoration theatre with *The Siege of Rhodes*, with scenery by John
Webb. The minute Rutland House stage, measuring only 18 ft by
22 ft 4 ins,[20] had single unchanging wing pieces. The design of the
stage-area, so close to the basic form of the scenic stage for the
masque, is the only solution to the problem posed by the size of the
hall. It makes practicable acting within the stage, behind the
proscenium. But it is not necessarily the fundamental form for the
Restoration theatres, which were equipped with a substantial forestage. The action of *The Siege of Rhodes*, though occurring within the
scenic stage, was played on the same area throughout with the
only changes of scenery taking place at the back-shutters. Thus,
though the play-space is now clearly separated from the audience-

area by the large and elaborate 'Ornament which encompass'd the Scene', the utilisation of the scenery as background and commentary, as a body of information to be read off and understood apart from the stage action, remained the same. But the methods of staging that Davenant adopted here remained the norm for the presentation of tragedy, while the Serlian-Jones-Wren tradition, with its emphasis on a separate acting-space, was the norm for comedy, at least until the 1690s. Restoration tragedy was based on theatrical illusion, the separation from the audience that was practicable by acting principally behind the proscenium; Restoration comedy emphasised its close connection with its audience – and hence its claim, through its *vraisemblance* in acting and locale, to comment on its audience's morals – by placing the action principally on the forestage. Realistic as many of the sets must have been, especially for London locations like the New Exchange, Hyde Park or Covent Garden, the actors aligned themselves with the audience, especially through the use of the aside, so that the audience perceived the realism of the set as mediated through the action of the hybrid being, the actor-character. The audience saw the actor as in a situation potentially analogous to their own, rather than in a totally fictive world. The achievement of the major Restoration stages, the Theatre Royal, Drury Lane, and the Duke's Theatre in Dorset Garden, was in creating a structure versatile enough to accommodate the opposing styles of comedy and tragedy. But the tendency towards the end of the period was to unify the two methods. The retreat of comedy behind the proscenium arch was caused not only by the desire of Christopher Rich for increased income (that caused him to reduce the forestage at the Theatre Royal) but also by the impact of the increasing power of the ladies, with their preference for tragedy, and the entire post-1688 audience, influencing comedy towards a drama of moral purity. The result was a sentimental comedy, that is, a comedy of increasingly romantic illusion, becoming like a tragedy whose scenic practices were also those necessary for romantic fiction.

It is by now generally accepted that the longitudinal section by Wren now in the library of All Souls, Oxford, is closely related to the Drury Lane theatre that Wren almost certainly designed (plate 4). The drawing may well differ in details and it is extremely sketchy as to the arrangement behind the proscenium line, but in essentials it would appear to be accurate.[21] The design of the Dorset Garden theatre, based on such evidence as we have, would appear to be similar.[22]

Wren shows a forestage with a front curving outwards to a depth

Wren: design for Theatre Royal, Drury Lane

of 3 ft 6 ins, in all 20 feet deep on the centre line to the proscenium, and by rather risky extrapolation the width would appear to be about 30 feet. Cibber claimed that before the alterations the stage at Drury Lane was curved and 'projected about four Foot forwarder, in a Semi-oval Figure, parallel to the Benches of the Pit'.[23] This is exactly what Wren shows. Wren's manner of placing the forestage is most significant in its relationship with the basic architectural form of the audience-area. In spite of there not being seats at the side of the forestage, the two proscenium doors are made a part of the row of corniced pillars that mark off the side-boxes. The effect is of a continuous architectural motif that includes the forestage but confronts the scenic area behind the proscenium. The interior is divided in ornamentation by the proscenium arch which also bisects the overall internal length of the building.

In the 1690s, Rich wanted to increase the capacity of the House; Cibber mourned the change because it pushed the performers away from the audience by 10 feet. The 'Semi-oval' forestage was cut straight and Cibber noted that:

the former lower Doors of Entrance for the Actors were brought down between the two foremost (and then only) Pilasters; in the Place of which Doors now the two Stage-Boxes are fixt. That where the Doors of Entrance now are, there formerly stood two additional Side-Wings, in front to a full Set of Scenes. . .[24]

Cibber's meaning is here, as so often, unclear but it would appear that the new arrangement of doors and boxes was now like that which Vanbrugh initially adopted for the Queen's Theatre up to the proscenium, i.e. a stage-box, a door and the proscenium pilasters, on each side of the stage. Cibber also implies that the second proscenium door was now upstage of the proscenium (he does not imply that the proscenium itself was moved), so that most entrances were now made within the scenic stage. The effect of all this is obvious: to diminish greatly the utilisation of the forestage in exactly the fashion that Vanbrugh built into his theatre. The picture stage becomes the norm for all drama.

### The form of the scenic stage

Before going on to examine the differences between the ways that tragedy and comedy were staged, we need to know what the area behind the proscenium did look like. The contemporary terminology is interesting here, showing that the separation of the two areas was acknowledged. The normal term for the space that I have been calling the scenic stage is the 'scene'. Hence there are stage directions like '*Fran.* looks into the Scene'.[25] But there are in effect three major meanings for the word:

(i) A part of an act of a play
(ii) Scenery, as in 'cut scene' or 'The Scene with the Chimny in it'[26]
(iii) The scenic stage area.

Many usages, in combining two or more of the meanings, show how the term reflects dramatic practice. The emphasis in (ii) and (iii) is on the definition of place, an environment that *controls* the segmentation of the play; hence the usage to indicate that the scenery does not change, 'the scene continues'. At the centre of the link between (i) and (ii) is the nature of the 'act-segment' in the English tradition, related indissolubly to change of location and not the French and classical usage, where the scene changes with each exit or entrance. As I shall show at the end of this chapter, even where the scenery is not defined as simple index of place, the 'scene' can be a part of the play's structure of ideas.

The evidence for the details of the scenery within the scene is contentious. The best graphic source would appear to be the Wren section of Drury Lane. While it is comparatively clear what the forestage was like in this drawing, the scenic area is only sketched in. Wren shows four upright lines, each with a thick black line next to it, of decreasing size, the height being determined by a dotted line that is produced to a vanishing point by a door some 9 feet from the inside of the back wall. Behind the fourth line come three more bunched together. The distances between the lines are: proscenium to first line, 5 feet: first to second, 3 ft 6 ins; second to third, 3 feet; third to fourth, 2 ft 6 ins; fourth to the group of three, 2 feet. On the evidence of the masque-stage, the lines can be interpreted as indicating four wing positions followed by three back-shutters.[27] Beyond these three shutters there is no indication of any scenery whatsoever, though even the simplest stage for masques had some form of grooves for relieves behind the shutters. The Wren drawing would give a scenic stage of a total depth of 18 feet. But, unlike the stage for *The Siege of Rhodes* where the back-shutters are only opened in order to reveal a different set, the Restoration stage depended on the utilisation of the space *behind* the shutters as an acting area as well as scenic space. The shutters, large flats which moved in grooves across the stage to join in the centre,[28] open and actors are discovered behind, set against a further piece of scenery. A typical stage direction shows that the space behind the shutters must have been large enough to act in with ease: 'The Scene draws, and discovers *Hippolito* bound to a Tree, and two Robbers by him with drawn Swords.'[29] The scene involves a fight around the tree and the releasing of Hippolito. Wren's section, since it shows no shutters behind the group of three, must be sketchy when it comes to this area.[30] Even those theatre historians who cling to the Wren plan find they have to alter quite radically his distances in the scenic area if they are to fit in the facilities required by plays definitely staged at Drury Lane. Not only are discovery scenes extremely common but many plays have two or even three successive discoveries, necessitating further sets of shutters. If the sets of shutters only started 18 feet behind the proscenium then all subsequent discoveries are an inordinate distance from the audience. In fact, whatever arrangement is decided on for the upstage area, the practice of playing some scenes completely in the scenic area effectively gives the lie to the belief that all Restoration plays were acted in an undeviatingly intimate relationship with the audience. If the farthest upstage that the action ever reached was 35 feet from the proscenium, (leaving over 10 feet behind the last piece of scenery) then the front row of the audience would have been 50 feet from the actors, further than in many of the largest theatres now. Dramatists could make use of this massive variation in the distance of action from audience.

In the masque, the area around the shutters was used for the great machines (the clouds, *scena ductilis* etc); the conflict between the perspective scenery and the human actors who were disproportionately large was reconcilable through the acceptance of the grandeur of the symbolic image. But even in those Caroline plays that did use scenery, acting within the scenes was unknown. There is however a useful parallel from the stage developed by Furttenbach, the German designer. In *The Noble Mirror of Art* (1663), he shows a stage with a 12 feet deep area behind the grooves and shutters that he calls the 'rear pit' (*hindere graben*); this area is used either for machines or for acting, and Furttenbach recommends a strong flooring with braces 'lest they should bend with an actor on them'.[31] The set for this area is kept simple, 'When all the shutters are drawn aside there is a large opening to the inner stage, where a tapestried room like a hall may be shown.'[32]

Furttenbach's use of the phrase 'inner stage' must not be misinterpreted. Now that the inner stage is no longer thought of as part of the Elizabethan theatre, there must be no suspicion that it was part of the Restoration stage. The area behind the shutters is instead a deepening of the stage-area with the withdrawn shutters masked by their own set of side-wings. Illustrations of the Restoration stage, like *The Empress of Morocco* engravings or the frontispiece to *Ariane* (1674), show this continuity clearly; the artists are able to turn the wings into a continuous side leading to the back-shutters (implying a box-set) without letting the wings impinge on the perspective. The effect in the theatre was not the series of chinese boxes that 'inner stages' might imply. This continuity of the stage area is important since it leads to the vexed question of where the shutters begin. Richard Southern argued that Dorset Garden, and by implication the other Restoration theatres, had four pairs of grooves for shutters dispersed over the entire stage-area, each pair with its own pair of grooves for wings to mask them; in addition, he argued for a set of back-shutters at the rear of the stage.[33] The traditional interpretation had been to locate all the sets of grooves towards the back of the stage. If Wren's section shows four wings and three shutters, then, when the action was on the forestage, the scenery was at least 18 feet behind the actors and any discovery scene pushed the action back over this great divide, making the area sided by the wings a virtually unused and unusable chasm. One possibility is to interpret Wren's section as showing four single shutter grooves backed by three back-shutters.[34] There are three objections to this plan: first, the shutters were masked by wings which Wren does not show; second, the theory makes the scenic stage unduly shallow, giving an inordinate amount of space behind the scenery that would surely have been better utilised; thirdly, if the grooves were single as Wren shows, then the shutters would need to be removed from their grooves and different ones inserted for any play requiring more than seven sets. This objection can be met simply by doubling the grooves at each position.

Other opposition to Southern's plan is based on size: if the proscenium was 30 feet wide, then shutters at the first wing position would need to cover about 26 feet of open stage, necessitating a further 13 feet offstage at each side to accommodate them, hence leaving only 2 ft 6 ins each side between the drawn-off shutter and the side wall (the theatre being about 57 feet wide). There is of course no evidence for the exact width of the proscenium or for the steepness of the perspective and there is, on the other hand, ample evidence of cramped backstage conditions. But the point also shows how large and clumsy the shutters must have been, even those designed to fit in the smaller grooves towards the rear of the scenic area. It would seem only logical that the acting companies would have been in favour of any system that avoided manoeuvring these massive frames *during* performance. Like the scenery of the masque-stage, where the stage was always carefully designed to take all the scenery required, scenery in the Restoration theatres must have been pre-set for each performance.

There are significant parallels to Southern's scheme in some theatre ground plans. It is possible that the lines sketched right across the stage behind the proscenium in Wren's 'Bridges St' plan relate to shutters. More helpful is the evidence of the Teatro della Pergola (1656)[35] and of the Teatro S. Carlo (1737),[36] showing Italian theatres where the wings are interrupted by shutters which are masked by further wings. An illustration of a German setting of 1655[37] shows a plausible arrangement that might have been in use in England. It does not show any drawn-off shutters and, in any case, on an apronless stage one would expect the shutters to be set further back to avoid limiting the acting-area. Even clearer is the arrangement of the Schouwburg Theatre in Amsterdam constructed in 1664 (a year after Bridges Street) and substantially unchanged until it burnt down in 1772. The ground plan shows shutters over the whole depth of the stage and the design is further shown in engravings of the fire showing a set with shutters drawn across upstage of only the second wing position.[38]

But the European parallels are merely additional support. The best evidence for Southern's theory comes from Cibber's comments on the alterations. The change of the position of the second pair of proscenium doors so that it was upstage of the proscenium resulted in the removal of 'two additional Side-Wings, in front to a full Set of Scenes . . .'.[39] Cibber's meaning is unequivocal: the removal of the wings unmasked a set of shutters, 'a full Set of Scenes', which had to be abandoned, moving the *whole* stage picture further back and leaving the forestage split by the proscenium. Cibber regrets that effect since all action in the scene was now even further back and hence less distinct in detail than it had been before. Rich did not, and probably could not, extend the stage backward and hence 'every grand Scene and Dance' had to be less 'extended'.[40]

There remain two further considerations regarding the arrange-

ment of the scenic area: wings and perspective. Davenant's experience had led him from one extreme to the other in the use of wings.
In *Salmacida Spolia* he had had four wing slots at each position; at
Rutland House he had had to make do with single wings. I am extremely doubtful that Restoration practice was to use them as anything other than stylised pieces. The scene stock may have contained
no more than three commonly-used sets, one each for interiors,
streets and gardens.[41]

I cannot solve the problems of perspective so easily. When Pepys
had to take a box because the pit was full, he found 'that from this
place the Scenes do appear very fine endeed and much better then
in the pit' (19 October 1667). Pepys' comment shows that it must
have been virtually impossible for the scene-painter to keep the
perspective for all parts of the House. The perspective was, significantly, best from the level of the King's box. But a discovery scene
must have raised added complications, for a set of a prison, say,
which was right for the overall perspective would have been totally
out of proportion to a man chained far upstage. While such dis-
proportion had been functional in masques, Restoration scene-
painters had to abandon the perspective in order to maintain upstage proportion.

The 'scene' was then a deep area which surrounded actors playing within it with scenery, rather than with spectators – though the
audience, to be seen rather than to see, did eventually re-establish
the right to sit on and around the stage. The theory of acting, the
intentions of the dramatist, the relation of actor to audience were
all profoundly different when the action was carried on within the
scene. Restoration practice made upstage action equivalent to a
stronger divorce from reality and a weakening of the claim on
the audience to see the actors as individuals similar to themselves.
Tragedy chose this way, comedy so far as it could resist. The pro-
gressive 'modernism' of Restoration comedy clung to a denial of
the scenic stage and hence to an archaic mode of theatre. What remains now is to show that the characteristic methods of producing
the two forms were in fact different.

### The staging of tragedy and comedy

Dryden's *The Indian Emperour* (1667) is a typical example of the
staging of tragedy at the Bridges Street theatre. Less spectacular than
performances at Lincoln's Inn Fields, where Boyle's plays had set a

fashion for tableau discoveries and packed scenes,[42] a fashion that
was carried over into the staging of opera at Dorset Garden, Dryden's play makes full use of the scenic stage as an *acting*-area. Act
I scene ii is a discovery scene, in this case the Temple scene that
had been used in *The Indian Queen* (1665). Act II scene i makes
elaborate use of flying machinery[43] and traps, all of which seem to
have been located within the scenic area,[44] necessitating the setting
of 'The Magitians Cave' shutters in the middle grooves; the second
scene is a discovery and must therefore start far upstage. Act IV
scene i opens on the forestage against shutters of 'A Prison', set
shallow, which opens when '*Cortez* appears Chain'd and laid
asleep'.[45] Instead of Cortez coming downstage to act, Dryden
carefully directs Almeria to go upstage towards him, into the scene.
Later in the scene the action does appear to have moved onto the
forestage but the emphasis on the scenic stage as the place of the
action is reaffirmed at the end: after Cortez' soliloquy he 'Goes in
and the Scene closes upon him.'[46] He literally and symbolically re-
enters prison. Act IV scene iii is an elaborate discovery scene, 'A
pleasant Grotto discover'd: in it a Fountain spouting; round about it
*Vasquez*, *Pizarro*, and other *Spaniards* lying carelessly un-armed . . .'[47]
but it is immediately followed by a second discovery scene, yet
further upstage, using a deep prison scene from IV.i and showing
'Cortez discovered, bound: *Almeria* talking with him.'[48] Again the
action of the scene at least initially must have taken place in the
deep upstage area. Similarly the final scene of the play, including
the torture and death of Montezuma, is played against the same
prison set, is a discovery scene and is acted upstage for most of its
length, for the torture-racks are discovered upstage and not moved
during the rest of the scene.[49]

By comparison with this high proportion of acting within the
scene, the Bridges Street practice for comedy barely uses the scenic
stage at all. Sedley's *The Mulberry-Garden* (1668) is an example of the
normal mode of staging comedy.[50] There is only one possible discovery scene and that is of an unusual type. After the exit of Horatio
in II.ii (a scene which would be played against a stock interior set),
Sir Samuel Forecast and Wildish enter, in the street; after a short
conversation the text reads:

> [*They enter the Widows house.*
> *Wild* I show the way, sir.
> [*They find her looking upon her Husbands Picture,*
> *and does not see 'um.*  (p. 28)

If this is indicative of playhouse practice rather than the author's imagination, it implies that the shutters show a house-front; when the men enter the house, the shutters open and the widow is discovered. The rest of the scene is played downstage. Every single other entrance onto the stage is made through the proscenium doors directly onto the forestage. Even more strongly indicative of the forestage acting is the transition in III.ii. Everyoung and the three Prentices who are to cudgel Forecast are first seen against an interior scene. Without their leaving the forestage the text directs that the 'SCENE changes' (obviously to a set of street shutters) and 'Forecast coming by in his Chair' (p. 41). The scene is only practicable when forestage acting is the norm. In The Indian Emperor, the same characters move to a different place between Act III scene ii and scene iii; but Cortez and Orbellan have to leave the stage, then 'The Scene changes to the Indian Countrey, they return'. The shallow scene of the 'pleasant Indian Country' – already used in I.ii and II.iii – cannot be pulled across while they are still on stage, probably because they are acting within the scene anyway. To denote a shift of scene in tragedy a clear stage was necessary. The pressure of the conventions makes the scenery an environment for tragedy but a back-drop for comedy.

To show that the same processes were in use by the Duke's company, I have selected two plays, both performed at Dorset Garden in the same season, Otway's Alcibiades (1675) and Etherege's The Man of Mode (1676).

The published text of Alcibiades shows that the play took into account the available scenic resources of the Dorset Garden stage while making the maximum possible use of discovery scenes set and acted in the scenic area. After the curtain rises to discover a Palace for I.i,[51] there are successive discoveries for 'The Tent of a Pavilion Royal' (I.ii) and 'A Grove adjoyning to the Spartan Camp' (II.i). In II.i the emphasis on upstage acting is increased by a stage direction that Alcibiades should enter 'from the back part of the Scenes'. The sequence of events in Act V shows the method most clearly. In the first scene, there is a direction 'Enter a Chair of State with a Table by it, and upon that the Crown and Scepter' (indicating that the throne is pushed onto the stage downstage of the first shutter position). Far from implying forestage acting as the mode for the play, the device allows for the subsequent demands for discoveries later in the act. The second scene, 'a darken'd Tent', opens with the discovery of 'Timandra asleep upon a Couch' (1.157) and, in the course of songs[52] and the use of flying machines, the middle-shutters are drawn to reveal 'Elizium' (1.158).[53] At the end of the dream 'They all vanish, and the SCENE changes again to the Tent' (1.159). At the end of the Act this far upstage area is used, as so often in tragedy, for death-throes: 'The *Scene* drawn discovers Timandra on a Couch in the midst of her pains' (1.163).

By contrast, *The Man of Mode* contains only two discoveries. Even though the fairly elaborate set for the first scene – 'A Dressing Room, a Table Covered with a Toilet, Cloaths laid ready' – would be discovered when the curtain rose, Dorimant still makes his entrance through a proscenium door onto the forestage. The result is that he can immediately establish a close, confidential relationship with the audience. During the course of the play Etherege examines that relationship through the oscillations of Dorimant's control over the action and of the audience's sympathy for him. In III.iii, the forestage is used as the shifting place of action in different parts of the Mall while the set is constant; the fluidity of location is achieved without the need of a new set for 'another part of the Park'. Both the discovery scenes occur in Act IV. The Act starts with 'The Scene opens with the Fiddles playing a Country dance' (p. 55). It is not clear whether this is a discovery of musicians on stage or a direction to precede the scene, that is, this part of the Act, with the music coming from the music-room located above the stage. In either case, when the actors appear, they are not discovered on-stage but instead enter downstage 'as having just ended the dance'. In the next scene Etherege uses the same shutters as in the first scene of the play and Handy is discovered 'tying up Linnen' (p. 68); even so, again, Dorimant and Belinda enter downstage. The placing of Handy in the scenic area is far from accidental; by this background position, Handy is literally 'behind the scenes' for Dorimant, the necessary convenience to ensure Dorimant's easy passage through society. At the same time Handy functions as a symbol, a reminder of the sordidness of Dorimant's sexual athleticism. The romantic illusion of love of which Dorimant and Belinda talk is simply not possible against this background, but is instead reduced to sex, to the 'irregular fit' that Medley calls it on his entrance (p. 70). This undercutting of romance will recur at the end of the play when Dorimant finds that he no longer has a pure language, devoid of the taint of his worldly cynicism, in which to tell Harriet that he *does* love her. Here it is partially embodied in the mute presence of Handy but made even clearer by the set used. The play opened in Dorimant's dressing-room and the scene emphasised the tension in Dorimant's conduct between his desire for natural behaviour and his care to be well dressed; within two speeches he can inveigh against unnatural dressing – which, as he emphasises, is the product of 'coxcombs' – and yet be pleased with Young Bellair's praise of his 'pretty suit'. Significantly the opening stage direction had pointed out the 'Cloaths laid ready'. The clothes, like the scenery, function throughout the play as indexes to meaning, as means for the audience to structure the play: Dorimant and Harriet are linked by rejecting the fussing of servants about their appearance; Dorimant and Sir Fopling are contrasted by the affected negligence of the one and the obsessive care of the other. Downes reported of the first performance that the play succeeded 'being well Cloath'd and well *Acted*'.[54] The care over the production was necessary. The set provides another control for the play. The first scene is an emphatic statement of the libertine's harsh, almost satanic cynicism, an aggression that the play renders of dubious value for success in life. This cynicism is an important aspect of Dorimant's whole relationship with Belinda, a relationship that he tries to consummate romantically in IV.ii even though it is enacted against this set, the visual symbol, the palpable locus of his power and desire to control and enjoy on his own terms. It is at home that he can plot against Mrs Loveit, Emilia and Harriet. His lodgings are after all the only place in which Dorimant is shown as secure; even the normal places of libertine control like the Mall now thwart him. This use of the dressing-room set shows one aspect of the use of scenery that I shall enlarge on later: the tension between the set as index of fictional location and as a part of the play's form, as a closed textual system. Through the discovery of Handy and of this particular set, Etherege makes the scenic stage function as metatext, undercutting the claims of the dialogue.

*The Man of Mode* demonstrates that when discoveries were used in comedy as dislocations of the normal staging form of forestage acting the dramatist could make them part of his purpose. Even in those comedies in which discovery scenes were more frequent the refusal to bring the actors down onto the forestage is intentional. Ravenscroft, for instance, in *The Citizen turn'd Gentleman* (1672), uses the scenic stage in Act V: 'The Scene draws open, and discovers *Cleverwit* sitting in state, *Lucia* on his right hand, and *Betty Trickmore* on his left, Attendants of Turks on each side the Throne' (p. 86).

The scene not only mocks the pretensions of Jorden through its re-interpretation of Molière in terms of the tableau discovery bel-

oved of Restoration heroic drama but it also points to the extravagant illusion and deceit of the romance world of the heroic play,
thus continuing the attack on the form launched in the prologue.[55]

In Aphra Behn's *The Roundheads* (1682), the scenic area is used for
the two council scenes (one of women and one of drunks), directly
parodying the pretensions of the Parliamentarians by paralleling the
great council scenes of tragedy, for example, in Otway's *Venice
Preserv'd* (1682), 'SCENE The Senate-house, where appear sitting, the
Duke of *Venice*, *Priuli*, *Antonio*, And Eight other Senators'.[56]

There are further examples of the use of the scenic stage for
specific parodies of tragic style in Otway's *The Souldiers Fortune*
(1681). In Act IV, 'The Scene opens the middle of the House [i.e. the
area before the middle-shutters] and discovers Sir *Jolly* and the Lady
putting *Beaugard* in order as if he were dead'.[57] The scene parodies
heroic diction, as in Beaugard's speech 'Sweet Creature, who can
counterfeit Death when you are near him?'[58] By the end of the scene
the action has again moved downstage so that Sir Jolly can bolt the
door to Sir Davy's Lodgings, i.e. a proscenium door. The scenic area
is used again in Act V where the action of tragedy is being mocked
(Beaugard's appearance as a 'ghost'[59]) and at the end of the section a
continuity of scene is accomplished by the direction to return to the
normal area for comedy: 'The Scene shuts, and Sir *Jolly* comes for-
wards'.[60] While directions of the opposite type (a discovery followed
by a move downstage) are fairly common, indicating the dramatists'
awareness of the need to move the actors onto the forestage, they
occur much more frequently in comedy than in tragedy.[61]

There is one author of comedy whose use of discoveries is posit-
ively obsessive, an exception to the rule so pronounced as to neces-
sitate consideration: Aphra Behn. In ten comedies – I have omitted
the farces – there are no fewer than thirty-one discoveries, many of
them needing much of the scene to be acted upstage. Certain of
them are necessitated by physical demands, like the discovery of a
man tied-up in *The City Heiress* (1682); some are to ensure spectacle,
as in the pageant of the elephant discovered right at the back of the
stage in *Sir Patient Fancy* (1678); three use the discovery for a night
scene, implying that the illusion could be conveyed more easily upstage,[62] for example *The Rover* (1677) 'Discovers *Belvile* as by dark
alone' (p. 46). But of the others, the vast majority – eighteen in all –
are discoveries of scenes of undressing, dressing or bedrooms.[63] No
other dramatist is even half as preoccupied with bedroom scenes
and Mrs Behn found it necessary to keep them upstage, partly at

least in order to separate the undressed actor/actress from the character. The Restoration styles of forestage acting encouraged the identification of actor and character simultaneously far more than does upstage acting.

Scenery and associated staging practices can, then, be made a function of the meaning of the text. This is far from saying that all writers of comedy made consistent use of the scenery in this way. In fact, one of the consequences of forestage acting was precisely that dramatists could disregard scenery. Shadwell, for instance, up to the mid-1680s, rarely indicates scenery in the scene-heading to the published texts, relying, it seems, on stock scenes for the most part. Frequently it does not matter for the scene whether its location is an interior or an exterior. The printed texts, with exceptions caused by the source of the printer's copy, tend to include the information only when it is useful or significant for the reader. Nonetheless many of the most important dramatists (Dryden, Wycherley, Etherege, Southerne and Congreve) clearly took great care over the use of scenery.

There is potentially a major conflict between the scenic demands of a dramatist and what the theatre's management can or will afford. Many of the devices that were used to make the scenery signify in the meaning of the play may have been based on economic necessity. The tension between conventions of practice, the demands of the author and the scene-manager's fidelity to the text, produced forms of scenic practice that, making full use of the separation created by forestage acting, structured the text for the audience.

### The text and the scenery

However much scenery had been in use before the Restoration,[64] the developments in the conventions of the use of scenery and the interpretation of the demands of the text were, to all intents and purposes, new problems. While resources for such a study are thin on the ground, there are available certain extremely valuable pieces of evidence: Davenant's *The Siege of Rhodes* as staged at Rutland House, Boyle's *Guzman*, printed in 1693 from the promptbook, and a number of playhouse prompt copies. (See Appendix A.) This body of evidence helps in two specific ways: Davenant's production provides evidence of an early tendency to a non-realist, non-environmental usage of scenery, pointing to the separability of the theatrical *gestalt* into interacting parts; the promptbooks provide evidence of the playhouse practice when confronted with an author's text.

Davenant, probably the closest link to the masque tradition and hence to a potentially symbolic interpretation of all stage machinery, found that even on the minute Rutland House stage, with so few changes of scenery possible, he could enact the drama in terms of the scenery.[65] When performed at Rutland House in 1656, the first Entry (Act) was preceded by music and showed scenery depicting Rhodes and its surrounds with 'the Turkish fleet making towards a Promontory'. Davenant uses the inverse of what was to be normal Restoration practice, by changing the scenery before the Act begins; after 1660 the scenery normally remained unchanged during the playing of the Act Music and was changed as the Act began. The effect of Davenant's method is to allow the audience to interpret the set before the action commences. The action of the Entry shows the reactions of various characters to the news, pictured in the scenery, of the Turkish invasion. One might expect the scene to take place inside Rhodes. Certainly the relation of action to scenery is not just one of place; rather the effect is of the scenery as motivation of the action, as the situation to which the characters respond. In this it is significant that the shutters show an event rather than a place; location is not passive and extra-temporal but instead is firmly rooted in the moment of the play's events. The strange sight of painted ships fixed and unmoving was effective precisely because the scenic picture on stage was not intended to be temporally co-extensive with the action.[66] Instead it represents the position, the moment from which the events originate.

Since the Ianthe scene of 1663 may well have been played against a new set, I move to the next section. The second Entry is preceded by a change of shutters to a scene of Rhodes besieged. The same characters, now definitely inside the town, are still talking against a back-scene showing the outside of the town; they are followed, against the same set, by Solyman and Pirrhus, members of the besieging force. The set is not only serving as temporal as well as locational index (signifying that Rhodes is now besieged) but, as locational index, it is generalised, non-specific. The significance of this is clearer if the set is compared with that for the first part of the third Entry where the action is played against the set of 'a Royal Pavilion . . . representing *Solymans* Imperial Throne'. The latter set is specific; it is intended to mark the fictive space before which the action does occur, within the illusion of reality; the former is a sign of the place which is inclusive, signifying 'Rhodes', not a particular place like a tent. This second, generalised, form is, of course, especially appropriate to the non-scenic stage. Bernard Beckerman has shown how most of Shakespeare's scenes are 'generalised' in this way (like Troy, Rome or Egypt) rather than being 'localised', (like the door to Aufidius' house, *Coriolanus* IV.iv) or completely 'unlocalised', (where does Ross talk to the Old Man, *Macbeth* II.iv?).[67] The mere fact of scenery virtually eliminates the entirely unlocalised scene but the generalised scene was extremely common after the Restoration: a set for Hyde Park did not need to change when the action moves from one part of the park to another.[68] The Restoration stage's generalised set, frequently a stock set anyway, was dissociated from the action in such a way that its significance is clear to the audience. If the action was played against shutters showing an inn then the audience recognised that the location was significant; the particular inn was unimportant, unless the dialogue mentioned it. There is no reason to think that the Restoration stage-managers had a different set for each of the twenty or more inns in which scenes are set. The specificity was in the dialogue, if at all. Beckerman's warning is as applicable to the Restoration stage as to the Globe: 'The generalised locale is not vague: it is extensive, it is symbolic and dramatically it is concrete.'[69]

Until the end of the 1656 text of *The Siege of Rhodes* the scenery is subsumed under these headings, either as generalised but temporally precise, or as specific. But at the end of the fifth Entry, Davenant makes one more change of style. After the Turkish attack has been repulsed, Ianthe and Alphonso, both wounded, are reconciled. The Turks are not defeated and the siege continues, as the shutters show,[70] but, in addition, the alteration from the shutters showing the assault provides an emotional relaxation of tension that is precisely what the action of the scene, the reconciliation, requires. While still providing the temporal and spatial information, the scenery demonstrates its ability to carry an emotional coding by virtue of its place in a syntagm, rather than through its status in relation to its own scene. The demand that this final technique makes of the audience is an observation of the scenery as a structural device, as a system interconnecting with the play's progress, as another code to help the audience understand.

In the case of *The Siege of Rhodes*, the coincidence of being author and producer allowed Davenant control over the scenery. The result was a collaboration with John Webb that was close to the interaction of author and designer that the masque sought to achieve. But for most plays, the author's demands were limited by resources, the size of the budget and of the scene-store. Most sets came from stock or were new pieces re-used. Hence, in Rawlins' *Tom Essence* (1677), there is a set called 'Malfey's Chamber' (p. 40), probably from a revival of *The Duchess*; the bedchamber from Otway's *Don Carlos* (1676) is used for Durfey's *Squire Oldsapp* (1679) p. 52, and Fuller's famous Elizium scene for *Tyrannic Love* turns up in John Lacy's *The Dumb Lady* (1672) p. 51. Other scenes are specifically marked as new, like, for example, 'The new Scene of the HALL' in Porter's *The Villain* (1662) p. 56. These new scenes are especially common early in the 1660s, as the companies built up a scene-stock.

Often, it is easy to see how the choice of scenes in a new work is conditioned by the availability of scenery in the theatre, particularly in opera where the demands are likely to be greater and exactly specified. When George Powell and John Verbruggen adapted Tate's *Brutus of Alba* in October 1696, they took careful note of the available scenes and machines. Four of the sets came from those made for Dryden's *Albion and Albanius* (1685), two from Shadwell's *Psyche* (1675) and one from Settle's *Fairy Queen* (1692). One further set was made by combining elements from *Psyche* and *Albion and Albanius*. Of the great machines in *Brutus of Alba*, there are three from *Albion* and one from *The Fairy Queen*; there is only one machine for which I cannot trace an earlier use. *Brutus of Alba* is simply a well-documented example of contemporary practice.

It seems to have been the practice for the manuscript or printed text to be given, early on in the preparations for production, to someone, probably the scene-keeper, to be marked up for possible sets.[71] Normally the shutters he suggested were the logical interpretations of the requirements of the scene. In *The Change of Crownes* (performed 1667), the only errors are in how frequently a particular scene had been used before, for example whether IV.ii is the first or second use of the 'outside of ye Court' scene.[72] But the sets indicated are as expected: 'The Scene Changed into a Monastery' becomes 'Scene Nunnery';[73] 'The Scene a Camp, a Pavillyon Royal' becomes 'A Camp Scene'.[74] For Cartwright's *The Lady Errant*, the prompt-copy notes scenery only for those scenes which do not have scenery specified in the text. When the scene indication is vague, the marker had difficulty and his choice is frequently arbitrary: in Cartwright's *The Ordinary* III.ii was variously marked as the 'New Hall', 'Covent Garden' and finally 'Red lyon feilds', though the text never mentions the last at all.[75] *The Ordinary* also shows how well used new sets were: the company, having decided to splash out on two sets, 'New Hall' and 'New Ordnary', uses them for five and six scenes respectively, using 'Covent Garden' three times and 'Red lyon feilds' twice for the rest of the play.

In spite of this evidence of fidelity to the text, some plays must have necessitated compromise. George Digby's *Elvira* (1667) demands one change that is impossible:

> Scene changes to the Laberatory. Here is to open a curious *Scene* of a Laberatory in perspective, with a Fountain in it, some Stills, many Shelves, with Pots of Porcelane, and Glasses, with Pictures above them, the Room paved with black and white Marble with a Prospect through Pillars, at the end discovering the full Moon, and by its light a perspective of Orange Trees, and towards that further end *Silvia* appears at a Table . . . (p. 60).

While the rest of the play is just about stageable as it stands, this direction is over the limit. Even if there were a laboratory set, it is very improbable that the stage floor would have been especially covered for a single scene, and the three-part set (Laboratory, pillars, orange-trees) is simply excessive. There are other problems with *Elvira*. In all there are over forty scenes requiring a dozen sets. Many of these scenes, in their brevity, imply a fluid form of staging in which a generalised set, like the 'Prospects of *Valencia*' used in II.ii (p. 18), covers a number of different places. This set could back the five different locations used early in Act III, all of which are described with the characteristic 'enter x as in y' formula.[76] But there is no time in a two-speech scene to establish place, implying that the author's specific detail is more likely to be theatrical maladroitness than an indication of actual staging. There are however many similarities in staging, as in style, to Tuke's *The Adventures of Five Hours* (1663), particularly in the flexible approach where more than one room in a single house is shown in succession. This suggests that there was a convention of seeing a generalised interior as indicating any part of that house, each move being shown by a clear stage. But *Elvira* also switches from interior to exterior of the same house with ease. This technique, achieved through the identification of proscenium doors with particular entrances to the 'house', is reminiscent of Elizabethan staging. It is also possible that the forestage was used as the street in front of a house and the scenic stage as the interior. Significantly, the primary use of these techniques of generalised interior settings is in plays of rapid physical action, like the Spanish plays, where other devices, like changing shutters without a clear stage, are also common. The only other play outside this tradition to use this form of fluid staging is John Caryll's *Sir Salomon* (1671). Caryll uses a form of continuous staging that allows a scene to shift from inside to outside at will. In Act II, Sir Salomon arrives outside his house but then sits and talks to Betty, now presumably inside without having left the stage. It is no accident that Caryll is also, like the writers of Spanish comedies, adapting from a foreign tradition – in this case Molière's *L'école des femmes* – where the stress on location in drama is not so great.

The best information on the stage-manager's and author's interpretation of interior and exterior scenes comes from Boyle's comedy *Guzman*. Pepys saw the play on its second performance, one more than Boyle's other comedy, *Mr. Anthony*, achieved, when he visited the Lincoln's Inn Fields theatre on 16 April 1669. After talking to Shadwell, Pepys commented of the play,

> it is as mean a thing, and so he says, as hath been upon the stage a great while; and Harris, who hath no part in it, did come to me and told me in discourse that he was glad of it, it being a play that will not take.

The play was almost completely ignored until 1693 when it was published, in folio, as a forgotten work of the great Boyle, with a dedication by Tate. The printer's copy was the playhouse prompt-book which Tate had seen[77] and many of the prompt-notes remained in the printed text. Boyle showed a care over scenery in all his plays[78] and the *Guzman* notes specifically mention sets used elsewhere in his plays: the garden scene, IV.vi, uses 'The Garden in *Tryphon* as a Back Scene' and 'The Q. of *Hungary*'s Chamber', used three times, II.iii, IV.ii, and V.ii, is taken from *Mustapha* I.ii. Boyle probably specified these sets himself – the coincidence of their both being taken from his own plays is most probably explained by this – and was obviously in close contact with the theatre. The company had two new scenes made, a Piazza, 'with Walks of Trees, and Houses round about it', also known as 'The new flat Scene',[79] and a 'Closet painted about with Mathematical Instruments and Grotesque Figures', also known as '*Alcanzar*'s Astrological Cabinet' or 'The new black Scene'.[80] The remaining six scenes are divided between 'The Scene with the Chimny in it' (II.i and IV.iii), 'A flat Scene of a Chamber' (II.ii and III.ii) and 'The Forest' (used for III.iv 'a Field with Trees' and IV.v 'a Grove of Trees'). The use of most of the scenes is consistent: for example the 'Queen of Hungary's Chamber' is always used for scenes set in Leonora's house. The scenic demands obviously stretched the Lincoln's Inn Fields' resources: seven different sets are used and some economies are made, as in the use of the forest set for two different but generalised locations. The problems come with the chimney set and the flat chamber: each is used for two different locations and each is used for Guzman's house. The latter problem is the easier. The stage-manager interpreted the text, which does not indicate the location for either scene, first as a living-room and then, because of a line of text,[81] as a bedchamber, both being located as the dialogue would tell the audience, inside Guzman's house. The change in fact keeps the scenery in more precise harmony with the action. But the flat scene had already been used to back a scene in Piracco's house ('Enter *Oviedo* to *Piracco* in his Chamber' p. 12) and the Chimney scene is soon used for '*Francisco*'s House', (p. 30). Part of the reason for this may have been the limited resources of the stage, necessitating the use of one fewer interior than the text required, though all theatre historians agree that the system could accommodate eight sets either at one time (Southern) or by replacement (Langhans), but the method is an unusual compromise. We are accustomed to seeing a set defined as a single place; the Restoration stage-manager had no compunction about making a set do double duty and, more importantly, the Restoration audience could perceive the locations as different. But the double use of the set makes it possible for the audience to read the repetition as a sign of the interconnection of the events of the two scenes. That obviously does not happen here – *Guzman* is one of the least subtle plays I know – but elsewhere the possibility was used. In the *Belphegor* promptbook, for instance, two different sets are used for Montalto's house, 'A noble Roome' (II.ii, fol. 13b) and 'ordinary' (III.ii, fol. 21a).[82] The Smock Alley promptbook for *Henry IV Part I* links the King and the rebels by using the same set for the council scenes of Act III.[83]

The Restoration staging practices made available to the dramatist a variety of potential resources for providing a systematic commentary based on the information offered by the scenery. The next section provides an example of how the scenery can affect a play when used to the full.

### The scenery of Etherege's 'She Would If She Could'

Etherege's *She Would If She Could* was first performed at Lincoln's Inn Fields on 6 February 1668. The text was entered in the Stationers' Register on 24 June and was probably published shortly after. There is no evidence to connect Etherege with the printing and the play appeared without dedication, preface, prologue or epilogue. He does not appear to have cared about the printing of any of his plays.[84] Copy was probably Etherege's manuscript as prepared for the playhouse use. It shows traces both of playhouse practice and of fictive illusion unconnected with the stage. The text does however allow for the reconstruction of performance.

As Dale Underwood first noted, the play's ten scenes provide a structure showing the polarity of the play's worlds, the libertine world and the Cockwoods' home. The locus of the action moves between the two areas:

> [The Cockwoods' home] becomes indeed the antithesis and finally the nemesis of them [sc. the libertine values]. The setting of the play has accordingly its own polarity. And as the heroes and, on either side of them, the dupes pursue their several actions through the comic curve which moves from undertaking to fall, they do so by shuttling between the two poles, whose values stand as thesis and antithesis.[85]

For once Underwood's analysis is less subtle than his material, for Etherege ensured that both the main axes of his dramatic conflict – libertine/dupe and male/female – are structured within the formal scenic pattern in parallels showing the power of libertine as well as dupe rendered vulnerable.

The first form of polarity of place, libertine/dupe, though I shall suggest that it is here subtly ambiguous, is extremely common in Restoration comedy. To take only one example, Wycherley's *The Country Wife*, for all but two scenes, changes between Horner's lodgings and Pinchwife's, the two locations defined in the play as sexual excess/success and sexual failure, impotence as disguise and impotence in fact. In addition, the subordinate status of the serious couple, Harcourt and Alithea, is exacerbated by their dispossession; they are not firmly associated with any particular locale.

It will be helpful for the analysis to give all the scene locations as they are recorded in the original text.

I.   i   A Dining-Room
I.   ii  Sir *Oliver Cockwood*'s Lodging
II.  i   The Mulberry-Garden
II.  ii  Sir *Oliver*'s Lodgings
III. i   The *New-Exchange*. Mrs. *Trinkit* sitting in a Shop, people passing by as in the *Exchange*
III. ii  Sir *Oliver*'s Dining-Room

III. iii    The Bear
IV.  i     A Dining-Room
IV.  ii    New Spring-Garden
V.   i     Sir *Oliver*'s Dining-Room

The play opens in Courtall's rooms. The opening was by 1668 already traditional, the rake-hero dressing or waking but, in either case, in control both of his world and of the sympathies of the audience.[86] The first speeches, whether pronouncements on the state of the world *ex cathedra* as here and in *The Country Wife* or a confidential exposition in conversation with the audience as in *The Man of Mode*, make full use of that closeness to the audience that forestage acting encouraged. The 'hero' sets out from an initial position, established by the staging, in which his actions seem laudable and his ideals beyond question. The first scene shows Courtall's power at its strongest. He has no trouble with any of the unexpected arrivals and Freeman and Mrs Sentry are appropriately dispatched to closet and wood-hole. The action of the scene plays out the contrast between true libertinism (Courtall) and the comedy of the dupes' aspiration to two libertine conditions, drunkenness (Sir Oliver) and promiscuity (Lady Cockwood). The dupes' aspirations to promiscuity are qualified by the emasculation of language in Lady Cockwood's periphrases and a problem of stamina on the part of Sir Oliver – he has to take 'cantharides'.

It will assist the analysis of the staging if I move immediately to v.i. The set is obviously that used in III.ii and IV.i; the fictive location is in all three the Cockwoods' dining-room. But the scene location also implies that the set is the same as that used for I.i (in fact the scene-headings for I.i and IV.i are identical). The exactness with which the room is specified as the 'Dining-Room' shows that this is another example of the one-set-for-two-places device. This patterning is borne out by the repetition in v.i of the pattern of hiding established in I.i: Freeman is again the first to be hid and again he is put in the closet; Courtall is hidden under the 'Table and Carpet' specifically called for in the scene-heading, rather than being put in the wood-hole.[87] There are further parallels: Lady Cockwood's opening cynicism ('if they had kill'd one another I had then been reveng'd.' p. 72) reflects one aspect of Courtall's libertinism in Act I, especially his attitude to Lady Cockwood,[88] but further brutalised as a sign of the degradation of libertinism in the play. But Lady Cockwood's ineptness in organising the hidings in v.i marks a distinction from the opening scene, indicating her lack of control when compared to the suave efficiency of Courtall in Act I. The two scenes mark opposing poles that through the parallel of the set have been shown to have merged: the difference between Courtall and Lady Cockwood, between a male libertine and a female one, is far less than the initial propositions of Act I had led the audience to believe.

Since the same set of shutters backed I.i and IV.i, they must also have been used for the other dining-room scenes, III.ii and V.i. Thus four of the six scenes set in lodgings were certainly unified by the set. There remain then only I.ii and II.ii.

The shift from the opening scene to Act I scene ii is also a form of structured parallel. Freeman and Courtall opened the play with a discussion of the tedium of life and the decay of debauchery and easy game (they use the hunt/trade imagery that is fundamental to the rake's social conduct). Lady Cockwood opens the second scene by worrying whether Sentry has been debauched. She confuses the libertine language of religiosity ("'Tis too late to repent') with the 'honest man' language of chivalry ('he has more honour'), debasing both in the way that the trade imagery of Courtall debased his claims as 'honest man'. From the beginning, Lady Cockwood's voracious promiscuity with its continual frustrations is shown as a form of female rakishness analogous to the male libertine. The satanic ambiguity of Lady Cockwood – she more than anyone else is referred to as a 'devil' – is an application to the female libertine of one of the central problems associated with the male rake, reaching its summit in the satanic grace of Dorimant.

As soon as the manifold similarities between Lady Cockwood and Courtall are perceived,[89] it is clear why the twin axes of male/female and libertine/dupe cannot be superimposed. Lady Cockwood is female, libertine *and* dupe; Courtall and Freeman are 'heroes' insofar as they can change from being libertines. To be a rake, especially at the wrong time, is in this play to come close to being a fool. What disqualifies Lady Cockwood and Sir Oliver and Sir Joslin is that rakishness is limited by one's age. They have gone on too long – Courtall at the end of the play can use them as a warning not to. The play sets up a standard by which one of the characteristics of the dupe is his belief that he is a free agent, in control of his actions. As the play proceeds, the audience is shown that those areas which the rake-hero might reasonably expect to control, be they places in town or stage-devices, work against him until the rake must abandon his claim to social control and revert to a pre-social, 'natural' problem, the problem of remaining constant. Just as the other major objection to Lady Cockwood's promiscuity is linked to a social taboo, so the play denies promiscuity to the rakes. Etherege is far from uncritically accepting the premise that the male alone has a fundamental supra-social right to sexual freedom. The libertine falls from his ambiguous social position, the disdainful observer and the frantic pursuer, into a pre-social state.

The scene-heading for I.ii, the scene where the revaluation of the rake in the light of Lady Cockwood begins, is generalised. It seems possible, though I would not be more definite than that, that the room in Sir Oliver's lodging that is shown is the same set that I have established was used for the other four scenes in the lodgings and that therefore six of the play's ten scenes were played against the same set. If the polarity of the dupes' house was, as would be logical, kept evident by a constant set then the parallel with the opening location and the contrast between the four scenes set in public places and the six home scenes would be all the stronger.

The odd characters in this structure are Ariana and Gatty. Unlike the rakes and the would-bes, they appear for much of the play to be in control of the situation. Every time they encounter the men in public, social places, in the park or the Exchange, they win hands down. When viewed from the world of the Cockwoods, the role of the unmarried girl seems to be one of restriction; in the town at large, the girls show that the society which tended to exalt the power of the man can still be controlled by women. From their first appearance, Ariana and Gatty usurp the rake's normal role as audience's confidant: they talk cynically about the fools at the playhouse – pointing up the play as performance[90] – and they disguise themselves so that the audience recognises them and the rakes do not. Significantly, two of the occasions on which the girls are discomfited, when they 'shriek and exeunt', are in scenes set in the Cockwoods' house, the locus of libertine demands. The four public scenes are not then set in the world of libertine values but instead are associated, through the triumph of Ariana and Gatty, with the libertine's fall. The locales which were known as the places for assignation and promiscuity show those libertine values under fire. The realism of the sets – and the sets for the Mulberry Garden, the New Exchange and the New Spring Garden were certainly recognisable representations of places so close to the theatre – is mediated by the use the play makes of them. They are places reinterpreted by the values and actions of the play so that the audience perceives them as bound up with the pattern of the play. In the Mulberry Garden scene (ii.i) the girls' rapid exits and re-entrances show them in control of the forestage area and its possibilities as well as the Mulberry Garden itself, and its world of disguise and repartee. In iii.i where the scenic stage is used for the first certain time in the play, the discovery of Mrs Trinket and of the shops of the New Exchange means that when 'All go to the Shop to look upon Ware, but *Courtall* and *La. Cockwood*' (p. 35), the girls are associating themselves with the locale as a commentary on the predicament of Courtall. At the end of the scene, they show their control by the ease with which they embarrass Courtall. In iv.ii, the men are discomfited by their belief in Lady Cockwood's forged letters. In this scene, the girls again 'shriek and run off', this time accompanied by Lady Cockwood. The disruption of the girls' control over the public world that this exit shows is the direct parallel to the end of the play. Much as iv.ii ends with the brutal irruption of aggressive libertinism, the duel of swords replacing the duel of wit, so the pattern of the private scenes against the dining-room set, the pattern of libertine control, is disrupted in the play's coda. In v.i after the men come out of the closet and the girls 'shriek and run out' yet again, the play's direction of complication is at last reversed and the knots begin to be tied. The libertines' role is by this stage severely undercut; made dupe-like, the libertine must accept his fall into the state of grace and, as was common, the fall takes place in the opposing camp, in the dupes' home. But Etherege sees this event as a criticism of the nature of the male. The girls freely acknowledge the stripping away of social pretences and deceits but remain dubious of the male's constancy. Courtall is now devoid of bravado, though he will return to it in his viciousness towards Lady Cockwood ('pray/Intertain an able chaplain' pp. 90–1). While hoping that the month's trial may be carried off successfully, he now sees the natural inconstancy of the male much as the girls do: 'If the heart of man be not very deceitful, / 'Tis very likely it may be so' (p. 89). The conditional phrase shows his new distrust of himself. Any resolution of the play is clouded over by Courtall's doubts. Left finally to his own resources, the rake appears almost as ridiculous as Lady Cockwood. The would-be rake's fall has provided an ironic parallel to the rake's fall; the old are grotesquely similar to the young.

The dynamics of *She Would If She Could*, the parallels and conflicts which generate its action, are all present in the tensions set up by the scenery. The set functions as index of place, as commentary on the action and as syntagmatic chain in ways that determine the play's course. The scenery is not simply re-emphasis of information elsewhere in the play. It is instead a device aiding the audience in their understanding of the play's meaning. It is a primary part of the perception and comprehension of the play.

# Performance: actors and the cast

Between the playwright and the audience comes the theatre. In examining the specific nature of the theatre's intervention, one becomes increasingly aware of the Restoration theatre's vaunting of its own self-consciousness. The battles of Brecht or Georg Fuchs, the attempt in Fuchs' slogan to 'rethéâtraliser le théâtre'[1] were past history in England.[2] The tradition needed little effort to revive it after the Restoration. Isabelle comments at the end of *The Wild Gallant* (acted 1663, revised 1667):

Come Nuncle 'tis in vain to hold out now 'tis past remedy: 'tis like the last Act of a Play when People must marry; and if fathers will not consent then, they should throw Oranges at u'm from the Galleries: why should you stand off to keep us from a dance?[3]

Over thirty years later, at the end of *The Way of the World* (1700), Witwoud comes in amazed,

Hey day! what are you all got together like Players at the end of the last Act? (p. 86).

The effect is the same, a part of the continual and almost obsessive foregrounding of the theatricality of the event. In addition, through the claims of the *vraisemblable* established by the genre, it is part of the world with its own theatricality. Theatricality and reality are interwoven. In a way that the eighteenth-century drama had to eschew, because of its concern with an honesty that is socially inept and idealistic, Restoration comedy accepts the theatrical and, in particular, acting as something outside morality, as a neutral process. Acting was not evil *per se*, but was at the centre of the absurdity of existence. For wits it could be social grace, for puritans social hypocrisy. Nonetheless, the awareness of acting as device results in an emphasis on the individual actor; his significance in the audience's perception of the play is correspondingly increased. As Webster described earlier, in his character, 'An Excellent Actor',

by a full and significant action of body, he charmes our attention: sit in a full Theater, and you will thinke you see so many lines drawne from the circumference of so many eares, whiles the *Actor* is the *Center*.[4]

The extent to which the personality of the actor intervenes in the drama marks out two limits of dramatic form. Fuchs writes of the alternative processes as a choice between the vitalising of the text, 'the literary subject matter', by the actor and the use of the actor 'as a vehicle for the transmission of ideas, as material . . . together with other material objects'.[5] Both Edward Gordon Craig and Brecht saw the actor as a human and humanist disruption, a sentimental corruption of the pure idea, especially when his contact with the audience constituted a destruction of the playwright-creator's control. For Craig, Irving's 'good-natured contempt' for the audience was precisely what made him 'the nearest thing ever known to what I have called the Ubermarionette'.[6] Brecht's concept of *verfremdung* places in the foreground the fact of representation, of the device, but through an elimination of the direct intervention of the actor as individual, as 'flesh and blood'.[7] The elimination of the actor's personality removes any obstruction to the audience's dispassionate consideration of the event. Brecht's political purpose is achieved theatrically by the same means as those called for by Craig's aesthetics; human actions that the audience may view sympathetically inhere in the character not the presenter, and are present only insofar as the individual is politically correct.[8] In the Restoration theatre, as this chapter shows, the status of the actor was the reverse of Brecht's approach. The reality of the actor, emphasised by his spatial connection with the audience, functions as evidence that the action of the play is at least analogous to reality. He mediates the play, through the part he plays, to the audience, guaranteeing its truth and relevance. Insofar as the actor 'fits' the part, the part is true, is real. There is a parallel in Fuchs' concept that it is the actor who is the mediation that can create the work of art by providing the means to reach that moment 'when the audience is aroused by it and thus finally convinced of its truth'.[9] The actor's intervention in the process of performance is thus a part of a developing human reality that the idealistic comedy of the eighteenth century has to avoid. But the extent of that intervention in performance is part of an ideological commitment. Through the retention of the actor's personality, Restoration comedy posits from the outset a society that, in its warm humanity, is essentially corrupt and impure; it allows for the existence of evil. The presentation of virtue must therefore be either a product of total control over the methods of that society (the approach that leads to Mirabell in *The Way of the World*) or a hollow supra-social ideal figure (the approach that leads to Fidelia Grey in *The Plain-Dealer* (1677) and also to the sentimental hero).

The intervention in performance is in part derived from the actor's intervention in the creation of the play itself. The practice of writing parts for an individual actor opens the way for various literary, personal and theatrical influences as embodied in the actor himself to work – and be made by the author to work – on the text as performed. At the end of this chapter, I shall be examining the effect of the casting in Farquhar's *The Twin Rivals*. Without looking at the cast, the critic can only see the interaction of the play with Farquhar's own work and a limited theatrical context. But the play depends for its meaning on the transformation of a particular series of established patterns, many of which are made apparent only through the casting. The audience must see the actor as an individual and understand his significance.

### The actor and the audience

The relation of actor to audience is in the first instance defined by the nature of the acting. Formal, artificial and unnatural acting tends to concentrate the audience's attention on the representation, emphasising the performance, not the action represented. Naturalistic acting feigns ignorance of itself, pretending that performance is action. Only when a naturalistic style is combined with a controlled fragmentation of the dramatic illusion is there a renewed awareness of the play as play. The evidence for the style of acting in comedy in the Restoration is limited. There is a long history of caricatured acting that modern productions think appropriate to Restoration comedy; their style is based on a misunderstanding of the problem of balance between natural acting and the forms of social artifice. The hundreds of seventeenth-century books describing the correct manner of comporting oneself in society, many translated from the French, point to a codification of social behaviour into consciously defined patterns of conduct. While, to us, these long descriptions of how to bow and how to sit, complete with diagrams and illustrations, are as superfluous and ridiculous as Victorian books of etiquette, the patterns were so strongly accepted by the society, especially as embodied in the practices of the court culture, as to be thought of as natural. Only the young or the outsiders needed to be taught. The line between a natural easy formality of public behaviour and a disregard of social forms is as strong as that between formality and an excessive punctiliousness, an affected formality, like that of Trim in Shadwell's *Bury Fair* (1689). The comedies explore over and over again the two concepts of the 'natural', the social ease and the Hobbesian pre-social naturalistic aggression, in the same way that, for example, Charles II himself combined the rituals of majesty with the freedom of instinctual action. The formality of society is reflected in the forms of the comedy; there is a correct way of being witty, of talking with a masked lady, of conducting an affair and that way is not merely a bookish repetition of others' brilliance but an individual's originality combined with a knowledge of the limits of social procedure. The expression of emotion in action became a part of the inflections and variations on a series of ritualised events. The 'decorums' were a *modus vivendi*, a pattern of social interaction that allowed men the opportunity of the relapse into the pre-social natural only when drunk. The whole question of the rake's reintegration into society at the end of a comedy is dependent on the extent to which society is prepared to find the two aspects of the natural compatible with each other and with society. The rejection of full-blooded libertinism in the comedies of the 1680s and after is a mark of a new, more rigid set of limits on real, as opposed to theatrical, acting. Just as it is possible to prove 'the consonance of the comedies with other popular literature of the period, and the consonance of both with period graphic sources',[10] so it is abundantly clear that the form of behaviour in the comedies was consonant with the form of behaviour of man in society, rendered theatrical and therefore more extreme. Insofar as the form of action in society was based on a formal drama of movement, so the drama was analogous to society. The acting style, except for the fools, was naturalistic; that is, it conformed to the conventions of social decorum.

Cibber describes in a famous story how he saw Nokes:

giving an Account of some Table-talk to another Actor behind the Scenes, which a Man of Quality accidentally listening to, was so deceived by his Manner, that he ask'd him if that was a new Play he was rehearsing?[11]

Unlike the anecdotes of actors appearing mad when rehearsing tragedy, Cibber views the comic style as a heightened extension, a raconteur's representation of reality. The language is probable, though formal. Exactly the same attitude is taken by 'Sir' John Hill in his treatise *The Actor*:

It is a general, and, allowing only for a very few exceptions, an indispensible rule, that the actor, in comedy, is to recite as naturally as possible: he is to deliver what he has to say, in the very same manner that he would have spoken it off the stage, if he had been in the same circumstances in real life that the person he represents is plac'd in.[12]

This sort of imaginative consideration of the similarity of a comic situation with a possible real event is completely alien to tragedy in the period and hence the tragic style of acting cannot involve this sort of identification. Given such a mode lasting as late as Hill, writing in 1750, it is not surprising that references to the acting style of comedy are few. Gildon comments, in the guise of Betterton, that:

The *Comedians*, I fear, may take it amiss, that I have had little or no Regard to them in this Discourse . . . Besides, as some have observ'd, that Comedy is less difficult in the Writing; so I am apt to believe, it is much easier in the Acting . . .[13]

But, while the acting style for the principals was natural, the descriptions of the style of acting of the fools show that they tended towards a caricature of the social patterns, towards a distortion of the 'natural' that is itself a parallel to the distortion of the norms practised by the real fools. 'Natural' clearly had the sub-meaning of 'normal' attached to it. Hill writes of the actor employing 'a certain set of extraordinary affectations which are the distinguishing peculiarities of the character he performs'[14] and that, to act Clincher, 'a man can never act it well, who does not very widely depart from natural playing'.[15] Certainly, for many actors, their physical shape contributed to the form of their acting, their unnatural naturalism. Cave Underhill was brilliant at the 'dry, heavy Characters', and he looked the part:

his Face very like the *Homo Sylvestris*, or *Champanza*; for his Nose was flattish and short, and his Upper Lip very long and thick, with a wide Mouth and short Chin, a churlish Voice, and awkward Action.[16]

All Underhill's parts accepted this appearance. It would have taken a strong nerve for a dramatist to cast him as a hero.

By contrast, the form of acting in tragedy was highly rigid and codified into strict forms. Gestures were formalised and melodramatic with much emphasis on the hands. Gildon can list the right ways of picturing the various emotions. His description of this rhetorical style is in strict accord with the gestural index provided by Bulwer's *Chirologia* and *Chironomia* (1644). The links of oratory and acting are shown by Bulwer's frontispiece to *Chironomia* (subtitled 'The Art of Manuall Rhetorique') which shows Roscius the actor with Demosthenes. The style of movement in tragic acting was stiff, representative of a limited range of practicable emotions with no gradations in between – though there do appear to have been exceptions, particularly Betterton's significantly more restrained style. The vocal technique owed much to the style of preaching and canting. The voice was used musically with a whining, nasal tone that must have risked droning monotony.[17] The canting tone was frequently mocked in comedies, as, for example, in Durfey's *Love for Money* (1691), where Jiltall's false artificial vow ('I vow I shall') in Act IV is marked to be spoken '*In a Tone*' (p. 48). Again, the restraint of Betterton's tragic style is repeatedly remarked upon and descriptions of ranting rarely mention him. Nonetheless, in one of the most vicious of all the prologues of the period, Powell, Betterton's rival, waging the war of the theatres with a disproportionately high degree of personal animus, mocked Betterton's voice and age:

Wou'd it not any Ladies Anger move
To see a Child of sixty five make Love.
Oh! my Statira! Oh, my angry dear,          (Grunting like Betterton.
Lord, what a dismal sound wou'd that make here. (Speaking like a Christian.[18]

It was one of the things that Hill later specifically remarked on: 'no actor ought to attempt parts of this kind [lovers], if he be past that period of his age in which loving would be proper in real life'.[19] But the Restoration did not follow this practice. The complex reasons for this lead us closer to the place of the actor in the play: age was unimportant because the style of acting was not one in which the identification with the part was total; the actor never stopped being an actor. Hence, as an extension of the audience's recognition of the actor as individual, the actor kept his own parts. It adds up to the basis for the Restoration theory of casting, the strong link between the actor and his parts, the concept of the correct and accurate performance.

The problem of the actor losing himself in his part is at the root of most theories of acting. The actor must, and *does*, retain consciousness of himself in performance. But the idea that he forgets himself on stage is one that recurs again and again, particularly where the separation of actor and audience is most marked. The classic attempt at a rebuttal of the theory of the actor's self-awareness is Archer's book *Masks or Faces?* (1888). The attempt to erect such a theory is an act of compensation for the audience's attempt to lose consciousness of itself, to construct for itself a new fictive world which it observes unperceived by the actors – 'fourth wall theatre'. Traditionally, the effect is dependent on, for instance, the avoidance of the direct aside, one indication that the action is conscious of itself as representation rather than presenting itself as a new reality to be observed. The theory is dependent on the degree to which the theatre is an escape from the world of the audience or a rigidly separated representation and commentary on it; its connection with particular changes in theatre history, especially such aspects as the darkened auditorium and the silent decorous audience, is clearly marked.

The idea that the actor forgets the audience surfaced especially strongly in the eighteenth century. In the Restoration the theory was different. When Flecknoe wanted to describe Burbage, he praised him as

a delightful *Proteus*, so wholly transforming into his Part, and putting off himself with his Cloathes, as he never (not so much as in the Tyring-house) assum'd himself again until the Play was done . . . [20]

Flecknoe's intention is not to suggest that Burbage's identity was forgotten on stage but to emphasise the consistent unbroken method of characterisation that Burbage used – not only acting while he was speaking – so that the part could be seen, particularly in tragedy, as a whole. Hence the successful interaction he describes between actors who had 'such Poets as these to instruct them, and write for them' and the poets who had 'such docile and excellent Actors'.[21] Burbage did what 'Betterton' takes particular care to congratulate Mrs Barry on: 'And I have frequently observ'd her change her Coutenance several Times as the Discourse of others on the Stage have affected her in the Part she acted.'[22] To enter into the part only means to act even when silent! If Mrs Barry was so exceptional as to warrant noting, then most other players must have remained themselves and abandoned their roles whenever they were not actually speaking.

By 1710, Gildon wrote that:

the Action of a Player is that, which is agreeable to Personation, or the
Subject he represents ... An *Actor* therefore must vary with his Argument, that is, carry the Person in all his Manners and Qualities with
him in every Action and Passion; he must transform himself into every
Person he represents ...[23]

Gildon is writing against those actors who seemed to make no
attempt at characterisation. His emphasis is not on acting as disguise
but as *representation*, with the actor playing within the bounds of
theatrical decorum prescribed for the type of role. Even Hill recognises that the actor, while being appropriate to his role, must be to
some extent outside it:

When a man gives us all the wit and drollery of a comic character, without
himself sharing in the diversion he affords us, the insipid coldness is easily
perceiv'd ... when the actor can bring himself to share the pleasure with his
audience, he is always sure to please.[24]

The actor must harmonise with the character, must link himself to
the audience in its appreciation of the character and hence mediate
between the audience and the fiction.

Samuel Foote's analysis of two different comic styles marks a new
stage in the theory:

cast your Eye on the *Abel Drugger* of G. [Garrick] and the *Abel Drugger* of C.
[probably William Collins]. I call the simple, composed, grave Deportment
of the former Comic, and the squint-ey'd grinning Grimace of the latter
Comical. The first obtains your Applause, by persuading you that he is the
real Man. The latter indeed opens your Eyes, and give you to understand,
that he is but personating the Tobacco-Boy: But then to atone for the Loss
of the Deception, you are ready to split with Laughter, at the ridiculous
variations of his Muscles.[25]

I find it difficult to believe that Garrick ever persuaded an audience
that he was anyone but Garrick, yet Foote's distinction is between
the Restoration style, the Comical, and the new style, the Comic. The
latter relates to a new attitude towards the actor's own involvement in
his role, a sensibility which affects the audience's understanding of
the performance.[26]

This theory could however be carried to ludicrous extremes:

A Man who suffers himself to remember that he is a *Player* upon the
*Stage*, must in that *Instant* be *out*, and the Audience will *see it*, whether he
*perceives* it or not.[27]

The rebuttal comes from Diderot, in *Paradoxe sur le comédien*, and in Dr Johnson's remark on Garrick: 'And if Garrick really believed himself to be that monster, Richard The Third, he deserved to be hanged every time he performed it'.[28] I have pursued this problem because of the curious connection with other changes in the theatre; the rise in a theory of the actor lost in his part matches a rise in a theory of the actor's sensibility that parallels the move to performance behind the proscenium arch.[29] The closer the actor is to the audience the stronger is the audience's recognition of the actor as an individual behind the role. Hence when Hill recognises that the comic actor need not feel[30] he is recognising the natural contact of comedian and his audience. The consideration of role-playing in social life that is a fundamental part of the critique of society offered by Restoration comedy is inseparable from the recognition of that comedy as performance. Samuel Butler's attack on the player is in relation to his similarity to the fundamental corruption of society: 'When he is off the stage he acts a gentleman, and in that only makes his own part himself'.[31] But Butler is also aware of the possibility of the counterfeit being taken for the real, of the subordinate taking over,

He is but a puppet in great, which the poet squeaks to, and puts into what posture he pleases; and though his calling be but ministerial to his author, yet he assumes a magistery over him, because he sets him on work, and he becomes subordinate accordingly.[32]

Butler voices the fear of the actor and of social disguise that Restoration comedy seeks to accommodate and respect:

All ornament and dress is but disguise, which plain and naked truth does never put on . . . His prime qualifications are the same with those of a lyar, confidence and a good memory; as for wit he has it at second hand, like his cloaths.[33]

The puritanical fear of acting thus becomes an expression of the fear of being unable to separate the real from the counterfeit.

In comedy in the Restoration, the actor was not only known to the audience but was also frequently referred to or described on stage. In Wycherley's *The Gentleman Dancing-Master* (1672) Monsieur de Paris and Hippolita debate the relative merits of the actors, Nokes and Angel,

*Monsieur*  I diddè go to the *Italian* Academy at *Paris* thrice a week to lean to play de Fool of Signior *Scaramouchè*, who is the most excellent

*Personage* in the World for dat Noble Science. *Angel* is a dam
*English* Fool to him.
*Hippolita*  Methinks now *Angel* is a very good Fool.
*Monsieur*  Nauh, nauh, *Nokes* is a better Fool . . .  (p. 35)

Nokes had particular success playing French or Frenchified fools;
Downes describes his performance as Sir Arthur Addle in a production of John Caryll's *Sir Salomon*.[34] Nokes obviously played Monsieur
here and his self-praise is behind the function of the passage. The
audience's perception of Nokes is a tertiary level of role-playing
beyond Mr Parris as Monsieur de Paris, just as Hippolita and
Gerard have to perceive and establish a positive ground for their
affection beyond the hypocrisy and histrionics of their surroundings.
The further link between play and society in terms of role-playing is
proved through the awareness of the theatre as theatre, of acting as
acting.

In Dryden's *Secret Love* (1668), there is a lengthy description of
Florimell that is also a description of Nell Gwyn who played the
role,

Such an Ovall face, clear skin, hazle eyes, thick brown Eye-browes, and
Hair as you have for all the world . . . A turn'd up Nose . . . a full neather-
lip, an out-mouth, that makes mine water at it; the bottom of your cheeks a
little blub . . .[35]

The audience is forced to recognise the particular actress behind
the description and thus to see the theatricality of the complexities
of Dryden's plot.

In Otway's *The Atheist* (1684) Beaugard's description of Porcia,
though he 'never saw her in my Life', is comic because it is an inaccurate
description of Mrs Barry – whom Otway knew particularly well,
though not as well as he would have liked – who was playing the part:

Her Eyes black, sparkling, spriteful, hot, and piercing . . . Her Hair of a
delicate light Amber-brown, curling in Huge Rings, and of a great
Quantity.[36]

Aston however described her as having 'darkish Hair, light Eyes'.[37]
The manuscript for Wilson's *The Cheats* shows that even where the
parts were not predetermined for particular actors this type of effect
was created in performance. Mopus describes her sweetheart and the
manuscript leaves a blank with a direction that she should 'here
describe the person that Acts Bilbo'.[38]

Certainly, then, the player was identified by the audience and known to them. This was made possible by the strength of the actor's link to his parts, his keeping them so that no one else could play them. As I shall show, this was the result of an extremely close connection between the author and the theatre company.

The actor owned and kept his own parts. Each part was a roll of paper containing his lines and minimal cues so that the actor had little idea of the rest of the play and any ad-libbing was particularly likely to throw the other actors out.[39] It was thus extremely difficult to act through a part; an actor had little idea what another might be about to say and rehearsal time was in short supply. When Elizabeth Weaver gave up acting in 1664 she 'brought in all her parts' since, as she was pregnant, the company 'were glad of her absence, wishing the stage to be a place of credit, and not one that persons of honour would avoid'.[40] The parts have a physical existence which has to be taken into account. Betterton's library, sold off after his death in 1710, included 'Eleven Bundles of Plays and Parts of Plays, each containing 24 – MSS'[41] which undoubtedly contained his parts. When, on an actor's death or retirement, the parts were redistributed, the process involved the physical handing over of the manuscript parts. Hence when Cibber describes Powell as being 'now in Possession of all the chief Parts of *Monfort*'[42] he was so in this double sense. The ownership of one's parts was a moral right in the theatre. When Anne Marshall returned to the theatre in 1667 as Mrs Quin, after a two-year absence, she found her old parts redistributed. She complained to the Lord Chamberlain, who ordered the company:

to admit Mrs Anne Quin one of his Ma[ties] Comedians to Act againe at ye Theatre Royall and that you assign her all her owne parts which she formerly had & that none other be permitted to act any of her parts without her consent.[43]

Before Betterton's rebellion, the Patentees attempted to weaken the power of Betterton and Mrs Barry by taking away some of their parts. Powell, ever ambitious, eagerly took up some of Betterton's, Betterton being disinclined to protest, but Mrs Bracegirdle refused to compete with an actress whose style was so different and 'refus'd acting any Part that properly belong'd to her [i.e. Mrs Barry]'.[44]

Even though the incompleteness of the records poses problems, this retention of control over one's own parts can be seen in the careers of many actors, for instance Betterton himself. Only in the 1690s, thirty years after he began acting, does he begin to alter the type of new role he takes on, and therefore changes his part in some earlier plays. He changes from being Caius Marius in Otway's play to being Marius Senior, from being Troilus in Dryden's adaptation to being Thersites. But he still chooses Valentine in *Love for Love* for his farewell performance in 1709 as a right, though by this stage he normally let Wilks take the role.

This continuity of casting can be tested by examining successive casts for the same play. A copy of *Julius Caesar*[45] has a manuscript cast for performances around 1675 and a printed cast for revivals around 1684. Kynaston still plays Antony and Griffin Casca, but other roles are changed. Hart's retirement and the union of the two companies gives Betterton the chance to play Brutus at last. Wintersell's death gives the part of Octavius to Perin, Mohun's retirement Cassius to Smith, Rebecca Marshall's retirement Calphurnia to Lady Slingsby and so on. The only actor who appears twice but in different parts is Goodman who is promoted from the very small role of Decius Brutus to one appropriate to his importance in the company by this stage, Caesar himself.

The only other occasion on which an actor might give up his part would be when a senior member might choose not to act in a Lenten performance.[46] This is the most probable explanation of the casts in a British Library copy of Durfey's *Madam Fickle* (press mark G 18953(2)). The copy has a few marks indicating possible preparation for a prompt copy in what is probably the same hand responsible for one of the manuscript casts. The cast would seem appropriate to a period around 1691, at the beginning of the careers of Powell and Verbruggen. The second manuscript cast in the same copy keeps Bright and Trefusis in the same roles, has Sandford as Sir Arthur Oldlove, the part he created, and switches Verbruggen and Powell around as Bellamore and Manley. The absence of Betterton, Mountfort and Mrs Barry probably indicates a Lenten cast of about 1691.

The continuity of possession is connected with the concept of a continuity of performance. Downes, praising Betterton's Hamlet records that,

Sir *William* (having seen Mr. *Taylor* of the *Black-Fryars* Company Act it, who being instructed by the Author Mr. *Shakespear*) taught Mr. *Betterton* in every Particle of it; which by his exact Performance of it, gain'd him Esteem and Reputation, Superlative to all other Plays.[47]

The key word is 'exact'. There is a single right way of performing; all succeeding performers work in the shadow of the previous actor, and only a remarkable actor like Betterton shakes off the weight of tradition when he wants to. Even so, though he was greater than Hart, Goodman and Mountfort, his predecessors as Alexander in Lee's *The Rival Queens*, 'when, from a too advanced Age, he resigned that toilsome Part of *Alexander*, the Play for many Years after never was able to impose upon the Publick'.[48] John Dennis believed that this overbearing quality of the original performance restricted subsequent actors' success:

most of our Poets having had either the Address or the Weakness ... to write to the Manners and the Talents of some particular Actors, it seems to me to be absolutely impossible, ... that any Actor can become an admirable Original, by Playing a Part which was writ and design'd for another Man's particular Talent.[49]

Others saw in a particular actor the repository of an entire dramatic corpus, the range of a theatrical style. Settle praised Hart in ecstatic hyperbole:

This I may modestly say of him (nor is it my own particular Opinion, but the Sense of all Mankind) that the best Tragedies on the *English* Stage have receiv'd that Lustre from Mr. *Hart*'s Performance, that he has left such an Impression behind him, that no less than the Interval of an Age can make them appear agen with half their Majesty from any second Hand.[50]

The identification of an actor with a role is extended into the consistency with which sequels were cast. Wherever possible, though the vicissitudes of theatrical politics often made it difficult, the same actor would reappear in the same role in the second play. This pattern can be seen in plays by authors as various as Mrs Behn, Farquhar, Cibber and Vanbrugh, and Durfey.

In *The Rover* (March, 1677) and *The Second Part of the Rover* (January, 1681), Mrs Behn took care over the repeated casting. In both plays Smith plays Willmore the Rover himself, Underhill is Blunt; very few of the important characters reappear in *Part II* and there is therefore no part for Betterton, Mrs Quin, Mrs Betterton and so on. Significantly, Willmore's destined match in both parts is played by Mrs Barry (Hellena in *Part I*, La Nuche in the sequel). The consistency of pattern, Smith and Barry as the central couple, is maintained even though the exigencies of the source, Killigrew's *Thomaso* (1664), has forced Mrs Behn to use a new heroine, along with the switch of locale from Italy to Spain. The audience's perception of underlying structure, the inevitability of a match between Smith and Mrs Barry, is allowed to carry over between the parts. Mrs Behn can profit from this to underline the alternatives: Willmore is forced to marry Hellena but his bargain with La Nuche is achieved without marriage – a reflection of the degradation of the heroine into a prostitute (no rake marries a whore and remains hero) and of the increasingly extra-social position of the rake in the comedies of the 1680s. Beaumond and Ariadne at least make a serious attempt to resolve the problem of marriage; they will try, 'if possible, to love so well to be content to marry; if we find that amendment in our hearts, to say we dare believe and trust each other, then let it be a match'.[51] But for Willmore, there is no re-integration into society, no end to the 'banished Cavalier's' wandering: 'You have a hankering after Marriage still, but I am for Love and Gallantry'.[52]

The stupendous success of *The Constant Couple*, with as many as fifty performances in five months,[53] made Farquhar write a sequel immediately. *Sir Harry Wildair* appeared around April 1701, about eighteen months after *The Constant Couple*. Though conceived with the original cast in mind, changes in the Drury Lane company forced Farquhar to allow for some alterations. The casting of Wilks as Wildair, Norris as Dicky,[54] and Mrs Verbruggen as Lady Lurewell stayed the same. But Powell, frightened by Wilks' success,[55] had moved to Lincoln's Inn Fields and the part of Standard had to be handed elsewhere. Mills was given the part since his role in *The Constant Couple*, Vizard, did not reappear in the sequel. The greater placidity of Standard in *Wildair* is a direct result of this change. Mills probably took over the role of Standard in *The Constant Couple* at this time as well; he was definitely playing the part by March 1707 when he is listed in a cast, and must have played it in the dozens of revivals from 1701 onwards.

In *Sir Harry Wildair*, the use of casting to establish the audience's expectations can be seen again. Mrs Rogers played Angelica in *The Constant Couple*. At the opening of the sequel it appears that Angelica has died but Mrs Rogers comes onstage as Beau Banter. Though at this time there is a rise in the practice of using actresses to play men's roles,[56] the tradition of the temporary assumption of breeches is so strong that, combined with the principle of continuity of casting, the audience undoubtedly felt uneasy about the truth of Angelica's disappearance and were not reassured by Beau Banter's consanguinity to the missing girl. They anticipated the denouement in the theatre in much the same way that the reader must have done when presented with a cast list with Mrs Rogers doubling Beau Banter, a Ghost and Angelica herself! The casting creates the necessarily comforting atmosphere of a play which is a celebration of accepted comic forms.

Similarly consistent casting links Cibber's *Love's Last Shift* (1696) and Vanbrugh's *The Relapse* (1697). Cibber as Sir Novelty, Verbruggen as Loveless and Mrs Rogers as Amanda all reappear. The casting of Mrs Verbruggen is an example of the conscious ironic attempt to work against the real marriage of the actors. Loveless (Verbruggen), in his flight from the restrictions of monogamy, a state he considers contrary to the nature of man, finds himself trying to commit adultery with Berinthia (Mrs Verbruggen). The nature of the pursuit of sin is exposed, as in Dryden's *An Evening's Love*, as a search after an image of the female which is in effect identical. Adultery is only a disguised form of constancy at another level of existence in a world of endless disguise. Mrs Kent as Young Fashion is again the cause of Sir Novelty's downfall though in a very different form from Mrs Flareit in *Love's Last Shift*. Vanbrugh, by this contrast, explores the other side of the fop; Sir Novelty's sex-life may be reduced to paying for what most gentlemen expected to get free but when it comes to a choice between the ties of blood and the love of money the fop's essential viciousness is revealed. For Vanbrugh as for Jonson the line between folly and evil was very thin.

Durfey wrote the first two parts of his trilogy from *Don Quixote* for the United Company and they appeared around May 1694. Part II profited by the first's success[57] and Durfey retained as many as possible of the original cast: Bowen, Bowman, Verbruggen, Anne Bracegirdle, Mrs Knight, Mrs Leigh and Mrs Verbruggen all have the same roles. The only part to be changed was that of Sancho Panza, transferred from Doggett to Underhill, whom it suited better. By the time Part III appeared in November 1695 the company had split and Durfey's play stayed with the now desperately depleted Drury Lane company. Only Mrs Verbruggen was available to repeat her role, as Mary the Buxom. The play was a catastrophic failure in spite of Purcell's music and Mrs Verbruggen's performance.

The casting of the linked plays shows how the use of normative casting establishes patterns that the audience used as patterns of expectations, anticipations of form dependent on the relation of actor, genre and part. In himself, the actor provides patterns that the dramatist has to use and which, if used subtly, can provide a route for the exploration of central themes in the play.

*The actor and the playwright*

In 1711, John Dennis commented that:

Most of the Writers for the Stage in my time, have not only adapted their Characters to their Actors, but those Actors have as it were sate for them. For which reason the Lustre of the most shining of their Characters must decay with the Actors.[58]

In investigating the ways in which the playwrights used the re-sources of the company, one becomes increasingly aware of the limiting effect on the playwrights of having only one or two small companies available, particularly when the range of available types of part is in question. Small companies tend to emphasise the re-stricted range of an actor's abilities by making him play a succession of roughly similar parts.

The transmission of parts in the pre-Restoration theatre com-panies was even more rigid. In Webster's *The Duchess of Malfi*, per-formed in 1614 but not published until 1623, the text has the two successive casts printed together: Ferdinand passes from Burbage to Taylor, the Cardinal from Condell to Robinson and Antonio from Ostler to Benfield. As this shows, the extremely restricted nature of the company with its small number of senior actor-sharers meant that, in order to continue to be able to cast and perform particular plays, the departure of one actor necessitated his replace-ment with an actor of a similar type, a Burbage with a Taylor, Kemp with Armin, Pope with Lowin and so on. Even though the differences between Kemp and Armin undoubtedly underlie the more cynical Shakespearean fool that emerges around 1600, Armin was still re-quired to play the more light-hearted Kemp fools when the earlier plays were revived.

The best attempt at large-scale analysis of the casting in the Shake-spearean theatre is still provided by the work of T. W. Baldwin, even though one must handle his work with care.[59] Baldwin, having established the list of actor-sharers and its changing membership, defined a 'line' for each actor, a particular type of role for which he was fitted, on the basis of isolated verifiable casting, chance descrip-tions within a play and the transmission of parts. Baldwin posited that the author, as employee of the company, had to fit his play to the number and range of styles of the actors in the company. On this basis, Baldwin constructed cast-lists for all the plays of Shakespeare and Beaumont and Fletcher. Baldwin was, of course, working largely in the dark, without detailed cast-lists such as we find in printed plays after the Restoration, and he was prone to extravagant claims for the rigidity of the system. Nonetheless, his results, used cautiously, provide some guidelines and warnings for the path I am about to follow.[60]

Baldwin's definition of lines was extremely rigid but, in fact, the exigencies of fitting the actors to the available roles result in a number of compromises. In particular, the premise that the chief actor always took the largest role results in a far greater range of roles for him than Baldwin's description of the lines would allow.[61] The chief actor, Burbage until replaced by Taylor in 1619, naturally tends to take the largest and choicest part, even when it might conflict with his 'line'; the result is that the playwrights naturally tailored their plays to fit him. Thus Baldwin allots Prospero to Burbage, though within Baldwin's terms it is not really Burbage's style, on the grounds that he was too old for other parts in the play, while still allotting him the youthful roles of Philaster and Amintor in *The Maid's Tragedy* around the same time. Baldwin's decision over Prospero was right but for the wrong reason, just as Parrott's objection is too sweeping: 'Once more it seems more likely that the chief part went to the leading actor, regardless of "line"'.[62] It is not that the casting is 'regardless of line' but that it is not the line to which Shakespeare wants to draw attention. Burbage was Prospero because of his status in the company; he was the principal actor, the theatre's chief officer and organiser, the duke of the players' commonwealth. The casting is vital to the purposes of the play.

Baldwin's work directs us to three major areas of Restoration theatre practice, the precise nature of the relationship between the author and the company (given the authors' new independence it is different from the usual connection in Elizabethan theatre), the extent and rigidity of the actor's line, and the effects particular actors may have had on the course of the development of a type of drama.

Again and again, in prefaces and dedications, playwrights draw attention to the brilliant acting of a particular individual and point to the way they have fitted the part to that actor's abilities. Southerne praised Mrs Mountfort's performance in *Sir Anthony Love*:

as I made every Line for her, she has mended every Word for me; and by a Gaiety and Air, particular to her Action, turn'd every thing into the Genius of the Character.[63]

He praised Mrs Barry as Isabella in *The Fatal Marriage*:

I made the Play for her part, and her part has made the Play for me; It was a helpless Infant in the Arms of the Father, but has grown under her Care; I gave it just motion enough to crawl into the World, but by her power, and spirit of playing, she has breath'd a soul into it, that may keep it alive.[64]

In the same dedication, Southerne shows how the availability of an actor may predispose the author to alter his story to fit the talent. He regretted that his desire of 'coming to the serious part' did not allow him to write a larger part for Mrs Bracegirdle, though,

I should have been very well pleas'd (if it had been possible to have woven her into that Interest) to have had her Company to the end of my Journey.[65]

Others were less scrupulous about their responsibility to their dramatic purpose. Certainly Mrs Behn's motives in casting Angel as Haunce in *The Dutch Lover* (1673) were not so high-minded; she complains of his ad-libbing,

My Dutch Lover spoke but little of what I intended for him, but supply'd it with a deal of idle stuff, which I was wholly unacquainted with, till I had heard it first from him; so that Jack-pudding ever us'd to do: which though I knew before, I gave him yet the part, because I knew him so acceptable to most o'th' lighter Periwigs about the Town.[66]

Nahum Tate's *Cuckolds Haven* (1685) had little success in performance because Nokes was not available,

The principal Part (on which the Diversion depended) was, by Accident, disappointed of Mr. *Nokes*'s Performance, for whom it was design'd, and only proper; which caus'd a Retrenchment of whole Scenes in the Action, that are in this Copy inserted.[67]

In addition to this evidence of the care and concern of playwrights, there were many actor-playwrights. Lacy, Medbourne, Betterton, Powell, Mountfort, Haines, Underhill, Harris and Cibber all wrote plays.[68] Most of them include plum parts for the author, but, in any case, display their close knowledge of the resources of the company. Lee, Otway and Farquhar were all failed actors. One actress, Elizabeth Leigh turned her hand to writing, providing a plot-scenario which she sold to Elkanah Settle to complete, at a fee of half the proceeds of performance. The merging of the companies led to litigation and when the play, *The Ambitious Slave*, eventually appeared in 1694, it failed to reach a third day.[69] Actors who turn playwrights obviously have a particularly good sense of the nature of the companies and in their adaptations of early plays – which constitute much of their work – they show how these facts can alter the nature of the play.

An extreme but nonetheless useful example of this close link with the companies is provided by Cibber's *Woman's Wit* (1697). The preface needs quoting at length:

Another inconvenience was that during the time of my Writing the two first Acts, I was entertain'd in the New Theatre [i.e. with Betterton at Lincoln's Inn Fields] and of course prepar'd my Characters to the taste of those Actors, and they having the two most Experienc'd, I might there . . . have expected a more Masterly Performance. In the middle of my Writing the Third Act, not liking my Station there, I return'd again to the Theatre Royal, and was then forc'd, as far as I cou'd with nature, to confine the Business of my Persons to the Capacity of different people, and not to miss the Advantage of Mr. *Doggett's* Excellent Action; I prepar'd a low Character, which . . . I knew from him cou'd not fail of Diverting; I have seen him Play with more success I own, but ne're saw any Man wear a truer face of Nature; and indeed the two last Acts were much better perform'd than I cou'd have propos'd in that other House; the difference is only this, had it been there I had propos'd some Scenes more of a Piece with the former Acts . . . I was forc'd to write to the Mouths of those I knew wou'd speak as well as they cou'd, and not think themselves above Instruction . . .[70]

Though Cibber's insouciant naivety is only too characteristic, it is clear that writing with particular actors in mind was, to him, the only proper way to write a play. 'Of course' he wrote to the taste of the actors; he was 'forc'd' to change the play when he changed companies; he could not 'miss' using Dogget. Unwilling to throw anything away, Cibber simply changes direction. The play of course falls apart. Harland and Cibber as Longmere and Longville are trying to cope with parts intended for actors like Betterton and Verbruggen and Leonora is a Bracegirdle role ill-suited to Mrs Knight. Olivia, the role given to Mrs Cibber, does not appear until Act III and is a late addition. Even worse is that the two scenes with Mass Johnny,[71] the role of a 'Disobedient School-boy'[72] written for Dogget, are overlong and completely irrelevant – apart from being singularly unfunny.

This is not to say that all plays were written with particular actors in mind, especially where the author is an infrequent or non-professional playwright. But nearly all the major dramatists seem to have taken care over the casting of their plays. To a large extent this was a result of the mechanics of Restoration play production. There was no director to intervene between the actor and the playwright, a concept that actors frequently find unnecessary even now. William Redfield, writing during rehearsals for *Hamlet* directed by Gielgud, remarks:

What irritates me is to see theatre people embrace a directorial concept (which is filmically appropriate) instead of an actor-and-playwright concept (which is theatrically appropriate).[73]

In the Restoration, rehearsals were directed by the author, often aided by the theatre-manager, especially when, as so often, the manager was also an actor.[74] Like Bayes in *The Rehearsal* or Marsilia in *The Female Wits* (performed 1697), the author could coach his actors through their parts. Gildon, speaking as Betterton, shows that, even where the author did not attend the rehearsals, the better the actor the more willing he was to consult. Though the younger actors,

take it . . . amiss to have the Author give them any Instruction; and tho they know nothing of the Art of Poetry, will give their Censure, and neglect or mind a Part as they think the Author and his Part serves . . . Whereas it has always been mine and Mrs. *Barry*'s Practice to consult e'en the most indifferent Poet in any Part we have thought fit to accept of . . .[75]

This working relationship must have made the author ensure that the actors were pleased: as Calista comments in *The Female Wits*, 'I hope you will find the Characters to your satisfaction' (1704, p. 21).

The sad case of Richard Flecknoe shows how important an author could consider the casting to the success of his play. Flecknoe's *The Damoiselles a la Mode*, was published, at his own expense, in 1667. The acting companies had turned the play down and Flecknoe's pride was hurt:

For the Acting it, those who have the Governing of the Stage, have their Humours, and wou'd be intreated; and I have mine, and w'ont intreat them; and were all Drammatick Writers of my mind, they shou'd wear their old *Playes* Thred-bare, e're they shou'd have any *New*, till they better understood their own Interest, and how to distinguish betwixt good and bad.[76]

But, in giving the list 'Of the Persons Represented', Flecknoe gives the 'Actors Representing them'.[77] He gives the names of those 'I intended shou'd Represent them, that the Reader might have half the pleasure of seeing it Acted, and a lively imagination might have the pleasure of it all intire'.[78] Flecknoe's play is carefully though unavailingly suited to the actors of the King's company.

As a final example, I shall consider the playwriting career of John Dryden. Dryden started writing under the auspices of the King's company. Up to 1667, all his plays were produced by them except *Sir Martin Mar-all* which was acted by the Duke's company. This was partly from a desire to use the talents of Nokes in a different type of play, since, as Downes says,

He Adapted the Part purposely for the Mouth of Mr. *Nokes* . . . All the Parts being very Just and Exactly performed, 'specially Sir *Martin* and his Man, Mr. *Smith*, and several others since have come very near him, but none Equall'd, nor yet Mr. *Nokes* in Sir *Martin*.[79]

Dryden stayed with the Duke's company to collaborate with Davenant on *The Tempest* adaptation, which was also a huge success. The King's company, seeing a chance, entered into a formal agreement with Dryden in May 1668 that he would provide them with three plays a year in return for $1\frac{1}{4}$ shares of the theatre's profits, estimated by the players to be worth £300–£400 a year.[80] In spite of never keeping to this extremely heavy schedule, Dryden stayed with the company until its fortunes declined so far that it was pointless to continue. Though Dryden was probably the first playwright to have such a contract in the Restoration, he was certainly not the last. Arguments over Dryden's contract revealed similar arrangements between Lee and the King's company and Crowne and the Duke's.[81] Durfey probably had a similar agreement in the 1670s,[82] and Settle had a contract with the King's company just before the Union of the companies.[83] Much as Dryden's brief sojourn with the Duke's company spurred the King's company to make the contract with him, so Cibber's flirtation with the secessionists over *Woman's Wit* encouraged Rich to stop him looking elsewhere again as a playwright while he was acting at Drury Lane. The elaborate agreement between Rich and Cibber specifies Cibber's receipts on a third and sixth day of performance, dependent on the size of house on the day following a benefit, and his rights over subsequent printing. It also records that:

Item it is agreed between the Parties to these Presents, that the said Colley Cibber shall bargain and sell unto the said Mr Rich his Heires, or Assignes all such other Play, and Plays as the said Mr Cibber shall hereafter write to bee acted only by the Company under the Government of the said Mr Rich his Heires, or Assignes, upon the like Termes, and Considerations aforesaid during the said Mr Cibbers being an Actor in this Company aforesaid, and that the said Mr Cibber shall not During his being an Actor in such Company write any Play, or other thing whatsoever for any other Company . . .[84]

This agreement, rigid as Rich could make, served, like the others, to restrict the author to a particular group of actors. In Dryden's case the heavy schedule was such as to force him to pay especial regard to the advantages the King's company had to offer but, in any case, Dryden always seems to have noted the strengths of his actors. Again and again, his plays seem to have been formed in a particular way solely so as to take advantage of a brilliant actor or a current theatrical success.

In *Secret Love* (1668) and *An Evening's Love* (1671), the structure of the plays revolves around the successes of Charles Hart and Nell Gwyn as the founders of the 'gay couple' style, a point to which I shall return shortly. In *Tyrannic Love* (1670) the whole tone of the play is twisted by the ironic casting of Nell Gwyn as the saintly Valeria, thus establishing that the hint of over-extended bombast, of hyper-heroic melodrama does veer over into self-parody. Without the Epilogue to serve as mediation between the illusion and the fact, those critiques of the play as nonsense would almost be justified.

In *The Conquest of Granada* the black-and-white pattern of morality for the women is possible through the patterns already established in contemporary tragedies by Rebecca Marshall and Elizabeth Boutell, a pattern that recurs even more forcibly in the 1690s with Barry and Bracegirdle. Benito in *The Assignation* is moulded around the whimsy of Haines. Rebecca Marshall's line of evil women recurred when she played Nourmahal in *Aureng-Zebe*. *The Spanish Friar* is dependent on Anthony Leigh as the friar, *Amphitryon* on the Nokes-Leigh pairing as Sosia and Mercury. Even at the very end of Dryden's career, Mrs Barry as Cassandra in *Cleomenes* (1692) was a stupendous success in a part intended for her from the start.

A full-scale analysis of the casting of Dryden's plays would reveal an assiduous care in practice that reflects the preoccupations frequently expressed in his letters. In August 1684, Dryden wrote to Tonson that,

for the Actors in the two plays which are to be acted of mine, this winter, I had spoken with Mr Betterton by chance at the Coffee house the afternoon before I came away: & I believe that the persons were all agreed on, to be just the same you mentiond. Only Octavia was to be Mrs Buttler, in case Mrs Cooke were not on the Stage. And I know not whether Mrs Percivall who is a Comedian, will do so well for Benzayda.[85]

The plays in question were *All for Love* and *The Conquest of Granada* which were both to be revived. Dryden's concern was as great for a revival as for a first performance, in this case because the retirement of Mrs Boutell necessitated a new Benzayda and no good choice was available. Dryden was concerned about the cast long before a play was finished. He comments in a letter to Walsh in May 1693, while writing *Love Triumphant*,

This morning I had their chief Comedian whom they call Solon,[86] with me; to consult with him concerning his own Character: & truly I thinke he has the best Understanding of any man in the Playhouse.[87]

For Dryden, as for his fellow dramatists, the casting was a vital early step in the creation of the play, for on it depended the audience's pleasure and perception of the structure. But the casting depended on the nature of the actor, on what he could or could not act, on the nature of his 'line'.

Every actor has his limitations. Restricted by appearance, voice or temperament, there are certain types of roles which are simply impracticable for him. By continuing to play a certain limited range of roles, an actor can affect a play simply by going outside that range. This concept of range is not in the mind of the actor, but in the mind of the audience; through their acquaintance with his type of part, the audience anticipates, from the presence of an actor, certain structures of dramatic event that can, at the dramatist's will, be fulfilled or frustrated. The casting thus follows or destroys notions of genre. In part, this development of pre-existing structures, of genres, is dependent on the audience's continual acquaintance with the patterns. It was true, for instance, of such series as Brian Rix farces or 'Carry On' films, descendants of the restricted range of characters and actions that made up the *lazzi* of *commedia dell'arte*. We can trace its effects in certain film genres: one cannot imagine a villainous John Wayne, a moral Clint Eastwood or a good Lee Van Cleef within the genre 'Western'. Once established, a 'line' can be directly parodied: Jean-Pierre Léaud, who so often plays the role of a sexually-confused young man, mocks his own role in Truffaut's *La Nuit Americaine*.

In the Restoration, the sense of limitation was far stronger. It was necessary if the actor was to survive the system. He would need to memorise hundreds of parts and be able to act them with minimal re-rehearsal. In a company with only a dozen leading players, he would still need to retain a distinctive individuality. The 'line' was then a direct help to the actor: it gave him a place in the company, a set of parts that were defined as his.

Any exposition of the nature of the 'lines' will necessarily be a distortion of a complex process, the result of an intricate relationship between author, actor and company. Any analysis of the effect of an actor on the historical development of a genre will probably be an inadequate simplification. Even where the change may be clearly divined, the burden of proof will often be beyond the limits of the evidence. One effect of the Union will serve as an example. Those comedies written for the United company (1682–95) tend to require more actors than those written before or after. My own counts show that most plays up to 1682 tend to fall within the range of ten to fourteen named and cast roles while those between 1682 and 1695 tend to fall in the range of thirteen to eighteen, with some having over twenty roles. Durfey's *The Commonwealth of Women* (1685) needs at least twenty-two actors, including nine women, a number that was out of the question before the Union. Similar problems occurred at Drury Lane after the secession of Betterton, when the small size of the company and their lack of experience forced them to act only plays with small casts, so that certain stock plays were beyond them. A full presentation of the relevant statistics might 'prove' this but on what grounds is one to show that the comedies of the Union period also produce an effect of ensemble comedy with many more *major* parts than before? Even if the data were quantifiable, the causes of the theatrical change are a mass of elements as diverse as the dramatists' concern to explore the notion of 'society', the vastly increased pool of actors available, the relative shortage of dominant stars to distort the emphasis and the nature of the theatre audience. In establishing a notion of specialisation then, one is less concerned with the restrictive notion that may have been present within the company, than with the links that the audience could perceive, the similarities that made one part a role for Bracegirdle, Hart or Underhill and for no one else.

The only significant attempt at an analysis of lines in the Restoration appears in an article by Ben Ross Schneider.[88] Unfortunately, Schneider started by selecting a set of roles through what he believed to be their similarities and then tested how well actresses fitted them. The result is a series of parts that do not belong together, traced over a period of sixty years during which the preconceptions that attach to the 'line' alter fundamentally. One must dismiss a system which can place in the same category Angelica in *The Rover*, Melantha in *Marriage A-la-Mode*, Olivia in *The Plain-Dealer*, Ruth in *The Squire of Alsatia* and both Lady Wishfort and Mrs Marwood from *The Way of the World*. These parts do not constitute a 'line' at all. Schneider's method is insensitive not only to the relationship of disparate roles but also to the effect of an individual actor at a particular moment. Thus he cannot perceive the significance of the variations on his group of 'young Coquette-prudes' that are worked by the parts assigned to Barry or Bracegirdle in the 1690s[89] or how important to the development of the drama of the 1690s was the subtle shift between 'heroine' and 'coquette-prude' in the roles of Mrs Verbruggen. The rule must be to start with the actor and consider the development of the line as an historical process in relation to that actor. The actor precedes the role.

Certain actors remained firmly linked to a very limited range of possible roles. Samuel Sandford, described by Aston as 'Round-shoulder'd, Meagre-fac'd, Spindle-shank'd, Splay-footed, with a sour Countenance, and long lean Arms'[90] was 'a villain from necessity'.[91] Sandford's form provided an automatic means of coding for his roles in tragedy, and this coding was made to serve a moral function. Cibber recognised how Sandford's appearance became a symbol of dramatic purpose, of a pre-Collier morality: 'The Spectator too, by not being misled by a tempting Form, may be less inclin'd to excuse the wicked or immoral Views or Sentiments of them.'[92] Sandford's speciality in tragedy was recognised as early as 1662 with his success as Malignii in Porter's *The Villain*, a ten-day wonder. He was still playing villains in the 1690s. Cibber's description of Sandford's attempt to play an honest statesman, even if apocryphal, is evidence of the significance that the audiences, in Cibber's view, attached to the coding by type:

A new Play (the Name of it I have forgot) was brought upon the Stage, wherein *Sandford* happen'd to perform the Part of an honest Statesman: The Pit, after they had sate three or four Acts in a quiet Expectation that the well-dissembled Honesty of *Sandford* (for such of course they concluded it) would soon be discover'd, or at least, from its Security, involve the Actors in the Play in some surprizing Distress or Confusion, which might raise and animate the Scenes to come; when, at last, finding no such matter, but that the Catastrophe had taken quite another Turn, and that *Sandford* was really an honest Man to the end of the Play, they fairly damn'd it, as if the Author had impos'd upon them the most frontless or incredible Absurdity.[93]

The casting of Sandford against the type he had established was not just an infelicity of production but a fundamental destruction of the patterns of expectation, of genre, and of the viability of the specific play as moral, truthful and probable work of art. Not surprisingly, the dramatists often made the casting against type a significant part of their plays' alteration of accepted norms of character. Sandford's practice in tragedy is a classic example of the pre-determination of dramatic effect. Seeing him, the audience expected to know how to cope with some of the problems the play might offer.

Sandford's restrictive type can be matched by others. Elinor Leigh specialised in servant roles, as well as playing a vast number of roles of promiscuous women like Lady Temptyouth in Mrs Pix's *Deceiver Deceived* (1698), Lady Laycock in Betterton's *The Amorous Widow* (1670s), or Mrs Bisket in *Epsom Wells* (1673). Even those actors who played the fools, like Leigh, Underhill, Nokes and Jevon, established certain characteristic limits. Leigh's roles were the jovial fool with an added specialisation in cunning clerics,[94] Underhill's the long-faced solemn fool like Lolpoop in *The Squire of Alsatia*, Jevon's the light-footed trickster – he was directly responsible for a stream of Harlequin-like characters in the late 1670s.

But, while Sandford's line in *tragedy* is distinctive, his roles in *comedy* are not consistent over his long career. For many years his comic roles tended to match his tragic ones and he played characters like Wheadle in *Love in a Tub*, or Cheatly in *The Squire of Alsatia*, but towards the end he began to take on roles of foolish old fathers like Sir Lawrence Limber in *The Richmond Heiress* (1693) or Foresight in *Love for Love* (1695), as roles more commensurate with his age. The difference shows the importance of separating out the comic and tragic roles; the type established in one is not transferable to the other unless specifically recalled in the play, as Wilks' tragic roles are in Farquhar's *The Constant Couple* by Wildair's (Wilks') quotations from *The Rival Queens*. There are two separate traditions, two lines for the actor. The tragic line need not affect the comic at all.

The change in Sandford's comic roles over a period of time is precisely what one finds in the comic roles taken by Betterton. At the beginning of his career, in the early 1660s, Betterton plays the quasi-heroic roles in comedy, like Beauford in *Love in a Tub* (1664). By the late 1660s and throughout the 1670s Betterton established himself as the leading rake-hero actor for the Duke's company, creating the leading roles in plays like *Epsom Wells* (1673), *The Countrey Wit* (1676), *The Virtuoso* (1676) and of course Dorimant in *The Man of Mode* (1676). Exceptions to this are intentional, like the would-be rakishness of Sir Salomon in Caryll's play (1671). By the end of the 1680s, the decline in the rake-hero is matched in Betterton's choice of parts as the rake begins to be seen more often than not as a cynical manipulator rather than a carefree man-about-town. Betterton had created the role of Don John in Shadwell's *The Libertine* (1676) and Nemours in Lee's *The Princess of Cleve* (performed around 1682) and their influence leads towards the darker roles, such as Lovemore in *The Wives Excuse* (1692), Polidor in *The Married Beau* (1694) and hence the villain roles, Maskwell and Fainall, in Congreve. In the 1690s Betterton begins to take some smaller roles including some of old men, not only Heartwell in *The Old Batchelour* (1693) but also Vanbrugh's Sir John Brute (1697) and Sir Timothy Tallapoy in Rowe's *The Biter* (1705). By 1707, he could appear without dislocating the play, as Morose in *Epicoene*. Any attempt to see Betterton's wide range of parts as evidence of 'versatility' fails to see his career as a slow development, a changing pattern linked to the changes in comedy and in Betterton's own preferences. While never having such a clear line as Underhill, Betterton's choice of roles followed a pattern, a reflection of the changing attitudes towards the acceptability of the ideals of the characters he played.

Although those who never rose above minor roles, or those who were just beginning to act, may have escaped, every significant actor in the Restoration had some clearly defined type of role in comedy and another in tragedy at each stage of his career. The task of the analysis is to disentangle that line and show how it affected a play at a particular juncture.

The continuing effect of a new characteristic, a new line may result in a fundamental change in the drama. The actors' intervention becomes not simply an available vehicle to be combined with the dramatist's purpose but the essence of that purpose. In themselves the actors can constitute a new possibility of form.

Frequently the intervention is strongest when two actors develop a pattern of dramatic relationship, often as a pair of moral alternatives, which can be perceived through a series of plays. There are frequent examples in the Restoration. In later chapters I shall look at the effect of the casting of Mrs Barry and Mrs Bracegirdle,[95] of Elizabeth Boutell and others in particular plays. For the moment, a brief analysis of the effect of Charles Hart and Nell Gwyn in the late 1660s will provide a good example of how this interaction worked.

The notion of the 'gay couple', the picture of the witty hero pursuing the wittier heroine to the accompaniment of streams of accomplished repartee, lives at the heart of the conventional concept of Restoration comedy. Bonamy Dobrée, describing the dialogue in *Marriage A-la-Mode*, pronounces that 'Every argument in favour of extra-marital relationships is brought forward with extraordinary wit, the arguments surely used by every wild gallant of those days, but as surely never so pithily stated.'[96] However much one might wish to note changes in the various guises in which it appears in later years, however much one might wish to establish its roots in Shirley, Brome or Davenant, the 'gay couple' was the most distinctive new contribution to comedy of the 1660s, the first new change in the comic form in the Restoration.

While this process, this breakthrough, has been traced by Robert Hume, his chronological progress through the plays of the 1660s is achieved without reference to the theatres.[97] But that the change in the comedy is bound up with the acting of Hart and Gwyn is painfully obvious. The emergence of the pattern shows how the competition between the companies and the presence of particular actors affected the work of the dramatists, and made the plays what they are. Equally clearly it shows how the pattern even develops through contact with drama written *before* the pattern is formed.

From the beginning, Davenant's actors, the Duke's company playing at Lincoln's Inn Fields, specialised in plays of intrigue and cross-wooing. All their early successes that point towards the form, such as Tuke's *The Adventures of Five Hours* (1663), depend on multiple pairs of lovers to generate plot. It is still characteristic of their drama in the two pairs of Etherege's *She Would If She Could* (1668). By contrast, Killigrew's actors, the King's company playing at Vere Street and then in the first Theatre Royal in Bridges Street, began to achieve success in plays which centre on a love-plot, concentrating the audience's attention solely on the main couple. Their first attempt at this technique, Dryden's *The Wild Gallant* (first performed 1663), was not successful. To Pepys, the fault was that the acting lacked the requisite dash and the play 'so little answering the name, that from beginning to end I could not, nor can at this time, tell certainly which was the wild gallant'.[98]

James Howard's *The English Mounsieur*, performed by July 1663, specifically avoids having two pairs of comparable lovers by gently mocking Comely's affection for the country-girl Elsbeth. The Welbred-Lady Wealthy plot is similar to the central plot of Dryden's play in having an impoverished hero, but here it is the widow rather than the hero who has to be forced into marriage. Nearly a year before *Love in a Tub* (1664), Howard shows a widow who must be bullied to the altar and a battle of wit based on the problem of who is to dominate in marriage and how the individual's independence – and love – can possibly survive afterwards. At this stage though, the play does not appear to have been successful. Further moves towards the form were made in Rhodes' *Flora's Vagaries* (first performed 1663), with its efficient heroine. But the development of the form was halted for two reasons: lack of actors to play the parts properly and the spectacular success of the rival company in Etherege's *Love in a Tub*, the effective fruition of the widow-suitor approach.

The last attempt at establishing the new form in the King's company before plague closed the theatres was in James Howard's *All Mistaken, or the Mad Couple*, performed in May 1665.[99] The subtitle is a clear indication of the style, even though the play has a double plot. Philidor and Mirida, the mad couple, come together with a sense of inevitability that denies the obstacles that in subsequent comedies were to be recognised as part of the problem of marriage and society. But Howard's play was probably the first to take advantage of the presence of Hart and Gwyn in the company and was possibly performed by them both at this time.

In spite of her relatively public private life, Nell Gwyn's career at this time is unclear. She had been cast as Paulina, a small part of a prostitute in Thomas Killigrew's *Thomaso*, probably around November 1664,[100] and as Melina, a servant, in *The Siege of Urbin* by his brother William at about the same time. At this time then she was obviously starting her acting career. Her true potential as an actress was not realised until after the plague – though her other potential had been realised by Charles Hart, her Charles the first, somewhat earlier.

On 5 June 1665, the Lord Chamberlain closed the theatres because of the plague. They remained closed until December, 1666. When the theatres re-opened, Nell Gwyn was immediately cast as the witty heroine to star opposite Hart in a series of revivals of those plays that had been partially successful earlier. She now appeared as Lady Wealthy in *The English Mounsieur*[101] and as Flora in *Flora's Vagaries*.[102] Though no certain performance of *All Mistaken* is listed until 20 September 1667, Pepys' comment when he saw it on that day, 'I do not remember that I have seen [it]', might refer to an earlier revival (or, possibly, the first run of performances). A revival was made inevitable by the tumultuous success of Dryden's *Secret Love* (late February, 1667). The roles of Celadon and Florimell were written expressly for Hart and Gwyn – as the description of Florimell-Gwyn quoted earlier shows[103] – since they were by now rivalling Davenant's spectacular scenery as the leading attractions of the theatre.

It has occasionally been suggested that Nell Gwyn played the part of the Second Constantia in Buckingham's adaptation of *The Chances* (February 1667).[104] Hart certainly played Don John and there are clear elements of what was becoming known as their characteristic roles in the play. The great enlargement of the Second Constantia's role is apparently motivated by theatrical rather than dramatic reasons. It would appear to be the first major role written for Nell Gwyn and designed to link her to Hart as a sort of 'gay couple'. Nonetheless *Secret Love* was the first play to make them equals in the performance.

Dissatisfied with the Fletcherian romance form he had used for *The Rival Ladies* (1664) Dryden turned to the double plot model whose effectiveness had been proved by Howard's *All Mistaken*. But Dryden retrieved the lower plot from farce by mixing the pastoral with a serious analysis of the problem of reconciling marriage and fidelity, placed in a society clearly analogous to London. Dryden redrew Howard's broad characters, adding a refinement and sensitivity that made them relevant to the audience's concerns, while still keeping the high plot separate. The production was a huge success. The high plot was cast in strength, with Rebecca Marshall, the great tragedienne, as the Queen. But the audiences came to see Nell Gwyn and Charles Hart. Pepys was completely bowled over by Nell Gwyn's performance:

and the truth is, there is a comical part done by Nell, which is Florimell, that I never hope ever to see the like done again by man or woman. The King and Duke of York was at the play; but so great performance of a comical part was never, I believe, in the world before as Nell doth this . . .[105]

The company quickly followed up that triumph. For the rest of that season and most of the next, almost every performance of a comedy at the Theatre Royal was designed to make use of Hart and Gwyn and their successful formula. In the period up to the end of May 1668, there are records of performances of *Secret Love* (six), *The Surprisal* with Nell Gwyn as Samira (four), *All Mistaken, The English Mounsieur* and *Flora's Vagaries* (two each). In addition, there is a revival of *Philaster* in November 1667 with Hart as Philaster[106] and

Nell as Bellario, and of *The Wild Goose Chase* in January 1668, probabby with Hart as Mirabell and Nell as Oriana.

Also in 1667, probably about March, Dryden's revised version of *The Wild Gallant* appeared. Significantly, one of the few additions that we can identify is the scene with Lady du Lake and the three whores (IV.i).[107] Dryden not only increased the bawdiness to fall in line with the aggressively anti-romantic tone of the revised play and the new style of drama but also included this scene as part of a move to emphasise the fragility of the central relationship. Constance's hold on Loveby's affections is now rendered dubious by his return to whoring. Her control is dependent on her presence, a concept that is central to *Secret Love* and *An Evening's Love* where the disguises of the heroine act as a barrier to the rake's inconstancy in love, in deed – though not in intention. The failure of the hero in the love-test is necessary so that the rake can be humiliated into marriage. I suspect that in the revised play Hart played Loveby, Rebecca Marshall Constance and Nell Gwyn Isabelle, the wittier and more aggressive of the two women.[108] The Hart-Marshall-Gwyn trio underlies *The Chances* as well.

By the time the next *new* comedy was produced at the King's theatre, Sedley's *The Mulberry Garden*, in May 1668, the leading wit parts of Wildish and Olivia were ready made for Hart and Gwyn.[109] As in Dryden's *Secret Love*, Sedley used a double plot but he placed it firmly in England – the play was after all performed after *She Would If She Could*. The courtship scenes are models of the Hart-Gwyn repartee pattern, ending in Act V with a discussion of the dangers threatening love after marriage, an awareness that is now fundamental to the form.

The last new play of the season was Dryden's *An Evening's Love* (June 1668). Though a success, Pepys heard from Dryden's publisher, Herringman, that 'Dryden doth himself call it but a fifth-rate play'.[110] Dryden had marked out for the rival Duke's company two new lines that could follow their successes with Spanish drama. *The Tempest* adaptation (first performed 1667) provided the ground plan for a combination of comedy and scenic splendour that was more fully exploited in Shadwell's later operatic version. *Sir Martin Mar-All* (1668) picked up the possibilities suggested by the two low plots of *Love in a Tub* and generated a form of buffoon comedy that was guaranteed to please. *An Evening's Love*, in spite of the location of the action and some concern with questions of honour, is not really a Spanish play. Not even the use of a play by Calderón as source can disguise the fact that the play's centre is the acting of Hart and Gwyn, their pattern of male pursuit and female victory, the blocking of the hero's lust by the heroine's ingenuity and the heroine's acceptance of the hero in spite of his failure to be constant.

Dryden's preface, with its defence of comedy of wit against the attack of Shadwell in his preface to *The Sullen Lovers*, is a manifesto for the King's company and its distinctive form of comedy. In spite of the preface's objections to the form's tendency to farce, an objection more appropriate to the Duke's company and Dryden's work for them, the defence is mounted through an emphasis on the moral and socially responsible concerns of the drama. Seriousness is shown to be compatible with wit. Dryden denies the artificiality of the choice of writing either wit comedy or Jonsonian humour comedy.

The play is a culmination of the development of a new comic form for the King's company as an alternative tradition to the Spanish, buffoon and operatic possibilities being explored at Lincoln's Inn Fields. One can see *She Would If She Could* as a triumphant exception, as an exploration of a mode that their rivals had made popular, but not as a type of comedy Davenant's company and his authors were prepared to pursue. This was primarily because they did not have two stars comparable to Hart and Gwyn.[111] Nell Gwyn's innate wit and vitality combined with the experience and grace of Hart produced in itself a new form of drama. Without them it could not have existed. What was new was not simply having women on stage but a woman who could credibly rival male wit.

The theatre practices that this chapter has outlined are intended to lead towards the analysis of the plays in later chapters. For the moment it will help to see how casting can affect a play in performance.

### The casting of Farquhar's 'The Twin Rivals'

Farquhar's *The Twin Rivals* was first performed at Drury Lane on 14 December 1702. The play was not a success – the next known performance after the initial run was in November 1716 – and Farquhar's preface to the play when it was published attempts laboriously to answer each successive criticism while maintaining that his original purpose was:

to improve upon [Collier's] invective, and to make the Stage flourish by vertue of that Satyr, by which he thought to suppress it.

I have therefore in this Piece, endeavour'd to show, that an *English* Comedy may Answer the strictness of Poetical Justice . . . [112]

As we shall see later in the case of Richmore, Farquhar's comments in the preface are not necessarily to be taken at their face value. It appears from this that Farquhar is attempting to construct a morally acceptable comedy, which is to include the presentation of evil on the stage – something Collier could never accept. But the play itself is a series of interlocking patterns, each mocking and parodying the next. *The Twin Rivals* presents the possibility of a Collierist comedy ironically. Farquhar conjures up patterns of virtue only in order to show that they cannot succeed in comedy. As he says in the preface, with a wry tone, a moral play does not even satisfy the citizens:

a certain Virtuoso of that Fraternity has told me since, that the Citizens were never more disappointed in any Entertainment, for (said he) however Pious we may appear to be at home, yet we never go to that end of the Town, but with an intention to be Lewd. (*Works* I 286)

The problems in which virtue finds itself are solved by the use of a series of theatrical tricks which have nothing to do with morality. But the theatrical conventions, borrowed from the form of comedy which *The Twin Rivals* is apparently rejecting, are themselves subverted by the alteration of the patterns of casting which had been established in the years up to its first production. The casting conjures up the generic expectations of comedy, only in order to overturn them.

Farquhar had himself tried being an actor in Dublin (giving up after a near-fatal stabbing on stage), and was a great friend of Robert Wilks, whose career also began with Ashbury at Smock Alley. Wilks' London success was founded on the parts Farquhar wrote for him, especially Sir Harry Wildair in *The Constant Couple*. Certainly Farquhar's acquaintance with the Smock Alley players led him to write for them when, as most did, they turned up in London: of the actors in *The Twin Rivals*, Bowen had been in Dublin for one season in 1698–9; Mrs Hook was there from 1698–1702 and had only recently arrived – as had Farquhar, in 1698 – Husband had left in 1700 and Wilks in 1699.[113]

But Farquhar's personal knowledge of the members of the acting company for which he worked was strengthened in his plays by his awareness of the doubleness of the audience's perception of the actor, as individual and as character. In *A Discourse on Comedy*, published in his book *Love and Honour* early in 1702 and probably written about the same time as *The Twin Rivals*, Farquhar uses the commonsense argument to rebut the Collierist attack on disguise. While watching *The Rival Queens*, the audience sees Alexander the Great,

Yet the whole Audience at the same time knows that this is Mr. *Betterton*, who is strutting upon the Stage, and tearing his Lungs for a Livelihood. And that the same Person shou'd be Mr. *Betterton*, and *Alexander* the Great, at the same time, is somewhat like an Impossibility, in my Mind. Yet you must grant this Impossibility in spight of your Teeth, if you han't Power to raise the old Heroe from the Grave to act his own Part. (*Works* II 341).

The casting of *The Twin Rivals* was done with great care for the patterns of expectation the conventional comedies of the previous few years had established. With a vicious disregard for the audience's susceptibilities, its reluctance to accept change, Farquhar turns most of these expectations upside down.

The cast in 1702 was:

| | | | |
|---|---|---|---|
| Elder Wou'dbe | Wilks | Constance | Mrs Rogers |
| Young Wou'dbe | Cibber | Aurelia | Mrs Hook |
| Richmore | Husband | Mandrake | Bullock |
| Trueman | Mills | Steward's Wife | Mrs Moor |
| Subtleman | Pinkethman | | |
| Balderdash ⎱ Alderman ⎰ | Johnson | | |
| Teague | Bowen | | |
| Clear-Account | Fairbank | | |
| Fairbank | Minns | | |

Many of the smaller parts are cast unexceptionally: Mrs Moor usually played servants; Pinkethman, known as 'Pinky', was a clown in the Jo Haines mould. It is perhaps surprising that Fairbank did not play the part of Fairbank the goldsmith. Drawing attention to names in such a way was quite common. In Farquhar's *The Recruiting Officer* (1706), Bullock was cast as Bullock, a part carefully tailored to his line; Bright was cast as Dullhead in *Win Her and Take Her* (1690), as Dullman in *The Widow Ranter* (1689) and again in Crowne's *The English Frier* (1690), and his name may have been punned on as Glisten in *The Revenge* (1680). It is possible that Farquhar intended the audience to see the name Fairbank as a connection between Lord Wou'dbe's goldsmith (Fairbank the character) and his steward (Fairbank the actor), the former as the high-principled though wealthy merchant, the latter as a man whose principles waver in the sight of money but whose conscience keeps re-asserting itself. Young Wou'dbe describes the steward as wanting 'courage to be thoroughly Just, or entirely a Villain – but good Backing will make him either.' (*Works* I 306). The merchant, in his financial security, is above such motives to change his morality.

The same sort of contrast between parts is established in the two roles played by Johnson: Balderdash refuses Young Wou'dbe a loan when he thinks him poor and the Alderman bribes him when he is known to be rich. The presence in the play of basically honest tradesmen is balanced, as the two brothers are balanced, by the dishonesty of other merchants.

Bowen was the natural choice for Teague. In November 1700, he had left the stage 'being convinc'd by Mr. Collier's Book against the Stage, and satisfied that a Shop-keeper's life was the readier way to Heaven of the two'.[114] But his conviction did not last and he rejoined Betterton's company, having a benefit night as Teague in Sir Robert Howard's *The Committee* on 6 March 1701. *The Post-Boy* remarked that:

it's the opinion of the best Judges in Town that no person in either of the Theatres can come so Near the Performance of the famous Original Mr. Lacy as he can . . . [115]

In the same notice *The Post-Boy* predicted Bowen's return to Ireland, but on 11 June he performed as Jacomo in Shadwell's *The Libertine* in a second benefit performance, this time at Drury Lane. He remained at Drury Lane until 1703 when he did leave for Ireland. It was therefore inevitable that the part of Teague in *The Twin Rivals* should be Bowen's. So extraneous is the role to the plot – that being part of its purpose in the play, as a reminder of old-fashioned comic devices – that Farquhar clearly included the part to take advantage of the known speciality of the new member of Drury Lane.

Bullock had by 1702 played two previous transvestite parts. In Dennis' *A Plot and No Plot* (May 1697), he played Sue Frowzy, 'A Campaigning Bawd just arriv'd from *Flanders*' (A4b). In the play, Bullock plays a good-hearted whore, bantering the pit and the boxes in the playhouse set of Act II, and discarded by the hero in Act V. There is nothing malicious about Frowzy or her plotting, nor is there about Kate Matchlock, another campaigning whore, in Steele's *The Funeral* (December 1701), also played by Bullock. Kate chatters on about the perils of campaigning and her nine husbands in the previous war. The playing of these parts by a man is little more than pantomine dame casting. It had previously been the speciality of Nokes, known as 'Nurse' Nokes from his performance in *Caius Marius*, Otway's adaptation of *Romeo and Juliet*. Nokes also played Lady Beardly, an 'amorous old woman' in Durfey's *The Virtuous Wife* (1680), and Megaera, wife to the Captain, in his *The Banditti* (1686). The tradition was tinged with geniality and the women parts were usually old, the butts for others' tricks. But Mandrake, the midwife-bawd of *The Twin Rivals*, is different. While others used cross-casting to minimise horror and perversion,[116] Farquhar emphasises the unnaturalness of his bawd by the casting of Bullock in the role. Funny though her dialogue can be, Mandrake's actions allow for rape, disinheritance and trickery on a non-comic scale. Her name points up her masculine villainy (man/drake) but also her ability to invert, to render insane the normal actions of others. She herself is like the mandrake root, a caricature of the human form, played by a man. Her nature, like that of Young Wou'dbe or Richmore, is irrevocably evil; like Young Wou'dbe, her figure, misshapen and gross, is an index to her moral character. As midwife and bawd, Mandrake controls and perverts her society; she is the perfect image of its confusion of roles in sex, just as Young Wou'dbe perverts its rules of primogeniture.

Robert Wilks was the great new star in the theatre. He had based his style of acting on Mountfort,[117] who 'gave the truest Life to what we call the *Fine Gentleman*'.[118] Wilks thus managed to establish himself as an actor always sympathetic to the audience. Cibber found that, though Wildair may be a character who deserves criticising, Wilks won the audience over:

in the Whole there are so many gay and false Colours of the fine Gentleman, that nothing but a Vivacity in the Performance proportionably extravagant could have made them so happily glare upon a common Audience.[119]

Wilks plotted his rise to fame carefully, taking over some of Mountfort's parts from Powell, to whom they had descended.[120] Powell, ambitious and 'uneasy at the Favour *Wilks* was then rising into',[121] left Drury Lane for Betterton's company. Wilks enhanced his success by ensuring his Dublin successes were revived.[122] With the tumultuous success of Farquhar's *The Constant Couple*, Wilks' career was guaranteed.

Based as it was on Mountfort's sympathetic manner, Wilks had to ensure that his acting kept that sort of sympathy, balanced between himself and the character. As a result,

Mr. *Wilks* very seldom, and always against his own Choice, assum'd any wicked or base Character upon the Stage ... in Comedy there was much less Variety, he seldom appearing in any other Character than that of the fine Gentleman.[123]

The emphasis here is again on a distinction between his comic and tragic roles.

Wilks' career was interwined with that of Mrs Rogers. In the late 1690s Jane Rogers' obsession with virtue led her to vow on stage, in the Epilogue to *The Triumphs of Virtue* (1697), that she would 'Study to live the Character I play' (A2b).[124] She thus established for herself a line of virtuous parts. Wilks however is supposed to have fallen in love with her and, after much 'Concern lest her Character should suffer',[125] she is supposed to have given in. The two had a great series of successes; even before her capitulation, Rich 'was obliged to let Mrs *Rogers* always act the Heroine in every Play where Mr *Wilks* was the Hero',[126] the demand coming from the audience rather than the actors. Certainly their affair was well known and Farquhar made great use of it in *The Constant Couple*.[127] Their private life became an analogy to, a pattern for comparison with their stage personae. Between 1699 and *The Twin Rivals*, the two played a series of 'gay couples', repeating the Hart-Gwyn pattern as William and Susanna Mountfort had in the early 1690s. Again and again one finds the pattern repeated in revivals and new plays, in Farquhar's sequel to *The Constant Couple*, *Sir Harry Wildair*, and in his Fletcher adaptation, *The Inconstant*. In Steele's *The Funeral*, they are relegated to being the secondary couple, Campley and Harriot, since the main pair, Lord Hardy and Sharlot, are far too serious for them.[128] Though in tragedy they may have tended towards those parts dependent on 'Sorrow, Tenderness, or Resignation' which Cibber saw as Wilks' *forte* in tragedy,[129] in comedy they are uniformly associated with the airy, happy parts. Even when Mrs Rogers acted without Wilks in Durfey's *The Bath* (May 1701), she still appeared as the 'Witty and good-natur'd' Sophronia.

Apart from *The Twin Rivals* only one other play distorts this pattern. Thomas Baker's *The Humour of the Age* (Drury Lane, March 1701) casts Wilks as Railton 'A Gentleman cheated of his Estate, and rails at all Mankind' and Mrs Rogers as Tremilia, 'A young, handsom, civiliz'd Quaker, attempted to be debauch'd by *Railton*' (A4b). The reference to Mrs Rogers' earlier career is unmistakable. Railton fails in his evil plot (unlike Wilks in his) and, repentant, he acknowledges to her 'You are all Piety' (p. 63).

If the Wilks-Rogers link is one of the strongest casting patterns in the period, another unites Wilks and Cibber. The major pattern here was as hero and foppish rival. In Cibber's own play, *Love Makes a Man* (Drury Lane, December 1700), the pattern is initially controverted, only to be re-established later. Cibber appears as the 'pert Coxcomb' (A1b) Clodio, Wilks as his elder brother, the serious student Carlos. Charino, father of Angellina, describe Carlos as 'a great Scholar, spends his whole Life in the University, and Loves his Study' and Clodio as having 'seen the World, and is very well known in the Court of *France*, a sprightly Fellow! ha!' (p. 2). Carlos' entrance is preceded by his library, Clodio's by a French servant. Carlos is a complete innocent, shy of women ('I never yet Convert with any but my own Mother' p. 13), and though he admires Angellina he retreats from her ('I have gaz'd too much – reach me an *Ovid*' (p. 14)). As in the Sandford anecdote,[130] the audience must by this stage have been wondering when Wilks would change. Persuaded by his uncle to come out of his shell, Carlos woos Angellina in front of his brother, abandons his books, beats Clodio in a duel and elopes with Angellina. Wilks reverts, as Carlos alters, to his normal type of part and for the last three acts, borrowed from Fletcher's *The Custom of the Country*, he plays 'the fine gentleman', again. Cibber's play is a fairly simple exposition of the tensions of the casting. Though not successful on its first run – lasting only four days – the play was frequently revived, being played on 13 June 1701 and 26 October 1702. It provides a plausible analogy to one course an audience might expect *The Twin Rivals* to take.

The Cibber-Wilks partnership was also well known in performances of *Volpone*. Cibber, as Volpone, chose the play for his benefit night on 19 June 1701 and Wilks, as Mosca, chose it for his on 12 June 1703. It is therefore probable that they were playing the same roles in the other known performances up to *The Twin Rivals*, 2 May 1700, 27 December 1700, 18 March 1701. The pattern is similar to the hero-fop relationship; again Cibber is duped by Wilks' cunning, though the malevolence of the Cibber part is new.

The patterns of casting thus established a series of expectations for the audience. Given nothing more than the title of Farquhar's new play, it would expect Wilks and Cibber to be the twins, the one a witty gentleman and the other a fool, and that Wilks would win

Mrs Rogers from under his 'brother's' nose. But Farquhar, from the raising of the curtain, turns expectation upside down.

Cibber is discovered dressing. There are immediately major disruptions of convention: Cibber is not the older brother; he is not a fop; he is hunch-backed. The normal pattern of comedy, one of the bases from which its attack on the disjunction between merit and the inflexible rules of society was launched, was that the rights of inheritance of the elder son, the tradition of primogeniture, were not necessarily justified. From Terence's *Adelphoe* to a play as recent as Vanbrugh's *The Relapse*, the witty younger brother usually wins in spite of the elder brother's inheritance. This archetypal form is destroyed initially by Cibber being *Young* Wou'dbe. But the inverse of the pattern commonly holds true in tragedy, where the younger's claim over his older brother is through his villainy.

Young Wou'dbe's opening lines, his disdain for the fussiness of dressing, automatically remove him from the status of fop and his naturalism links him to that massive complex of post-Hobbesian libertinism that is part of the rake's ethos:

Here is such a Plague every Morning with Buckling Shooes, Gartering, Combing, and Powdering, Pshaw! Cease thy Impertinence, I'll dress no more to day – Were I an honest Brute, that rises from his Litter, shakes himself, and so is Drest, I could bear it! (*Works* 1 293)

But if the brute wish is an attribute of rakishness, it is in the tragic form an attribute of villainy, the unnatural naturalism of Edmund in *King Lear*. The lines then, while appearing, out of context, as a perfectly conventional Sir Frederick Frollick-like opening to a rake-biased comedy, are undercut by being spoken by the non-rakish Cibber, the greatest actor of fools and fops of his day.

The rakishness of Young Wou'dbe is extended by the arrival of Richmore. The conversation now covers other characteristics of the fine gentleman, his desire to live outside of time and his chronic shortage of cash. The rake's ideal of being beyond the normal restraints of time is both a part of his programmatic naturalism and a result of his nocturnal pattern of life. But the denial of time links him directly to Falstaff, seen at this time as vicious and evil rather than funny and endearing: 'What have we to do with Time?' (*Works* 1 293) would be as appropriate to him as it is to Young Wou'dbe's aspirations. Either way, the characteristically flippant rejection of social graces is designed to bring the character into the audience's sympathies when spoken by a true rake. The rake's impoverished state is used from the very beginnings of Restoration comedy, for example in Loveby in *The Wild Gallant*. But Cibber is not a rake.

As hero, the rake has to be handsome and tall like Wilks. Apart from being short, Cibber was hunch-backed for the part of Young Wou'dbe. This is obviously a reference to *Richard III*, adapted by Cibber and first produced, with Cibber himself in the title-role, around January 1700. Cibber had intended that the title-role should have been played by Sandford but Sandford was with Betterton's company. Cibber therefore took the role himself, and imitated Sandford in the part as far as he could, even down to his voice with its 'acute and piercing' tone.[131] As Cibber's enemies gleefully noted, the audience could not distinguish between Cibber's acting and Richard's and disliked the reduction of Richard to a man who 'screamed . . . without Dignity or Decency'; Richard, which would have been the ideal part for a 'Comic-Tragedian', was all but hissed off the stage and at his death 'the good People were not better pleas'd that so *execrable a Tyrant* was destroy'd, than that so *execrable an Actor* was silent'.[132] The production was soon taken off and not revived until 1704 but Cibber's performance must still have been remembered. Young Wou'dbe and Richard III are both hunch-backs who turn lovers, both younger sons who aim to destroy their brothers.[133] In the hunch-backed, vicious rake with which the audience was presented at the beginning, Farquhar shows that the axes along which judgements are to be made are to be profoundly different from any of the conventional patterns. The contrast of witty rake and fop is impossible as soon as Cibber is shown to be playing not just a harmless fool but an evil villain, defined as such primarily by the hunch-back and its associations with Richard III, as played by Cibber.

The audience, confronted by Young Wou'dbe, is required to re-evaluate the grounds on which its approval had been granted to the rake-hero and to consider whether the rake's good looks had let his views be accepted in spite of their innate anti-social aggressiveness. In establishing this inversion, however, Farquhar is careful not to re-align figure and morality too strongly: the late Lord Wou'dbe, repeatedly held up in the play as an ideal figure of benevolence and virtue, was hunch-backed as well and the similarity is used by Young Wou'dbe as an added piece of self-justificatory rhetoric ('Then why shou'd not I be a Lord as well as he?' *Works* 1 295).

The first scene, in its importation of the values and expectations of tragedy into a setting of comedy and in its insistence on the Shakespearean analogues,[134] moves towards a species of mixed form, a Fletcherian tragi-comic mode, but one which demands of the audience a form of moral judgement that is foreign to the Restoration view of romance form.

Farquhar continues this dislocation through the casting of Jane Rogers as the serious heroine; she is not the witty cynical Aurelia, but Constance, compassionate even in her attitude to Clelia's pregnancy (*Works* 1 303). But the tragic tone of the main plot is already being subverted by the cynical comedy of Mrs Mandrake. Certainly, until the entrance of Wilks as the Elder Wou'dbe, the audience can no longer have any idea how to utilise their understanding of contemporary comedy, dependent on the separation of the tragic and comic modes, in order to cope with Farquhar's apparently furious attack on the comic hero, whose callous villainy is now shown as innate in the ideals of the libertine.

The first crisis comes in Act III. The first scene opens with Young Wou'dbe's levee. The scene is an obvious parallel to I.i, shifted now from the comparative squalor of Young Wou'dbe's lodgings where he was attended only by a valet, to the restrained opulence of Lord Wou'dbe's house, with Young Wou'dbe happy now to be dressed and to be surrounded by 'several Gentlemen whispering him by turns' (*Works* 1 314). The audience, used to seeing Cibber as a fop, is unsure whether they are seeing a villain in fop's clothing or vice versa. Either way, they must expect that Wilks' arrival will prick the bubble of Cibber's pretensions and that the handsome hero will stride on and take control.

The Elder Wou'dbe does stride on, but, far from being an apotheosis of the virtuous hero, he turns out to be rather dull, foolishly impetuous and socially inept. Unlike Sir Harry Wildair or Mirabell in *The Inconstant*, both of whom have been in France, the Elder Wou'dbe's visit to the continent has taken him to Germany and his pocket-book smacks of Teutonic thoroughness. In addition, his opening speech is in verse and stamps him as another sentimental hero, a refugee from Steele's mode of comedy transposed into a London that is more profoundly vicious than anything in *The Funeral* yet also a *comic* world in which providence plays no part. Elder Wou'dbe is certainly braver and more virtuous than Wilks' previous roles in Farquhar's plays but he is also far less socially and *theatrically* adept. Farquhar rebuts Collier's demands for a moral drama by proving that dramatic resolution is a theatrical process, not a social one, and that the conventions of drama, not the workings of divine providence, are what count in the theatre, whatever may be necessary in the world. Elder Wou'dbe is too virtuous and too naive to succeed in a comedy. With Wilks and Jane Rogers quickly shown to be destined for each other in a sentimentally tragic mode, Farquhar turns elsewhere to make his point.

The close parallels of the two major plots of *The Twin Rivals* are clear: both are triangles with a villain (Richmore and Young Wou'dbe), a rather gullible virtuous hero (Trueman and Elder Wou'dbe) and a vulnerable heroine (Aurelia and Constance). The parallels are further enhanced by each pair being friends, the girls being cousins as well, and by the fact that both villains rely on Mandrake. The two plots are differentiated in method, the romantic-tragic Wou'dbe plot contrasted with the straightforwardly comic Trueman plot. As the play develops, Elder Wou'dbe finds himself in increasingly desperate situations, until it seems that it would be impossible for him to extricate himself from the mess and that any escape will require the direct intervention of Providence to succeed. But the chaos is in fact resolved by the comic methods of the other plot.

Elder Wou'dbe tries to reclaim his estate, fraudulently claimed by his brother. As long as he follows a moral approach of honest action, he fails. When Teague, his own servant, is found to be the one who, impossibly, witnessed Lord Wou'dbe's 'last words' in Young Wou'dbe's forgery of his father's will, Elder Wou'dbe's position improves. It needs Teague, a typical comic servant alien to Elder Wou'dbe's serious world, to help him. Elder Wou'dbe's success is reversed when Mandrake, who has overheard the events, claims that Young Wou'dbe is the elder brother. Mandrake combines the theatrical cliché of hiding in the closet with a delightfully wicked willingness to lie. The first occurs extremely frequently in the comedy of the period, so that Elder Wou'dbe's defeat at this point is effected by the difference between his type of character and the form of drama in which he finds himself. The second is a fact of social life, the presence and power of evil, with which Elder Wou'dbe's strict moral code does not equip him to deal, as well as proving morality – *pace* Collier – theatrically viable. This reversal is a union of the theatrical and the social, the two forms of the real, that marks a new point in the play's development.

Inevitably, after this, the plot is resolved by an emphatically theatrical solution. Elder Wou'dbe, outwitted by his brother and taken by a constable, is discovered 'sitting and writing' in 'A Room miserably furnished',

> Virgil, *tho' cherished in Courts,*
> *Relates but a spleenatick Tale,*
>   Cervantes, *Revel and Sports,*
> *Altho' he writ in a Jayl,*

Then hang Reflections [*starts up.*] I'll go write a Comedy (*Works* 1334–5)

'Comedy' is precisely what happens from then on. Trueman turns up at all the right places at all the right moments, usually in disguise, in order to rescue Elder Wou'dbe from prison, save Aurelia from rape by Richmore, and defeat Young Wou'dbe's plots. Luck and comic expertise count for far more than providence and virtue. Although Farquhar denies Collier's demands by this comic coincidence, he recognises that comedy cannot in the end control evil, even though it can promote the audience's recognition of it. Young Wou'dbe storms off to:

Poverty and Contempt –
To which I yield as to a milder Fate
Than Obligations from the Man I hate.   (*Works* 1 350)

Richmore, on the other hand, appears repentant and resigned to marry the pregnant Clelia – a classic scene of villainy overcome by remorse. But Farquhar's preface wilfully extends the characters beyond the play's resolution into the 'real', the putative social world beyond the play:

I see nothing but what is very general in his Character, except his Marrying his own Mistress; which, by the way, he never did, for he was no sooner off the Stage, but he chang'd his Mind, and the poor Lady is still in *Statu Quo*...   (*Works* 1 287)

Congreve, in *The Double-Dealer* (1694) lets a strange form of reality intrude upon and overturn the comic ending. The accidental meeting with Mellefont that arouses Cynthia's suspicions is an event made plausible by the restricted world, the claustrophobic limitations of the gallery. The play, as comedy, is destroyed; there can be no dance, no neat resolution, but instead a scramble of revelations and entrances with a dubiously affirmative ending. Farquhar refuses to allow his play's resolution to be destroyed in this way and he therefore rigorously excludes the reality of evil. Young Wou'dbe leaves and Richmore is unrepentant once 'off the Stage'. The workings of providence that the Elder Wou'dbe praises at the end are, in the terms of the play, so much wishful thinking:

Chuse a brave Friend as Partner of your Breast,
Be active when your Right is in Contest;
Be true to love, and Fate will do the rest.   (*Works* 1 350)

Having proved that evil, reality and comedy can only mix im-
perfectly, Farquhar turned to a new method of social drama in *The
Recruiting Officer*.

Farquhar uses the casting of his play as a background which places
*The Twin Rivals* in an exciting tension with its own comic clichés,
with the conventional forms of comedy. Demanding that the play
should be recognised as play, he disrupts the audience's comfortable
preconceptions, both dramatic and moral, through the focus of the
casting. Actor as individual and as character are both necessary for
the drama; the audience must see both Betterton and Alexander.

# 4

## Performance and the published text

In most studies of drama, there is a fundamental and yet unstated belief in a sequence, a chain of events underlying the creation of the play: the playwright writes a text, the text is performed, the play is subsequently published, the play is read. In the classic distinction between 'drama as literature' and 'drama as theatre', the point of application, the places on the chain to which criticism attaches itself, are to the text either as written or as performed. Most attempts to locate the tensions implicit in the study of drama are, in fact, a distinction between writing and performance, that is between the two modes of production of the text. My emphasis is on the alternative group, on the distinction between reading and seeing, between the two modes of consumption of the text. Raymond Williams, writing of the nature of the text for the drama of 'visual enactment', the category in which he places Restoration drama, describes the tension between text and performance as either exactly prescriptive or one where 'the text does no more than prescribe an *effect*, of which the *means* must be worked out in performance'.[1] In this, he is using 'text' to represent the text written by the author. But 'text' need not be an author's manuscript. Stage directions in the text are usually 'effects' whenever the text is part of a later segment of the sequence, the published play.[2] The text that is available to be read nearly always exists *after* performance. To a large extent, the text as published in the Restoration is a record of what happened in past performances, not a suggestion of what might happen in future ones. After all, the nature of the play as published is not a suggestion for future productions so far as most readers are concerned. In modern practice we can easily distinguish between a normal published text, designed essentially to be read, and, say, a 'French's acting edition', designed to be acted in the future.

Although in his later writing, Professor Williams does try to locate the text in the interstices between making and receiving the work, he substitutes for the concept of text as object the notion of text as

notation.[3] But notation still contains the concept of a future performance. The text as notated awaits the moment in which it becomes
actual by the performance of the notation. Printed music, as notation, is designed to be performed and it is the performance to which
the audience listens. There is, of course, the ability to read music
and reconstruct an imaginary performance. In this case, the result is
certainly analogous to what I shall show as the pattern of reading
plays in the Restoration: it connotes comprehension of certain performance conventions, even outside the moment of performance,
sufficient to apply them to new, unheard pieces. But the practice
in music is restricted to experts. For most of us, performance is a
necessary intervention in the chain. This intervention indicates the
extent to which the notation still locates the musical text in the area
of writing, not of its reading.

The problems start when the connection of the published text to
the performed text is only dimly perceived. Text is not only a pre-
condition of performance, a socially or generically determined
event, determined ultimately by the writing. My intention in this
chapter is to concentrate on a different practice, the practice of
reading, in order to explore later the connections that that practice
has with the practice of watching performances. Only through the
correct perception of these two practices can they be combined
into a perception of the object, the play, to which they bear witness.
The previous chapters have been concerned with the mode of presentation of the play in the theatre. My task now is to demonstrate
from the play quartos themselves how they offer themselves to be
read. The form itself is revealing; it is its own best evidence. Printers
and publishers knew how to exploit their market. They presented the
plays that they published, in spite of differences in the provenance
of copy, in a manner that balanced the economics of publishing, the
author's ideals and public taste. Even where there is excellent
evidence that the playwright closely supervised the publication of
his plays, making corrections at all stages of publication, the published format is rarely changed.[4] The plays, widely sold and widely
read, assumed a public published form that conveyed their connection with performance, as well as their status as a book, as literature.
We must first find out what that form was, how the small stitched
volume made its purpose plain.

*The mode of presentation of the published play*

The Restoration format for published plays emerges from a history
of alternate traditions. From the very beginning of the publication

of plays in England, there are a number of different attitudes towards the status and purpose of the play-text. On one side is the direct assertion that the play is printed in order that it can be used for future performances, the text as play-script. Between 1530 and 1570, at least twenty plays were published with directions on how to perform them, in particular how the vast numbers of parts, often thirty or more, could be divided amongst the small numbers of actors in most of the contemporary acting troupes.[5] Thomas Preston's *Cambises*, for example, has thirty-eight roles which can be taken by as few as six men and two boys, with judicious doubling. Again and again, one finds texts with a notice proclaiming that 'six may easily play this interlude' or something similar. Bevington shows how this pattern was used, as it had to be, by the dramatists to produce particular effects in the plays, but he refers to the plays as 'published for use by the troupes'.[6] But the plays were not only read by company managers looking for scripts. The reading public, which must have been, at the very least, an analogous group to the play-going public, could use these texts in order to reconstruct the mode of performance. The effects that Bevington analyses would have been perceptible to the reader through the combination of shared conventions and information as simple, for example, as the brackets indicating the doubling in the lists of characters. If the good and the bad characters were played by the same actor then that fact was as available to the reader as to the spectator at one of the performances the texts were designed to encourage.

Occasionally, though rarely, the play, though a 'script', shows signs of literary effects. In *Godly Queen Hester* (*c.* 1561), Hester is described only as 'a maiden' on her first entrance, a piece of literary suspense that is strictly analogous to the dramatic suspense of the entrance of an unidentified character. Neither entrance, on stage or on the page, gives away the secret of the maiden's identity immediately.

However, this tradition of play-scripts vanished by the time the professional stage firmly established itself in the 1580s. Subsequently. as we shall see in the case of Richard Flecknoe, play as script can be linked to an anticipation of performance by one *particular* company.

On the title-page of *Damon and Pithias* (1571), the printer proudly announces:

Newly Imprinted, as the same was shewed before the Queenes Maiestie, by the Children of her Graces Chappell, except the Prologue that is somewhat altered for the proper use of them that hereafter shall have occasion to plaie it . . .

This announcement occupies a middle ground between two traditions. The printer is aware that future productions will need to make
alterations because of the occasional nature of the original performance. But he knows that part of its sale will depend on the
accuracy of its link to a prestigious performance. The text hovers
between being a record and a script. This tradition of the text as a
record obviously becomes extremely strong in the printing of
masques and entertainments, where the performance is not to be
repeated. The reading of the text is seen as an attempt to recapture
the glories of one particular day; the text is like a large souvenir
programme, whether the buyer was present at the original performance or not. The text is accurate insofar as it includes everything
that happened then, so that it can be a substitute for those who were
not present.[7]

As early as *Gorboduc* (1570–1), this practice is applied to plays.
This text, published to correct the inaccuracies of an earlier edition,
although the play was 'never intended by the authors thereof to be
published' (A2a), takes pride in its exactness: the title-page defines
it as 'set forth without addition or alteration but altogether as the
same was showed on stage before the Queenes Maiestie, about nine
yeares past, *vz.* the xviij. day of Ianuarie. 1561'. Here again, of course,
it is the court performance that is referred to. The stage directions
in the text are written in the past tense indicating that the text is, as
it were, already a part of history, a history of performances. But
obviously this practice leads directly to the form of the title-page,
common throughout the pre-Restoration period, which links the
text to *past* performances at a particular theatre, e.g. 'As it was acted'
or 'As it hath been acted'. The form 'as it *is* acted' is very rare. The
text exists in the past; the reading as a re-creation of performance
that is implied by this form is a re-creation of one that has gone.
Implicitly, the separation from current performance leads to the
establishment of the printed play as a literary form, fixed and unchanging, rather than one in which performance is necessary to the
comprehension of the text. The status of the text as history releases
the text from the status of ephemera. In such circumstances, acting
is seen as little more than a simple grace to the play, rather than
an integral part of the drama. The text can move from theatre-text
into a different form.

The idea that the text is therefore available for a different form of
perception, reading, takes over strongly by 1600, though it had been
present as early as 1566. Lewis Wager's *The Repentaunce of Marie*

*Magdalene* (1566) was recommended as 'very delectable for those which shall heare or reade the same'.[8] But in 1600, Ben Jonson, in the forefront of the attempts to redefine the status of drama, had *Every Man Out of His Humour* published with a notice on the title-page that the text contained 'more than hath been Publickely Spoken or Acted' and, also for the first time, with the addition of 'the severall Character of every Person'. Both devices move the play away from the theatre and support the other assertion of the title-page that the text is 'as it was first composed by the Author B.I.'. It is the mere fact of extending the text that is significant. The literary play-text is not restricted by the temporal or, occasionally, moral limitations of the public stage.[9] Hence, as here, satire against the court, impossible to perform in public, can be included, as well as scenes that would drag on stage.

This tendency is taken up fairly frequently thereafter. Barnabe Barnes in *The Divils Charter* (1607) leans in both directions: the text is 'As it was plaide before the Kings Maiestie, upon Candlemasse night last' but it is also 'the more exactly rewewed, corrected, and augmented since by the Author, for the more pleasure and profit of the Reader'. By the time of the first publication of *The Duchess of Malfi* in 1623, the equivocation is even more pronounced: the title-page defines the non-theatrical nature of the text ('The perfect and exact Coppy, with diverse things Printed, that the length of the Play would not beare in the Presentment')[10] but the text is the first to be printed with a cast-list assigning the actors to their roles, and also includes the succession of parts, so that the contemporary reader could match the play to his experience of it as spectator.

Jonson's other innovation in *Every Man Out*, the 'Character', an extended description of each part in the dramatis personae, was not followed up as frequently until after 1660. The lengthy descriptions provide for the reader a mass of information that was not available on stage. Most important, it gives the reader information on the nature of a character in advance of his appearance. Jonson is unusual in providing such preview descriptions in the main body of the play as well.[11] It was this device that Dryden singled out for particular praise: when a character is described in advance, 'even from their first appearance you are so far acquainted with them that nothing of their humour is lost to you'.[12] It is this 'acquaintance' that is of a different nature when the description is only in the published text; the character begins to be made human, deepened, especially as Jonson, in *Every Man Out*, uses events not in the play to describe the characters. Shift, for instance, is said to fall 'under the executions of three shillings, and enters into five-groat bonds'.[13] The characters through the descriptions are established in a real world that is opposite to the awareness of the character as acted. Devices of this type tend to make the play literary not so much in the sense of untheatrical as in a novelistic, fictional way. Either way, the publication moves the experience of the text away from action, allowing character to be perceived as essentialist and definable *ab initio*, rather than only perceived in and through the action of the play itself. Character in *Every Man Out*, as is innate in the concept of the humour character, is a given, a premise from which the action emerges. The descriptions aid this process.

This device is one of the more extreme methods of separating reading from seeing but, of course, many authors explicitly disparaged the whole process of publication, considering it inappropriate to drama. In particular, Marston and Thomas Heywood were annoyed that any of their plays were published.[14] But the contrary tradition, from which they sought to dissociate themselves, reaches its first climax in Jonson's publication of his plays in the folio of 1616 as *Works*, thereby giving rise to a host of 'work/play' punning epigrams. *The Works*, in itself, is a claim that the plays should be considered as literature, an extension of the dignity that prefaces and dedications had begun to confer. It also implies a selectivity in the audience to which he appeals, a wealthier and more discriminating one than would buy or would acknowledge buying the normal cheap play-quarto. The motto from Horace on the title-page, 'contentus paucis lectoribus', is an indication of the superior stance that Jonson was adopting. Unlike a play in the theatre, the plays in the Jonson folio would not seek out a wide audience; Jonson would be content with few readers. Again, the text is not linked to the current theatre but to an earlier one, as Jonson lists the principal actors in the plays, many of whom were dead by the time of publication. The claim of dignity is extended by the division into classical scenes, the listing of all characters at the head of the scene, prefatory poems and all the other devices that Jonson had already used in the play-quartos since *Sejanus*.

Jonson's bid for status and authority, the right of an author to separate his plays from the indignities of the public stage and universal indiscriminate audiences, is followed by the Shakespeare folio of 1623. It leads towards the other collections, such as the Beaumont and Fletcher volume of 1647, which also includes scenes cut on stage. In the quest for dignity and literary status, the published text was moving further and further away from the stage, at least in the most prestigious publications.

When the theatres closed in 1642, the theatre public was forced, in spite of the occasional play performances, to rely largely on the published plays. The demand was so keen that prices went up: in 1653 *Two Noble Kinsmen* was not available for under two shillings.[15] But the play-texts were rooted in theatre conventions that had vanished or were, at best, no longer present. Plays, especially those newly published during the Interregnum, could not be linked to the playhouse practices.

Much of the continued publication of plays was the direct result of the work of Humphrey Moseley who published dozens of plays by Beaumont and Fletcher, Suckling, Cavendish, Brome, Shirley, Massinger and others. As in the Restoration period, the publication of drama centred upon one man. Significantly, in addition, Moseley continued and enlarged the practice of binding up unconnected quartos as collected editions, as for example those of Marston and Chapman in 1652. The effect was to increase the demand for plays as literature, dignified and separate from the stage. The entire period, with its suspension of actual performance, encouraged the movement. As Louis Wright comments, 'The focusing of attention upon the reading of plays ... tended to increase the prestige of drama as *literature* ... By that time, drama had come to occupy a literary position as honorable as that held by fashionable romances and non-dramatic poetry.'[16]

Though the moves towards the end of the period were primarily away from the theatre, producing a concept of the play as a reading text with only incidental and tangential connections with the stage, at the same time there was some evidence of an increased connection with the stage through the listing of actors and their assignation to roles.[17] In the period between the publication of *Malfi* and the Restoration, sixteen plays for the public stage appear with assigned cast-lists[18] and they were significant enough as a departure for the antiquarian James Wright to be able to name eleven of them in 1699 in his dialogue on theatre history, *Historia Histrionica*.[19] After the Restoration, and ever increasingly as the century continues, this becomes the norm.

In fact, almost all plays originally intended for and performed on the London stage after the Restoration are published according to a conventional form. Most have dedications, most have cast-lists,

most have at least traces of indications of scenery, most have the
necessary stage directions. The playwright Edward Howard commented in 1668 that 'the Impression of Plays, is so much the Practice
of the Age, that few or none have been Acted, which fail to be display'd in Print; where they seem to put on the greater formality of
Authors . . .'[20]

With such a large degree of uniformity as was present, it is easy
to see how the conventions for reading, for decoding the conventions of printed drama were established. That equilibrium between
the stage and the study, between the play as drama and the play as
literature that I have analysed for the earlier period was now heavily
reweighted in favour of the theatre. The act of reading is to be a
re-creation of the events of the stage. John Harold Wilson describes
the published play as 'a book of fifty to sixty quarto pages, which
was offered for sale, sewn and without covers, for sixpence; it was,
in effect, a paperback convenient for a daring young girl to hide
under her pillow'.[21] But this type of reader, attractive though she is
to imagine, is not representative of the main market that was aimed
at. All the evidence suggests that those who bought plays were fundamentally the same group as those who saw plays. It is only natural
that Pepys, an avid theatre-goer, should also be an avid play-buyer.
The action of reading can therefore be a re-creation of the stage
performance since the reader knows the conventions of watching.
The amount of information needed to perform that act of reconstruction is minimal, at least within the recognised possibilities
of what a reading could offer. By analysing the elements of the
published volume, it will be possible to see how this re-creation
is made possible, and how it is in part contradicted by other elements. Taking the quarto form of pieces is a prelude to seeing how
the whole works.

The Restoration play-quarto usually announces on its title-page
that the text is 'as it is acted' at whichever theatre it was. In itself, this
denotes a change from pre-Restoration practice, the 'as it hath been'
form described earlier. The Restoration form of words indicates
that the reading is adjacent to, simultaneous with the possibility of
seeing the play on stage. It does not place that performance as
automatically anterior to publication. Often, a pre-Restoration
play revived has its new title-page changed. *The Duchess of Malfi*, for
instance, in 1623, was described as 'As it was Presented . . .'; in 1664,
this became 'As it was Acted by his late Majesties Servants at BLACK

FRYERS with great Applause, Thirty Years since. And now Acted . . .';
in 1678, the play, complete with the contemporary cast starring
Betterton, is announced as 'As it is now ACTED AT THE Dukes Theater'.
Durfey's *Love For Money* (1691) was first published with an ornament
on the title-page; in the third and subsequent states, the ornament
is replaced by the conventional formula. The implication is that the
early states actually ante-dated performance and the quarto was
corrected when performances had begun.[22]

There are rare exceptions to the formulaic announcement, the
finest being James Drake's *The Sham-Lawyer* (1697) which announces
'As it was Damnably ACTED at the Theatre-Royal' with the word
'Damnably' picked out in black-letter.[23] There were, of course, a
certain number of plays published without being acted but the title-
pages clearly differentiate them; thus John Banks' *The Island Queens*
(1684) is 'Publish'd only in Defence of the Author and the Play,
against some mistaken Censures, occasion'd by its being prohibited
the Stage'.

While at the beginning of the period one finds publication taking
months or years, increasingly the time between first performance
and publication diminishes. The major change seems to occur
around the middle of the 1670s. By the 1690s it is often a matter of
one month or less from first performance to publication and general
availability.[24] The force of the present tense, 'as it *is* acted', effectively
increases towards 1700.

The practice is most marked for the publication of operas. Some,
even early in the period, are printed almost simultaneously with
production: Shadwell's *Psyche* was first performed on 27 February
1675 and advertised in the Term Catalogues in the same month;
George Powell prefaces *Brutus of Alba* (1696) with a note that *anticipates* the poet's nights, the third and the sixth. Certainly, for some
of the operas, libretti were on sale in the theatre during the first
performances; for the Dryden-Davenant *Tempest*, the *Songs and
Masques* were printed especially for use in the theatre.[25] Only very
rarely is there evidence for such a practice occurring for an ordinary
play. But Edward Ravenscroft's *The Italian Husband* (1697), a run-
of-the-mill tragedy, was advertised in *The Post Man* for 14/16 December 1697 as to be published 'To morrow' but that 'They will be sold
this evening at the Theatre', in advance, as it were.

There is however one slight piece of evidence to indicate that
play-texts might have been used in the theatres, rather as today we
might use an opera libretto, to follow the performance in the text.

Pepys, on 31 December 1660, records:

> I went out and in Paul's Churchyard I bought the play of *Henery the fourth*.
> And so went to the new Theatre . . . and there saw it acted; but my expecta-
> tion being too great, it did not please me as otherwise I believe it would;
> and my having a book I believe did spoil it a little.

I suspect that it was spoiled not just because Pepys owned the book –
that would not provide grounds for complaint – but because he
followed the play with the book. Pepys' disappointment is under-
standable; one cannot 'have a book' and watch a play at the same
time with any great success.

Pepys' problem is at least some evidence for the use of the printed
play as part of the experience of watching the play. Frequently
Pepys buys a copy of a play close to a visit to the theatre to see it.
He bought *The Indian Emperour* on 28 October 1667 and saw the
play again on 11 November; he bought *Secret Love* on 18 January
1668 and saw it again on 24 January. Again, this implies a combination of the two experiences.

Play publication, before the Restoration, was kept separate from
performance, partly of course because of the risk of piracy. After
the Restoration, publication becomes increasingly an adjunct to
performance, as the title-pages proudly proclaim. This was emphasised by the practice of printing the cast-list. James Wright commented that 'I wish they had Printed in the last Age . . . the Actors
Names over against the Parts they Acted, as they have done since the
Restauration. And thus one might have guest at the Action of the
Men, by the Parts which we now Read in the Old Plays.'[26] Clearly,
the cast-list helps the reader, knowledgeable in the type of acting of
each of the major actors, to reconstruct the performance. A Betterton
part could only be performed and hence only read in a Bettertonian
way. The information establishes for the reader a pattern of prediction, a range of expectation identical to that used in the theatre.
In a slightly different context, a report of an amateur performance
in 1674 matches the young actors to the professional actors' parts:
'. . . Peg Gardiner and Ury who acted Harris and Batterson's parts
in that play came off with great applause and all w[th] as little prompt-
ing as ever I observed at the Theater . . .'[27] The remarks show the
extent to which the actor is as important as the role in the play.
Certainly, by the 1690s, at the time at which the omission of an
assigned cast is becoming rare, the process coincides with the drawing together of first performance and publication. Again, the published play is linked with performance.

However, although the cast of the original performances was given, the action of reading that play at a distance from that performance became instead an act of historical reconstruction. Later reprints do not revise or update the cast-lists, except where the publication is a Restoration revival of a pre-Restoration play. Almost the only example of such a change occurs when Mrs Hughes, cast as St Catharine in the first edition of Dryden's *Tyrannic Love* (1670), was replaced by Mrs Boutell in the second edition (1672), a change identical to that which apparently occurred with the part of Theodosia in *An Evening's Love*.[28] The effect of this fixity in the cast is to fix the first performance as that which 'realised' the play most fully, a tendency that is analogous to the effects that could be achieved through the casting. Given the tendency for a cast to remain the same for many years, that printed cast-list was likely to remain accurate. Nonetheless to some extent the cast-list becomes history.

But the publication of the cast-list can also alter the perception of the play. The reader, able to check back, can see whether a particular character will or will not appear. He knows that in *She Would If She Could*, Madam Rampant will not in the end appear;[29] he knows that in *Sir Harry Wildair* Angelica will reappear alive and no ghost; in Southerne's plays, peopled with characters who hover on the edge of appearing, the cast-list indicates which ones actually will.

Following Jonson, the cast-lists often include brief statements defining the characters. In the normal form this does little more than explicate the patterns of love and relationship and define the types of characters. To take a play at random, in Aphra Behn's *The Luckey Chance* (1687), the list tells the reader, for instance, that Bearjest is 'Nephew to Sir *Cautious*, a Fop' and that Gayman is 'A Spark of the Town, Lover of *Julia*'. Of course, the type of character is both implied by the identity of the actor (Jevon and Betterton, respectively) and a spark or a fop would be immediately recognised as such by the spectator. Equally well, relationship and affection are quickly made explicit in most plays – though not in *The Way of the World*. But these sketches can also anticipate information that is only given late in the play, for example that Belmour was 'Contracted to *Leticia* disguis'd'. They may define characters in a way that only later events prove true; the sketch becomes too much of an anticipation, in that it destroys the reader's discovery of character. Even in uncomplicated plays, this may alter effects: in Betterton's *The Amorous Widow*, Mrs Brittle is *not* immediately apparent as a 'Cunning, Intrieguing Coquet, that *always* over-reaches her Husband'.[30]

This destruction of the process of anticipatory suspense is carried over into the text itself. Each character is identified on appearance by stage direction or speech prefix, while in the theatre the audience may not be able to name a character until his identity is made explicit by statement or by gesture. The only way to maintain this process in the reading text is by altering the speech prefixes, as Shaw frequently does. This flattening-out of the experience of the text, this inevitable elision of the possibilities of suspense diminishes the act of reading as a 'dramatic' experience, 'dramatic' in the sense of excitement. In the Restoration, reading a play is usually analysed as a cerebral activity, a comprehension of the text that overcomes the distortions of the theatre's demands for emotional empathetic involvement.

The description of character, at its most extended, as in Jonson, is fairly common. Significantly, Tuke thought it necessary to point to his use of it in the third, revised, edition of *The Adventures of Five Hours* (1671):

> though it be unusual, I have in a distinct *Column*, prefix'd the several *Characters* of the most eminent *Persons* in the *Play*; that being acquainted with them at his first setting out, he may the better judge how they are carried on in the whole *Composition* (A3a–A3b).

Tuke's emphasis on the descriptions as 'characters', that is as moral judgements on individuals, connects with his notion of the roles as people, living entities rather than dramatic stereotypes. Hence, he can write of 'being acquainted' with these 'persons', constructing a fictive reality that moves the play away from performance towards fiction. This type of fiction is rarely carried over into the text of the play itself, though it may inform a whole play, either through the play's non-theatricality as in Digby's *Elvira*, with its extravagant stage directions, or through its demands on the audience, as in *The Way of the World*.

This sort of non-theatrical information is also available in the dedication. Frequently, of course, the dedication is used to connect the play to performance, commenting on good or bad aspects of the production. Frequently, too, the dedication offers a critical exposition of the author's position, though not often at the length of Dryden. But in both cases, the prefatory material serves to limit, to define the way in which the play is to be approached, reducing the freedom of the reader to control his experience of the text.

When we look at the acting-text of the play itself, it is clear that the play-text does make reference back to the theatre. Almost every time that the published text differs from the performed text, the dedication draws attention to it. George Granville in the preface to *Heroick Love* (1698) sees this almost as an obligation: 'It may be necessary to inform the Reader, that after the first Representation of this Play, the Conclusion was altered' (A2a). He then proceeds to explain the reasons for the alteration.

Shadwell, in *The Lancashire Witches* (1682), distinguished the censored passages by having them printed in italic, to vindicate himself against the censors. Shadwell sees this as an accident of performance, about which the reader has no need to worry, except in order to reconcile the published text with the banned performed one.[31] More extreme is the note to the reader in the 1676 text of *Hamlet*:

This Play being too long to be conveniently Acted, such places as might be least prejudicial to the Plot or Sense, are left out upon the Stage : but that we may no way wrong the incomparable Author, are here inserted according to the Original Copy with this Mark " (π2a).

The effect of the distinction is to separate out two texts, an acting version and a reading-text. The reader, unlike the spectator, is allowed to encompass both. The reading-text is that designed to reveal the full beauty of the language and the structure; the acting version merely gives the bones of the play, without disrupting its forward movement, 'plot or sense'.

Of course, alterations in the stage-text can occur for numerous reasons: a text could be simply too long,[32] or an actor might have been unavailable[33] or the death of the author could have given the actors too much freedom to alter the text.[34] Only very rarely is the text cut for publication. Crowne, in *The Destruction of Jerusalem* (1677), cuts the play because of his friends' advice but still believes that the reader would know better than the spectator: 'And, Reader, if you will please to peruse that Scene carefully, you will find he is no such formidable person as imagined' (a1a).

In describing such alterations I have assumed that the text used in the theatre was a fixed entity. In fact, actors did alter their parts as they wished. In particular, farce actors ad-libbed furiously.[35] But when, during the Collier crusade, informers sat in the audience to record every oath, their records, turned into evidence in the prosecutions of the actors, show that the ad-libbing was no more extreme than one would expect. When Dogget and Underhill were prosecuted in 1701 for using blasphemous phrases during a performance of *Love for Love* on Christmas Day, 1700, the phrases quoted in the indictment show some cuts from the 1695 quarto and the addition of a sprinkling of oaths – five references to God that Congreve did not write.[36] They seem to me to be unremarkable alterations for a play that had been in the repertory for five years.

In two particular respects the published text tries to return to the playhouse, in the recording of certain eccentricities of pronunciation and in the reproduction of certain playhouse rhythms of speech.

Whenever a Frenchman appeared on the Restoration stage, he was expected to talk a strange gibberish. From Monsieur Raggou in Lacy's *The Old Troop* (1664) to Foigard in *The Beaux' Stratagem* (1707), English is offered deformed into a reproduction of Gallic stupidity and the deformation is repeated in print.[37] Crowne, in *City Politiques* (1683), writes a strange phonetic form of speech for Bartoline but has to explain it at length to the reader 'because otherwise he will hardly understand much of the Lawyers part . . . but when this reidiculous way of spelling is familiar with him, it will render the part more pleasant' (A2b). In effect, the reproduction of this eccentric language requires that the reader tries to hear the part as Tony Leigh spoke it, since it is printed 'in that manner of spelling, by which I taught it to Mr. *Lee*' (A2b). This device works against the published text's tendency to eliminate the acoustic elements of the words.

The primary aid to reconstructing the rhythmic sound of the dialogue, especially in those more serious passages where emotion takes over, is in the printing of prose in a form of bastard verse. It is significant that this does tend to occur whenever the language of the scene as a whole is approaching the sentiments or diction of heroic drama. The more one analyses these passages, the more one is led to conclude that some of these represent a division of the speeches into speech-units, that is, that they are divided up in the way an actor might treat the text in order to speak it. The reader is thus enabled to recover that pattern of speech.

Vanbrugh makes ironic use of the tendency for this prose-as-verse to hover in some middle ground between ordinary speech and heightened heroic diction. In *The Relapse*, for instance, the emotional scene in the countryside on the temptations of the town is implicitly parodied by the prose-as-verse form:

*Amanda* Forgive the Weakness of a Woman,
　　　　I am uneasie at your going to say so long in Town,

I know its false insinuating Pleasures;
I know the Force of its Delusions;
I know the Strength of its Attacks;
I know the weak Defence of Nature;
I know you are a Man – and I . . . a Wife.   (B2a)

But the conventional form is sometimes affected by the exigencies of publishing. For Southerne's *The Wives Excuse* (1692), the publishing was shared and each publisher used a separate printer. The first half of the play was set completely as 'prose-as-verse'. The second printer took over at the beginning of gathering E and set the rest of the play solid, in order to save space. But the result was that some passages of blank verse are set as prose.

The stage directions in the published text are the minimum necessary to comprehend the action. Scenery seems to have been particularly noted whenever it was remarkable because new or significant for the action of the play. Most other directions are simple entrances or exits. There are a few cases in which the text has a profusion of stage directions which seem to refer to the details of actual performance. Thus Tuke's revision of *The Adventures of Five Hours* in 1671 has many more directions than the earlier text; most of them are ones that would have been observed in the theatre. Similarly, the reprinting of *The Prisoners* and *Claricilla* in the folio edition of Killigrew's plays in 1664 now gives the plays vast numbers of detailed directions that were not present in the 1641 edition.[38] These directions, as Wertheim noted, 'are more than the usual aids provided in contemporary texts for a reader's visualization of the play'[39] but his belief that the text derives its annotations from a promptbook is belied by the lack of anything approximating to such notes in such profusion in any of the surviving promptbooks. Most of the directions refer to gestures by the actors: in *The Prisoners*, for instance, the 1664 text gives the following sequence of directions, '*Gillipus* lays hold on her and pulls her', 'He pulls her', 'Still he pulls her, and she resists', 'He takes her in his arms, and sets her down again' (pp. 73–4); none of these had appeared in the earlier edition. Such notes are in fact remarkably similar to the type of stage direction in the published text of John Wilson's *The Cheats* (1664), directions that are *not* present in the promptbook. Nahm distinguishes between the two texts of *The Cheats* as a contrast between a reading-text 'in a finished literary style' and an acting-text that 'wastes little time in extras'.[40] I suspect that Wilson – and Killigrew – when preparing the texts for publication, added the comparatively extravagant numbers of directions in order to make the text even more of a record, a re-creation of what happened for the benefit of the reader. It is not an accident of the provenance of the printer's copy but part of a rather more extreme version of the contemporary practice.

The play-quarto is then a conventionalised record of the practice of performance. But, though the dramatists and publishers used the format of the play-quarto as a shorthand to refer to the mode of performance in the public theatres, there was still a distinction made between plays and literature. The significance of Jonson's gesture in publishing *Works* and the position of plays as a respectable form of literature can best be seen now by examining how plays were treated in the records of private libraries before and after the Restoration. This is an area of study that has long been ignored. I want here to indicate the type of information that is available from such sources. Much more detailed work still needs to be done.

A wide range of practice is implied among pre-Restoration evidence of book-buying. At one extreme is the massive collection; at the other, total absence. In the first group come people like Sir John Harington whose collection of 135 plays included 90 out of the 105 plays published between 1600 and 1610.[41] Harington's comprehensive collection specifically excluded all occasional drama like masques and entertainments. Into this group also comes Henry Oxinden's collection of 122 plays and the receipt from the bookseller Humphrey Moseley in 1640 for a customer's settlement of a bill for 67 plays.[42] John Buxton, a Grays Inn man of the 1620s, bought 'ffor my library' between 1627 and 1631 at least 37 plays plus an unspecified part of the batch of '30 playes and Poems' that he bought on 3 May 1631 for 15 shillings.[43] This steady acquisition of plays is also demonstrated in the collection by John Horne (200 plays).[44] The last large list to mention is that of Sir Edward Dering in his accounts books for 1619 to 1624. Dering's passion for amateur theatricals – including an adaptation of both parts of Shakespeare's *Henry IV* into one play – led him to buy plays in bulk but the records include at least 220 plays bought, though few are identified. What is significant is the combination in Dering's case of play-buying with play-going. In the period there are notes of twenty-seven visits to plays even though he was not usually living in London. In 1623, between 2 May and 9 December, Dering recorded 'seeing a play' eighteen times and bought 161 'playbooks'.[45]

More formal lists of libraries frequently include no plays at all.

As the editors of the catalogue of Lord Lumley's library comment, this library excluded the type of literature 'read by the uneducated man: the street ballad, the play, the broadside news-sheet'.[46] Plays were simply not respectable enough for a great library and therefore their absence from library catalogues does not necessarily indicate that the owner did not read or buy plays, only that they were not considered worthy of noting in the library records. William Drummond of Hawthornden read dozens of plays but few are known to have been in his library.[47] The library of Sir Thomas Bludder lists few important volumes of plays but conceals play-quartos as bound pamphlets.[48] We know from his book of expenses that Viscount Conway was buying plays in 1636 but virtually none are listed in the library of 6000 volumes in 1641–3.[49] The classic statements on this question of status are in Sir Thomas Bodley's letters to Thomas James in January 1612 during the establishment of the Bodleian Library. Bodley classes plays as 'idle bookes, & riffe raffes', putting them with 'Almanackes . . . & proclamacions'.[50] Bodley admits that 'Happely some plaies may be worthy the keeping: but hardly one in fortie' and, after distinguishing the triviality of English plays from the wisdom of Foreign ones, he lays down: 'Were it so againe, that some little profit might be reaped . . . out of some of our playbookes, the benefit ther of will nothing conteruaile, the harme that the scandal will bring vnto the Librairie, when it shalbe given out, that we stuffe it full of baggage bookes.'[51]

With the publication of the great play collections, starting with the Jonson folio, plays could be a part of a library. But play-quartos were still disdainfully treated.

After the Restoration, a typical man-about-town's library was lampooned as containing trivia: 'His whole Library consists of the *Academy of Complemets*, *Venus undress'd*, *Westminster Drollery*, half a dozen *Plays*, and a Bundle of *Bawdy* Songs in *Manuscript*'.[52] I doubt if this was very far from the truth. Jeffrey Boys, a Gray's Inn student, bought some law books in 1671. But he also bought Aphra Behn's *The Forced Marriage*, after seeing it on 9 January, and Mrs Behn herself sent him a copy of *The Amorous Prince* on 1 July. The moral tracts were spiced with *Hudibras* (bought on 12 July) and a 'French Play Book' (3 August).[53]

Others were buying more seriously. Again as earlier there are occasional large collections of plays. One gentleman's library, sold anonymously in 1697, included over 130 plays.[54] Sir William Coventry's library contained 87 plays bound in ten thick volumes while, separated from the others, there are the folios of Jonson, Shakespeare and Davenant.[55] There is a clear distinction between those libraries where the plays are bound up together into volumes[56] and those where one finds play-quartos simply bundled into odd batches like assorted paperbacks, listed under 'Bundles of tracts and Pamphlets' and sold in bulk.[57] In effect, it is only when the owner takes the trouble to bind up the quartos that they acquire dignity.[58] In many libraries, even where one would expect otherwise, there is no trace of plays at all. I find it improbable that there were no plays in Sir Charles Sedley's library but none were sold.[59] But there are many libraries which apparently contain no plays other than folios by Davenant or others.[60] The gigantic library of Richard Smith, in all over 8300 items, contains only one volume of plays, the Davenant folio.[61] The prestige of the folios, established from Jonson's onwards, was carried over into the Restoration.

It will be helpful to look at three individual libraries, Isaac Newton's, John Locke's and Samuel Pepys'. Newton's library was not particularly large and, in the state in which it is known to us, includes certain items that were not Newton's.[62] But still, to balance a collection of works by Jeremy Collier, there are a number of plays, including quartos of all of Congreve's, as well as such plays as *The Rehearsal*, the Dryden-Davenant *Tempest* and Trapp's *Abra-Mule*. Almost all the plays are in editions that are post-1700 so that the lists may not include any plays he may have bought earlier.

With John Locke's library, roughly similar in size to Newton's, there is a far larger representative sample of literature and drama, in spite 'of [Locke's] melancholy reputation with the literary critics'.[63] There are admittedly none of Dryden's works to set against the seven different editions of Terence but there are plays by Congreve, Cowley, Davenant, Tuke and others, as well as Beaumont and Fletcher (1647) and Jonson (1616). Locke owned a bound-up set of Wycherley's plays (1694) as well as a first edition of *The Plain-Dealer*. In addition there are a number of works stemming from the Collier Controversy, including *The Short View*.

In this context, Pepys' library can no longer be seen as so extraordinarily rich as it appears when viewed in isolation. It is much larger than Newton's and Locke's. It seems more a collector's library than a working library and Pepys certainly liked plays enough to collect them. Apart from collections of plays by Jonson, Shakespeare, Beaumont and Fletcher, Killigrew, Robert Howard and Cowley, the library contains about 65 English plays, a disproportionate number of which are pre-Restoration. Pepys weeded out his library; the final collection does not include many plays that he records buying in the diary.[64] Again, there is the distinction between respectable and everyday books. Pepys bought plays as part of his play-going activities; he did not buy them to fill up his ambitious library.

### Seeing and reading

On 31 May 1663, Pepys recorded in his diary:

And after dinner, up and read part of the new play of *The Five houres adventures*; which though I have seen it twice, yet I never did admire or understand it enough – it being a play of the greatest plot that ever I expect to see, and of great vigour quite through the whole play, from beginning to the end.

Pepys had been ecstatic in the play's praise when he had seen it;[65] but he recognised that seeing a play and reading it were not the same thing.[66] It is this distinction that I want next to explore.

There is only limited discussion in the Restoration of the difference between seeing and reading a play. Certainly there was occasionally an awareness of the need to discriminate between the types of response that were being called for, an awareness, at root, that the two activities were not identical. In spite of the re-creation of performance in the published text, playwrights also saw publication as a chance to rectify, not to make different, the false impression of the play brought about through mistakes in the attitude of the theatre audience. Gildon, in the preface to Aphra Behn's *The Younger Brother* (1696), sees reading as an area in which the faction that had damned the play on stage cannot operate: 'The unjust Sentence this Play met with before very partial Judges in the Acting, will, I'm pretty sure, be revers'd by the more unprejudic'd Readers' (A2a). The readers are unprejudiced – even apart from Gildon's flattery – because they have no reason to be otherwise. Factions exist only in the playhouse; outside, it is the individual reader who will make up his mind.

However, circumstances of the performance itself frequently made it impossible for the theatre audience to understand the drama. Often, the prefaces indicate that reading can therefore make up for such deficiencies. Thus the audience at Crowne's *Darius, King of Persia* (1688) could not understand the play because of the illness of Mrs Barry whose part in the fourth act was 'wholly cut out, and neither Spoke nor Read' so that, not surprisingly, 'the People went away without knowing the contexture of the Play, yet thought they knew all' (A1a). Oldmixon, in the preface to *The Grove* (1700), complains of the acting obscuring the perfections of the play; the audience had complained of the rushed and awkward ending to the play but 'they will now see if what he had writ had been spoken, every thing wou'd have appear'd clear and natural, which, to shorten the Entertainment, had been before broken and disorder'd' (π 3a). Reading becomes a correction of the mistakes; it makes possible understanding of what could not be understood before.

Wherever the acting or the scenery had been particularly fine, the dramatist's references to it imply that the reading of the play is necessarily a diminution of the splendour and vitality of performance. Edward Howard realised that published plays 'thus appearing, divested of the life of Action, which gave no small varnish to their figures, they suffer a more severe Correction from the Reader'.[67] At its most extreme, in Crowne's *Calisto*, the emphasis on representation of the masque is so strong as to separate the two possibilities, reading as reconstruction and reading as memory of a previously seen performance:

If you were ever a Spectator of this following Entertainment, when it was Represented in its Glory, you will come ... with very dull Appetite, to this cold lean Carkass of it ... If you have never seen it, then (perhaps) you may receive some pleasure ...[68]

All three of these attitudes to the reading of plays, the rectifying of prejudice, the better understanding, and the shadow of performed splendour, emphasise the extent to which the differences between seeing and reading are designed to be submerged into a concept of the play as separable entity. If, as seems common, both reading and seeing were held to be unsatisfactory modes of understanding, modes equally liable to error, though improved through repetition and overlap, then the implication of passages such as these was that the play was held to exist outside of the modes by which it was perceived. The conventional form of the statements of the prefaces does not hide the belief in the play as object. 'The play' then becomes something different from the play in performance or the play as read. The published text and the stage performance are seen as two ways, reconcilable to some extent, through which 'the play' is discovered. In fact, this theoretical approach was obviously not pursued to any great extent. Instead one tends to find a continual equivocation, a re-weighting of the relative merits of the two modes of perception. Occasionally one finds a detailed examination of the problem.

Richard Flecknoe, never very successful at getting his plays performed, oscillated between these possible attitudes towards the play-text according to the warmth or hostility of his relations with the acting companies. Thus *Love's Kingdom* (1664) is a text differentiated from that used for performance because the actors had mangled the text. The title-page announces it to be 'Not as it was Acted at the Theatre near *Lincolns-Inn*, but as it was written'. Flecknoe's willingness to publish is not in contradiction to his emphasis on the importance of acting. The process of reading is, for him, a re-creation of the acting. Reading a play, to Flecknoe, is not the creation of a fantasy world but an imaginative reconstruction of performance, even where the normal relations of text to performance have been disrupted. In *Erminia* (1661), he apologises for publishing the play before performance, a disruption of the status of text as memory and re-creation. But Flecknoe goes on to say, 'mean while a lively fancy may imagine he sees it Acted: and to help the imagination, I have set down the Scenes, the Habits, and Names of the Actors' (A3a). This belief is repeated in the preface to *The Damoiselles a la Mode* (1667), where the quality of the pleasure of the reader is seen as dependent on the imaginative skill with which the acting can be reconstituted: 'Together with the Persons Represented in this Comedy, I have set down the Comedians, whom I intended shou'd Represent them, that the Reader might have half the pleasure of seeing it Acted, and a lively imagination might have the pleasure of it all intire' (A7a).

Flecknoe's opinion here was mocked by Langbaine, who doubts that imagination can 'supply the defect of Action'. Langbaine aligns Flecknoe with a character in Horace,

Who fancy'd he saw Plays acted in the empty Theatre; but to others in their right Sences, all [Flecknoe's] Rhetorick could not have been able to perswade them that a Play *Read* (notwithstanding the utmost force of Imagination) can afford half the pleasure with that of a Play *Acted*, since the former wants the Greatest Ornament to a Play, *Gracefulness of Action*.[69]

Langbaine's distrust of the imagination is compatible with his position in all his writings but his comments in effect constitute a wilful misreading of Flecknoe's. There is no reason why 'Gracefulness of Action' should not be recuperable or imaginable by the reader provided that he knows the abilities and manner of acting of the actors assigned roles in the cast-list. It is only from the initial premise, that Flecknoe accepts, of the fact of the reading audience's knowledge of the details of contemporary theatre practice, that the re-creation can take place. Flecknoe does not begin to posit an alternative audience for the printed text. As he says, 'For my Printing it before 'tis Acted, 'tis only to give the Auditors their Bill of Fare beforehand; so far from taking away their Appetites of seeing it afterwards, as (on the contrary) if they like it, it increases it but the more'.[70] Flecknoe's idea recurs in Steele's preface to *The Conscious Lovers* (1723), with an added emphasis on the performance as the means of inculcating virtue: 'for the greatest Effect of a Play in reading is to excite the Reader to go see it; and when he does so, it is then a Play has the Effect of Example and Precept'.[71]

Only at one moment does Flecknoe suggest that seeing and reading are essentially different, and the passage is an anticipation of Langbaine, 'It will want much of the grace and ornament of the stage; but though there it be better seen, yet here 'tis better understood'.[72] This distinction between seeing and reading as one between pleasure and understanding is present earlier in the preface to Marlowe's *Tamburlaine*,[73] where the distinction is made between 'acceptable' and 'delightful', between the 'wise' readers and 'the vain-conceited fondlings' who watched it at the theatre. The distinction does not often occur in dedications to plays, though there is that repeated emphasis on the reader understanding parts of the play that the action had obscured. The reader is able to understand the play because almost every aspect of the meaning – rather than the simply pleasurable aspects of the play – is transferred into the published text. The play-quarto, as we have seen, can indicate everything necessary to 'make the reader understander'. This type of ability is not possible in the French tradition and Hédelin argues at length against including any information as part of the text that is not available in the dialogue alone. Hédelin's writings, touched on earlier, mark an important interim stage on the way to Dryden's exploration of the problem.

Unlike Flecknoe, Hédelin believes that the theatre is a place that is illusionistic, mimetic rather than conscious of itself as enactment. The reader uses his imagination in order to construct the fantasy-world. But Hédelin places a primary emphasis on the word, because the play 'cannot be known to the Spectators, but just as the Actors shall make it so; and the Reader can understand no more of it than the Verses or Expressions do inform him'.[74] For Hédelin, the communication of the play in the theatre is solely the result of the words spoken by the actors, so that 'either way all the Decorations, Clothes, or necessary Motions, for the understanding the Play, must be had in the Verses'.[75] Any extraneous part of the play when published is merely a concession 'to help the dulness of some Readers' but 'in all these Notes 'tis the Poet that speaks, which he is not allowed to do in this sort of Poems, and it cannot be done without interrupting the Reader in the midst of passions, and dividing his application, and so dissipating some of those Ideas which he had receiv'd already for the understanding and relishing the Play'.[76] For Hédelin the system of signification through which the theatre communicates its meaning must be totally embodied in the spoken word or it cannot exist at all.

Hédelin's emphasis on the primacy of language is found in England. Edward Howard, recognising the published play as less than the performed one, still sees what is left: 'the Press being in some manner the stages Tyring-House, where all Ornaments are thrown off, save native design and Language'.[77] This concept is central to Dryden's writings on the subject.

In two prefaces, to *The Spanish Friar* (1681) and *Don Sebastian* (1690), Dryden investigates the potential differences of the experience of reading plays and in both cases he uses part of Hédelin's argument, the ability of the reader to understand what is incomprehensible on stage, primarily through the reader's ability to understand the words of the dialogue. The reader can 'find out those beauties of propriety in thought and writing which escaped him in the tumult and hurry of representing'.[78] In *The Spanish Friar* preface, Dryden even values the experience of reading over that of the theatre, a part of his increasingly disdainful attitude towards what he saw as the stupidity of the audience: 'But as 'tis my interest to please my audience, so 'tis my ambition to be read: that I am sure is the more lasting and nobler design'.[79]

What Dryden recognises is that that discriminating judgement of language ('The purity of phrase, the clearness of conception and expression, the boldness maintained to majesty . . . '[80]) which he sees as by far the most important aspect of the kind of tragedy that he was trying to write at this point, could too easily be subverted by other parts of the theatrical experience of the play.

For if either the story move us, or the actor help the lameness of it with his performance, or now and then a glittering beam of wit or passion strike through the obscurity of the poem, any of these are sufficient to effect a present liking, but not to fix a lasting admiration.[81]

Dryden's demand that he should be praised when read is an alignment of his critical theory with drama as 'poem' rather than as theatre. Scenes such as the debate scenes of *Don Sebastian* can be seen in this light as moving the play towards epic, towards *The Aeneid*. But Dryden sees, as comprised within the practice of reading the play, elements that one would tend to associate only with performance, in particular the list of the virtues that are perceptible in reading includes 'the significancy and sound of words, not strained into bombast, but justly elevated'.[82] There are two significant implications of this: one is a matter for historical linguistics, the separation of meaning and sound; the second is the implication that reading is an interior vocalisation of the words, thereby indicating the extent to which that reading is analogous to a theatrical one. Dryden's reading is predominantly an aural not visual experience; the reader hears, rather than sees, what he reads. Silent reading had begun much earlier[83] but Dryden does not necessarily mean that the words are to be spoken aloud, only that the process of reading is automatically and simultaneously an imagined creation of the sound of the words. Hence Dryden attributes to language the primary place in the process of reading.

But Dryden also sees reading as discriminating judgement, as had been suggested in the preface to *Tamburlaine*. On stage, 'the propriety of thoughts and words . . . are but confusedly judged . . . The most discerning critic can judge no more of these silent graces in the action'.[84] It is a process of discovery, uncovering things that are obscured in performance, in order to judge them. Judgement, the criterion of aesthetic value, becomes of central importance by contrast with the unthinking, distorting pleasure that can be gained from performance. The theatre goes against the intellect, against rational judgement. In its turn, this suspicion on Dryden's part leads him to his perception of one of the major differences between reading and seeing.

I have already indicated his emphasis on performance as 'hasty motion', 'transient view', 'vehemence of action', 'the tumult and hurry of representing'.[85] Watching a play for the first time is like riding 'post through an unknown country'.[86] When *Don Sebastian* was performed, Dryden accepted that it would have to be cut and, with assistance from Betterton, 1,200 lines were 'judiciously lopped'.[87]

The story did not suffer except in a certain precipitateness, but Dryden realised that the first passages to go were the 'most poetical parts'. Dryden, as part of this chain of reasoning, saw that one of the major differences is a matter of time: 'every reader is judge of his own convenience; he can take up the book, and lay it down at his pleasure'.[88] In effect, Dryden is here concentrating on the matter of attention spans but this connects with one of the primary differences: on stage, time is out of the hands of the audience; in the study, it is controlled by the reader. Theatre time is strictly connected and represents the diachronic movement of the play; time is irreversible. In the study, time can be interrupted but it can also be reversed, short-circuited and speeded up. The reader can perform actions that ensure that reading is the discovery of meaning. In addition, Dryden defines reading implicitly as a second reception of the text, a corrective to seeing rather than a first perception of the play.

These two elements combine to place emphasis on the continual re-reading and re-watching of the text. Bernard Beckerman emphasises that 'plays should not be read, but *reread*'[89] but for Dryden reading is always re-reading. What happens when we read or watch a play for the second time? The first problem is that the work changes in our memory between the two experiences of the text. It is not the events of the text that are altered (the 'what') but memory changes the order, balance and significance of those events (the 'when', 'how' and 'why'). In his brilliant study, 'On Rehearing Music', Leonard Meyer shows that memory modifies unexpected events according to the 'psychological "law of good shape"', regularising and improving the structural patterns.[90] Meyer demonstrates that forgetfulness is a joy: it enables us to rediscover the vitality in a work too frequently heard.[91] The organising power of memory places the set of predictions within which the second experience of that work would function into a close relationship with the predictions used for the initial confrontation, closer than one might expect.

But our second experience of a work can be made irrevocably different by our knowledge of the solution. As Philip Edwards has shown, Fletcher's *King and No King* changes when we know that Arbaces is not royal after all.[92] Everything that had disrupted decorum is now explained. The second confrontation with a text reduces our tendency to false prediction. We know, however much we might hope otherwise, that Lear will die, that Oedipus will be blinded; but we can see the significance of our continued hope that Lear and

Oedipus will this time escape. We rediscover the original desire for a particular solution and understand rather better why that desire is not to be realised. In addition, the diminished concern about what is to happen allows the second reading to concentrate on the moment and also to observe as significant for the future what the knowledge of that future has already revealed to be significant (a circularity of perception across the entire expanse of the play). The entire basis of the second reading is that the reader now has greater control over the text, precisely what Dryden saw as implicit in the entire process of reading.

It is that control, made practicable by the diminution of the intervention of performance, that makes the experience of reading so different. It is the unevenness of performance that enables it to emphasise, to direct attention and thus to structure perception. Redundancy is set within the play's control of the audience's perception. The audience perceives how they are to connect the signs with structures of plot and meaning or with incidental delight. The published text is starker; the reader must not only understand, he must also connect. Reading replaces the incidental redundancy of *performance* with the redundancy of *the text itself*. This redundancy – as Dryden saw, of the poetry – is then in turn made part of a larger system in which that redundancy becomes the basis for comprehension of the moment of the play. As the individual line is better understood so the place of that line in the total structure of the play is grasped. The comprehension of the moment, the particular virtue of reading, is the beginning of the perception of structure that in theatre is controlled by the large movement of the text. This new redundancy is radically different.

The essential characteristic of this redundancy in reading is that it is generated not by the playhouse but by the author. In spite of the extremely strong degree of control that the playwright did exert over the production of his plays on stage, it is innate in performance – especially in repertory productions with conventionalised presentation – that the play is affected by aspects of performance that are not part of the play. At its most extreme, this means the actors or the audience disrupting the play. Pepys finds his enjoyment of *Heraclius* spoilt when the actors laugh and forget their lines especially with the excessive backstage noise,[93] and his enjoyment of *The Maid's Tragedy* spoilt when Sedley talks through the play, much as he enjoyed Sedley's conversation.[94] But anything that draws attention to something outside the play would constitute such a disruption. Even though much more is comprised within the notion of 'the Play' than is defined in the spoken words, performance still includes events that are not part of this concept of play. Though the work of the printer might affect the play, particularly with careless or eccentric presentation, the published text is less equivocally the work of the author; he includes just so much of the playhouse as he deems necessary. Dryden was right to think of reading as a purer form.

To end this chapter, I want to look at the way an author, under pressure from some outside forces, but still basically following his own critical principles, can try to change the way his plays could be read by adopting a different form of presentation.

### The Works of Mr William Congreve, 1710

On 9 November 1710, Congreve wrote to his friend Keally that 'I would send you my books, which will be published in a month'.[95] *The Works* was advertised in *The London Gazette* for 5/7 December. Though Congreve made minor revisions in the second edition of 1719–20, it is *The Works* of 1710 that provides the substantial alternative to the original quartos of the plays. Certain of the plays underwent revision in second and subsequent quarto editions, prior to 1710, but the quartos and *The Works* represent the twin poles of intention, the one substantially the text as record of performance, the other an entirely new approach to the presentation of Restoration plays as reading-texts.

There is ample evidence of Congreve's care over the 1710 edition. Tonson wrote to his son in 1729 that Congreve 'took a great deal of care himself in the 8° edition I printed. I believe that wil be the best coppy for you to follow'.[96] In the preface, Congreve defends his purpose in publishing as the natural desire of an author: 'It will hardly be deny'd, that it is both a Respect due to the Publick, and a Right which every Man owes to himself, to endeavour that what he has written, may appear with as few Faults, as he is capable of avoiding'.[97] But *The Works* is not to be thought of as a work of absolute perfection. For Congreve, 'This Edition . . . is only recommended as the least faulty Impression, which has yet been Printed; in which, Care has been taken both to Revise the Press, and to Review and Correct many Passages in the Writing'.[98] The purpose of this section is to examine the nature and purpose of these alterations and explore their significance for Congreve's aims in his plays.

The 1710 edition emphasises the form of the text as a 'reading edition' through a series of devices alien to the practice of the play-quarto. There is no way in which *The Works* could mediate the stage presentation because it does not represent the shared context within which that might be possible. All the 'French' styles of the edition serve to construct an ideal, imaginary and non-specific theatrical representation divorced from Drury Lane or Lincoln's Inn Fields. The whole force of the ordinary play-quarto, as I have explored it in this chapter, is towards a form of shorthand, providing a simple connection that the play-reader could make with his experience as play-goer. The play-quarto, as a body of conventions, could refer back to the theatre with a small gesture, as, for example, in its indications of scene-changes. A quarto is not uninformative because its devices are perfunctory. That perfunctoriness is an indication of its methods: it 'presents' the stage; it constitutes a combination of text and performance. *The Works*, as Congreve knew, was a new departure, an entirely original approach to the presentation of contemporary drama, of the text as text, a deliberate obscuring of the actual theatrical performance in search of what a non-playgoing reader might comprehend.

Many of the small verbal changes in *The Works* stem ultimately from the after-effects of Collier's attack on Congreve twelve years earlier. In April 1698 Collier published *A Short View of the Immorality and Profaneness of the English Stage*. Collier seized on the least suggestion of blasphemy. Lady Plyant, in *The Double-Dealer*, comments 'Jesu, Sir Paul, what a Phrase was there? You will be making Answers, and taking that upon you, which ought to lie upon me . . . ' (1694, p. 34). Collier brandished the profanity triumphantly: 'Lady *Plyant* cries out *Jesu* and talks Smut in the same Sentence'.[99] On 12 May, Luttrell recorded, 'The justices of Middlesex did not only present the playhouses, but also Mr Congreve, for writing the Double Dealer; Durfey, for Don Quixot; and Tonson and Brisco, booksellers, for printing them'.[100] The action of the Middlesex justices was only one of a number of prosecutions undertaken in the period following Collier's attack. Actors were prosecuted for blasphemous ad-libbing[101] and even for speaking lines that had previously been licensed. Poor George Bright was 'prosecuted . . . unknowingly' and fined the considerable sum of £10 with £10 costs after playing Old Bellair in *The Man of Mode*:

in y^e Conclusion of his part, these words are Exprest (Please you Sir to Commission a young couple to go to bed together a' Gods name) w^ch being Lyconed & permited, y^e said Bright did humbly conceive, y^t there was neither imorality or prophainess therein, y^e said Bright as well as sev;^ll others, having often Exprest y^e said words publickly on y^e stage, & no notice ever before taken thereof . . .[102]

By the time Congreve published his *Amendments of Mr Collier's False and Imperfect Citations* in July 1698, the threat of possible prosecution must have worried him. He acknowledges his fault in Lady Plyant's speech:

That Exclamation I give him up freely. I had my self long since condemn'd it, and resolv'd to strike it out in the next Impression. I will not urge the *folly*, viciousness, or affectation of the Character to excuse it.[103]

Some of the pamphleteers who responded to Congreve's *Amendments* doubted whether *The Double-Dealer* would ever reach another impression[104] but, when Collier himself published his *Defence of the Short View* in November, he indicted Congreve for inconsistency:

Well! Repentance is a very commendable thing, and I heartily wish Mr. *Congreve* may go Through with it. But I'm afraid this good Resolution of his went off in a little time: My reason is, because the *Double Dealer* was publish'd in 1694. and stands still in the First *Edition*; but the *Old Batchelour* has been Reprinted long since, the Sixth Impression of this Play bearing date 1697. And yet here in this last Edition we have the exclamation *Jesu*, used in a jesting way, by the fulsome *Belinda*. If Mr. *Congreve* was displeas'd with the Prophaneness in his *Double Dealer*, why did he not expunge it in his *Old Batchelour*? He can't deny but that Opportunity presented fair a great while together.[105]

When *The Double-Dealer* was reprinted in 1706, Congreve made a large number of revisions. The second edition thus marks a midway stage to the final form of *The Works* of 1710. In addition to Lady Plyant's 'Jesu', which was cut, Congreve deleted Lord Froth's 'Jesu' (1694, p. 7); Brisk's two self-deprecatory phrases, 'O Lord, Madam –' and 'O Jesu, Madam –' (1694, p. 16) became 'O dear, Madam –' and 'O Heav'ns, Madam –' and his further exclamation, 'O Jesu! Madam, you have Eclips'd me quite ...' (1694, p. 78), was appropriately trimmed. Over Belinda in *The Old Batchelour*, Congreve was more recalcitrant. Belinda, in mocking Heartwell's marriage, cries out '*Jesu*! how he looks already. Ha, ha, ha' (1693, p. 52). Even though the play went through a further edition, the seventh, in 1707, Congreve allowed the offending word to stand and it only finally disappeared in 1710.

In the *Amendments*, Congreve had used Belinda, with Miss Prue from *Love for Love*, as examples of the need to see that characters may be ridiculed:

> I only refer those two Characters to the Judgment of any impartial Reader, to determine whether they are represented so as to engage any Spectator to imitate the Impudence of one, or the Affectation of the other; and whether they are not both ridiculed rather than recommended. (pp. 14–15)

The central part of Congreve's claim is not simply that not all characters are good but that his drama is essentially moral. The audience is not only able but required to judge the characters. On this basis, Congreve's willingness to give up Lady Plyant's 'Jesu' is an abandonment of his position: characters must be able to speak without constraint so that they can damn themselves. In giving in, Congreve has lost one of the premises on which his drama was based.

Apart from words risking the charge of blasphemy, Congreve cut some – though by no means all – of the swearing. In *The Double-Dealer*, Careless's 'Pox I'm weary of guzling' (1694, p. 1) loses its first word and Brisk's 'Pox, Man' (1694, p. 2) becomes 'Pshaw, Man'. Sir Paul now laments that Lady Plyant has 'been an invincible Wife' rather than an 'impenetrable' one (1694, p. 20). Lady Plyant complains 'what have you to entertain any bodies privacy?' rather than 'what have you about you . . .' (p. 34). The Plyants suffer worse through the elimination of sexual references. The whole point of their castrated relationship is lost when Sir Paul is no longer 'render'd uncapable of using the common benefits of Nature' (p. 54), when Lady Plyant does not claim as grounds for divorce that 'there has hardly been Consummation between us' (p. 55) and when the rigidity of her code of practice for behaviour in bed disappears with the elimination of this entire passage:

*Lady Plyant* ... Well, remember for this, your Right Hand shall be swathed down again to Night – and I thought to have always allow'd you that Liberty –

*Sir Paul*    Nay but Madam, I shall offend again if you don't allow me that to reach –

*Lady Plyant* Drink the less you Sot, and do't before you come to Bed.  (p. 56)

*The Double-Dealer* explores the nature of lust as one of the centres of evil, a deliberate inversion of the usual status of the rake as heroic locus of superabundant sexuality and fertility. Its heroine is named Cynthia to counterpoint her chastity against the adultery of all three wives in the play. The deletions seriously damage the play.

Even more serious is the elimination of most references to hell and damnation. In Lady Touchwood's monologue in Act V, Congreve deletes 'Hell and Fire', ' a Hell of Torments, – but he's Damnation proof, a Devil already, and Fire is his Element'; 'Shame and Destruction' is changed to 'Shame and Distraction' (p. 68). She no longer attacks Maskwell as a 'Hellish' traitor (p. 73) and, at her final exit, she does not shriek 'Plagues, and Curses seize you all' (p. 79). Again the reason for the cuts may be legal in origin but the effect is to ruin the most important means by which the plot is resolved. Cynthia had announced in Act IV, at the point at which her nerves had caused her to suspect that her marriage would not take place, that Mellefont must defeat Lady Touchwood. Mellefont agrees 'unless the Devil assist her in *propria persona*' (p. 44). Cynthia accepts the condition:

Why if you give me very clear demonstration that it was the Devil, I'll allow for the the irresistable odds. But if I find it to be only chance, of destiny or unlucky Stars, or any thing but the very Devil, I'm inexorable ... (p. 44).

Lady Touchwood is defeated but only through the workings of chance, a chance meeting, a chance overhearing, a chance doubt. Mellefont's claim must rest in the proof that she and her accomplice are devils, and it is precisely that proof in Lady Touchwood's own words that Congreve eliminated.

The alterations to *The Double-Dealer* are not simply the polishing of odd phrases. Even while retaining some phrases that had given most offence in other of his plays, Congreve's blue pencil removes passages that drastically reduce the coherence and seriousness of his moral and dramatic purpose. The selectivity of the alterations – Mellefont can still accuse Lady Touchwood of having 'all the Host of Hell her Servants' (p. 62) – indicates that most of the changes were not made solely to avoid prosecution for blasphemy. In *Love for Love*, words like 'pox' and 'god' are allowed to stand more often than they are deleted. But Congreve believed that his collected works should be genteel pleasures, an ideal commensurate with his own claim to be a gentleman first and a playwright second. The search for a new type of interaction with the reader led him in this case to construct a play of new purity but far less significance. It seems appropriate that the new title-page in 1710 should include a new quotation, from Terence's *Heautontimorumenos*, which effectively indicates an alignment of Maskwell and the far less vicious Syrus, an alignment impossible before the changes in the text,

Oh I reckon this a Master-piece of my Cunning: In this Plot I triumph in having that mighty knack and faculty at Juggling as to cheat both of them, by telling the truth.[106]

A similar relaxation of seriousness occurs in *Love for Love*. The only major change is the deletion of almost all of Sir Sampson's last speech (p. 90). Sir Sampson now seems humiliated rather than furious, capable of being redeemed rather than totally irreconcilable. The effect is compounded by the fact that in the 1710 text he does not leave the stage. It is precisely his storming out, like Malvolio, that is the mark of his complete intractability. In 1710 his one remaining line ('You're an illiterate old Fool, and I'm another' 1 489) seems uttered more in sorrow than in anger, and, though silent, he is now present for the final dance. The cloud which his exit in Q1 had cast is now removed and the effect of Angelica's generosity is now inclusive, no longer excluding Sir Sampson himself.

In all four comedies, there is a continual tidying-up and regularising of the language to make it conform to more gentlemanly patterns of speech: 'a' becomes 'he', 'an' becomes 'if'; tenses are brought into line so that Tattle's 'have suffer'd me to take it' becomes 'have suffer'd me to have taken it'; inversions are re-inverted (Prue's 'are not you' becomes 'are you not').

Of course, the changes in *The Mourning Bride* were immense. In the preface, Congreve announced that 'The Tragedy of the *Mourning Bride*, in this Edition, is reformed in its *Numbers*, and by several little Variations and Transpositions in the Expression, intirely cast into Blank Verse; in respect of which Measure, it was before, in many Places, defective' (1710, I A3a). Dozens of lines are regularised and reformed. The quarto-text is clearly the better for performance; its lines have a greater verve and elan, an aggression that the later text lacks. But the text of 1710 has a pleasing conformity to classical orthodoxy: it looks more regular and more beautiful.

The effect is to make the play conform to canons of literary perfection that are not appropriate to drama on stage. Like the minor polishing in the comedies, the play is removed from the voice and given to the eye. The whole form of *The Works*, with its strong capitalisation and its heavy punctuation, reduces the lightness and fluidity of Congreve's stage lines and places them in a weightier and more measured context. *The Works* has a solemn dignity that is alien to a play-quarto.

Increasingly, Congreve recognised in Roman New Comedy, and especially in Terence, a standard of drama that was precisely what he was seeking. *The Double-Dealer*, which points directly to Terence in its motto, includes in its preface a generalised defence of a particular aspect of the drama, the soliloquy. Congreve's defence is in terms of the closed nature of theatrical representation rather than as part of an address to the audience.[107] The preface also includes a vicious snarling attack on the imperceptiveness of the theatre audience. The play, in the approval of various aristocratic friends, 'succeeded before it was Acted' (A2a) and performance seems to have been nothing more than an occasion to misconstrue the play's purpose.

By the time of *The Way of the World*, the reference to Terence prefaces a sincere doubt about performance, now seen as vulgarisation:

The purity of his Stile, the Delicacy of his Turns, and the Justness of his Characters, were all of them Beauties, which the greater part of his Audience were incapable of Tasting: Some of the coursest Strokes of *Plautus*, so severely censured by *Horace*, were more likely to affect the Multitude; such, who come with expectation to Laugh out[108] the last Act of a Play, and are better entertained with two or three unseasonable Jests, than with the artful Solution of the *Fable*.   (A4a − A4b)

Congreve's choice in *The Works* is clear. He will no longer pander to the 'Plautine' tastes of the multitude. The play will instead have the purity, delicacy and justness that is Terentian. Like Ben Jonson searching for the few sensitive readers, Congreve can no longer rely on the right auditors happening to be in the playhouse. The only possible choice was to turn away from the playhouse itself by publishing the plays in a format that invented a new relationship to the reading of plays, denying the status of the text as a record of performance. He will leave restrictive stage conventions, patterns of speech and vulgarity of language to those who want them. Instead *The Works* is to be reading matter for gentlemen.

Editions of the works of Restoration dramatists were just beginning to appear. The Davenant folio had appeared in 1673 but there was a long gap before anyone else acquired such dignity. The first demand was for bound-up sets of plays with new general title-pages. Macdonald lists such sets for Dryden for 1691, 1693, 1694 and 1695, and comments that the demand was established 'by 1691'.[109] Hence when *Cleomenes* was published in 1692 the title-page announces, after Tonson's address, 'Where Compleat SETS of Mr. *Dryden's* Works,

in Four Volumes, are to be Sold. The PLAYS being put in the order
they were Written'. Similar bound-up sets of quartos with a new
title-page exist for Shadwell, Lee and Otway in the 1690s.[110] An
edition of Aphra Behn's plays appeared in 1702 that was similar
in format. But the major event was the publication of Dryden's *The
Comedies, Tragedies and Operas* in two folio volumes in 1701, making
up the first two volumes of the *Works* of 1701. August and dignified
though the Dryden edition was, its size stopped it from being recrea-
tional reading for gentlemen. Instead it makes its claim for a dignity
appropriate for a poet laureate and accepted 'giant of the age'; it
aims to raise its material, mere plays, to the status of literature such
as Dryden's poems or translations, in much the same way that Jonson
had over eighty years earlier. But this was not what Congreve wanted.

In 1704 an edition of Etherege's works appeared and was sold by
Thomas Bennet and Jacob Tonson. Tonson's slight involvement
in this edition implies a link with Congreve's *Works*. The Etherege
volume is octavo; it reprints the three comedies and follows them
by eight pages of poems. Unremarkable in itself, the volume implies
the sort of public for which Congreve was looking. The volume is
not one to be placed in a library unread, but instead to be read at
leisure. In the same tradition as the Etherege, though far grander and
more influential, was Rowe's multi-volume edition of Shakespeare
published by Tonson in 1709. Congreve's edition of his own works is
thus the second term in Tonson's magnificent series of small-format
reprints of what were for him the great English dramatists: Beaumont and Fletcher (1712), Otway (1712), Jonson (1716), Dryden
(1717), Vanbrugh (1719), Congreve again (1719), Shadwell (1720).
It is in this context that Congreve's *Works* aimed to be placed.

But the status as a reading-text rather than a memory of performance, combined with the desire to be a Terentian playwright, led
Congreve to divide the plays into 'French scenes'. In 1704, John
Dennis, in publishing *Liberty Asserted*, divided his play into scenes
according to the entrances and exits onto the stage. In the preface,
Dennis provided a justification by appeal to 'the Ancients and . . . the
Moderns of other Countries, and . . . our own *Ben. Johnson*', and by
defining the demand on the reader rather than the spectator, of the
perception of the plays:

I thought that agreeable Delusion into which the Reader willingly and
gladly enters, for the sake of his Pleasure, would be both greater and
easier if he were not put in mind of a Stage by *Entrances* and *Exits*, which
are nothing but Directions that are given to a Play House Prompter.[111]

Dennis enhanced this dimension of his play, the reading rather than theatrical purpose, by ordering 'the last Scene of the Play to be printed, which on the account of Length was left out in Acting, tho' it yet remains in the Playhouse-copy'.[112] But Dennis still recognised that the theatrical performance is the root of the play-text. He pays tribute to Betterton for his 'Hints' but 'as well as for his excellent Action' and he acknowledges that his play 'indeed receiv'd all the Grace and Ornament of Action in most of the principal Parts, and in all the Womens'.[113] He goes into raptures over the performance of Mrs Barry. In spite of the mode of presentation of the text as one divorced from the stage, Dennis goes out of his way to ensure that the reader knows about the cast and the performance. The text pursues two directions simultaneously.

The notion of the scene as defined by entrance or exit is enshrined in Restoration critical theory, with a distinguished ancestry. All major editions of Terence and Plautus were divided up in this fashion, from the *editiones principes* of the fifteenth century.[114] Ben Jonson started using the system in the quartos of *Cynthia's Revels* and *Poetaster* and perfected it for *Sejanus, Volpone* and *The Alchemist.*[115] Jonson's purpose was clearly emulation of the classical model and his folio of 1616 became in turn the new model for emulation. Comparatively few play-quartos followed the plan, though it was quite common in the first few years after the Restoration, especially for those plays written in the Interregnum and unperformed or published in a way unconnected with theatrical norms.[116] Nonetheless, the significance of this method as a mode of thinking permeated the critical orthodoxy. Dryden's *An Essay of Dramatic Poesy* (1668) has Eugenius defining without hesitation that 'it is to be accounted a new scene, not every time the stage is empty, but every person who enters, though to others, makes it so; because he introduces a new business'.[117]

For Hédelin, this meaning of scene is paramount; the word 'signifies that part of an Act which brings any Change upon the Stage, by the change of Actors'.[118] But he recognised that the technique was not used by the Greeks and was absent from the earliest copies of Terence and Plautus, because 'knowing that the whole *Act* could not contain above one sensible Action upon the Stage they judg'd very reasonably that there was no need of separating the Parts that should compose it'.[119] Scene, in French neoclassical theory and in its English counterpart, is a unit of action as much as of entrances.

Echard's translations of Terence and Plautus use 'scene' in this

way. Hence, Terence's '*Scenes* are always unbroken, so that the
Stage is never perfectly clear but between the Acts'.[120] Echard uses
the word in this way throughout his preface and notes.[121] He divides
his text of Plautus into acts and scenes 'according to the true Rules
of the Stage'.[122] But Echard does not divide his text of Terence in this
way 'because they are of no such use; only the Reader may take
notice that whenever any particular *Actor* enters upon the Stage,
or goes off, that makes a different *Scene*; for the *Ancients* never had
any other that we know of'.[123] The scene-divisions are unnecessary
because the strong internal logic of the drama diminishes the necessity of pointing up the changes of tack in the action, the introduction
of new business. Significantly, one of the major emphases in Echard's
attack on contemporary comedy is the same as Hédelin's: that
modern comedy lacks the necessary link between matter and form,

Then the *Matter*, and Discourse of our Plays is very often incoherent and
impertinent as to the main Design; nothing being more common than
to meet with two or three whole Scenes in a Play which wou'd have fitted
any other part of the Play ev'n as well as that; and perhaps any Play else.[124]

Congreve's declaration in the preface to *The Double-Dealer* is a clear
assertion of his agreement; nothing must be 'impertinent' and
therefore,

I design'd the Moral first, and to that Moral I invented the Fable, . . . I made
the Plot as strong as I could, because it was single, and I made it single,
because I would avoid confusion, and was resolved to preserve the three
Unities of the Drama, which I have visibly done to the utmost severity.[125]

But Echard's avoidance of the scene divisions maintains a fluidity
and verve that give his translations the vitality of contemporary
comedy. The classical authority that the scene-divisions confer does
not need to be expressed in the printed text.

For Congreve, classical authority was precisely what he did desire.
*The Double-Dealer* had announced the unity of time and place; *The
Way of the World* proudly proclaims 'The Time equal to that of the
Presentation' (1700, a2b).[126] The division into scenes was the logical
next step, analogous to the purifying of the language.

Certainly, as, for example, the preface to *Love for Love* shows,
Congreve always thought of a scene in the classical sense. He announces there that he allowed the cutting in performance of 'one
whole Scene in the Third Act' (A4a) and, as Gosse has shown, it is
a 'French' scene that was omitted.[127] But a remark of Gosse reveals

how the divisions can intrude and obstruct: 'The French method of scene division, however annoying to the casual reader, is of inestimable value in calling attention to a play as an acting script and in emphasizing its dramatic structure'.[128] If it was 'annoying', then that was precisely what Congreve had tried to avoid, and, if it recalled the stage, the disaster was compounded. But, as we shall see, one effect of this method, when imposed on a play not originally constructed in this way, is to blur entrances and exits and to make of each scene a unit with a separable weight of meaning, rather than to accept the fluidity and over-arching structure of the act as unit. As Hédelin warned, unmotivated scene-divisions make every scene 'as it were an *Act* by it self'.[129]

The effects are particularly marked in *The Old Batchelour* where the subtlety of the connection between the Fondlewifes and the park in Act IV (marking out Vainlove's gullibility as parallel to Fondlewife's) tends to be submerged by the apparent significance of the scenic unit. In this play too, Congreve's conscious 'de-theatralisation' produces moments as inelegant as my term to describe them. In Act I, Wittoll and Bluffe are not 'seen' by the reader to 'cross the Stage' (p. 8), but instead Bellmour remarks 'I see he has turn'd the Corner, and goes another way' (*Works* I 17). In Act II, Betty is present throughout Araminta's conversation with Belinda, so that her comment 'Did your Ladyship call, Madam?' (*Works* I 34) becomes redundant. Instead of the entrances and exits of the Footman and Betty flowing across the dialogue over Belinda's indecision, highlighting her affectation, they are grouped by the ends of scenes iv, v and vi. Similarly, the Footman is irrelevantly on stage throughout II.vii so that he can give the final line of that scene. In Act III, Vainlove's exit line 'Well, I'll leave you [Bellmour] with your Engineer [Setter]' (*Works* I 49) is made meaningless as he does not leave until Bellmour does, at the end of the scene. In Act IV, the servant is apparently present throughout Bellmour's soliloquy on his disguise (IV.vi). The theatrically necessary delay between Bellmour's hiding in the chamber and Laetitia's opening the door to Fondlewife disappears because the direction 'Bell. goes in' is cut and is now implicit in the end of the scene (IV.xv), two lines further on.

In Act V, Heartwell and Lucy are not directed to 'appear at *Sylvia*'s Door' (p. 44), but instead are assumed to be there because of Bellmour's comment. Again Congreve's concern is to reduce the visual element, the re-creation of performance that the conventional play-quarto draws attention to. In V.xi, Sharper's exit is uselessly delayed until the end of the scene; in v.xii, the Boy is present during Heartwell's soliloquy (Congreve cut Heartwell's 'Leave me' as well as the exit); in v.xiv, Sharper does not go out and bring in Bluffe and the others but summons them instead.

Almost every one of these changes is necessitated solely by the scene-divisions. None of them adds anything to the play; most detract. Theoretic demands work against Congreve's own dramaturgic skills so that if the play is visualised as read, it appears rather inept. Congreve's careful defence of soliloquy in the preface to *The Double-Dealer* is rendered nonsensical by the observed soliloquies here. Congreve's pursuit of his ideals has pushed his most 'conventional' play into a theoretic straitjacket.

In the other comedies, Congreve's change of theory had preceded practice and the changes are fewer. In *The Double-Dealer*, the exit of Froth, Brisk and the others at I.v is justified by the introduction of a *liaison de vue* (Froth's 'here is Company coming' *Works* I 171), which gives classical correctness to what would otherwise be a clear stage in the middle of an act – a point that on stage would not matter at all. Minor adjustments are made in the exits at the end of II.ii and III.i. The pattern of hiding in Act IV now involves three ridiculously short scenes (xv, xvi and xix). At the very end of the play, the exit of Lady Touchwood is delayed until after Lord Touchwood's sentence on her ('Go, and thy own Infamy pursue thee') and is now simultaneous with the irruption of Maskwell hauled in by Mellefont. Here again the stage direction that points up the switch in the theatre audience's attention, Mellefont's entry 'from the other side of the Stage', is deleted.

In *Love for Love*, the scene-divisions leave on 'stage', characters who ought not to remain there. In II.iv, the Servant, Angelica and the Nurse are present for Foresight's brief soliloquy 'Why, if I was born to be a Cuckold there's no more to be said –' (*Works* I 355).[130] Tattle no longer ends the act with a single line *before* rushing off in pursuit of Prue ('Exit after Her' 1695, p. 33); they both leave at the same point. The song in III.iii is now apparently sung by Tattle as no singer is brought on stage. I have already discussed the change in Sir Sampson's last exit.

In *The Way of the World*, the care over scene-divisions is twice beneficial. The division after III.x for the exit of Mincing links the phrase 'the Town has found it' with 'What has it found?' rather than with 'their Folly is less provoking than your Mallice' as the misplaced exit in Q1 produced (p. 40).[131] In v.viii, Sir Wilfull 'Goes

to the Door and Hems', instead of going out to bring in Mirabell, a
pattern of exit and immediate re-entrance that, as we have seen,
Congreve tries to avoid. Barnard considers that this may be 'a detail
of the original staging',[132] but, even if it is, its presence is primarily
for neo-classical, rather than theatrical, reasons.

But other changes are as messily untheatrical as the ones examined before. Hence Peg's exit in III.iv is shifted, leaving no time for
her to fetch Foible before III.v. Millamant's laughter is now more
contemptuous because it sounds in Sir Wilfull's presence (IV.iv)
and the great moment immediately after, when Mirabell, stealing
in, completes Millamant's couplet, is altered because Sir Wilfull's
exit is now simultaneous with Mirabell's entrance.

Very rarely does Congreve realise the effect of an alteration and
change the dialogue accordingly.[133] In spite of Gosse, the 1710 text
is clumsy 'as an acting script' in a way that the quartos were not.[134]
No one would guess from *The Works* that Congreve was a brilliant
theatrical craftsman, a skilled man of the theatre.

In the search for what would constitute a reading edition, Congreve's need to elevate his drama led him to choose the wrong models. In refusing to offer his readers plays as plays, Congreve found
that he had no useful precedent to follow. His particular brand of
classicism was not compatible with the plays that he had written and
unlike Shaw, he sought to provide a reading-text by stripping the
plays down rather than by adding to them. Congreve's feeling that
the theatre was a limiting form comes to its climax in *The Way of the
World*. There the limits of the theatre audience's receptivity are
marked out in order to be transcended. The play's anti-theatricality
takes on meaning solely in performance, by reference to the theatre
it battles against. The double nature of the text combines in that play
so that it must be read to be seen, seen to be read. But the root of
the play is still the theatre, not the bookshelf.

# 5

# Text and performance (1): the comedies, 1691 to 1693

Every year the playhouse received new play-scripts; the managers of the company selected from them for performance, cast them, designed the sets, rehearsed and performed them. But the cycle is affected by the demands which the playwright may make on the resources of the company. Often there is a tension between the intentions of the playwright, writing with a particular company in mind, and changes in that company: actors leave and return; financial pressures limit the number of new sets that can be made, and so on. This tension between the dramatic concerns of the author and the theatrical restrictions of the company can best be examined in terms of a small period of time, seeing the effects play by play. This chapter explores the complicated relations between the United company and the new comedies, between the theatrical and the dramatic, in two theatre seasons, 1691–2 and 1692–3.

There is a second reason for such a study. My main purpose in the preceding chapters has been to demonstrate how complex the significance of performance can be. But few plays are as subtle as *The Twin Rivals*. Nonetheless, it is the third-rate – and worse – that defines the normal theatrical conventions. This chapter starts and ends with one of the greatest, and most under-rated, Restoration comedies, Thomas Southerne's *The Wives Excuse*. Even though there is no space to examine the play as fully as it deserves, I hope at least to indicate the conventions within which it is located in the theatre company and the nature of contemporary comedy against which it must be set, for its context is not *The Way of the World* or *The Man of Mode* but *The Wary Widow* and *The Female Vertuoso's*.

In recent years, there has been increasing attention given to the conditions of the theatre in the period from Betterton's secession in 1695 until 1710.[1] At the same time there has been a growing recognition of a change in the practice of comedy somewhat earlier, around 1691. Arthur Scouten, for instance, decided that 'a second period of the comedy of manners did develop in the final decade of the century, after a lapse of seventeen years. It commenced with the production of Thomas Southerne's *The Wives Excuse* in December 1691.'[2] Although I would not want to see Southerne's play as an unprecedented beginning, the plays in these two seasons do indicate a strong revival of a satiric comedy concerned with the actions of contemporary society.

In all, nine new comedies were performed in the two seasons, 1691–3; I list them here with the month of their first performance:

| December 1691 | Thomas Southerne | *The Wives Excuse* |
| January 1692 | Tom Durfey | *The Marriage-Hater Match'd* |
| November 1692 | Thomas Shadwell | *The Volunteers* |
| February 1693 | Thomas Southerne | *The Maid's Last Prayer* |
| March 1693 | William Congreve | *The Old Batchelour* |
| March 1693 | Henry Higden | *The Wary Widow* |
| April 1693 | Tom Durfey | *The Richmond Heiress* |
| April 1693 | George Powell | *A Very Good Wife* |
| May 1693 | Thomas Wright | *The Female Vertuoso's* |

All were published shortly after the initial performances and all, except *The Wary Widow*, have cast-lists in the published text. Since any cast for *The Wary Widow* would be pure speculation, a phrase like 'except for a possible appearance in *The Wary Widow*' must be imagined to punctuate the chapter at appropriate intervals. (For casts, see Appendix B.)

In addition two plays were published that, so far as I can establish, were not acted. Jo Haines' *A Fatal Mistake*, published in 1692, is a burlesque tragedy based on Buckingham's *The Rehearsal*. Reuben Bourne's *The Contented Cuckold*, also published in 1692, is a comedy of unimaginable awfulness.

I have artificially divided analysis of the casting and of the use of the scenery in the study of these nine plays. The first is used to analyse chronologically the changes in the theatre company;[3] the second is treated much more briefly, as an ahistorical recapitulation. It is with the theatres, with what the theatre audience saw and heard, that I am concerned.

### The actors and the plays, 1691 to 1693

The United company was finding it difficult to get an audience. Perhaps the monopoly of the London Theatre by the company was itself a major factor; *The Lacedemonian Mercury* commented 'When the Two

Houses were up, 'twas observable the Town had better Plays, and the Players better Audiences' (7 March 1692). Internal dissension, mismanagement and low morale in the company did not help. Nor did the decline in royal patronage, particularly after the death of Queen Mary in 1694. The theatre was decreasingly a centre of aristocratic society. The war was taking too many men away from town,[4] a theme that reappears in the plays. Henry Higden's *The Wary Widow* opens with Jack Scaredevil 'in a Fantastick Habit as just return'd from the *French*-Camp' mourning the deserted spaces of London: 'The Play Houses are silent; the Bowling-Greens abandond' (p. 1). In the prologue to *Greenwich Park* (1691), William Mountfort bewails the lot of the actors:

> Sad Days for us, when War's loud Trumpets sound,
> Nothing but Beaux and Parsons will be found:
> Look to't, you Men of Battel, of Renown,
> They'll claw your Ladies off, when you are gone:[5]

The appeal to the ladies in the audience which becomes so strident at this time may, in part, be a direct result of the disproportionate number of women in the audience that a city at war would contain.

The prologues and epilogues now have a distinct note of panic. In 1690, George Powell complained that the theatre-managers, in their search for an audience, increased the number of new plays, in the hope that novelty would be an attraction in itself:

The time was, upon the uniting of the two *Theatres*, . . . a new Play cou'd hardly get admittance, amongst the more precious pieces of Antiquity, that then waited to walk upon the Stage: And since the World runs all upon Extremes, as you had such Scarcity of new ones then; 'tis Justice you should have as great a glut of them now . . . [6]

To Mountfort, desperate times called for desperate measures:

> With the sad Prospect of a long Vacation,
> The Fear of War, and Danger of the Nation;
> Hard have we toil'd this Winter for new Plays,
> That we might live in these tumultuous Days.[7]

The playhouse was for a time flooded with new drama. In the season 1690–1, there were thirteen new plays (seven comedies, five tragedies and one opera) compared with seven the previous season (three comedies, three tragedies and one opera). Eventually, as we shall see, the managers turned to spectacular opera to bring in the audience and nearly bankrupted the company in the process.

But the dramatists, particularly in their comedies, had turned back to satire. Durfey's comments show that he believed in satire as the function of the theatre. The vices of the theatre audience are the subject for drama:

> Vices like these are here disgrac'd,
> And with Satyrick stroke defac'd:
> . . .
>
> In brief a mixture of all sorts,
> Sit daily here to view the Sports,
> And oft by *Satyr* bluntly us'd,
> Generously pay to be abus'd . . . [8]

The anonymous epilogue to Shadwell's *The Volunteers* (1693) takes exactly the same line:

> SHADWELL the great Support oth' *Comick Stage*,
> Born to expose the Follies of the Age:
> To whip prevailing Vices, and unite
> *Mirth* with *Instruction*, *Profit* with *Delight*.   (A4a)

This almost obsessive iteration of a satiric purpose, the recognition of general social corruption that the drama sought to reform, is located by Bancroft in his prologue to *Edward III* (1691) as one new way of reviving the waning interest in the stage, but also as the original purpose of drama:

> Plays were at first design'd to Lash the age,
> By shewing all its Vices on the Stage,
> . . .
> But for the space of Twenty years and more, ⎞
> You've hiss'd this way of Writing out of door, ⎟
> And kick and winch when we but touch the sore. ⎠
> But as some Fashions long since useless grown,
> Are now Reviv'd and all the Mode o'th'Town,
> Why mayn't the Antient way of Writing please,
> And in its turn meet with the same Success?   (A3b)

This revival of a satiric, critical drama, of 'Restoration comedy', is based on a re-examination and a frustration of the norms of contemporary drama. Expectation is at risk. It was not perhaps the best frame of mind in which to search for a reluctant audience.

In the middle of Southerne's *The Wives Excuse*, Welvile announces to

the rake Wilding and the foolish husband Friendall that he is writing
a play called *The Wives Excuse*. Welvile is unsure how to end the play
and, according to their interests, the two others advise him. The
doubt revolves around the honesty of the wife of the title: is she to be
honest or not? For Welvile, her honesty would be a tribute to the
ladies of the audience; for Friendall, her adultery would be realistic
and match the true desires of the ladies. The scene calls attention to
the play's own plot while calling into doubt the conventions according to which the play thus far appeared to have been written: the
play becomes open-ended. At the same time, the scene shows how the
place of the individual in society is drastically limited by the attitude
of that society; action and its significance become determined by
others, by Welvile, Friendall or Southerne. Society takes over and
individual freedom is permitted only under its ironic, sardonic gaze.
Character is shown as socially determined in a savage way that places
truth and the power of society in an ironic counterpoint to morality.
The attitude is closely bound up with the play's self-awareness of its
own manoeuvres, Southerne's highlighting of the play's performing
itself.

This restriction on character is linked to the cast directly in the
epilogue. The play ends with the wife honest but the epilogue emphasises that this is not realistic. With the audience, cuckolding is both
fashionable behaviour and social justice: 'And most of you more
justly us'd than here'. The 'metled Sparks' in the pit are shown to be
annoyed that the play refuses to succumb to these pressures:

> Why, when the means were in the Lady's hand,
> The Husband civil, and the Lover near,
> No more was made of the Wife's Character?
> Damn me, cries one, had I been *Betterton*,
> And struts, and cocks, I know what I had done;
> She should not ha' got clear of me so soon.          (A4a)

The phrase is not 'had I been Lovemore' but 'had I been Betterton'.
It is not just the character in the play who has failed; Southerne has
disrupted the whole pattern of comic form and expectation that was
established through the conventional casting. For the audience,
Betterton somehow stood for successful rakishness.

Most of the casting is conventional. Joseph Williams plays the rake
Wilding; Mrs Corey plays another old woman like the Aunt in
*Greenwich Park* (1691) or Belliza in *The Amorous Bigotte* (1690). The
purity of Anne Bracegirdle as Sightly and the serious platonic love of

Kynaston are both expected. Anne Bracegirdle's role does however involve her in rumours of promiscuity, as if the actress's reputation, as well as the character's, were in doubt. Frequently in lampoons of this period it is suggested that Anne Bracegirdle was not as pure as she claimed. Tom Brown, in one of his *Letters from the Dead to the Living* (1702), has William Mountfort complaining of backache: 'pox on you, says he, for a bantering Dog, how can a single Girdle do me good, when a Brace was my Destruction?' (*Works* (1715), II 224). The clear suggestion is that Mountfort and Bracegirdle were lovers. Brown's lampoon is ten years after the event, but *The Player's Tragedy*, an anonymous *roman-à-clef* published in 1693 giving a fictionalised account of Mountfort's murder, indicates an affair as well:

Bracilla [Bracegirdle] . . . is believ'd at last, to have found all her cold indifference melt at the secret and well-mannag'd Advances of *Monfredo*'s [Mountfort] Love. (p. 4).

The device is a normal one for fiction but it is emphasised in the novel that the affair was adulterous:

How happy she made him in private I shall not dare to Divine; yet the Publick Favours she bestow'd, discover'd she cou'd ill conceal the Passion she had entertain'd for him, in whom a Wife had so Powerful a Claim.
(p. 5).

Even if Mountfort was not actually having an affair with Anne Bracegirdle, the rumour of such an affair seems to have been common: Hill, Mountfort's murderer, certainly believed that Mountfort was his rival for Mrs Bracegirdle's favours.[9] Hence Mountfort/Friendall's pursuit of Bracegirdle/Sightly becomes part of a theatrical relationship as well as a dramatic one. The intermeshing of the social group on stage and off depends on such a pattern; after all, an actress's reputation was well known and her 'Reputation, as well as Person is exposed for the Pleasure, and Diversion of the Audience'.[10]

Bracegirdle's reputation works on the character of Sightly, just as much of the play is generated by the tension and conflict between reputation and truth. When Wellvile tells Mrs Sightly that she ought to tell Mrs Friendall about Friendall's pursuit of Mrs Sightly – one of the massive chains of interconnecting demands out of which the play is constructed – he argues that there is a parallel drawn by society between Lovemore's pursuit of Mrs Friendall through friendship with her husband and Sightly's 'affair' with Friendall through friendship with his wife,

*Sightly*    This is not only to be accountable for our own conduct, but to answer for all the indiscretion of the Mens.

*Wellvile*  You must, Madam, for those Mens you allow to be so near you.

(p. 35)

Reputation is out of the control of the individual, irrespective of one's actions, but controlled by society's expectation aroused by context, by juxtaposition, by pattern. It is this that underlies the central struggles of the play, the attempts by Lovemore to seduce Mrs Friendall by disparaging her husband: as Witwoud, the bawd, says, 'For the World will believe, she turns such a Husband / To the right Use, whatever she says to the contrary' (p. 10). The play's pattern takes shape through its disruptions of expected relationships, made predictive for the audience by conventional comic form, embodied in the acting history of the four stars.

William Mountfort played Friendall. Below Betterton, Mountfort was the most important actor of the company. In the preceding season, 1690–1, his comedy *Greenwich Park* was produced and he took leading roles in nine new plays, as well as revivals. Even Alexander Davenant was forced to reimburse him for his labour and gave him twenty guineas 'upon account of his extraordinary Study for the service of the y$^e$ Theatres'.[11] There was nothing surprising in Mountfort acting a foolish fop in *The Wives Excuse*. He had created with great success the title-role in Crowne's *Sir Courtly Nice* (1685) and was famous as Sparkish in *The Country Wife*; Colley Cibber's later success in both parts was due, he acknowledged, to 'the Advantages I receiv'd from the just Idea and strong Impression he had given me from his acting them'.[12] As Sir Courtly, in particular, part of Mountfort's success was based on his brilliance as a singer: 'For he sung a clear Counter-tenour, and had a melodious, warbling Throat, which could not but set off the last Scene of Sir *Courtly* with an uncommon Happiness . . .'[13]

Mountfort's singing ability was frequently commented upon. Monfredo in *The Player's Tragedy* 'cou'd Sing, Dance, and Play on the Musick' (p. 6) and *The Ladies' Lamentation for their Adonis*, an elegy on Mountfort's death, comments:

His flute, and his voice, and his dancing, are rare,
And wherever they meet, they prevail with the fair.[14]

Another contemporary satire explicitly links Mountfort's singing ability with his performance as a beau in comedy, 'He that like *Monfort* Sings, . . . / That Thing's a Beau.'[15] The Music Master's despair at the prospect of having to perform Friendall's song (p. 10) is an ironic inversion of Mountfort's fame as musician. The audience is being reminded that it is Mountfort who is acting Friendall.

But Cibber indicates that one of Mountfort's strengths in his performance of fops was his ability to hide himself. As Sir Courtly Nice, for instance, 'his whole Man, Voice, Mien, and Gesture was no longer *Monfort*, but another Person'[16] and the excellence of his performance was in proportion to his ability to eradicate himself: 'had he not kept his Judgement, as it were, a Centinel upon himself, not to admit the least Likeness of what he us'd to be to enter into any Part of his Performance, he could not possibly have so completely finish'd it'.[17] The direct emphasis on Mountfort's singing, as well as the pattern that is suggested by the casting of Mrs Mountfort, indicates a tension between the actor and the role, between the character and the social pattern. The final triumph of Friendall is a total disruption of the fate of fools in comedy; it is also an ironic disruption of Mountfort's place in the theatrical system.

Brilliant though Mountfort was at acting fops and fools, he was also brilliant as the witty rake; as Cibber comments, 'in Comedy, he gave the truest Life to what we call the *Fine Gentleman*'. Mountfort's ability to combine the two roles is remarkably unusual: 'He had . . . a Variety in his Genius which few capital Actors have shewn, or perhaps thought it any Addition to their Merit to arrive at; he could entirely change himself; could at once throw off the Man of Sense for the brisk, vain, rude, and lively Coxcomb, the false, flashy Pretender to Wit . . .'.[18] It is clear that Mountfort's fame was at this time based on his performance of rake-hero roles. In particular, in the seasons up to 1691, Mountfort had established his theatrical reputation as the witty rake of comedy pursuing towards marriage his own wife, Susanna Mountfort. The two had re-created the predictive inevitability of union that had been the achievement of Charles Hart and Nell Gwyn over twenty years earlier. The Mountforts appeared opposite each other in, for instance, Carlisle's *The Fortune Hunters* (1689), Shadwell's *Bury Fair* (1689), as Antonio and Morayma in Dryden's *Don Sebastian* (1690) and in Mountfort's own *Greenwich Park* (1691), a play in any case closely patterned on *The Fortune Hunters*. By 1691, the theatre audience would expect that any time both Mountforts appeared in the same cast, they would woo each other and end the play together.

In *The Wives Excuse*, that prediction becomes the basis for the play's final irony. Mrs Mountfort played Witwoud. It is the first time that she had been cast in a new play as an evil, isolated, aging bawd. Witwoud's problem is her despair at her own unattractiveness: 'I am sorry to find, that every Man / Has not a Design upon me' (pp. 23–4). In the end, Witwoud substitutes herself for Mrs Sightly partly in order to ruin Sightly's reputation, and partly out of the sexual frustration of her own life. Mrs Mountfort does end by having sex with her husband, masked and unrecognised. The predictive pattern is fulfilled but only ironically and, immediately it is known, Friendall is distant and respectful, 'Madam, I beg your pardon for some Liberties I have taken with your Ladyship' (p. 53), an attitude which Witwoud, when recognised, repeatedly evokes. Earlier in the play Wilding 'declines into a respect to her' (p. 23) when she unmasks. Mountfort formally rejects Mrs Mountfort, moments before the dramatic rejection of wife by husband, the separation of the Friendalls is enacted. Mrs Friendall is rejected by a fool and a fop who is triumphant in his discomfiture, rather than humiliated. The fool is found to hold power. The double pattern, of play and cast, is fulfilled, but in a fashion directly contrary to the patterns expected.

Mrs Barry played Mrs Friendall and Betterton her lover Lovemore. In itself the pattern of aggressive rake and honourable wife naturally moved towards tragedy; the relationship of Mrs Barry and Betterton in comedy was founded on that. It is parodied in revivals of *The Man of Mode*, when tragedy comes to mean Mrs Loveit's (Elizabeth Barry's) rantings. In Lee's *The Princess of Cleve*,[19] Betterton and Barry are, as Nemours and the Princess, in a situation identical to that of *The Wives Excuse*. The nobility of the Princess emphasises by contrast the uncontrolled sexuality of Nemours. But the Prince of Cleve is a worthy match and the tragedy is generated by his honour and his death. In *The Wives Excuse*, it is Mrs Friendall who has to ennoble her husband's actions by her natural dignity and honour. The Princess of Cleve is alone by the end of the play, Mrs Friendall from the beginning. But Mrs Friendall's isolation at one extreme of the moral hierarchy of the play is paralleled by the isolation of Witwoud at the other. Increasingly in the course of the play, their situations are made parallel until in the maskings of the final scene, Mrs Witwoud takes Mrs Friendall's place with her husband, through her disguise as Sightly. Both Witwoud and Mrs Friendall are married to Mountfort/Friendall.

In linking Mrs Barry's performance to the pattern of *The Princess of Cleve*, it should be clear why Betterton was cast as Lovemore. Betterton was still the most important actor in the company. Perhaps through discontent with the management of the patentees, he rarely appeared in new plays at this time. Wrongly, I suspect, the patentees ascribed this to failing health combined with a disproportionate belief in his own power. Betterton, they complained, 'hath put himselfe into all great pts in most of y^e Considerable plays Especially in y^e Tragedys' and yet 'a Man at 60 is not able to doe That w^ch he could at 30 or 40'.[20] Betterton rarely performed in comedy. Apart from the operatic *Amphitryon* (1690), his last known part in a new comedy was as Bellamy in *Bury Fair* (1689). But, especially in view of his performance as Dorimant in a revival of *The Man of Mode* the following year, it is clear that Betterton still embodied the cynical single-minded egocentric rake better than any other actor. Betterton's appearance evokes the rakes of the 1670s directly, but now caught in the play's dilemma between acceptability to the play's society and ethical rejection by the audience. Far from being sympathetic, Lovemore is a rake whose presence and persistence becomes increasingly irritating to the audience as his attempts on Mrs Friendall's virtue continue.

Lovemore demonstrates that the premise of the libertine or, in tragedy, heroic role is that all individuals are in fact conformable to the libertine's perception of them; no woman can, to the libertine's mind, resist the force of his lust. But Southerne demonstrates that the libertine is caught, trapped in his social behaviour by his chosen role and that that role is not all-conquering, however much society may malign the resisting individual.

The social role given to an individual is shown to be a strait-jacket that restricts the individual's range of action. Welvile is a good example. Disillusioned by the apparent change in Sightly to promiscuity – that is, he assumes society's evaluation of her to be correct – his misconception of her and her role leads him to try to alter his own. He attempts to become a Wilding or a Lovemore, even though that is out of his own character and Kynaston's. Sightly's rejection is savage but necessary: 'the encouragement you are pleased to make, from other Peoples Base Opinion of me, shall teach me to despise you' (p. 43).

Welvile reverts to his role and attempts to move the play to a resolution. But his own case is shown to be fixed and static, fixed by his own psychology into a perpetual unfulfilled desire: Sightly rejects his offer of marriage, 'This is too sudden to be serious: when you're in earnest, you won't need an answer' (p. 54). Welvile has in fact been serious for 'these seven years' (p. 32) but he is trapped in his role.

It is precisely these roles, predetermined at one level by society and at another by the casting (and hence by the comic form), that are seen as producing the play's final stasis. Lovemore must still be hopeful of winning Mrs Friendall; it is in his character to be so ('What alteration this may make in my Fortune with her, I don't know', p. 54). His optimism is juxtaposed with the unchanging status of Mrs Friendall, separated but not divorced ('I must be still your Wife, and still unhappy'). Friendall is as free as he always has been. The separation does not in fact change anything; the endless social round continues as before; as Friendall says to his wife, 'I only article that I may have a freedom of visiting you, in the round of my acquaintance'. The casting offers ironic reflections of the comic pattern – the Mountforts do come together at the end – and the patterns are those that the cynical realism of the society has prescribed.

From satiric comedy of this complexity to a play by Durfey might seem a long way. Durfey himself described *The Marriage-Hater Match'd* as 'a Mixture of all digested with Comical Turnes to the last Scene'.[21] But the play is not just the catch-all that Durfey disarmingly claimed; it is also a fascinating re-examination of the methods of contemporary comedy through a re-examination of the nature of the stock character, viewed as a Jonsonian humour. It is precisely the interaction of actor and character, and of character and plot that bemused the contemporary audience. *The London Mercury* wondered 'Why does the same Author make the Heroe of his Play, debauch a Parson's Daughter in the first Act ... and marry her the Lords knows how in the Fifth?' and it demanded,

Whether in Justice he is not obliged to present Mr. *Dogget* (who acted *Solon* to so much Advantage), with half the Profit of his Third Day, since in the Opinion of most Persons, the good Success of his Comedy, was half owing to that admirable Actor? (26 February 1692).

Dogget was known as Solon thereafter. Dryden, writing to Walsh on 9 May 1693, records meeting the players' 'chief Comedian whom they call Solon'.[22]

The materials of *Marriage-Hater* are conventional and necessarily the casting is so as well. Mountfort played the 'wild witty Gent. of the Town', Sir Philip Freewit, Anne Bracegirdle the loving Phaebe, Elizabeth Barry the proud widow Lady Subtle, Bowman yet another fop, Lord Brainless, and so on. A pamphlet satire on Durfey and his play, *Poeta Infamis, or a Poet not worth hanging* (1692), admitted,

'tis true, thy Play is altogether surprizing, and very unnatural; the several neat turns of a Play, I confess do keep the Minds of the Audience employed with Expectation, Hope and Desire, but I'm sure they don't end in Satisfaction ... (B2b)

This dissatisfaction is part of Durfey's purpose. Character as Jonsonian humour becomes obsessive and inescapable. Berenice simply cannot stop herself teasing her suitor Darewell, even though she recognises that her behaviour may result in losing him. She explains herself by claiming that 'The time of Wooing is a Woman's own, / But when she's Married once, her time is gone' (p. 28); but her manoeuvres and flightiness are a result of her own 'freakish' nature rather than the result of a desire to test Darewell. Sir Philip's distaste for marriage is so extreme that he vomits at the thought of it. Even Phaebe, who recognises the irrationality of her love for Sir Philip, cannot stop. In any case, her love is not the trusting love of the seduced woman, but a cloyingly possessive demanding affection that is as distasteful as Sir Philip's rejection of her.

The role of Phaebe is established on the convention of Anne Bracegirdle's playing virtuous women. Durfey then enlarges the psychological obsession with virtue and its resolution in marriage, until it becomes a humour. The standard comic desire of virtue (marriage) and the standard comic treatment of seduced women (no marriage) come into direct conflict and both are in tension further with the disguise of Phaebe as a boy. She is pursuing the man she loves, disguised but, strangely, with the shared knowledge *by both* that she is in disguise. The two patterns, virtue seduced and disguise, are combined *because* they are not compatible, and the play investigates the consequences for the rake and the girl.

The prologue itself establishes the incommensurability of Bracegirdle and breeches:

> *Bracegirdle* ... Would the Play were Damn'd:
> I shall ne'er wish the Poet good Success;
> For putting me into this nauseous Dress;
> A Dress, which of all other things I hate ... (H4a)

This is then combined with Bracegirdle's own reputation, when, after establishing a connection between dress and modesty, she announces

> Let all loose Dresses to loose Minds belong,
>     Men, nor their Garbs did e'er my Credit wrong.
> *Mountfort* That's much, faith having known the Stage so long.

A similar combination is made with Sir Philip. Mountfort of course was cast as the rake but this rake is brutish and revengeful. From the beginning there is something odd about a rake 'who being Jilted by Lady *Subtle*, whom he once Loved, professes himself a *Marriage Hater*' (a2b). Most rakes are not jilted, and are marriage-haters anyway, jilted or not. The causal connection between the two, marriage-hater because jilted, is doubly disconcerting. In effect, Freewit becomes a man whose wildness and wittiness are based on a desire for revenge and an avarice that is as obsessive as his dislike of marriage. His actions are then explicitly opposed to the normal sequence of action for the rake-hero. He is never motivated by love and his concern with money is the inverse of the free-wheeling generosity of the type. The obsessive humour subverts the sympathetic attitude on which our acceptance of the freedom of action of the rake is founded.

What the play explores, then, is the exhaustion of a mode of drama. Character no longer has any meaning as a concept of *vraisemblance*; instead all forms of social activity are based on role-playing, the enacting of social set-piece scenes. This is particu-larly true when the fools are allowed full rein. Leigh, as the laugh-ing fool Van Grin, and Mrs Corey as Lady Bumfiddle are allowed long scenes to make plain their respective humours so that the play, as plot, is held in stasis, while the play, as acting of character, is demonstrated.

In the end, the characters force marriages on each other. There are no fewer than seven marriages at the end, all of them disillusion-ing. Even Lady Subtle ends up only with the foolish Van Grin and seems content to have married a fool with money. The fools marry the maids but it is not the prospect of these improbable marriages that we are left with but with Comode's statement, 'Well Sir, the Law will give us Allie Money, and that's all we care for –' (p. 51). Even when it does appear that two fools have married each other, the truth is different. Lord Brainless marries La Pupsey for money and finds she was an actress:

Ld Brainless   A Player, hahaha, why now you Rave, Màdam, – *Darewel*, thou
canst witness the contrary of that, thou toldst me her Breeding
was such, that she has been familiar with Kings and Queens.

Darewell   Ay my Lord in the Play-house, I told ye she was a High Flyer
too, that is, I have seen her upon a Machine in the *Tempest*.

Ld Brainless   In the *Tempest*, why Then I suppose I may seek her fortune in
the *inchanted Island* . . .   (p. 50)

The pattern has moved back into the reality of the theatre and the
casting is again the spring for the manoeuvre. La Pupsey was played
by Charlotte Butler, her last part in a new comedy before leaving
for Ireland. Mrs Butler was not appropriate to the part of an affected
woman besotted with her howling lapdog. But once the cheat is
revealed, the purpose of the casting is clear. On one side was
Charlotte Butler's comic line as a cunning, intriguing prostitute,
as Jiltall in *Love for Money* (1691) or as Levia in *The Amorous Bigotte*
(1690), for example. La Pupsey is shown to be exactly that, a woman
intriguing for a title. On the other, Charlotte Butler was famous
as a singer. Although she is not recorded as playing in any known
production of *The Tempest*, the play may have been revived in 1692
and she would probably have sung in it. She was to sing in *The Fairy
Queen* later that season; in *The Wives Excuse* she was brought on
stage just in order to sing one of the songs. She was therefore a
regular performer in semi-opera and machine-plays. As with the
other parts, the casting is the means of defining the difference of the
humour from the stock character that the humour distorts, the
character predicted by the casting. The casting explains the movement of the plot to its improbable resolution, laying bare a society
that uses social trivialities to mask its obsession with wealth.

On 2 May came the first performance of the long-awaited opera
*The Fairy Queen*. Looking back, one can see the importance of this
production for the United company. The production was enormous-
ly expensive; Luttrell recorded that 'the clothes, scenes, and musick
cost 3000*l*'.[23] Even Settle had to admit, in the preface to the published
text, 'If this happens to please, we cannot reasonably propose to our
selves any great advantage, considering the mighty Charge in
setting it out, and the extraordinary expence that attends it every
day 'tis represented.'[24] But its financial failure put the company deep
into debt and forced changes. Cibber placed the blame primarily

on the previous opera spectaculars, *The Prophetess* and *King Arthur*, which had encouraged the patentees to undertake *The Fairy Queen*: 'every Branch of the Theatrical Trade had been sacrific'd to the necessary fitting out those tall Ships of Burthen that were to bring home the *Indies*. Plays of course were neglected, Actors held cheap, and slightly dress'd, while Singers and Dancers were better paid and embroider'd.'[25] Henry Higden, whose play was produced the following season, complained of the company's off-hand attitude, a direct result of this debt: 'I may well say *Unadorn'd*, for there was nothing done for the advantage or decoration of this Play: not a farthing expended. When I had given them leave to Act it, I was told it was theirs, and they would Cooke it according to their own humour.' (A4a)

In the season 1691–2, because of the preparations, the company offered fewer new plays than in the previous one. In the following season, the company attempted to recoup their losses with eight new plays, only one of which was a tragedy. Comedy, particularly when set in London, was much cheaper than tragedy in terms of sets and the 1692–3 season was marked by a mood of economy.

Shadwell's *The Volunteers*, the first play of the new season, raises few problems in the casting. Most of it re-emphasises the set of conventions on which the drama enlarges. Shadwell's play is a confirmation of the ideals of his society, a celebration of the virtues of volunteering. Indeed the virtues are seen as so transparent, so self-evident that the casting must be kept simple and self-evident as well. If good and evil are plainly perceptible, then the casting must not obscure the sentimentalist simplicity of the epistemology.

For one good couple, Hodgson was cast opposite Anne Bracegirdle, as they had been in *Love for Money*. Powell as Hackwell Junior was placed opposite Susanna Mountfort, a pattern that, tried here for the first time, was repeated quite frequently after Mountfort's murder, in an attempt to make of the two a new leading couple. It is not clear why Mountfort did not act in *The Volunteers*. *The Ladies' Lamentation for their Adonis* says of Mountfort 'But no quality fop, / Charms like Mr Hop'.[26] Cameron suggests that 'Hop' refers to the dancing-master in *The Volunteers* and that the part may therefore have been played by Mountfort.[27] In the published text, there is no indication who played Hop. It is an improbably small part for Mountfort at this stage of his career, appropriate to him only because of his dancing ability. I think it unlikely that he was in the cast.

*The Volunteers* was the last new play in which Tony Leigh appeared. The double nature of Blunt, as beneficent presiding deity watching over and stage-managing the revels and as the somewhat foolish old-fashioned man, is characteristic of Leigh's parts, the good-natured fool. The real foolishness to which Blunt belongs is kept in the background, the drunken Cavalier officers whose example of past volunteering contrasts with the sober goodness of Hackwell junior and Welford. Blunt is therefore weighted in the audience's sympathies away from his foolishness. It is one of the clearest indications of the play's drift away from conventional satire towards a revaluation of all the characters according to the implications of volunteering and patriotism. Even Bowman, as the arch-fop Dainty, is allowed some dignity because he volunteers. The play redefines our stock responses to actors and roles, according to a scheme that emphasises the good implicit in those roles, a scheme that is beyond the bounds of the traditional comedy within which it appears to operate.

On 9 December 1692 William Mountfort was murdered while trying to prevent the abduction of Anne Bracegirdle by Captain Hill and Lord Mohun.[28] Less than a fortnight later, Anthony Leigh died, some said of grief. *The Gentleman's Journal*, in its December issue (published no earlier than January, 1693), remarked 'We are like to be without new Plays this month and the next' and ascribed the delay to the two deaths. When Southerne's *The Maid's Last Prayer* finally reached the stage late in February, the choice of cast was affected by the double disaster. The deaths were a major factor in the changes of status of a number of actors, with consequent effects on new plays. Many of Leigh's parts descended to Bright.[29] But Bright was never as successful as Leigh and the roles are spread among Bowen and Bowman as well. In Southerne's play, Leigh's death would seem to be responsible for Underhill taking his first part in a new comedy for some time. But Mountfort's death was the more serious. Williams had left the stage in August 1692. The patentees encouraged him to return, at a great rise in salary, but he proved to be unreliable: the patentees later claimed that 'yᵉ last year Mr Powell & Mr Verbruggen did Act his pts above 30 times'.[30] In any case he was probably not available when the rehearsals started. Powell, who took over most of Mountfort's roles, was cast as Granger. Verbruggen was still too inexperienced, only playing small parts like Nickum, Sharper and Bonavent in this period; he is cast here as the malevolent Garnish, a curious cross between power-

seeking rake and fop. John Freeman had proved to be fairly undistinguished as an actor in comedy. In part, then, it seems in
desperation, the company cast Bowman as Gayman, an experiment
that proved not to be worth repeating, once Williams had returned.

But Bowman's playing of Gayman does point to one of the play's
central ambiguities: how can one tell the wit from the fool? Garnish
is foppish but he does have sex with Trickitt, which is more than
Granger manages. Garnish's shadowy malevolence – the way he
sneaks on to the stage to enter conversations – points to an altera-
tion in the status of fop, an alteration only partially prefigured in
Courtall in *The Wives Excuse*. When Gayman does finally make love to
Lady Malepert in the dark, she is not capable of distinguishing
Gayman from Sir Ruff Rancounter even though she wishes it were
Gayman:

> Love! what can'st thou not do in a Woman's Heart!
> That brutal thing, whom, as I thought, I loath'd,
> Thy gentle Fires have softned by degrees
> and melted into *Gayman*:
> Night be still my Friend, let me not see him,
> and I will think it was my *Gayman* still.   (p. 48)[31]

In the same way, Gayman's fury in the same scene comes from Lady
Malepert's inability to see that good love-making ought to be
beyond the capabilities of Sir Ruff:

The Lady receiv'd me for Sir *Ruff*: but when I think of the pleasures that
came after, that she shou'd still mistake me, for that bargaining Booby of her
Bawds providing; I don't forgive her; The furious riot, the expense of
Charms, the prodigality of Life, and Love (too vast for Nature's Bounty to
support another hour) might have inform'd her better.   (p. 48)

Side-by-side on stage, neither knows that the other is really right,
that illusion and reality are the same. The identity of their illusion
and the reality ought to be satisfying but, with truth mistaken, it is
only frustrating. The irony hinges on the confusion of wit and fool
that is marked by the casting of Bowman as a wit.

For most of the cast, Southerne uses a similar pattern of characters
to that of *The Wives Excuse* but degrades them. The whole play views
society as more diseased, more corrupted. Trickitt, the parallel part
to Mrs Sightly and also played by Anne Bracegirdle, is fairly virtuous
in appearance but in fact is prostituted to money: 'There's not a
Rogue so nauseous, but is welcome to her for his Mony' (p. 2).

This is one of the very few non-virtuous parts taken by Anne Bracegirdle. The unusual nature of this piece of casting is an indication of the extent of Southerne's satirical disgust for his society. As so often, one of the first indications of the play's satire is in a tension between actor and role. Similarly, Lady Malepert (Mrs Barry) is a Mrs Friendall who has already capitulated and is now prostituting herself solely for money.

This universal corruption, shown through the obsession with money as in *The Marriage-Hater*, has affected the characterisation of Lord Malepert, whose position in the play's structure is analogous to Friendall. Malepert is a fool who is gulled by all; there is no moment of triumph. The fop/rake ambiguity of Mountfort is replaced by the fool complete of Dogget.

Wishwell, the bawd who controls Lady Malepert, is closely parallel to Witwoud in *The Wives Excuse*. Like her, she is no longer attractive but is the way to the beauty of others: 'While I am Mistress of *Malepert*'s Beauty, I am not very sensible of the loss of my own: For her sake I will be Courted' (p. 10). Significantly Wishwell explains her position in a scene exactly parallel to Witwoud's solo scene. Each is the first scene of Act II; each has the woman discovered seated (Wishwell 'at her Toylett', p. 9), musing on her condition. But Wishwell was not played by Mrs Mountfort. Instead, possibly at Betterton's own instigation, the role was played by Mrs Betterton. This was the only new part Mrs Betterton took in these two seasons; as the patentees complained, 'She not appears in any pts to y^e satisfaction of y^e Audience'.[32]

Susanna Mountfort was cast as Lady Susan, a part much older than those she usually played. It is tempting to ascribe the reason to her pregnancy. Her daughter, Mary, was baptised on 27 April 1693[33] and the birth presumably accounts for her absence from the cast of *The Richmond Heiress* in that month. For *The Maid's Last Prayer* she was already at least seven months pregnant. But she was eight months pregnant when she first played the much younger role of Belinda in *The Old Batchelour*. The true reason would seem to be the shortage of women to play older roles. The part was fitted to her physical appearance: Lady Susan is a 'Youthful Virgin of five and forty, with a swelling Rump, bow Leggs, a shining Face, and colly'd Eyebrows' (p. 3) and Mrs Mountfort, who 'would make no scruple of defacing her fair Form to come heartily into [a low part]',[34] was described by Aston as having 'thick Legs and Thighs, corpulent and large Posteriours'.[35] Lady Susan combines the bawd figure with the coquettishness that Mrs Mountfort appears to have begun to adopt at this time, as in Cibber's famous description of her as Melantha in *Marriage A-la-mode*.[36] But, if Mountfort was originally cast as Granger – which Powell's appearance in the role would make likely – then the connection between Granger, Trickitt and Lady Susan is similar to the connection between the three players in *The Wives Excuse*. At the end, Granger's rejection by Trickitt leads to his rejection of Lady Susan in terms that point to a theatrical pattern of expectation that is frustrated:

La. Susan  Oh Law! Mr. *Granger*, what if you, and I, should make it the Double Marriage?
               [To Granger *who leaves her*]
Granger   'Tis an Old Play, Madam, and will never take.   (p. 56)

*The Maid's Last Prayer* sees society as nauseous and distasteful. Its satire depends on its ability to vulgarise and degrade anything that that society might value. In the process, the actors, especially those like Anne Bracegirdle who were primarily associated with a pattern of virtue, were made ridiculous. The satire affects the actors as part of the society it is seeking to attack.

Congreve's *The Old Batchelour* was first performed on 9 March, 1693. It was a staggering success. Richard Boyle, Earl of Cork, wrote to Congreve's father on 11 March:

Your sons play was Acted on Thursday last & was by all the Hearers applauded to bee the best that has been Acted for many yeares, Monday is to bee his day which will bring him in a better sume of money than the writers of late have had, for the house will bee so full that very many persons of Quality cannot have a Seate all the places having been bespoken many days since . . .[37]

I shall be examining the particular ways in which Congreve uses his casts in a later chapter but it should already be clear how such a study will view this play. For example, the disruption over Mountfort's death led to Powell taking over the rakish role of Bellmour, playing opposite Mrs Mountfort. The Mountforts must have indicated the link to the 'gay couple' pattern in Bellmour and Belinda. The death of Leigh and the consequent shortage of actors to play buffoon roles may have led to the reappearance of Jo Haines in the company to play Bluffe. Betterton, the aging actor of rakes, was cast as Heartwell, the cynical aging outsider, the rake grown old indeed. The links of these, and other, connections of cast to play are firmly embedded in the development of the acting company at this time as I have traced it. Congreve, in spite of beginning his play before ever coming to London, made his revisions firmly match the play to the theatre.

By directing the audience to consider the tension between the actor and the role, the playwrights established their satire as an attack on the conventional forms of comedy, forms that were in turn seen as extensions of society's criteria of orthodoxy. As society assimilates drama, makes it respectable, so the dramatist must alter his comic form, make it strange and self-aware and thus make the audience aware again.

From the prologue onwards, Durfey's *The Richmond Heiress* makes plain its intention of deforming comic expectation for its satiric purpose, principally by altering the assumptions on which stock characterisation and hence stock plots were based, continuing the argument of *The Marriage-Hater Match'd*. As Dogget says, using an old trope but with a cutting edge,

> I am to Act a Madman in the Play,
> A Part well tim'd, Sirs, at this time of day,
> All are craz'd now – Beaus, Warriours, Citts, Projectors;
> The World's the Stage, and all Mankind are Actors.   (A3b)

Everything in the play is governed by acting, by role-playing. Acting is falsifying; only the representation of that falseness, the truth of the duplicity can bring about the resolution. Almost obsessively, the play is constructed out of scenes in which actors play parts, disguise themselves or their intentions.

Dominating the disguise and the intrigue is Dogget as Quickwit. The part is analogous to Brainworm in Jonson's *Every Man In his Humour*, a servant using intrigue and disguise with gay abandon and being rewarded for his wit and skill at the end. But at the end of *The Richmond Heiress*, Quickwit is the only one to be rewarded. The play can celebrate its own theatricality through Quickwit but there can be no marriage, no comic or social resolution, because all the other disguises have been revealed as covering corruption and self-seeking fortune-hunting, egocentricity on a huge scale. Character, that is, a part played by an actor, is revealed as acting a social role, usually dishonestly. Quickwit alone comes to occupy a position of ethical neutrality, a master of intrigue without the malevolence of the others. Dogget has barely appeared on stage as Quickwit, after the prologue, before he is reminding the audience that he is Dogget; he can, he claims, 'turn my Face into a Changling Grimace, and act like *Solon* in the Play' (p. 2). No one could act Solon but Dogget and the speech enforces on the audience recognition of the actor, of the role-playing.

With the appearance of Sir Quibble Quere, social gossip about the theatre is turned directly into self-conscious indications of the process of acting, of the performance of the play itself. Sir Quibble's endless questioning includes references to fourteen actors, of whom no fewer than ten were in the cast of *The Richmond Heiress*. The other four, Betterton, Nokes, Haines and Kynaston are mentioned at the beginning and end of the list, framing the others, relating the play to the real playhouse that is separate from the play.

Most of Sir Quibble's queries are answered by the play itself. 'Does Mr *Sandford* Act the Villain still prithee?' (p. 4) is answered by Sandford's appearance as the unvillainous, superstitious comic doctor, Guiacum. 'Jolly *Cave Underhill*' is playing jolly Dick Stockjobb, whose happy uxoriousness is deflated in the course of the play. Mrs Barry is not the Queen as in *The Spanish Fryar* but the frustrated 'Female plain-dealer' Sophronia. Powell's 'new Part' (p. 5) is as Tom Romance, not a great rake but a rake and fool. '*Bowen* too, a notable Joker', as Frederick (Williams) interjects, plays Cunnington, whose joking has already been revealed to be malicious. 'And Mrs *Bracegirdle*, prithee where is she now?': in the asylum, feigning madness as a desperate expedient to avoid the predators forcing her into marriage.

Sir Quibble also wants to know about Dogget, 'what's become of him, prithee?' (p. 5): Dogget is standing opposite him. The reference to Dogget includes another mention of his performance of Solon. Finally Sir Quibble refers to Bowman (Shenkin), Bright (Sir Quibble himself), and Hudson (that is, Hodgson who played Hotspur). Hotspur, like Frederick, is a good example of the way the play degrades conventional types. Hodgson tended to play the good friends, sober, upright gentlemen. But Hotspur is not a sober, upright gentleman; he is both a brash friend, whose aggression causes more problems than it solves, and at the same time a man who can be bribed by Tom Romance to keep quiet. For Hotspur, revenge on Mrs Stockjobb becomes the motive for his actions, and the revenge, like Dorimant's on Mrs Loveit, is seen as self-interested rather than in the interests of truth.

In the end, it is only for the foolish Stockjobbs that the play can be resolved. That in turn is possible only because the conventional comic form's attitude towards the merchant and trade is proved to be consonant with the whole materialist self-seeking society. As the disguises are removed, Dick Stockjobb can reject his wife and stay within the bounds of comedy. Fulvia, the Richmond heiress, decides to remain single, justified by the revelation of the motives of her suitors. But the decision is tinged by precisely the same self-seeking that she had rejected: 'Since such a general defect of honesty corrupts the Age, I'll. no more trust Mankind, but lay my Fortune out upon my self, and flourish in contempt of humane Falshood' (p. 63). Anne Bracegirdle remains single and virtuous and the comedy triumphs in its refusal to end with marriage – even Quickwit rejects Marmalet, for the present. But the triumph is hollow, undercut by the principals' inability to see themselves: when Fulvia comments that 'My eyes in contradiction to the World, have ever (scorning Interest) fix'd on Merit' (p. 64) she conveniently forgets her mistakes over Frederick's honesty. The tension between actor and role leads directly to the tension of the conclusion.

*The Richmond Heiress* is the last of the new comedies of the season to use the casting for complex dramatic purposes. The last two plays cast as they need to and as they are able to in order that they can be performed; they do not investigate the meaning of the final cast.

Powell's *A Very Good Wife* is plagiary on a grand scale. Gildon noted that it was 'taken whole Pages together out of *Brome*'.[38] It is in fact made up of vast chunks of three plays, Brome's *The City Wit* (1630) and *The Court Begger* (1640), and Shirley's *Hide Park* (1632), taken with minimal verbal alteration and with no acknowledgement.[39] Powell's main purpose was to provide a good part for himself. Thus Brome's Crasy, 'a young Citizen falling into decay', is raised to Courtwit, 'A Gentleman, who by his Generous Temper, has wasted his Fortunes, and put to his shifts'. Powell as Courtwit dominated the stage and demonstrated his versatility in disguises.

Powell's dominance was enhanced by the absence from the cast of most of the major actors. Annabella, the very good wife, was Mrs Mountfort, again playing opposite Powell as the new 'gay couple'. In effect, the plot takes as a premise their affection – they are married *and* in love – rather than showing them moving towards love and marriage. Apart from Michael Leigh, as Jeremy the clever servant, none of the other parts are likely to divert the audience from rapt attention on the brilliance of Powell.

All the casting is predictable. Hodgson plays another noble gentleman. Verbruggen is still in the background as Bonavent. The play made large demands on the company for fools and so Cibber was given his largest role so far as the foppish son Aminadab. Haines turns up again as the meek citizen Sneaksby. In all, the cast was young and vigorous, all the play could ask for.

Thomas Wright's *The Female Vertuoso's*, the last new comedy of the season, appeared in May 1693. An adaptation of Molière's *Les Femmes Savantes*, the play is, apart from the ending, a fairly conventional example of the anglicisation of a French play. The conventionality of the approach meant that the casting should also be conventional. Wright's play is a useful way of seeing how the company's composition had changed since 1691. Though the roles were based on Molière's, they conform to expected types of Restoration parts and as such matched quickly and easily with the actors then available.

Thus Witless junior, the foolish Cambridge scholar, is inevitably a part for Dogget, linking straight back to his success as Solon. Underhill as Sir Maurice Meanwell is 'married' to Mrs Leigh, as a husband who has power over his wife, provided that she is not present. It is the same pattern as the relationship of Drydrubb and Siam in *The Maid's Last Prayer*. The two, senior members of the company, are ranged against each other in a struggle for independence. Lady Meanwell, the dominating wife, is an inevitable part for Elinor Leigh, matching her performances as Mrs Hackwell and Mrs Sneaksby. The female virago, once a characteristic role of Mrs Corey, has descended to Elinor Leigh as of right. Lovewitt, her daughter, was given to Mrs Rogers, a role to match Teresia or Mrs Squeamish, sharing with the latter a fervid desire for sex masked by an obsessive abhorrence of reference to it.

Wright's play posed a problem in the central couple, Clerimont and Mariana, a pure, idealistic pair whose love is honest and untroubled. Mariana was of course played by Anne Bracegirdle, whose claim on the virtuous parts was unshakeable, but she plays opposite George Powell. In *Love for Money* Bracegirdle as Mirtilla was matched with Hodgson as Young Merriton, and in *The Volunteers* the same pattern was used. But though Hodgson continued to get virtuous parts, his status in the company had not grown. Instead the ambitious Powell had put himself in a position where he was rapidly becoming almost indispensable as male lead. In the six comedies published with casts since Mountfort's last role, Powell appears in every single one and always in important parts. Insofar as he was rivalled, only the unreliable Williams posed a threat. Hodgson was given only the small part of Meanwell, Sir Maurice's honest upright brother.

By the end of the 1693 season, the United company was significantly short of actresses to play older women. Because of the retirement of Mrs Corey and the virtual retirement of Mrs Betterton, the parts were allocated to younger actresses who were more or less suitable. Mrs Mountfort had however begun to establish for herself a line perhaps rather more appropriate for a widow than gay young heroines. The new line was as a coquette, like, for instance, Belinda. She played Catchat, 'a stale Virgin', because she was establishing her claim to the part of any woman 'who fancies every Man is in Love with her' (A4b).

In *The Wives Excuse*, the disruption of one element of a pattern produced part of the meaning of the drama; in *The Female Vertuoso's*, disruptions in the theatre company do not disturb the easy tenor of the play. It is in plays like *The Female Vertuoso's* that the norms of casting are established, forming the conventions of expectation that in succeeding seasons can be turned back on themselves, creating the basis for a satiric drama.

### The scenery and the plays, 1691 to 1693

Unlike the changing composition of the theatre company, the stock of scenery for comedy in this period is constant. With the emphasis so firmly on economy, the dramatists had to make use of the available resources, usually efficiently and occasionally subtly. There is a temptation to confuse dramaturgic skill in the use of scenery with dramatic excellence. Efficient use of resources is not of itself an aesthetically valuable quality. As I shall show, some of the plays in this period do what is necessary to ensure that the scenery is appropriate, but in a few cases the scenery provides a part of the meaning of the play. Dramaturgic skill means that the scenery is used negatively; the audience is required only to note that the scenery does not obtrude. Dramatic effect depends on the scenery being noticed. In the one, it is an accessory that theatrical practice makes necessary, a redundant index to location; in the other, the audience is made aware of the scene and the scenery as part of the structure of the play. Instead of analysing the use of the scenery in the plays according to their chronological sequence, I shall order them, roughly, according to their progress from the simple dramaturgic to the complex dramatic.

The simplest use, degree zero of scenic art, is that adopted by Powell in *A Very Good Wife*. Every so often, as the scene requires, the scenery changes. With such vast debts to pre-Restoration drama, that is to a theatre without scenery, it is hardly surprising that Powell's cobbling did not concern itself with the niceties of scenery. The action is all firmly on the forestage; the play does not have a single discovery. Powell's stage directions merely indicate scenery so that something will appear in the scenic stage, but he is not interested in what.

By contrast, Henry Higden, in *The Wary Widow*, emphasised that his play was fiction, divided from the audience, by using a large number of discoveries. The action, as a result, takes place *within* the fictive locations of the scenes. In particular, the scenes with Leonora, the forlorn heroine, tend towards tragedy and are firmly located upstage. After Leonora throws herself onto a couch and 'the *Scene* Closes' (p. 21), Lady Wary and her maid come on, on the forestage, 'as in the Street'; the following scene begins with a discovery of Leonora onstage, lying on the same couch. The scenic stage is used to convey the permanence and continuity of the play's reality: Leonora is where she was during the intervening brief scene.

For Higden, scenery is necessary as an indication of the place where the action occurs, rather than, as for Powell, a drop against which or in front of which the play is acted. But Higden's play appears all the worse whenever he allows spectacle to take over from dramatic purpose. Suddenly, with no justification, the audience is presented with the set of a ship and sailors and hornpipes. The plot falls apart, revealing the play's essential lack of pretension to be anything more than simple entertainment.

Durfey's approach to the question of scenery is not much more subtle. Neither *The Marriage-Hater Match'd* nor *The Richmond Heiress* reveal much interest in scenery. In the published texts very few locations are marked. *The Marriage-Hater* indicates that iii.ii takes place in '*Bumfiddle's* Lodgings', because it is the only scene to move outside Freewit's or Lady Subtle's houses. *The Richmond Heiress* marks only the first scene and two unlocalised discoveries. It therefore emphasises its move outside London, away from the centre of the conventional comic world. The country is less blatantly motivated by money, less scornful of the traditional virtues. The choice between the town and the country can no longer be made automatically in the town's favour.

*The Marriage-Hater* uses its two most important locations to emphasise the vulnerability of the rake and the widow. Both are particularly vulnerable in their respective homes. Phaebe cheats Sir Philip best in his lodgings; *Poeta Infamis* noted the fact in amazement, wondering 'that any man should let his Wench into his Closet, where the Writings, and Jewels . . . were, when he had fall'n out with her just before' (p. 12). Similarly, Lady Subtle is besieged by fools at home and marries Van Grin.

In *The Female Vertuoso's* and *The Volunteers*, the question of the house that Durfey had touched on here becomes of primary importance. The scenery begins to define, almost independently, the meaning of the play.

In *The Female Vertuoso's*, only three short scenes do not take place in Sir Maurice's house; all three are concerned with the subplot of Witless junior, the foolish suitor. In the main plot, what begins as a typical marriage-plot with various blocking figures (Lady Meanwell, Lovewitt and Catchat) is resolved into a struggle between Sir Maurice and his wife for the right of possession of the house itself. The easy resolution of Molière's play, with the wife disillusioned and acquiescent, is replaced by separation of husband and wife. The play prepares for this struggle by its emphasis on Sir Maurice as 'honest', 'rich' and a 'Citizen'. Both his wife and her daughter mock his mercenary antecedents: his description of the poetaster Jingle as 'the very scandal of his Trade' provokes his step-daughter to reply 'His Trade! Fough, how Citizen-like is that Expression!' (p. 25). Sir Maurice is not ashamed of his status and he can seriously and correctly define the ideal of an exemplary wife, 'a Living Pattern of Virtue, and Discretion to all about her' (p. 25), an unusual statement for a citizen in Restoration comedy.

By Act v, most of the obstacles to the marriage of Clerimont and Mariana have been removed. But Sir Maurice cannot tame his wife. Furious at the young couple's lack of wit, Lady Meanwell announces that 'this illiterate Couple shall never come into my House' (p. 50) and that 'therefore, Sir *Maurice*, think of another Habitation for your self'. The demands of wit have led her to break up her own marriage. Clerimont offers Sir Maurice his own home, thereby introducing a new off-stage location, and Sir Maurice is content to 'retire with you into *Essex*' (p. 51). Sir Maurice, a citizen, gives up his house in London and moves to a gentlemanly retirement in the country with a hero whose desire for the gay life of London is minimal. Lady Meanwell is left in possession of the house, the symbol of Sir Maurice's wealth.

But the control over the fictive location, the house, is not the same as control over the comic scene, the stage. Sir Maurice may have been thrown out of his house unceremoniously, but it is Lady Meanwell who must leave the stage. The comic convention of the expulsion from the stage of the intransigent blocking character is too strong, embracing Malvolio, Mrs Loveit, Olivia and Fainall, for example. Sir Maurice retains control of the comic resolution. Wright has begun to explore the tension between the set as locus of the play's fiction and the stage as locus of the play as performance. Lady Meanwell wins one and her husband the other; the comedy is undisturbed.

While Wright concentrates on a single house, Shadwell, in *The Volunteers*, contrasts two, Major-General Blunt's and Colonel Hackwell's. The two houses become, in the course of the play, the twin poles of the play's argument, distinguishing between Cavalier and Puritan, happiness and sadness, honesty and cheating, inclusion and exclusion, and so on. In the end, the good controls the bad by absorbing the evil characters into itself.

Early in the play, Hackwell's son, disinherited by his father, is invited by Blunt to stay: 'Look you young fellow, answer me not, but with your Leg' (p. 7). The phrase refers to Morose in Jonson's *Epicoene* but it is more than the reaction of a doctrinaire Jonsonian. Like Kastril, who at least begins *The Volunteers* as the inverse of his namesake, the roaring boy of *The Alchemist*, Blunt is the inverse of Morose. Morose spends most of his time trying to throw people out of his house, while Blunt wants them to stay. Morose is reduced to passivity, while Blunt rushes around furiously, stage-managing the distribution of the characters in his house. Before the men can overhear their mistresses admit their love, they are pushed into a closet by Blunt and it is Blunt who drags the girls back into the room after they have tried to run out. Blunt controls the stage.

By contrast, Colonel Hackwell is controlled by his wife, no stage-manager but a consummate actress. His house is the place of delusion, self and greed. The language of his house is deceptive and cheating, while at Blunt's, the imagery of volunteering extends to both fool and gallant. When asked to give up war for love, even Sir Nicholas Dainty can speak sincerely: 'Not for the World Madam, What? set aside my Honour? that cannot be for all the Treasures upon Earth' (p. 43). In Hackwell's house, such a statement would be a sham.

But Blunt's house does contain its 'Dark Room', the place for discovery. It is there that, while checking over his stockjobbing papers, Hackwell discovers that he is cuckolded. Blunt enters with servants and lights, literally illuminating the scene. Hackwell is incorporated into Blunt's group and rejects the darkness that had characterised his house. Mrs Hackwell, in leaving, explicitly associates herself with the darkness: 'I will hide my head in some dark hole, and never see the light again' (p. 55).

Shadwell, through the differentiation of the two houses, combines the two trends in the play, its sentimentalism and its satire. Blunt's house is as exemplary as the analysis of Hackwell's world is satiric. The two are embodied in the play's scenic structure, in the antithesis of place.

In *The Old Batchelour*, the structure of the scenes becomes one of the central methods of the play's articulation of its meaning. The play uses the traditional sites of Restoration comedy but the scenery is subservient to the scenes. The scenic structure achieves a juxtaposition of similar actions in different places that brings disparate characters into conjunction. Sequence, the chain of combination of dramatic events, becomes the mode by which the evaluation of the various modes of action can be achieved. Congreve's method is then radically different in its approach to structure. It uses the set as only one determinant of the meaning of the sequence; it displaces the authority of the scenery. But a full exposition of this method must wait to be made in conjunction with Congreve's other comedies in a later chapter.

With Southerne, the question of scenery and scene are re-articulated in relation to the stage itself. Southerne, in exploring the interconnection of individual and society, locates his drama in the interstices of the connection of stage and play.[40] *The Wives Excuse* conducts its analysis of society in the midst of the society it uncovers. The stage itself, located in the theatre, reconnects the fictive and the real by linking the audience to the stage world. As the two groups, the real and the fictive, coalesce, the individuals are isolated even more completely.

Initially the play establishes the most extreme separation of the two worlds. After the prologue, the curtain rises on an unconventional scene, 'The outward Room to the Musick-Meeting. Several Footmen at Hazard, Some Rising from Play' (p. 1). The scene was played in front of a drop-scene, that is an additional curtain placed in one of the groove-slots.[41] The drop-scene was ambiguous; it was both flat and curtain. The first scene is similarly ambiguous: the footmen and pages discuss their masters and ape them. In effect, it is both the first scene of the play and, at the same time, another prologue to the main action. It is both a scene with scenery and a prologue before the curtain. In consequence, the scene has an ambivalence that is also characteristic of much of the play: it is both extremely realistic in its detailing of society and yet extraordinarily theatrical in its presentation as an introduction. The footmen reappear in the course of the play, now as silent choric figures, referring the audience back to their comments at the opening. Witwoud's footman, for example, who complained of everlasting errands, is sent off with a stack of messages in Act II. The opening scene distances and objectifies the society that is to be analysed, placing it for the audience through the servants. The servants mediate the action for the audience, telling them the truth about the characters, something that the characters themselves are often shown to be incapable of understanding.

The drop-scene was occasionally used in tragedy to highlight a tableau scene; its use allowed the maximum space for the composition of the tableau. Southerne uses it in precisely the same way: 'The Curtain, drawn up, shews the Company at the Musick-Meeting' (p. 5). The members of the society already described are fixed upstage during the performance of an Italian song; it is a tableau that allows the audience to apply the descriptions already heard to the individuals now seen. The man talking to a young girl must be Wilding; the fool must be Friendall and the woman embarrassed by his actions must be his wife, and so on. The song has become a device that by *its* doubleness as realism and theatricality provokes the audience to understand the play.

Only one of the important characters is missing from the group, old Mrs Teazall, who, by her behaviour at the end of the play, demonstrates her alienation and separation from this society:

*Mrs Friendall*  Good Mrs *Teazall*, not so censorious: Pray where's the harm of a little innocent diversion?

*Mrs Teazall*  Innocent diversion, with a Pox to't! for that will be the end on't, at last: very innocent diversion indeed; why, your Musick-meetings, Dancing-meetings, Masquing-meetings, are all but pretences to bring you together.  (p. 52)

Mrs Teazall is right, as Mrs Friendall, above all others, should know; after all, Lovemore has always tried to seduce her at such meetings. But Mrs Teazall demonstrates that she fails to understand the basic articulation of this society. Throughout the play, fact, meaning and event are not dependent on truth but on the public nature of the knowledge. It is only when something is known to have occurred – or believed to have occurred – that it is 'true', within the terms of the society. As Wilding tells Mrs Teazall about her niece Fanny whom he has seduced: 'You won't bring it to *Westminister*, I hope, to be decided, who has most injur'd her; I, by being civil to her, or you, by telling it to all the Town' (p. 53). It is not wrong, in this society, for Courtall to tell Welvile about Wilding's approaches to Mrs Sightly but it would be wrong to tell everyone at once; gossip, intrigue and malice are not public statements, 'telling it to all the Town'. Reputation becomes the key. Friendall is a fool but he must be seen publicly to be one; as Mrs Friendall says, ''tis with the tendrest Concern for my own Reputation, that I see my Husband daily trifle away his So notoriously, in one Folly or other of the Town' (p. 10). Witwoud's venom is based not on her own perception of the reputation of her state, but because 'I am declining in my Reputation; and will bring every Woman, of my Acquaintance, into my own condition, of being suspected at least' (p. 45). Witwoud's emphasis on 'condition' indicates the restricted nature of the social role, an aspect of the play I touched on earlier and which becomes the climax for Mrs Friendall, isolated and helpless ('This hard Condition of a Woman's fate', p. 54). But the tension here between the social and the individual is made manifest in its guise as the separation of private/public throughout the play.

After the song, the company 'advance to the Front of the Stage' (p. 5). They fill the forestage and move fluidly over it. Southerne offers fragments of conversations as the socially cohesive group circles around. Frequently a snippet of conversation is followed by a direction that indicates the speakers' re-integration into the whole group, for instance, 'mingles with the Company' or 'They mix with the Company' (p. 6). Privacy of statement becomes virtually impossible and all relationships are subsumed into implications, hints and subtleties. But the social group, the 'company', is totally interconnected, as in the long causative chains of the plot. The long chains are woven through the members of the group (mixing and mingling) so that Ruffle is explicitly brought in from outside the group by

Lovemore to prove Friendall a coward by challenging him to a duel. Only Lovemore knows who Ruffle is, and he identifies him to Welvile, the 'writer' of the play. The strangeness of Ruffle's presence is analogous to the play's emphasis on Fanny's youth, her recent introduction into the society, and the newness of Friendall's marriage ('My Master has been married not a quarter of a year', p. 2). This emphasis on the public social group is in conflict with place. It is not only the public places that are the locations of public action. Instead 'public' comes to mean wherever more than two or three are gathered together. Hence Friendall's house can be the place for a public scene (e.g. IV.i) and St James's park can be relatively private for the assignation in Act v.

The conflict of private and public is explicitly linked to the theatre. Whatever Mrs Friendall knows privately of Friendall's cowardice is not public and the public acknowledgement of Ruffle's apology to Friendall is to be 'to Night in the Side-box, before the Ladies' (p. 28), that is in the theatre itself, the location of the real as well as the fictive society. The play thus defines the theatre as the locus of its argument.

Once the company has claimed the forestage and therefore carried the social group virtually into the laps of the audience, the actions on stage are defined by their difference from the full stage, from the presentation of that controlling gathering. Individuals, for instance, are conspicuously isolated. Act II opens with Witwoud discovered, seated 'at a Table' (p. 14), some way upstage behind the grooves used for the street scene at the end of Act I. Witwoud's despair at her own isolation is therefore combined with her physical isolation from the audience and the society on stage. The society's control over the stage area extends to become control over the individuals on it. When Welvile wants to speak to Mrs Sightly alone (p. 41), the company moves behind the scenes ('Scene draws, shews Tables and Cards ... The Scene shuts upon 'em', pp. 41–2), almost as if the society has granted permission for the interview to take place. No sooner has Welvile made a fool of himself than 'the Company rises from play, and comes forward' (p. 43). Welvile's position is analogous to Friendall's after being struck by Ruffle, 'the Company come about 'em' (p. 13).

At the end of the play, the masks which conceal identity and motive are removed in a process that re-emphasises the connection between public and private, between company and individual, as it has been explored as a domination of the stage area – the stage itself as the locus for action, the mediation between the fiction and the reality. There are three successive 'discovery' scenes. Welvile, who has already been identified, through his 'writing' of the play, as the author, the manager of stage-events opposed to the manoeuvrings of Witwoud, engineers the last, far upstage: '*Scene* draws, shows *Friendall* and *Wittwoud* upon a Couch' (p. 53). The last discovery of the plot is the last 'discovery' on stage. The theatrical term is made to refer back to the mechanics of the plot and points to the theatrical basis of the discovery, the Mountforts together. Stage and world are combined; the real place is the locus for the fictive action. But at the same time the reality of the theatre pushes the play towards the audience. They are implicated in the play's actions, in its analysis of society; they are both analyser and analysed. Echard commented later that 'Our modern Comedies generally end with a multitude of Actors; . . . it is undoubtedly a Perfection that the Ancients seldom or never aimed at'.[42] Southerne makes the full stage, the whole society, the object of his satire.

In marking the extent of the difference between Powell's and Southerne's use of the scenery, the gap of theatrical practice has been pushed to its greatest extent. Both Powell and Southerne are efficient, expert at the techniques of the contemporary stage. Clearly, without the establishment of the mode of utilisation of scenery that Powell embodies, the subtlety, even the possibility, of a technique like Southerne's would be impossible. After all, the raw material is the same for both, a stock of scenery and a need to put some sort of scenery into the stage area. But the gap, as with the casting, is the difference between merely using and making that use a necessary part of the meaning of the drama. As Edward Gordon Craig saw,

The reason why you are not given a work of art on the stage is not because the public does not want it, not because there are not excellent craftsmen in the theatre who could prepare it for you, but because the theatre lacks the artist – the artist of the theatre, mind you, not the painter, poet, musician.[43]

# 6

# Text and performance (2):
# Wycherley's *The Plain-Dealer*

When, in 1725, John Dennis looked back to the audience of the 1670s as an apex of intelligence, his praise was mitigated by his awareness of its fallibility even then:

I must confesse the Town was now and then in the wrong, Deluded by the enchanting performance of soe just and soe great an Actour, as Mr Hart or Mr Mohun, or by the opinion They might have of a celebrated Authour who had pleasd them before. But then there were several extraordinary men at Court who wanted neither Zeal nor Capacity, nor Authority to sett them right again . . . When these or the Majority of them Declard themselves upon any new Dramatick performance, the Town fell Immediately in with them, as the rest of the pack does with the eager cry of the stanch and Trusty Beagles . . . And when upon the first representations of the *Plain Dealer*, the Town, as The Authour has often told me, appeard Doubtfull what Judgment to Form of it; the foremention'd gentlemen by their loud aprobation of it, gave it both a sudden and a lasting reputation.[1]

It is easy to appreciate the Town's confusion. They knew – or thought they did – what to expect from a play about plain-dealing. They knew what to expect when they saw Hart, Kynaston, Mrs Boutell and Rebecca Marshall on stage. They knew what to expect when they read a dedication or heard a prologue. In each case, indeed in every part of the play, their expectations were thwarted, turned back on them. Expectations founded on their experience of contemporary comedy and theatre practice, on their judgement and morality were suddenly proved to be inapplicable. Things no longer meant what they wanted them to mean, or rather, not *only* what they wanted. The evaluation of any action, the perception of event, the nature of the significance of language were presented as elusive, no longer susceptible to the application of the frameworks within which social and cultural determinations of meaning would operate.

Satire is bound to be disturbing, but nothing as profoundly disrupting had confronted the theatre audience from a Restoration dramatist. It became easiest to pay lip-service to the play's greatness and avoid its implications. But the play demands to be taken on its own terms, placed in the context of contemporary theatre practice, so that its own methods of pointing out its difference can be seen. Wycherley's project is too large to admit of compromise.

### The dedication and the prologue

The proverb says 'Plain Dealing is a jewel'.[2] The meaning is clear: plain-dealing means to speak out, to tell the truth bluntly and honestly, however unpalatable it may be. It stands in opposition to fawning, lying, time-serving social behaviour. The plain-dealer, by definition, will not pretend, will not mince words or use rhetoric as a disguise. The plain-dealer has no use for, no connection with fiction. The audience in the theatre and the reader of the published text have no doubt that plain-dealing means not feigning. But even before the play itself starts, Wycherley confuses the audience, disorientates them, by joining the two incompatible ideas, plain-dealing and pretence, around the dual concept inherent in the word 'acting', doing something and performing, pretending to do something in a play.

The problem is posed through the confusion over the identity of the speaker of the dedication and prologue. Author, actor, and character are intertwined; the audience is dubious about the relative authority of the various voices. The author becomes part of his own play; the actor becomes part of his character; the role steps out of the play and demands to be accepted before the play has even begun. The act of speaking the prologue, or of writing the dedication, is made both a pretence and, at the same time, a genuine action. Immediately the audience is placed in a position in which judgement is impossible and thereby Wycherley begins to cast doubt over the entire procedure of judgement, of evaluation and of the determination of the nature of a sign, verbal or gestural, spoken or acted. Plain-dealing, an idea that had seemed so simple, so straightforward, is found to cover a multitude of possibilities, mostly incompatible.

In any case, plain-dealing and dedications are irreconcilable opposites. Dedications use truth and flattery indiscriminately, for personal advantage. A good dedication is one that is well-written, not necessarily true, in its flattery; indeed, truth – in the plain-dealing sense of frankness – is out of place:

> Plain-dealing is, you'll say, quite out of fashion;
> You'll hate it here, as in a Dedication. (Prologue, A3b)

But a dedication, if not true, is at least supposed not to be ironic. What Wycherley offers instead is an urbane, witty, ironic, paradoxical and, occasionally, savage statement and then tries to suggest that this mixture of mind-bending logic and subtle double-meaning is plain-dealing. For the first time in a published Restoration play, the play begins in the dedication.

Wycherley's only previous dedication had also been ironic. Barbara Villiers, now Duchess of Cleveland, the dedicatee of *Love in a Wood* (1672), was well known to have become Wycherley's mistress after the success of his play.[3] The tone of the dedication is, on the surface, fairly conventional; it is perhaps wittier, more paradoxical and certainly less subservient than many. Wycherley excuses any breaks in the norm with standard phrases about being young and a 'new Author', as well as with a conventional recognition of his dedicatee's supreme wit and beauty. But beneath this, there is an undercurrent of double-meaning: the 'favours I have receiv'd from you' included sex, and hence Wycherley was doubly 'concern'd not to have your Graces Favours lessen'd' (A2b). There is also play on her 'obliging all the world, after the best and most proper manner' (A2b) and on the 'Generosity in your Actions, which others of your quality, have only in their Promises' (A3a). The dedication hinges on the acceptance by society of the combination of sexual and poetical dependence, a witty paradox that can be expressed through a single group of words, 'favour', 'generosity' and others.

But the double nature of *The Plain-Dealer* dedication is compounded by the ambiguity of the speaker. In *Love in a Wood*, Wycherley was author and lover; now, the writer of the dedication is both author and character. Yet the character is not the plain-dealer the reader expected. Ian Donaldson recognised the ambiguity of author and character but sought to link it to Manly directly:'the urbanely ironical voice of the Dedication, though it is lighter, on the whole, than that of Manly, frequently gathers his tone, and it attacks, as Manly attacks, the hypocrisy of women'.[4] But urbane irony is not Manly's style, at least for most of the play, and the attack is mounted, as plain-dealing could not be, from a position of hypocrisy. This dedication is pretence from first to last, from the addressee, 'my LADY B–', a bawd, and the first line, 'Tho I never had the Honour

to receive a Favour from you'(†1a),[5] to the final glorious confusion of 'But you, in fine, Madam, are no more an Hypocrite than
I am when I praise you' (†3b), a line so convoluted and plural as to
be virtually impossible to pin down. To call this plain-dealing is to
play a game with the reader, a game that disrupts expectations of
what is to follow: is Manly going to be a plain-dealer like this?

For the rest of his life, Wycherley's friends called him Manly and
the Plain-Dealer with utter seriousness. Dryden writes of 'The
Satire, Wit, and Strength of Manly *Witcherly*'.[6] Granville sums up
his note on Wycherley by claiming that,

In Mr. *Wycherley*, every thing is *Masculine* ... Like your Heroes of Antiquity he charges in Iron, and seems to despise all Ornament, but intrinsick
Vertue; and, like those Heroes, has therefore added another Name to his
own; and by the unanimous Assent of the World, is call'd The *Manly
Wycherley*.[7]

Fairbeard introduced Lady Drogheda to Wycherley with 'Madam ...
since you are for the *Plain Dealer*, there he is for you'.[8]

But it is worth distinguishing these examples from Wycherley's
own later use of the phrase. He often uses it in a tone of cultured
modesty, to ward off tributes, wondering about the compatibility of
the label with praise. He writes to Pope, for example,

'so that, you have obliged me to be vain, rather than not think you, a
Plain-dealer.[9]

or, on two occasions to Dennis,

But I fear I am forfeiting the Character of the Plaindealer with you; and
seem like vain Women or vainer Men, to refuse praise, but to get more ...
But when you talk of Store of Delights you find in my *Plain-Dealer*, you cease
to be one ...[10]

His other habit is to differentiate between the plain-dealer and his
own identity, almost as if the term comprises a public mask that he
can use:

Yours, by the names of the plain-dealer, and Wm Wycherley.[11]

but I am Yours, not as a feigning lying Poet, but a true plain Dealer, (especially) when I tell you I am, (my Dear Mr Pope) Your most obliged Friend,
and real humble Servant, W. Wycherley.[12]

These private uses display a witty detachment, a self-deprecatory
amused stance, that is poised and tongue-in-cheek. The effect is of a

man toying with others' descriptions of him, denying gently its applicability to himself. It is elegant, courtly almost, in a way that others' uses are not.

More significant, however, are the Juvenalian lashings of the mad preface to Wycherley's *Miscellany Poems*, (1704) all in the name of plain-dealing. The preface carries wit built around paradox to an extreme point of savagery. It is a thirty-page tirade against those 'Who were my *Criticks*, before they were my *Readers*' (p. iii). The preface explores paradox in the way Rochester did in Alexander Bendo's Bill: statements are made, justified, inverted, justified again; contrary positions are held simultaneously, and all the time the attack continues. The ending is absolute confusion:

for, if Mens Understandings are judg'd Good or Bad, by the Choice of their Friends, speak of me as if you were my Enemies, to oblige me to be your Friend; say, if you will, I am no Poet, since a Lover of Truth, and no Wit, since the

PLAIN DEALER                                             (p. xxx)

It is not the multiplicity of paradoxes so much as the use of the persona that is important. The mask is an uneasy amalgam of wit and disgust, the satirist implicated and corrupted within the society by the furious nature of his righteous indignation. The whole is in contrast to the gentler, wry Horatian pose of the frontispiece portrait of Wycherley with its Virgilian tag, 'quantum mutatus ab illo'.

A similar process is at work in *The Plain-Dealer*. The dedication has quotations from Juvenal, from the vicious misogynist Satire 6 († 2a) and contrasts that with the title-page's Horatian motto, a motto that is consonant with the wit of the dedication. The two models of satire are presented, in the play as well, as moulds according to which Manly and Freeman might initially be viewed. But, if the dedication, in quoting from Juvenal, seems to include Manly within its Horatian–Freeman frame, it also denies its link to Freeman, in being signed by the plain-dealer. The conflict is incompatible with plain-dealing.

The dedication's convolutions of wit, its entire pose of self-satisfied paradox, add up to a denial of plain speech. Words are allowed a freedom of reference, particularly sexual reference, that goes far beyond plain-dealing. The sexual freedom for language is to be the sexual freedom of the poet in the brothel, like Jerry's 'free ingress, egress, and regress to and from your Maids Garret' (p. 92). But the freedom of language is an artifice, a rhetoric that is led back into the theatre. In the theatre, virtue cannot make a statement because there it would look like pretence. Acting makes action unevaluable:

But why, the Devil! shou'd any of the few modest and handsome be alarm'd? (for some there are who as well as any deserve those Attributes, yet refrain not from seeing this Play, nor think it any addition to their Vertue to set up for it in a Play-house, lest there it shou'd look too much like acting.) (†2a)

So, to prove himself a plain-dealer, the plain-dealer does the reverse, he pretends. But in the midst of this acting, of rhetoric and pretence, Wycherley the plain-dealer calls for an ally: 'tho, as the Plain-dealer *Montaigne* says' (†2a). Montaigne is invoked to judge on sex, to support the witty Wycherley's plea for free and frank admission of sexuality. The essay 'Upon some verses of Virgil' is used lavishly in the dedication. There are three direct quotations and a mass of derived material. Occasionally in the play itself, Montaigne is implied. Thus, for instance, Manly's complaint that 'if you are a Cuckold, it is your Friend only that makes you so' (p. 14) is a prophetic indication of the course of the play (Manly as Vernish's cuckolder and vice versa) and the idea is paralleled in Montaigne 'For, to what friend dare you entrust your grievances, who, if hee laugh not at them, wil not make use of them, as a direction and instruction to take a share of the quarie or bootie to himself?'[13] The enmity between Olivia and Vernish in Act v is parallel to Montaigne's observation, 'I have . . . seene husbands hate their wives, onely because themselves wronged them',[14] here inverted, as well as to the quotation from Juvenal in Wycherley's dedication.[15] In the dedication itself, for instance, the desire for Lady B–'s protection to help the play into ladies' closets (†1b) is parallel to Montaigne's statement: 'It vexeth me, that my Essayes serve Ladies in lieu of common ware and stuffe for their hall: this Chap. wil preferre me to their cabinet.'[16]

But the direct quotation from Montaigne, 'Els envoy leur conscience au Bordel, & tiennent leur contenance en regle' (†2a), also re-appears in the play. When Fidelia describes Olivia to Manly, she says that Olivia 'has impudence enough to put a Court out of countenance, and debauch a Stews' (p. 58). The passage is particularly close to Florio's translation of the passage in Montaigne: 'They send their conscience to the stews, and keepe their countenance in order'.[17]

The Montaigne of 'Upon some verses of Virgil' is the quintessential plain-dealer not only because of what he says – the frank sexuality which is in itself a contradiction of both the dedication and Manly's deviousness – but also because of his style. Montaigne was seen as refusing to use masks and disguises in his writing. Halifax's assessment of his style is particularly explicit: 'He scorned *affected Periods*, or to please the mistaken Reader with an empty *Chime* of *Words*. He hath no *Affectation* to set himself out ...'[18] Montaigne, then, embodied stylistically the right position of linguistic purity, the absence of pretence, from which to attack the abuses of custom; as Daniel saw it, Montaigne 'hath made such bolde sallies out upon/ *Custome*, the mightie tyrant of the earth'.[19]

Montaigne seemed to offer the Restoration a concept of the transparency of the sign. The word, as in Hobbes, would have a single and necessary connection with the object signified. This emphasis on the word as *signifié*, as index of the truth of external reality, is precisely in line with the conventional concept of plain-dealing. But it is also at the opposite extreme from the plain-dealing of this dedication with its delight in the interplay of referents, the freedom of the *signifiant*. Montaigne's supposed ideal of the one-to-one correspondence belongs to the type of wit that the dedication pointedly ignores. That type of language is based on the premise of the clarity of the object, the easy transposition of perceived meaning into language. It is that type of language, that possibility of reliance on language, that the play confuses and removes. The dedication establishes instead a norm in which linguistic or social events are over-determined in their meaning by the multiplicity of their signification. If Montaigne as an authority seems ironically out-of-place, too much a plain-dealer for this dedication, then for him, as for Manly himself, Wycherley/Plain-Dealer reminds the reader 'an Author can as easily make any one a Judge or Critick, in an Epistle, as an Hero in his Play' (†2b). The dedication puts Wycherley into the play, removes him from his dominance over the play's morality and epistemology and makes him part of the unstable play-world in which decisions are to be made.

The second element of the text that is available only to readers is the dramatis personae (A4b). The sketches of the characters are for the most part conventional except for the three principal men. Vernish's friendship with Manly is total, '*Manly's* Bosome, and onely Friend' and perhaps therefore excessive, heroic and unworldly. This absolute friendship goes uncomfortably with the massive emphasis, in huge type, on 'THE SCENE, LONDON'.

Freeman's gentlemanly and bankrupt background, 'a Gentleman

well Educated, but of a broken Fortune', is a conventional phrase for any rake from Loveby, the wild gallant, onwards. Gentlemen in plays are often penniless – it is often in fact a mark of that gentility – but they are also uncompromising, proud and witty; they do not fall into the category of a 'Complyer with the Age'. Compliance and compromise are not witty activities; they imply a subservience to the society, an integration into the whirl of commonplace existence that libertine wit and gentlemanly natural superiority were intended to avoid. The reader cannot be sure how to regard such a figure, how to come to terms with the juxtaposition of wit and compliance.

This pairing of opposites is precisely what one finds in the description of Manly himself: 'Of an honest, surly, nice humor, suppos'd first, in the time of the *Dutch* War, to have procur'd the Command of a Ship, out of Honour, not Interest; and choosing a Sea-life, only to avoid the World.' (A4b). The entire passage is built out of contrasts. 'Honest' and 'surly' are attributes of plain-dealing, though 'surly' has an undercurrent of arrogance, as well as blunt and rough. But 'nice' is a perfect Empsonian complex word; there is one group of contemporary meanings of strict, precise, scrupulous and finely discriminative (*OED* 'nice' 7) and another group indicating tender, delicate, effeminate and unmanly (*OED* 'nice' 4). The word therefore includes the idea of unmanliness, an inversion of the name. There are similarly irreconcilable aspects to the combination of the honour of commanding a ship and the desire to escape from the world. The one is a social ideal – Manly does not fall in with the corrupt practices but does what the world should do – while the other is a complete denial of the forms of society, a total and excessive rejection. The description moves from the heroic, through the social ideal of perfection to the extra-social and Manly, Wycherley suggests, combines all these. There are similar doubts raised over the names themselves. Can a free man be compliant or would that be a limitation on his freedom? Does varnish (Vernish) go against the notion of a true friend, implying only a superficial affection? Can manly be nice?

The prologue is the first point at which reader and spectator come together in their experience of the play. On to the forestage walked Charles Hart, already in costume as Manly. The fact that he is in costume establishes visually the ambiguity that surrounds the prologue. In the text the speaker is Manly himself, 'Spoken by the Plain-Dealer' (A3a). But, while Wycherley and Manly have been

confused in the identification of the writer of the dedication, the
prologue confuses actor and character, intertwines them in the
ambiguity of the lines themselves. It is necessary that Wycherley,
the authorial presence, should be removed from this procedure.
The playwright is intrusively present in the published text, present
in a way that is irrelevant to the presentation of a play on stage.
Hence Wycherley is distanced from the text on stage and Hart/Manly
takes on a separate existence. The speaker of the prologue places
Wycherley as 'Our Scribler' and as 'the course Dauber of the coming
Scenes', an entity separate from the 'I' who addresses the audience
directly.

The prologue opens with a deliberately under-punctuated couplet, emphasising its ambiguity:

> I The PLAIN-DEALER am to Act to Day:
> And my rough Part begins before the Play.

The lines can be understood as an acknowledgement by Hart of his
assumption of the role; the prologue is an act, a part of the theatrical performance. But, if the lines are spoken by Manly, they are
an admission that the plain-dealer is an actor too, that in the play
he will pretend as well as do. This whole double emphasis on theatrical practice affects the prologue's mockery of the fops and sparks.
The prologue, in any case a self-conscious piece of rhetoric, is now
defined as feigning. It is not the actor who is insulting the audience
but the plain-dealer who is acting out his name. The audience is
presented with the problem of the duality of the speaker. This is
not the actor or the author *hiding* behind a persona, a mask, but
instead consciously pointing to the mask, reminding the audience
of its existence. The elusiveness of the identity of the speaker disrupts the normal way of grasping the meaning of a statement. As
the audience will see, it is virtually impossible to understand the
nature of an action, particularly if the description is given by an
unevaluable source. Words are completely opaque, a substance
through which the object is glimpsed, but their opacity is a result
of the plurality of their signifying. The opacity only clears when
the nature of the actor/speaker as a pre-determining and compre-
hensible consciousness is available to the audience and its moral
judgements and systems of values. If character is no longer fixed,
if it is no longer possible even to say whether a statement is by a
character or an actor, then the basis of evaluation collapses.

It is as if the consensus of judgement is itself at risk; the whole means by which social meaning is produced is undermined. Wycherley begins to explore that risk in the prologue, with its emphasis on the incompatibility of Hart/Manly/Wycherley – that curious hybrid – and its authoritative rejection of what 'You'll say'. But the rejection of the opinions of society is also a theatrical gesture and the prologue emphasises that theatricality:

> I, only, Act a Part like none of you;
> And yet, you'll say, it is a Fool's Part too. (A3b)

Wycherley places that description of Manly at the end of a list describing his treatment of the other characters in the play:

> But the course Dauber of the coming Scenes,
> To follow Life, and Nature only means;
> Displays you as you are; makes his fine Woman
> A mercenary Jilt, and true to no Man;
> His Men of Wit, and Pleasure of the Age,
> Are as dull Rogues as ever cumber'd Stage:
> He draws a Friend, only to Custom just;
> And makes him naturally break his trust. (A3b)

The equivalence between the stage and life that is used here is transposed into an emphasis on the role of Manly ('I, only, Act a Part . . .'). But Manly is talking of himself and claims an arrogant right to truth:

> The onely Fool who ne'r found Patron yet;
> For Truth is now a Fault, as well as Wit.

The entire standpoint of the prologue is revealed as being constructed out of Manly's egocentrism and at the same time out of the doubleness of acting. Both Manly and Hart are pretending.

The prologue sees acting, a form of social hypocrisy, as widespread; it is not only Manly who acts but simply that his role is unusual. As Wycherley said in a later poem,

> Why are harsh Statutes 'gainst poor Players made,
> When Acting is the Universal Trade?[20]

But the poem also points to the distinction that is operated in the prologue between Hart, the honest man because acknowledged as an actor, and Manly, and society in general which may not acknowledge its role-playing,

> But 'twixt the World and Stage this Diff'rence lies,

> Play'rs to reform us wear a known Disguise;
> We no such warrantable End can boast,
> But still are Hypocrites at others' Cost.[21]

For Manly himself, the stage is a special place where he acts out his role as honest man in contention with the rest of the world. But the prologue also shows how the success of that honesty is dependent on the theatre, a fictive, unreal resolution,

> And where else, but on Stages, do we see
> Truth pleasing; or rewarded Honesty?

The prologue ends with a conventional appeal for favour:

> If not to th' Honest, be to th' Prosperous kind:
> Some Friends at Court let the PLAIN-DEALER find.

But it is the character as well as the actor who asks for court praise. The confusion of plain-dealing and wit in the dedication has become the paradox of a plain-dealer appealing for friends at court. The prologue merges acting and pretence, doing and performing, actor and character, and subverts the basis from which meaning can be assessed.

### The cast

Given this emphasis on the ambiguity of the actor and the role, the casting functions primarily to bring into play the double pattern of casting, in comedy and in heroic drama. The principal actors are marked out by the applicability of their casting in heroic drama to their situation in *The Plain-Dealer*, but the heroic mode is now transferred to a comic world in which the values and rewards, the unworldliness and simple morality of heroic drama are totally inappropriate, savage parodies of the actual processes of the play. The casting provides a pattern through which the audience can predict the moral relationship of the characters but the predictions prove to be at variance with the play's own interpretation of events. The double schemes – comedy and heroism – are incompatible both with one another and with the play itself.

In the smaller roles there was no problem. Letice was probably played by Ursula Knight, rather than Frances Maria Knight, whose acting does not fit with this role.[22] Novel was played by Clark, a young actor usually cast as a gentleman in comedy, but whose career was only just beginning. Clark, together with actors like Perin, Wiltshire, Sheppey, Goodman and Griffin, seems to have joined the company around 1673 when the King's company was desperately trying to rival the huge successes of the Duke's company. Griffin (Vernish) had had few parts before and most of those had been in farce. He was to play Manly himself in 1700. Charlton (Jerry) had similarly been restricted to parts in farces in new plays. Jo Haines, who had supposedly been a contemporary of Wycherley's at Queen's College, Oxford, was cast as a fool and a fop, Lord Plausible, a role much like Sparkish, his part in *The Country Wife*. Both roles are men who indulge their affectations, fools who disguise their egocentricity with a pretence of good-humour. The good that they believe of themselves matches the good they affect to believe of others – the two parts belong together. Hence, long after Haines, Dicky Norris played both parts in productions between 1715 and 1723.[23] Cartwright, who appears to have been a singularly versatile actor was cast as the aging fool Oldfox, again a role fairly similar to his part as Sir Jasper Fidget in *The Country Wife* (1675).[24] Mrs Corey as the Widow Blackacre is playing a role in line with her speciality, old viragos. In *Love in a Wood*, for instance, she had played Mrs Joyner, the bawd, another organising woman like the widow.

This tendency for Wycherley to use actors in similar roles is the operation of a double system; the strength of the individual actor's line is matched by the author's establishment of a range of parts to suit the company's resources. With this type of repetition, the differences stand out all the more clearly. In his two previous plays for the King's Company, Wycherley had cast Mrs Knep as Lady Flippant and Lady Fidget, both examples of the radical dissociation of language and action, appearance and desire. Both women use words to mean precisely what they want them to mean: 'Honour' means 'sex', abhorrence indicates desire, and so on. They liberate words from fixed meanings and use them as arbitrary symbols capable of redefinition whenever they wish. Language, the process of cultural signification and definition, is inverted and made redundant; actions speak louder. In effect, both women display an attitude that belongs to Olivia in *The Plain-Dealer*: a promiscuous freedom in the use of language. Eliza stands apparently at the opposite extreme; for her, words are not arbitrary but ought to have a single signification. She is the female exponent of the Montaignean cool rational transparency of discourse. As such, she is isolated throughout the play in a way that Lady Flippant and Lady Fidget eventually are not. Though they are separated from morality almost throughout their plays, they can be reconciled with comic form; Eliza cannot. The casting deliberately inverts Mrs Knep's status in Wycherley's plays.

To some extent, a similar pattern marks the casting of Charles Hart. In comedy, Hart's forte, stemming from his partnership with Nell Gwyn, was as the young rake. Hence, in *Love in a Wood*, Hart, as Ranger, holds together the various strands of the action; Ranger, though often imperceptive, can be reformed and occupies the clear middle-ground in the hierarchy of morality and social success in the play. Significantly, Kynaston, cast as Valentine, is placed high above Hart, in touch with the pastoral, heroic, unreal world that Ranger gently parodies. A similar relationship between the two actors is used in *The Country Wife* where, however one evaluates Horner's (Hart's) success and moral worth, Harcourt (Kynaston) is clearly by far the most virtuous of the men in the play, working solely and seriously towards marriage.

In comedy, Kynaston was almost always cast in a serious role, rarely as a gay rake and never when Hart was also in the cast. Wycherley's earlier pattern was therefore conformable with current practice in comedy. Comparing that with *The Plain-Dealer*, we can see that Wycherley makes this firm model disturbingly dubious. Manly's unbridled sexuality is in part that of a libertine like Horner – with whom he shares a denial that most women can be anything other than sex-objects – and Freeman is in part the voice of social ideals. But even to enunciate this is to see how far Wycherley has moved. Freeman's social actions are barely desirable and Manly is a libertine without the critical intelligence. The list of qualifications to the model would be endless but the basic pattern still contains sufficient traces of the comic paradigm for this to be recalled, expected and frustrated. Yet it is primarily in relation to heroic drama that the casting of Manly, Olivia and Fidelia was important. After all, Rebecca Marshall (Olivia), in particular, rarely played in comedy. What happens when heroic drama and its patterns are transposed into a world, strange to them, normal for comedy? Manly and Fidelia are in many respects refugees from another world, another drama.

The heroic drama itself was changing. Dennis, in the passage about the first performance of *The Plain-Dealer*, also comments that,

When The Town too lightly gave their aplause, to Half a Dozen Romantick, Ryming, whining Blustring Tragedies, . . . then Villers Duke of Buckingham writt the *Rehearsall*, which in a little Time opend their eyes, and taught them to Despise what before They rashly admired.[25]

The major change seems to have occurred at precisely the time of *The Plain-Dealer*. Prologues and epilogues now attack and mock heroic drama as frequently as their conventional targets like farce. Duffet's burlesques provided a staple part of the King's Company's fare, a repeated attempt to mock the opposition's successes with spectacular heroic plays. In *The Mock Duellist*, Belon attacked the unnaturalness of heroic diction,

> His easier Scene no big-Swoln rumbling speaks,
> That while you look on't, like a Bubble breaks,
> Tumbling along with an amazing noise;
> But his accoast is gentle Nature's voice. (Prologue, (1675) A4a)

The prologue to *Piso's Conspiracy*, performed by the Duke's Company, indicated that the burlesques were having effect,

> Besides Our Men Players are out of Heart
> Of being seen in an *Heroick* Part:
> What, with Prince *Nick*, and t'other House-Gallants,
> They have run *Hero's* out of Countenance? (1675, A2a)

Duffett had made all tragedy appear like farce.

The epilogue to Shadwell's *The Virtuoso* points to the heroes of such drama as ridiculous; they are superhuman in battle and idolise women,

> Though they can laugh at danger, blood and wounds;
> Yet if the Dame once chides, the milksop Hero swoons. (1675, O3a)

But Shadwell also comments on the lack of realism in tragedy, indicating how impossible the transposition from Granada to Greenwich would be:

> These doughty things nor Manners have nor Wit;
> We ne'er saw Hero fit to drink with yet. (O3a)

This is Wycherley's point entirely and a consistent concern of his plays. Prior to *The Plain-Dealer*, it is most strongly present in the interaction of high pastoral heroics (Valentine and Christina) with

the corrupt world of London in *Love in a Wood*. In the prologue to
*The Country Wife* (1675), Hart points to himself as heroic actor, the
multi-talented Almanzor figure, that Horner parodies:

But though our *Bayses* Batles oft I've fought,
And with bruis'd knuckles, their dear Conquests bought;
Nay, never yet fear'd Odds upon the Stage,
In Prologue dare not Hector with the Age,   (π2a)

Transposed to normal society, heroism becomes hectoring and
boasting. Of course, that hectoring is precisely what Hart/Manly's
prologue does dare.

The shadowing of comedy by the heroic was almost inevitable with
the appearance on stage together of Hart, Mrs Marshall and Mrs
Boutell. Throughout the 1670s, culminating in Lee's *The Rival Queens*
(1677), the two women were paired as the embodiments of good and
evil, light and dark – in hair as well as morality. In *Nero* (1674), for
example, Mrs Marshall as Poppea was contrasted with the chastity
of Cyara (Mrs Boutell). This pattern led inevitably to Roxana and
Statira. The pattern is there, though subdued, in the contrast
between Lyndaraxa and Benzayda in *The Conquest of Granada* (1672).
The contrast was complicated by a tendency for the characters
played by Hart and Rebecca Marshall to be madly in love with each
other. When Mrs Marshall's role is evil, the love is only on her side:
hence Lyndaraxa is passionately in love with Almanzor, and Nourmahal with Aureng-Zebe. But often the love is eventually recipro-
cated, for instance Cortez and Almeria (*Indian Emperour*, 1667),
Caesario and Gloriana (*Gloriana*, 1676), Porphyrius and Berenice
(*Tyrannic Love*, 1670).

Perhaps the best example outside heroic drama of the complications introduced into these patterns of expected relationship is
Dryden's *Marriage A-la-Mode* (1673). There, delicately and wittily,
Palamede (Hart) is shown in love with Doralice (Mrs Marshall),
but he marries Melantha (Mrs Boutell). But the play does not explore the casting as a heroic pattern. It is the heroic concern with
honour, in fact the introduction of the whole system of values of
heroic drama, in Manly and Fidelia that indicates that Wycherley
is referring to the casting of heroic drama.

In this pattern, the virtuous Mrs Boutell frequently found herself playing in breeches. Breeches parts were extremely common
throughout the Restoration. J. H. Wilson estimates that of 375 new
plays between 1660 and 1700, 89 contained at least one breeches

role.[26] Certainly throughout the 1670s, Elizabeth Boutell cornered the market in this line. She appeared in breeches roles in both tragedy and comedy. Her first certain stage appearance was in breeches as Aurelia in Joyner's *The Roman Empress* (1670). Before *The Plain-Dealer*, she was disguised as a man as Melantha, Benzayda and Margery Pinchwife, in addition to various roles in revivals. The strength of the line is so strong that the confusion of sex is almost inevitable with Mrs Boutell on stage. But, though she bridges the two forms of drama, it is the obsessively heroic-romantic mode of Fidelia that determines her relationship with Hart in this play.

Mrs Marshall and Mrs Boutell together provided a pattern. Lust against virtue was compounded by virtue's disguise and lust's attractions. It was little more than a machine that was nudged and set in motion. The simplicity with which the moral pattern could be observed – the unreal morality of the heroic drama – was dependent on the hero's clear and positive embodiment of 'correct' morality.

The cornerstone in the pattern is Hart himself. Settle's extraordinary tribute, in the dedication to *Fatal Love* (1680), has already been quoted in chapter 3. It indicates Hart's dominance over the stage. Much as Hart in comedy established himself as socially enticing, the tempting heterodoxy of the rake, so Hart in tragedy was the embodiment of virtuous and energetic heroic morality. The problem is that any retrospective consideration of Hart as Manly risks erecting into a principle what Wycherley intended to be a pre-conception to be altered in the course of the play. Thus Davies comments that Hart,

was, in person, taller, and more genteel in shape, than [Mohun] . . . From Mohun's generally acting grave, solemn, and austere, parts, I should have cast him into that of Manly in the Plain Dealer; but it seems Hart claimed it . . . In the same author's Country Wife, Pinchwife, a part not unallied in humour to Manly, was acted by Mohun . . .[27]

Davies' association of Pinchwife and Manly is an indication that, for him, Manly is to be rejected, an obsessed figure to be reviled by polite society. It is impossible, once the connection with Pinchwife is accepted, to see Manly as virtuous but unsocial; such a view in effect rejects everything that Hart stood for in the play.

Davies was not the first to make the connection. In the period after 1715 Barton Booth appeared in both roles. But society changes: the attitude towards Manly in 1676 is not necessarily the same forty years later. To refer back from Booth's doubling is to use an alien model. In effect, the play poses a series of problems over Manly himself or in a comparison of Manly and Freeman (along such axes as morally acceptable and socially successful behaviour). The problems must be resolved within the models for that acceptance or that success, within a juxtaposition of the play and contemporary expectations. But the models have already been rendered incompatible by the presentation of a model of heroic virtue (Hart and Mrs Boutell), a model of comic moral probity (Kynaston), and one of success in society (Hart as rake). It is the combination of the different generic models and the inter-reflections of that juxtaposition that in relation to casting indicates the over-determination, the excessive plurality of the play's signification.

Wycherley sets out in the play to indicate a plurality of models, merging opposites in the audience's awareness. The effect is that *all* models – or none – are seen as acceptable. The stereotypes are impossible if they are seen as limiting – as the combination of Pinchwife and Manly would be. Casting Hart as Manly introduced so many possibilities that it frees the play. The destruction of the generic patterns began as soon as *Hart* as Manly walked out onto the forestage to deliver the prologue.

## The play

The prologue done, the curtain rises and onto the forestage 'Enter Captain *Manly*, surlily; and my Lord *Plausible* following him: and two *Sailors* behind' (p. 1). The play opens then with Manly being aggressive, blunt and honest, but the aggression is justified by the object of his distaste. Plausible, the fop and arch-complier, replaces Philinte from *Le Misanthrope* in this opening attack on 'ceremony'. The degradation of the adversary in the debate on contemporary *mores* from the rational Philinte to the foolish Lord Plausible indicates a greater distaste for the world than one finds in Molière but, more significantly, it also justifies Manly's conduct. Even though Manly emphasises his extra-social nature as an 'unmannerly Seafellow' (p. 2), his position here as accurate analyst of the corruption of social behaviour, as satirist, ensures that his struggle against the forms of that society will appear heroic. There is an abrupt juxtaposition between a fop, embodying worldly practice, taken out of any comedy, and the extraordinary nature of Manly. Manly here sees the world accurately because he is outside it and can discriminate in his judgement of it. He justifies his separation from the world through his heroic belief in his ability to be just: 'I that can do a rude thing, rather than an unjust thing' (p. 2).

The scene, then, establishes from the beginning the parodic distance of *The Plain-Dealer* from *Le Misanthrope*. Molière's play is recalled so that Wycherley can mark his distance from it. Through the alteration of Philinte into Plausible, Wycherley is able to offer Manly as a more attractive and justified idealist. Manly begins to acquire the attributes of detached supra-social observation traditionally, in comedy, the prerogative of the rake, and to combine this with a heroic virtue. Unlike Alceste, Manly has already been to the wilderness; he has established his right to be a critic of society by the fact of having been outside it. The scene offers the audience elements of both sides of Hart's acting, as rake and as hero, and through juxtaposition with a fool, establishes the acceptability of both.

But the juxtaposition of heroic Hart and comic Haines hints at ridicule. No audience could have forgotten the famous story of Haines' mocking Hart during a performance of Jonson's *Catiline*. It is unclear whether the event was supposed to have taken place in 1668 or 1672 but, in either case, Hart and Haines had rarely acted together since.[28] There must inevitably have been a hint in their joint appearance that Haines was ridiculing Hart, that Manly is rather too pompous and arrogant, a bubble ripe for bursting.

While Manly is revealing the falseness and hypocrisy of Plausible, the sailors stand silently by. When they come to speak, after Manly has left 'thrusting out my *Lord Plausible*' (p. 3), they offer a commentary on the action that has just occurred as well as on events that precede the opening of the play. For the first of many times in the play, an event is discussed and shown to be open to a variety of interpretations. It is clear that Manly's ship has sunk, but the motives and results, the meanings of the relationship of that act to the individuals involved in it, are not reconcilable. The audience is offered conflicting moral assessments of the action; its consequences are not reducible to a simple framework. The sailors disagree over whether the sinking was a good action. Sailor 2's concern over its harmful effects on others, especially 'black *Kate* of *Wapping*', is contrasted with Sailor 1's recognition of Manly's personal disaster in the wreck, a disaster evaluated in the sailor's terms, in the world's terms, as money lost. That loss of 'five or six thousand pound of his own' (p. 3) puts Manly back into contact with the realities of social existence, just before he is pictured as trying to escape from it.

The ideas are incompatible: Manly is not just an extra-social hero, he is also a man of some wealth, once worth £12,000. The delight in aggression ('I never saw him pleas'd but in the Fight', p. 4) reflects back on the dispute with Plausible. Manly himself is beginning to be shown as an accumulation of irreconcilable contradictions. The possibility of confining Manly to one generic pattern appears to diminish. At the same time, the process of moral judgement, the evaluation of others' discourse recedes. As the sailors' conversation just begins to show, evaluation of an event is dependent on the ability to define its meaning in reference to constructs acceptable to the individual. As soon as fixed meaning vanishes into a maze of multiples, into the plurality of the process of signification itself – all meanings equally correct – the nature of an act, as well as the signification of that act in language, becomes ambiguous. Not only is the distinction between acting as doing and acting as pretending to do threatening to blur – in the elaboration of the performance as performance in the identification of Hart and Haines – but all action is now becoming susceptible to doubt. Reality is no longer recuperable into pre-existent patterns of perception.

Of course, at this stage in the play, this process is merely beginning. The sailors disagree over the meaning of an event that is not seen in any case. But with the arrival of Freeman, the audience is shown that concepts about character can be altered through repetition in a new context. The scene with Freeman is a re-enactment of the scene with Plausible but the alteration of 'adversary' produces a radical alteration in the attitude towards Manly himself.

Manly reads Freeman's social actions as a tension between protestation and belief, a form of hypocrisy doubled by its insincerity of statement. For Freeman, Manly's belief in sincerity is valid but impractical and asocial: 'Why don't you know, good Captain, that telling truth is a quality as prejudicial, to a man that wou'd thrive in the World, as square Play to a Cheat, or true Love to a Whore!' Freeman's airy compliance is presented as a cross between social commonsense and Plausible-like compliance. The ambiguity is weighted according to one's stance, to the audience's preference for the heroic or the comic. In exactly the same way, generic preference places Manly as more or less of a fool or a hero. The extremes of the evaluative attitude begin to separate out. Manly's belief in the singularity of friendship starts to appear as either obsessive or as a reference to the friendship that underlies heroic action, like Damon and Pythias. Freeman's general friendship has the easy grace of the rake. Dorimant, after all, appears friendly towards Sir Fopling or Young Bellair, whatever he may say of them behind their backs. The attitudes of both Freeman and Manly imply that the self is separate from the rest of humanity, whether openly stated (Manly), or only behind others' backs (Freeman). If Freeman recalls the rake's superiority, he is also a sailor, as extra-social as Manly in that respect. It is no longer possible in this scene to be decisive in one's attitude towards the actors. Kynaston, the highly moral actor, is now shown to be one for whom the world is simply a place to be used, a maze to be negotiated with maximum compliance and minimum involvement. Hart, the hero, is now shown to be a social incompetent, whose cynical and accurate perception of the way the world goes is bedevilled by the impossibility of implementing his ideal. As Freeman recognises, he has, as an ally, the entire practice of society to set against Manly-ism: 'You are for *Plain-dealing*, I find; but against your particular Notions, I have the practice of the whole World' (p. 7). Significantly, Manly sees Whitehall as a performance: 'there they seem to rehearse *Bays*'s grand Dance' (p. 7). The social ceremonies are part of a parodic drama (*The Rehearsal*) that burlesques the theatrical and social response to the type of drama with which Manly the hero is associated. The grand dance is acting as pretending, the form of acting that is opposed to clarity and transparency, the single meaning of social signification in which Manly believes. Freeman's worldliness makes his desire to adopt Manly's style and show himself a true friend impossible: 'pray believe the Friendship I promise you, real, whatsoever I have profest to others' (p. 7). Freeman can no longer make a statement and have it believed as true: the continued confusion of action and pretence has disqualified him from the possibility of making a true statement. But, in any case, Manly shows at this point, at the end of the conversation, that he simply will not accept mere statements: Freeman may say it but will he do it?

Fidelia enters and the distinction of saying and doing is promptly applied to her. Caught by the nature of her own position, she is an ambiguous being. Just as Manly's words are variously interpretable according to the moral evaluation of his character – a circular process since the words define the evaluations at this stage – so Fidelia does not say what she means since she is not what she seems. Her lines throughout this scene are a classic example of the doubleness and paradox associated with Fletcherian romanticism: the heroine disguised as a man *can* love 'better than any man can love you' (p. 8). Fidelia stands as a sign that cannot be decoded by the other characters since, at least until Vernish meets her, stage convention renders her disguise impenetrable. While Fidelia represents a simple passion, a simple way of viewing others – her love for Manly is absolute – she is herself a lie, a plural sign, a girl-boy.

Though Fidelia is so clearly an exile from another type of drama, a naïf in London's corrupt and corrupting world, analogous to Margery Pinchwife, her attachment to Manly does not imply a simple attraction felt by similar exiles. Manly is barely more aggressive to Olivia later than he is to Fidelia from the very beginning. This aggression motivated by Manly's hatred of a coward, stands out beyond the stage disguise. It does not, of course, in its immediate source, *Twelfth Night*. Wycherley's audience is required to mark out a distance between Orsino's affectionate treatment of Viola and Manly's contempt for Fidelia. Juxtaposed with Fidelia, Manly belongs to a type of drama in which aggression is the sole possible response·to the presentation of ideals opposite to the hero's. One thinks directly of the automatic changing of sides that is obligatory for the heroic or romance character whenever his position in a framework of moral relationships is altered. But though Fidelia's 'cowardice' provokes Manly here, Manly's character cannot be defined in terms of a black-and-white morality. If aggression is morally justifiable through ignorance in a heroic play, it becomes an index of stupidity when transposed to London. Nonetheless, this single-minded heroic virtue is impractical, not wrong.

The heroic tends to belittle the rakish, making compliance a pejorative term. But Freeman's position in the play's hierarchical structure is so far still high, dependent solely on *how* he uses society for his own ends. If mockery of the world led him to the right wife all would be well. An intelligent woman, a witty wife would set Freeman against Manly's excessive and vulnerable passion for Olivia. But the Widow Blackacre is not what anyone would expect. This is the crucial moment at which Kynaston is permanently displaced in the play from being the repository of social wisdom. That kind of expertise, in Freeman's case, now appears as the abandonment of any interest or belief in love or intelligence. Woman, for Freeman, is a source of income, a way out of his poverty. On this basis, the witty gentleman denies in marriage any normal function, as the fulfilment of love or the perpetuation of wit in society. Money has become the ultimate end of the gentleman's endeavours. Freeman had stood for a mode in which pretence was a way of action. Initially, Freeman's position appeared to embody ridicule as opposed to Manly's severity; he exemplified the Horatian motto on the published play's title-page: 'Ridiculum acre / Fortius & melius magnas plerumque secat res'. But his position is shown to be untenable; it leads only to the widow. The motto is no longer a controlling attitude to the play; instead it joins the ever increasing group of preconceptions overturned, of patterns unfulfilled. If Freeman's wit can produce only the Widow, his wit is an arid performance.

Fidelia, left alone, shows that her perception of the nature of love is to combine verbal demonstration – like Freeman's assertion of friendship or his wit – with physical proof:

> She has told him she lov'd him; I have shew'd it,
> And durst not tell him so, till I had done,
> Under this habit, such convincing Acts
> Of loving Friendship for him, that through it
> He first might find out both my Sex and Love . . .     (p. 13)

Fidelia's trust in the clean separation of speech and act has already been made doubtful by the connection of both with pretence, with acting. But her naïve trust in the accuracy of Manly's perception of event is yet to be disputed. By the end of Act I, the audience knows that, for Manly, assertion may mean proof. Fidelia's hope that he may see through her disguise is ridiculous. When Freeman questions Manly about his relationship with Olivia, Manly shows that he trusts her statements, even though he will not trust anyone else. Freeman's incredulity is unanswered and unanswerable: 'But how come you to be so diffident of the Man that sayes he loves you, and not doubt the Woman that sayes it?' (p. 14). Manly is again shown to be of a 'nice humor', discriminating arbitrarily where he pleases, capable of justifying that discrimination only through generalised reference to large idealistic statements that seem increasingly dubious. If the audience expects to see Manly learn how to evaluate character, Fidelia's in particular, to see Hart loving Mrs Boutell, it must accept that that is only possible through a resolution which disdains to concern itself with the evident impossibilities and irresolvable elements of the audience's own judgements on the characters.

To some extent, in this survey of Act I, I have anticipated the procedures of the play. But, it seems to me, its increasingly disconcerting and frustrating events, that shifting way in which nearly all the characters – especially Manly – waver in and out of the audience's sympathies and moral approval, are all processes begun in Act I. The two principal areas of discrepancy, a distance between speech and act, and a blurring of doing and pretending to do, are both present from the beginning. What happens is that the possibility of restricting this interplay, of holding onto a single meaning becomes more and more of a chimaera. The audience has lost its privileged status. Whatever it does know about the manoeuvres and devices of the play, as, for example, the true sex of Fidelia, is counterpoised by its inability to use that knowledge, to make it a base from which to predict the movement of the play.

As soon as Act II starts any conventional heroic triangle that might have existed between Hart-Marshall-Boutell, Manly-Olivia-Fidelia, is made impossible. Olivia's opening line *could* have come straight from Manly: 'Ah, Cousin, what a World 'tis we live in! I am so weary of it' (p. 15). It has Manly's weariness and generalised disgust. What is only partly present is the peculiar rhythm of Olivia's drawling speech, its emphasis on exclamation and on definition through adjectives, that is found in her second statement: 'O hideous! you cannot be in earnest sure, when you say you like the filthy World'. Olivia's mode of treating language is histrionic, just as her analysis of the fops ( pp. 19f) is a performance. Later in the play, she describes how she tricked Manly: 'I knew he lov'd his own singular moroseness so well, as to dote upon any Copy of it; wherefore I feign'd an hatred to the World too, ... ' (p. 71). Olivia functions in relation to Manly as an actress, a mimic giving a performance that copies the original. Doing and pretending are indistinguishable. Affectation in her own life is only another form of the performance, but there actress and role are merged. For Olivia, acting and pretending, affectation and performance are equally real. Olivia is so far from the passionate heroine that Mrs Marshall usually played opposite Hart – she is not even as level-headed as Doralice in *Marriage A-la-Mode* – that it seems now that the play has no complexity of plot to offer. Manly, the audience expects, will learn Olivia's true nature and turn away. But again this pattern is based on a preconception of Manly's ability to act on his knowledge; the audience's commonsense is not necessarily compatible with Manly's.

Olivia's language offers a disjunction between statement and style, a disruption of surface meaning and the subversion of that meaning through manner. Against her affectation is set the honesty and transparent language of Eliza. Throughout this scene, Eliza offers a Montaignean frankness, an acceptance of the naturalness of the world. But her enjoyment of the world is only apparently reconcilable with the approval of it. It relates more strongly to the audience's evaluation of the real world than to anything that is presented on stage. Apart from Eliza herself, the play's world is peopled with fops and fools; we are never shown these 'other Women' Eliza speaks of, for whom 'the World ... has such variety of Charms' (p. 15), and we cannot take their existence on trust. The isolation of Eliza, most marked in her separation from her logical partner, Freeman,[29] makes her ethical superiority vulnerable. It becomes even more marked in the discussion of *The Country Wife*.

This scene, Wycherley's next manoeuvre in the assault on the audience's safe preconceptions, is a debate on the signification of meaning in language. The critique is far more than a joke or a game. In reminding the audience that it is a play, another by Wycherley, Wycherley at the same time extricates himself from it, denies responsibility for it and his status as moral arbiter. He becomes, as he was in the prologue, a 'Scribler' or a 'course Dauber'.

The problem in the critique is that while Olivia's response to language is farcically over-emphatic, her awareness of the nature of meaning is right. In this debate, Eliza is left some way adrift of the reality of the social use of language. Eliza's attitude towards social behaviour is that modesty is not the same as ignorance but is a pretence of ignorance: 'so may a Lady call her own modesty in question, by publickly cavilling with the Poets' (p. 24). At a bawdy play, Eliza's ideal does not indicate that she understands the bawdy but sits through it unblushing, pretending not to understand, pretending not to be embarrassed. There is no suggestion by Eliza that the embarrassment is what is wrong, only the obvious indication of it. This is as much artifice and pretence as 'those grimaces of honour, and artificial modesty' (p. 24). It is still disguise, however modest.

In the same way, Eliza conceives of language as limited in the multiplicity of its referential meaning. For her, the name 'Horner' is simply a name. Her belief in the harmlessness of language's references would be acceptable if, as Montaigne did, she recognised that language spins off into infinite associations. But for Eliza, meaning is to be drastically delimited by the word in context. For Olivia, a word is the key to the expression of desire; the name

'Horner' for her unlocks the restrictions on appetite:

Olivia   O fie, fie, fie, wou'd you put me to the blush anew? call all the
         blood into my face again? But, to satisfie you then, first, the clan-
         destine obscenity in the very name of *Horner*.
Eliza    Truly, 'tis so hidden, I cannot find it out, I confess.
Olivia   O horrid! does it not give you the rank conception, or image of a
         Goat, a Town-bull, or a Satyr? nay, what is yet a filthier image
         than all the rest, that of an Eunuch?
Eliza    What then? I can think of a Goat, a Bull, or Satyr, without any
         hurt.
Olivia   I, but, Cousin, one cannot stop there.
Eliza    I can, Cousin.
Olivia   O no; for when you have those filthy creatures in your head
         once, the next thing you think, is what they do; as their defiling of
         honest Mens Beds and Couches, Rapes upon sleeping and waking
         Countrey Virgins, under Hedges, and on Haycocks: nay, farther –
         (p. 24).

Eliza sees nothing 'clandestine' in the word at all, obscene or not;
Olivia can only see obscene connections. For Eliza the animal images
are arid connections, they do not function as symbols of sexuality.
If one goes back to *The Country Wife*, it is obvious that Horner's name
is connected to animalistic sex as well as cuckolding. The name
*is* a symbol; it connects with other patterns of meaning and makes
them relevant to the use of the word in the play. Horner *is* a goat
and a town-bull in his attitude towards sex; he *is* a satyr in his
cynical analysis of society, as well as his sensuality. Up to the point
at which Olivia 'cannot stop', she is right in her reading of the name.
Eliza's reluctance to read and interpret the name marks a connection with Mrs Knep's other roles for Wycherley. Distinct though
Eliza is from Lady Flippant and Lady Fidget in her attitude towards
physical sex, all three aim to use a language that is ostensibly pure.
For the latter two, the purity is debased by their own double thinking
on the nature of meaning. For Eliza, the purity is shown to be too
limited; language is not as simple as that. Eliza is not Wycherley's
own voice.

But, equally well, it is not as complex as Olivia makes it:

I say, the lewdest, filthiest thing, is his *China*; nay, I will never forgive the
beastly Author his *China*: he has quite taken away the reputation of poor
*China* it self, and sully'd the most innocent and pretty Furniture of a Ladies
Chamber; insomuch, that I was fain to break all my defil'd Vessels. You see
I have none left; nor you, I hope.  (p. 24)

Olivia's confusion is at the level of the linguistic sign itself. Horner, in the 'china scene', had made the word 'china' as *signifié* a cover for a play on 'china' as *signifiant*, making the word mean 'sex'. The word, Tweedledum-like, means exactly what he wants it to mean, that is, two different things to the two on-stage groups, the women and their guardians. But Olivia confuses the word with the object. For her, the word's unequivocal link with the object means that the sullying of the one involves damage to the other.

Eliza's response is to ignore the question as posed within the play and separate the play from society: 'You'll pardon me, I cannot think the worse of my *China*, for that of the Play-house' (p. 25). It is a separation that has already been offered satirically in the prologue ('And where else, but on Stages, do we see . . . ') and rejected. If the play has no connection with the world then it cannot exist as the moral and didactic satire that Wycherley made of his other plays. Eliza purifies the playhouse's use of language by purging it of social applicability. Her denial of the connection between stage and life is a denial of everything that the play has so far had to say about 'acting'.

But while Olivia's actions, breaking all her china, are stupid and extreme, she is accurate in her understanding of the effect of sexual innuendo and double meaning on the use of words. Words do not exist in a one-to-one relation with objects, with the thing signified. It would be easy to give a long list of 'innocent' words that have acquired an inseparable sexual meaning that makes their pure use almost impossible. The sign acquires a plurality of connections to different systems of reference in society, connections that deny its apparent simplicity. Meaning is socially corruptible.

It is at this stage in my argument, even though out of its dramatic sequence, that the purpose of the widow Blackacre plot can best be explored. The principle of litigation is that there should be some resolution, some compatibility between the actions of the law and the necessary and appropriate justice. Events, in law, are held to be susceptible to an analysis that can define their single meaning, one that can then be interpreted as right or wrong. The law itself is a series of statements intended to be clear and exact, even though their application to an individual case may need clarifying. But litigation, in *The Plain-Dealer*, has come to mean litigiousness and to be associated with empty rhetoric. Legal action means making money for the lawyers: even on his death-bed Wycherley believed that, commenting 'I know the world well Enough if I present these

Gentlemen [lawyers] with their ffees or what is fitting . . . They will not take [the trouble] amiss'.[30] What has vanished in the play, what has become as extra-social or as idealistic as Manly himself is any concept that the law in action means the discovery of the truth. Westminster Hall is the ultimate location of the corruption of the language. The widow's cases are carried on through perjury and filibuster; some of them are bought and thus have no direct relation to the widow herself. Litigation is no longer an attempt to establish the truth of conflicting evidence. Even when Freeman uses law against the widow, it is as a cheat. His suit – itself a pun on his suit of marriage – is a 'Choak-Bayl Action' (p. 91), a subterfuge to encompass his designs on her for a jointure in settlement. Law is as much a pretence as 'china'; it does not mean what it seems to mean. This pretence affects all the legal language in the play; coloured with its obsessive sexual innuendo it abounds in a verbal fertility which mocks its own aridity. Thus, for instance, the widow's body becomes a piece of land and sex with her is to be achieved through the law's device for claiming possession: 'Ay, ay, Mother, he wou'd be taking Livery and Seizen of your Jointure, by digging the Turf' (p. 12).

With Olivia, the distance of language from reality, its arbitrariness as a sign, has begun to collapse; with the widow, her cousin, language has lost all status as a medium for the definition of reality. Linguistic signs are no longer what they seem. The law is merely another form of acting and pretence at the level of language, but one that is more fundamentally corrupting. When the widow briefs her lawyers (pp. 40–3), she is like a director in rehearsal, preparing and marshalling her case and advising them on their mode of performance: 'Come, Mr. *Quaint*, pray go talk a great deal for me in *Chancery*; let your words be easie, and your Sense hard, my Cause requires it: Branch it bravely and deck my Cause with flowers, that the Snake may lie hidden . . . ' (pp. 40–1).

It is in Westminster Hall too that Manly is able to demonstrate his comprehension of the world. He opens the act complaining 'How hard it is to be an Hypocrite!' (p. 37) and closes by giving a superbly polished performance as hypocrite, disposing of impertinents with a massive display of wit and socially cynical expertise. Standing on the forestage, he forces the pursuers to merge back into the scenic area, to rejoin the background, the world of which they are a part. But his achievement in that sequence is exactly the opposite of truth-telling. Abuse, even when true, does not help; only socially expedient lies enable him to rid himself of the troublesome acquaintances. Lies, in the corrupted temple of truth, have become the means of revealing the truth, making plain the characters of others. Manly shows himself to be adept at using language in the way that lawyers do, falsifying for personal advantage. But paradoxically, his rakish witty brilliance, his denial of himself as plain-dealer, makes him more human and certainly much more sympathetic than he had ever been before in the play. For the first time, Manly appears as a rake, and takes the rake's place on stage, mediating between the audience and the events in the scenic stage. The static social satire makes Manly into an expositor, above the machinations of the world he merci- lessly dissects. It is at this point that Manly comes closest to embody- ing a comic ideal of dispassionate superiority, the rake observing all. It is achieved primarily through the dramatic device of placing him between the audience and the 'Several crossing the Stage' (p. 55); he explains the stage picture of the world to the audience.

When Manly reverts to plain-dealing – behind the back of those he now mocks – Freeman agrees with his opinions. Being poor, they are both dispossessed, separate from the world of 'Ceremony, Embra- ces, and plentiful Professions' (p. 55); neither has yet lied or cheated sufficiently to eat:

> But now, the Lawyer only here is fed:
> And, Bully-like, by Quarrels gets his bread.   (p. 56)

Act III, in spite of its minimal concern with advancing the plot, establishes that concern with the definition of meaning so vital to the rest of the play. Although the prediction of event was subverted throughout the first two acts, the end of Act II offered a new set of predictions. When Manly and Olivia curse each other (p. 31), the play suggests to the audience that the curses will be carried out: Olivia does suffer from 'the Curse of your Husband's company on your Pleasures; and the Curse of your Gallant's disappointments in his absence; and the Curse of scorn, jealousie, or despair, on your love: and then the Curse of loving on'. But while the play offers these events as the future pattern of the plot, they form, in fact, only a small part of the events of Act III. Fidelia's mission to Olivia is displaced by the reality of Westminster Hall.

The first climax to the play comes in Act IV, in the night scene in Olivia's lodgings. It focuses upon two enigmas: does Manly have sex with Olivia? and what is Fidelia's true sex?

As one reads the various recent critics on *The Plain-Dealer*, it is quickly apparent that they fall neatly into two groups, those who

believe that Manly does have sex with Olivia off-stage in the bedroom and those who believe Manly decides against it. A recent
article[31] has shown that both interpretations are intrinsically
consistent and that both can be followed through the whole play
without encountering contradiction. The key moment is Manly's
first line on his return to the stage from the bedroom: 'I have
thought better on't' (p. 74). Is the 'it' that Manly has decided
against sex or the public revelation of the sex that has taken place?
Some recent editions place a full-stop after 'on't',[32] making the
ambiguity stronger. The first edition has only a comma, thereby
making the attraction of 'on't' to 'I must not discover my self now'
all the stronger. But, while that implies that 'it' is 'discovery', in
the following line, 'if I barely shou'd publish it', 'it' is more likely
to mean 'sex'. Adams concludes that Wycherley's purpose was to
make the audience aware of their moral position by the nature of
their choice; Wycherley's aim was 'to cynically give the playgoers a
chance to damn themselves by their reactions to his play'.[33] But
Adams's is only a partial understanding of the significance of the
passage. The real problem is the difficulty of *knowing* what happened.
Wycherley is questioning the basis of the use of language to signify
event. Even though the decision between sex and no sex cannot be
made, the play proves that the choice does not make much difference
to the assessment of Manly: in one way, he is a hypocrite in his later
discussion with Vernish of having had sex with Olivia (p. 88), if he
did not;[34] in the other, he is a debased animalistic sensualist, an
uncontrollable figure of lust.[35] Both interpretations tend to disparage Manly, to make him a figure to be rejected.

Both lines have a close connection with Hart. Manly boasting to
Vernish is analogous to the rake boasting of his conquests to his
friend. Significantly, throughout that scene (pp. 81–8), Manly finds
it possible to talk, to banter and to indulge in witty repartee with the
fools that surround him. He is hardly even impatient in discussing
satire and wit with Novel and Oldfox (p. 85), and is in fact eager to
return to the discussion, after being interrupted by Fidelia: 'I must
stay here yet awhile for my Friend. But is Railing Satyr, *Novel?*'
(p. 86). Manly the hypocrite is then a perversion of Manly/Hart as
a rake. Manly as sensualist is a Hobbesian re-interpretation of the
appetite-driven characters of heroic drama, an Almanzor without
the honourable ideals. This side of Manly is closely linked to that
other aspect of Hart's career, the super-hero of heroic drama.

But just as hypocrite and sensualist reflect rake and hero, they also reflect on the duality of 'acting' on which I have commented so often. As sensualist, Manly is condemned for doing; as hypocrite, he is condemned for pretending, for performing as an actor. If he is true to his own desire, he is wrong, because it deceives Olivia; if he suppresses that desire and plays the social game of boasted sexuality, he is wrong, because he deceives himself. Either way, Manly cannot win.

The events in the bedroom are an enigma with only a single moral solution. Wycherley has made the moral signification of an event single even where the event itself is plural, and, in addition, incompatibly plural – there cannot have been both sex and no sex! The dilemma is made doubly acute for the audience because it is totally reliant on what is said in order to reconstruct the events off-stage. In the confusion over Fidelia's true sex, the enigma is acute for the characters onstage because each one believes that he or she has had the necessary physical evidence to decide. In the case of the bedroom scene, the audience has been dislodged from its position of privileged omniscience; in the case of Fidelia, the stage itself provides the answer, Mrs Boutell is a woman.[36] The audience knows that answer from the start. Yet Vernish is seen onstage establishing Fidelia's sex when he 'Pulls off her Peruke, and feels her breasts' (p. 75), and Olivia believed that she knew the sex of the 'gentleman'. Vernish can be talked out of his belief. Sensory impressions are no longer to be trusted. Language, that instrument of falsification, is given absolute control.

Before the final scene of the play comes the triumph of Freeman. In part, it is based on a legalistic jargon that obscures the true nature of the agreement.

*Widow*  Have a care, Sir, a Settlement without a Consideration, is void in Law: you must do something for't.

*Freeman*  Pr'ythee then let the Settlement on me be call'd Alimony; and the Consideration our Separation ... (p. 92)

Naming is now a device to replace truth with a socially and legally viable fiction. It no longer contains the concept of defining. Freeman's settlement does leave him free. He has gained an annuity of £300 and will have his debts paid. In addition, he does not need to marry or, more distasteful task, go to bed with the Widow. Freeman's success is out of all proportion to his place in the play. So strong has been the audience's feeling of contempt for the widow-hunting, for this capitulation to the lowest of society's games, that

Freeman's triumph has no relation to the moral attitude towards his activity. During the play, the character of Freeman has steadily become unattractive: more and more, Freeman's ideas, the social expression of how harmonious social existence is to be achieved through a modicum of lying, have been undercut and made unacceptable by the actions to which they have given rise. Surprisingly, the rejection of 'Freeman-ism' has been clearest when juxtaposed with Manly; Freeman's knowledge of the ways of the world has not added up to a moral superiority. Freeman has shown no way in which his praise of the world might be viable. Manly's cynicism, in its turn undercut by *his* actions, nonetheless seems to be a more accurate picture of the world as it is. Freeman has shown himself to be blind to the implications of his ideals for himself; his actions are a subversion of the pretence and hypocrisy that is a fundamental part of his social behaviour. Only through Manly does Freeman learn to disparage bowing to the wealthy for food (p. 56).

The audience's doubts over the acceptability of Freeman's success are small in comparison with their doubts over Manly's. In a conventional sequence of darkness and light, leading, literally, to the illumination of identity, the characters learn the true basis of the patterns of relationship that had subsisted between them. Wycherley associates this discovery with an extra-social group, the sailors. Just as the sailors had helped Freeman steal the widow's papers, so when the people arrive at Olivia's lodgings, they are 'lighted in by the two Sailors with Torches' (p. 94). The sailors who had commented as a chorus on Manly at the beginning of the play now stand as silent witnesses to his discovery of his own stupidity. The sailors do not belong to the society in which the other characters move. They are part of the outside from which Manly appears, the sea and the overseas Indies, as well as Wapping.

Wycherley's emphasis is also on the public nature of the discovery. All the principal characters with the solitary exception of Oldfox are present for the revelations. Manly had said after the first bedroom scene that he would wait, 'I am without Witnesses' (p. 74); the shaming of Olivia can only be done in public. Her double adultery (cuckolding Manly and Vernish, each with the other), places her beyond society's limits of acceptable behaviour. But the doubts about the nature of proof mean that the 'facts' must be publicly accepted before they can be proved. In private, before Eliza, Olivia and Vernish avoid the truth of the adultery; in any case, the enigma of Fidelia's sex makes the claim unprovable. But in the final scene, it no longer matters whether Olivia did have sex with Manly or not; even her intention to do so is unimportant. What the public shame does is to produce a belief in the event through context and through language, that is through the two means which the whole play has cast into doubt.

Olivia's departure is the final parodic inversion of *Twelfth Night*. Fidelia pimping for Manly was a degradation of the relation of Viola to Orsino; Olivia's exit is, as it were, a change that leaves Malvolio in control. Manly's manner is more fundamentally a form of self-isolation than Orsino's love-sickness; it is closer to being an imbalance, based on a trust in his own self-sufficiency, that is a humour – a 'nice humor' – like Malvolio's pride.

At the moment of revelation, Manly is shown to be a fool. However many different types of character he may have embraced before, rake, hero, wit, sensualist and hypocrite, his ignorance about Vernish makes him a fool complete. Friendship founded on verbal protestations is found to be a pretence. The title that Manly had cherished in Act I comes to be that of 'a Rascal . . . a man of that extraordinary merit in Vilany' (p. 96). Manly now embodies a tension between the rake's success in London and the hero's safety outside it. He can leave the world to give Fidelia the wealth she deserves: 'you deserve the *Indian* World; and I wou'd now go thither out of covetousness for your sake only' (p. 96). He can stay in the world: 'stay in this ill World of ours still'. Either decision is open to misconstruction. Wycherley's solution is an extraordinarily theatrical one: the revelation of Fidelia's wealth, not her sex, is the true resolution of the enigma she posed. She is named 'Grey', a shadow on the edge of the stage, a morally neutral device liable to produce unexpected solutions. The unreality of the discovery of the heiress is no more than the unreality of the breeches disguise. The wealth is real but a pretence, a theatrical truth that belongs to a set of romantic drama conventions, the conventions to which Fidelia's ideals and breeches have already indicated that she belongs. The line goes directly back to the prologue,

> And where else, but on Stages, do we see
> Truth pleasing; or rewarded Honesty?
> Which our bold Poet does this day in me.  (A3b)

If the theatrical ending were to be all, then one would expect that the imponderabilities and incompatible elements of the character of Manly could be united by excessive reward. That would assume that Manly could now be made capable of speaking the truth, a sign that he deserved Fidelia. Instead he produces another example of the confusion of language. Freeman can be a *'Plain-dealer* too', because of a single statement, in spite of everything the audience has learnt in the course of the play about Freeman's lack of plain-dealing and the dangers of trusting statements. Manly bandies around the name of 'friend' with little proof that it is earned: 'I'll say I am thy Friend indeed'. But the most extraordinary misuse comes in the final verse lines:

And, for your two sakes, tho' I have been so lately deceiv'd in Friends of both Sexes;
> I will believe, there are now in the World
> Good-natur'd Friends, who are not Prostitutes,
> And handsom Women worthy to be Friends. (p. 96).

Manly in fact gets the lines the wrong way round. What he means is 'good-natured friends worthy to be friends and handsome women who are not prostitutes'. The descriptions and the objects have become inverted. Manly has not been incorporated in society. Language is still an imprecise, uncontrollable tool which blurs what it aims to define.

It is left to the widow to speak the epilogue and appeal for justice. The appeal is tempered with rhetoric ('If not the Poet here, the *Templer* spare' A4a) and with paradox ('For Playes, like Women, by the World are thought / (When you speak kindly of 'em) very naught'). Widow Blackacre, the parody of the law, praises the audience as 'the Judges learned in Stage Laws'. But *The Plain-Dealer* has taught the audience that judgement is a fraud, that there are few means by which we can guarantee knowledge and none at all by which we can talk about it. The act of praise becomes, in the stage society and by extension the real one, another form of pretence. The epilogue carries the play out again to the world. Acting on stage – doing and pretending to do – is no more ambiguous than acting in society. Social perception has been revealed to be governed by the ability to use pre-existent definitions, ones that place Hart as hero or rake. In removing the comforts of expectation, Wycherley disturbed the neat lines of separation on which society claims to depend: rake and hero, doing and pretending, actor and author and character are merged.

In Pepys' catalogue of his library, he lists a volume containing three plays, bound together, Wycherley's *The Plain-Dealer*, Shadwell's *The Sullen Lovers* and his adaptation of *Timon*. The volume is called '3 Practical Comedies'.[37] It is a curious term. In many ways the plays do go together: Stanford, Timon and Manly all reject their society and all are 'proved' wrong. But are the plays 'practical' because they mock society or because they define a need to be complicit with it? Is it Pepys the puritan or Pepys the epicure who terms them 'practical'? Is it another form of that acting in public at which Pepys was so good? It is an enigma like those in *The Plain-Dealer*. Wycherley has made his play defy categories, as soon as the play is linked to the world. Acting does not stop at the edge of the fore-stage:

> But the course Dauber of the coming Scenes,
> To follow Life, and Nature only means;
> Displays you, as you are . . .   (Prologue, A3b)

# Text and performance (3):
# the comedies of Congreve

Since all Traditions must indisputably give place to the *Drama*, and since there is no possibility of giving that life to the Writing or Repetition of a Story which it has in the Action, I resolved in another beauty to imitate *Dramatick* Writing, namely, in the Design, Contexture and Result of the Plot.[1]

Congreve's statement in the preface to *Incognita* indicates that from the beginning he recognised the primacy of theatrical representation over all forms of literature. But there seems to be an increasingly common view that Congreve begins as a man who 'had read more plays than he had seen',[2] and by 1700 abandons the stage, contemptuous of the audience.

Congreve wrote *The Old Batchelour* in the summer of 1689, between leaving Trinity College, Dublin and coming to London, and his experience of the theatre at that stage must have been limited. At Smock Alley, he might have seen recent London plays like Southerne's *The Disappointment*, Shadwell's *The Libertine*, Otway's *The Atheist* and the Dryden – Lee *Oedipus*,[3] but there is no evidence that he did. Congreve's library catalogue includes a number of plays that he might have bought before coming to London, if only by virtue of the date of publication. He might have read the folios of Shakespeare (541),[84] Jonson (44), Beaumont and Fletcher (42) or Killigrew (342). He is more likely to have owned at that time a 1687 bound-up set of Otway's plays in quarto (444). More probable still is that he owned and had read Rapin (509), Hédelin (10) and Dryden's *Essay of Dramatic Poesy* (406).

*The Old Batchelour* can be seen as a combination of a reader's experience of the English tradition of comedy and French neoclassical orthodoxy. Hédelin's name occurs with surprising regularity in discussion of Congreve's plays: Herbert Davis tries to show the influence of Hédelin on *The Old Batchelour*;[5] John Barnard links Hédelin with *The Double-Dealer*.[6] The French connection is held to become stronger as Congreve moves towards the unities and abandons the conventions of Restoration comedy. With the publication of the 1710 reading edition of the plays, Congreve is seen as taking the next inevitable step and abandoning the stage for ever: his audiences, after all, could no longer follow the plays. Congreve is placed firmly in a tradition that leads towards the novels of Fielding and Richardson.

But there is another side to the case. In that preface to his only novel, Congreve is describing the transposition of dramatic techniques into another mode (precisely the endeavour of Richardson). Between the first drafts of *The Old Batchelour* and its eventual performance came a long period of revision with help from Dryden and Southerne; Congreve was given author's privileges of free entry at the playhouse six months before the first performance.[7] Even after the relative failure of *The Way of the World*, Congreve wrote *The Judgement of Paris* and a part of *Squire Trelooby*, as well as taking a brief share in theatre management with Vanbrugh. For all the frustrations caused by imperceptive audiences, Congreve is, for at least as long as he was writing comedy, first and foremost concerned with the possibilities of the theatre.

Congreve's plays pose particular problems for the audience in performance, problems that cannot be reconciled with a view of the plays as moving away from the stage. The audience is deliberately confused, refused the security of expectation of what a play ought to do. The result is that the audience has to follow the chain of the play extraordinarily closely; they must pursue the syntagmatic sequence of juxtaposition and substitution. That sequence often refuses to obey traditional dramatic laws of procedure, denying rational motivation. Its movement is frequently metonymic rather than causative. Bewildered, the audience – so Congreve hoped – followed the play towards 'the artful Solution of the *Fable*'.[8] This kind of confusion, though strongly rooted in the experience of the plays in the theatre, is totally alien to Hédelin. Hédelin's view of all dramatic devices is that they should be clear. We can compare Hédelin's authoritative statement on disguise directly with Congreve. Hédelin states:

But if it be necessary that an Actor should be *incognito* both as to his Name and Quality, in order to his being known with more pleasure towards the end of the Play, then the Spectators must at least know that he is *incognito*; and in a word all confusion must be avoided . . .[9]

Congreve wrote to Catharine Trotter, commenting on her tragedy
*The Revolution in Sweden*,

> One thing would have a very beautiful effect in the catastrophe, if it were
> possible to manage it thro' the play; and that is to have the audience kept
> in ignorance, as long as the husband (which sure they may as well be) who
> *Fredage* really is, till her death.[10]

The greater the audience's ignorance the more it is affected. In
Congreve's comedies, actions that the audience had followed with
rapt attention are proved to have been made totally redundant,
their purpose already circumvented. Plots and plotting fail, while
the plot, the design of the play, is carried forward. Congreve's best
description of his method places the emphasis on the plot as the
expression of the moral and didactic purpose of his play,

> I design'd the Moral first, and to that Moral I invented the Fable, and do
> not know that I have borrow'd one hint of it any where. I made the Plot as
> strong as I could, because it was single, and I made it single, because I would
> avoid confusion . . .[11]

'Confusion' here means a confusion of purpose by dividing the
audience's attention between various plots. The audience is still
confused by the conflict between prediction and result in the events
of the play.

  The consequence of overvaluing Congreve's dependence on
Hédelin has been to allow critics to ignore the 'how' of the plays'
methods, the distinctiveness of Congreve's approach to comedy, in
pursuit of more and more refined and discriminating concepts of
'what' he was trying to say. The plays are increasingly described as
if they were indistinguishable from novels. The failure of the contemporary audiences to comprehend becomes the symbol of the
non-theatricality of Congreve's method. As I have already shown,
reading weakens the linearity of the plot, reducing its dependence
on its sequential presentation in time. But this sense of sequence,
of theatrical process, is fundamental to Congreve. This chapter
examines Congreve's four comedies by exploring a tension between
the audience's presuppositions and the events of the plays themselves, the tension between the predictions founded on the casting
and the action of the plays as seen in the scenic structure, in the
fictional event and the theatrical movement. The emphasis is on the
theatre.

Whatever help Congreve may have had in the final revisions of *The Old Batchelour*, the final cast was evidently chosen with care. In his preface Congreve praises the whole cast:

this Play . . . with all its Faults, which I must own were, for the most part, very industriously covered by the care of the Players; for, I think, scarce a Character but receiv'd all the Advantage it would admit of, from the justness of Action. (A2b)

It seems likely that *The Old Batchelour* was originally scheduled for performance in December 1692 but was delayed by Mountfort's murder. Almost certainly, Mountfort had a part in the first cast. Summers suggests that Mountfort was cast as Vainlove;[12] but Mountfort's particular preference for rakish parts makes Bellmour a more likely choice. Given that most of Mountfort's parts passed to Powell, Powell's presence as Bellmour in the cast of the first performance makes this likely. At the centre of the play, as Bellmour and Belinda, are Powell and Susanna Mountfort, the United company's new witty couple. They seem intended to embody the conventional forms of comedy, as if the comedy that *The Old Batchelour* was seen as revivifying was made practicable through the genuine joy at the union of Bellmour and Belinda, an unremarkable match but a promising one. Implicit in the pattern of the Mountforts or the new one of Powell and Mrs Mountfort is Restoration comic form, a form in which Bellmour and Belinda can replace the recognition of the limitations of their characters with a deeper understanding of their merits.

Opposite Powell and Mrs Mountfort were Williams and Anne Bracegirdle as Vainlove and Araminta. These two seem intended to hover as the serious alternative to the union of Powell and Mrs Mountfort. For Belinda is to some extent mocked: her affectation means that, as Congreve commented later, she is, in part, 'ridiculed rather than recommended'.[13] Congreve, in the throes of controversy with Collier, is of course overstating his case. But however witty, that is superficially attractive, she may be – and her wit *is* fine – the audience is perhaps encouraged to see a certain hollowness in her frenetic affectation, a hollowness that is increased by comparison with Anne Bracegirdle's performance as Araminta.

The two pairs of lovers ought to be moving along roughly parallel lines. Conventionally, the twin pairs, one rather more serious than the other, represented similar, or at least convergent, attitudes towards wit and marriage. Ariana and Gatty, to choose an obvious

example, disagree about how to live properly in town but the dis-
agreement is easily resolved and both end the play postponing
marriage. The wittier of the two men or two women is almost always
demonstrably the closer to the comic and ethical norm so that the
other is convinced by the arguments and acquiesces in the form of the
play. There had been hints of irresolvable tensions between the pairs
in earlier comedies. Dorimant, for instance, is contemptuous of
Young Bellair and there can be no simple ethical or comic solution
that would accept both Horner and Harcourt. But in both cases, it is
the more serious of the two who is pushed into a subsidiary position
in the action. It is for this reason that I was able to speak of the
audience expecting Williams and Bracegirdle, inevitably the more
serious pair, to hover around the action. But Bellmour and Vainlove,
in spite of their friendship, are not compatible. The audience might
have expected Powell and Mrs Mountfort to dominate the action, but
they found that they were required to judge two different manifesta-
tions of the basic split in the concept of the rake, the pursuer and the
observer. The ethical and comic alternatives grow further apart as the
play proceeds.

The choice is between Bellmour and Vainlove. On one side is the
extreme activity of Bellmour, on the other the fastidiousness and
passivity of Vainlove. Bellmour's actions are seen as following
limited and pre-set patterns that are prescribed either by Vainlove
(in the case of Laetitia) or by a comic device (the conventional disguise). The contrast is to some extent analogous to that between
Truewit and Dauphine in *Epicoene*. Truewit's activity is often in-
stigated by Dauphine – though Truewit like Bellmour is beyond
Dauphine's (Vainlove's) control. Dauphine's intrigues which silently
prepare the ground on which most of Truewit's actions are based –
like Vainlove's previous conquests of Silvia and Laetitia – are however presented as shadowy and dangerous. It is Truewit who is the
norm for comic action and comic ethics. When Dauphine demands
Daw's left arm, Truewit attacks him, 'How! Maime a man for ever,
for a jest? what a conscience hast thou?'[14] Dauphine's rejection of
Morose at the end is precisely lacking in conscience and humanity.
Similarly it is Bellmour who, as it were, does the things that comedy
requires, and it is Vainlove who stands outside the fall into marriage.
Bellmour and Belinda, in marrying, come to terms with society, just
as the Mountforts had always done in conventional comedy. Bellmour's marrying an affected woman is less ridiculous than the
marriage of Palamede and the foolish Melantha at the end of Dryden's

*Marriage A-la-Mode*. Vainlove's exclusion from the comic resolution is based on the audience's distaste for his sexual attitudes; his dislike of sex is almost foppish in its niceness. It is only a short step from Vainlove to Sir Nicholas Dainty: 'No, no, Sir, we never bring it to Enjoyment, If we can make a Lady fall in Love with us, or fall into Fits for us, 'tis all the Triumph we desire'.[15] We may suspect that Bellmour's activities are not grand and imaginative but Vainlove, the alternative, is seen as abnormally obsessive. Bellmour may be the rake who has capitulated to the demands of society rather than maintaining a detached stance, but the detachment, while giving the rake philosophical superiority, is in Vainlove's case also impotent and frustrated.

Congreve's method depends on the juxtaposition and contrast of seemingly unconnected characters. While Bellmour and Vainlove offer two different approaches to the activity of the rake in society, Heartwell combines the two. Heartwell, 'the old batchelour' himself, was played by Betterton. It was probable that Betterton would take a role in such an important production, but the choice of role is significant. Betterton does not play one of the young rakes; instead, older than Powell or Williams, he stands as a warning of what a rake becomes. Heartwell is a superannuated rake and, as such, he becomes gullible. His perception of everything, including himself, is soured by rakish egocentricity, now turned into vanity in isolation. Betterton, the actor of the great rakes of twenty years earlier – that is, of the time when Heartwell was young – is appropriate to Heartwell as a figure of fun. This is the first time that the aging Betterton takes a role in comedy that is his own age and the effect is to direct the audience's attention to Betterton himself. The comic convention is soured by Betterton as the comic Heartwell.

But, while Betterton the rake is mocked, Betterton the great tragedian is also necessary for the understanding of Heartwell's self-dramatising posturing, the libertine's pose rendered ridiculous. Heartwell, like Prince Volscius in *The Rehearsal*, who is also a parody of Bettertonian tragic roles, makes of his feet an emblem of his indecision: 'Well, why do you not move? Feet do your Office – Not one Inch; no, Foregod I'me caught –' (p. 20). This posturing is emphasised by a deliberate fracture of the dramatic illusion. Heartwell, married, soliloquises in rhyme and Bellmour points it out directly, 'Now *George*, What Rhyming! I thought the Chimes of Verse were past, when once the doleful Marriage-knell was rung.' (p. 52) The verse is not a dramatic device, a convention of theatrical practice, but an attempt by Heartwell to give his meditations an authority that quasi-heroic verse would provide. He really is talking in rhyme. But Heartwell's personal tragedy, as he sees it, or posturing, as the audience sees it, is undercut in turn by the brutishness of his misanthropy. His primitive obsession with appetite, itself characteristic of Betterton in comedy (Dorimant, for example), links Heartwell to the apotheosis of free appetite, Shadwell's Don John in *The Libertine*, another famous Betterton role, possibly revived as recently as 1692. Heartwell is not simply the misanthrope, the man jeering at the society from which he is excluded and from which he excludes himself, he is also an indication of the direction in which Vainlove's attitudes might lead him. In exploring his own revulsion, Heartwell eventually acts energetically in a way that Vainlove finds himself incapable of doing – hence the link to Bellmour the active rake – but the actions themselves are motivated by premises that characterise Vainlove's sexual indigestion, a physiological disorder that approaches a Jonsonian humour. In effect, the presence of Betterton in the title-role emphasises the play's concentration on the future, the permanent irresolution of Vainlove against the future accommodation of Bellmour. This is not the young viewing the old as fools but as themselves grown old.

Gerald Weales suggested that, in Vainlove, 'Congreve has touched on something more complicated than the stereotypical surface of his play allows.'[16] But it should already be clear that the play is not simply bland. Vainlove is a problem in the play but not an isolated one. Instead the play explores its difference from the stereotypical presentation of twin pairs of lovers, from the expected performance of Betterton, and also queries the ease with which conventional resolutions can be achieved. Congreve chooses the most difficult route to the solution of his 'fable'. He confronts comic vitality with some of its own darker aspects; he confronts the promiscuous and active rake with his detached and cynical self. Yet the end still moves further towards an integrated acceptance of social norms than the presence of Vainlove would lead one to expect.

The continual reflection and distortion of concepts of behaviour that is the basis of this movement is achieved through a distinctive use of the stage. The action of *The Old Batchelour* is firmly placed within the stage world. Characters are continually emphasised through their stage movements. Entrances and exits, presence and absence become more important than the scenic background. Parallels of place are less significant than parallels of action. Acts IV and V both open with Bellmour entering in his disguise accompanied by Setter. It is not the repetition of place that provides the theatrical structure but the repetition of the action. The place of the scene frequently seems arbitrary, particularly in the street scenes, but the juxtaposition and repetition never is. The play is a continuous whole unfolding on the stage, not in an imaginary London.

Act I concentrates on the men. It opens with the two gallants, the peaks of the socio-comic scale, and ends with a glimpse of Bluffe and Wittol, the two fools. The audience moves from witty rakishness to foolery. Hence, there is no hint of anything unnatural about Vainlove's behaviour until others are introduced. It is only late in the act that we are dubious about some of Vainlove's early statements: for example, when he told Bellmour 'my Temper quits an Amour, just where thine takes it up' (pp. 2–3). At the time the phrase seems innocuous. The decline in the status of the new male characters parallels precisely the decline in our approval of Vainlove's activities; the sequence of the comic form is the development of its own doubts about Vainlove as its 'hero'. The process of decline is extended right through the play: Wittol and Bluffe are seen properly in Act II; Setter, the next rung down the socio-comic ladder, a servant, appears in Act III; the final fool, a citizen, merchant fool, Fondlewife appears in Act IV. For the 'normal' conventional rake like Bellmour, the introduction of the fools marks the difference between him and them, the ever-increasing gap between the cultural verve and comic expertise of the wit and the ineptness in both spheres of the fool. For Vainlove, the fools are connected to the 'wit'; the moral, social and comic vulnerability of Vainlove's modes of action becomes more, not less, marked. Bellmour and Vainlove, opening the play together as equal friends, diverge as Vainlove's position increasingly converges with that of the fools.

The opening conversation invites an audience to identify the two as different aspects of the rake and indicates in Vainlove an elegant boredom. He is as much a contriver, and as malicious about his friends as a Dorimant. But in the course of the play he actually contrives very little. His actions as a successful rake, his seductions in particular, predate the play itself. It is Bellmour whose actions are shown. Where Vainlove does act, for instance over the forged letter, he acts wrongly. Bellmour too risks failure but his escape is through comic wit, a wit that can reconcile his promiscuity with his marriage, a wit that accepts the nature of the comedy itself.

Bellmour's soliloquy leads to the introduction of Sharper and

Heartwell. Sharper and Bellmour are clearly connected. Much as Bellmour is shown to be parasitical on Vainlove for his sexual activities, so Sharper is dependent on Bellmour for his financial ones. Bellmour, as Spintext, disguises himself as Vainlove; Sharper disguises himself as Bellmour. Both choose prey where success is assured. Just as this dialogue unites Sharper and Bellmour, so the introduction of Heartwell links him with Vainlove. Vainlove and Heartwell share an egocentricity that pushes them to a mock-tragic isolation. Both share a love-hate attitude to women. Congreve makes the latter evident through a verbal link. Vainlove, according to Bellmour, 'says I do the drudgery in the Mine' (p. 5), while for Heartwell, sex is a misery that lovers must undergo in the pursuit: 'Dressing, Dancing, Singing, Sighing, Whining, Rhyming, Flattering, Lying, Grinning, Cringing, and the drudgery of loving to boot' (p. 6). For both, sex is 'drudgery'; for both marriage is a dreadful prospect; for both independence comes to mean intransigence.

Act II provides a contrast between Bellmour (the rake-lover) and Sharper (the rake-trickster). When Vainlove does appear he is curiously quiet (pp. 16–18). But more important the act introduces the women and sets up an identical sequence of descent to that of the men, from Araminta and Belinda, through Silvia and Laetitia, from ladies to whores to cuckolders. This is not an ethical sequence – there is nothing vicious about Laetitia – but it is a social decline so closely parallel with the men as to interconnect in the sequence. Silvia, like Mrs Loveit in *The Man of Mode*, substitutes the fool for the rake and so emphasises their similarities. She and Lucy even replace one for the other in dialogue:

*Silvia* Whom mean you?
*Lucy* Whom you should mean, *Heartwell*.
*Silvia* Senseless Creature, I meant my *Vainlove*. (p. 19)

Heartwell's ridiculous debate with himself leads him to Silvia and immediately Vainlove's relationship with Araminta is juxtaposed as a ridiculous enigma:

*Vainlove* ... but I would –
*Bellmour* Marry her without her Consent; thour't a Riddle beyond Woman.
(p. 21).

The first appearance of Araminta and Belinda, the serious and the affected, comes immediately after the departure of the fools Bluffe and Wittol. Belinda's affectation is made all the stronger by the juxtaposition. Belinda's manner, her refusal to say what she means, the falseness of her public presentation of herself are closely analogous to Bluffe. But this is offset by her beauty and genuine wit: she is evidently Bellmour's match. There is a clear link to *Marriage A-la-Mode*. Melantha was one of Mrs Mountfort's greatest roles; Cibber used her performance to define her brilliance as an actress.[17] Melantha and Belinda, linked through Mrs Mountfort, are both women who indulge in their affectation. The social mask is however no longer a direct equivalent of foolishness, a distinction that becomes of increasing importance in Congreve's work.

By comparison with Bellmour and Belinda, Vainlove is at the mercy of Araminta's wit. He is barely able to complete a sentence when she is present (e.g. p. 17). Away from her, he becomes more of a fool than a lover. It is a contrast that is immediately enlarged on in the next act, in Heartwell's actions with Silvia. When confronted by love and a woman, rakes like Heartwell and Vainlove demonstrate that both action and inaction are equally liable to error. The false perception of the rake himself is the root of the mistake.

By this stage in the play, the two processes of the sequence are clear: on the one hand juxtaposition links disparate characters (Vainlove and Heartwell or Araminta and Silvia in their pursuit of Vainlove); on the other is the substitution of one character for another (Bellmour for Vainlove and Sharper for Bellmour). In Act IV, the two devices are used to the detriment of both the juxtaposed and the substitutors. Vainlove is revealed to be as imperceptive as Fondlewife and Bellmour is revealed as a failed intriguer.

No sooner has Laetitia persuaded Fondlewife to leave than Vainlove is tricked by the false letter from Silvia. That link has already been prepared for by the scene between Silvia and Heartwell in Act III. Again Heartwell mediates between Vainlove and the audience. Heartwell is deceived by Silvia; Vainlove will be deceived by her. Even before Vainlove is compared to Fondlewife, the fool has been linked to Heartwell. Heartwell sees money as a means of valuing love ('This buys all the 'tother – And this thou shalt have; this, and all that I am worth for the purchase of thy Love –' (p. 27)) and Fondlewife does the same ('I profess I do love thee better, than 500 Pound –' (p. 31)). Far from being just an outsider in the comic structure, Heartwell is the vital term in the sequence to prepare the audience's perception of Vainlove.

At the crucial moment, Vainlove has to choose between Araminta's social expertise and the evidence of the forged letter. It is precisely the combination of these two that places Vainlove in an impossible position. In the end his choice of action is based on a choice between his senses: 'Did I dream? Or do I dream? Shall I believe my Eyes, or Ears?' (p. 38). Vainlove decides to trust his eyes and is wrong. In the immediately following scene Fondlewife is caught in the identical dilemma, chooses to believe his ears (Laetitia's explanation) and is also wrong. Each is confronted by a situation in which the problem is caused by substitution (Silvia as Araminta in the letter; Bellmour as Spintext) and each reveals himself incapable of seeing through any but the simplest ruse. Vainlove had begun the play the equal of Bellmour. Now he can be compared with Fondlewife.

It is then the sequence that defines the true nature of the social intransigence of Heartwell and Vainlove. Their failure of social perception produces disruptions in what would otherwise be a simple comic resolution. As it is, neither can Bellmour and Vainlove both marry nor can Heartwell's ambiguous status (rake and fool) be fully resolved. Unlike the normal comic dupe Heartwell gets *un*married; unlike the normal pair of comic heroes, Bellmour marries and Vainlove does not. The comic form that the play revives is in the end ironically but inevitably inconclusive for both Heartwell and Vainlove.

The techniques that Congreve begins to develop in *The Old Batchelour* are the foundation of his dramatic method. They have a fluency and an elegance that is even more characteristically Congreve's than his prose style. But in this play, the movement of meaning is accomplished primarily through the unit of the scene. The juxtaposition of Fondlewife and Vainlove as two forms of imperception is accomplished through a change of place from the street to Fondlewife's house. The connection is achieved across the change of scenery. The scene is thus a theatrical unit marked visually by changing scenery. It is not the fictive place but the theatrical location, the stage itself, that changes.

There is one final device in the play that Congreve begins to use here but which becomes of greater importance in his later comedies. Bellmour's actions, his pursuit of Laetitia in particular, are seen by the end of the play to be curiously pointless. The play's action does little to move Bellmour and Belinda closer together. Although their agreement to marry is a contrast to the impasse between Vainlove and Araminta or to the failed marriage of Heartwell and Silvia, the action from their point of view is not that of a comedy of love and courtship at all. Belinda agrees to marriage in an offhand way:

O my Conscience, I cou'd find in my Heart to marry thee, purely to be rid of thee. – At least, Thou art so troublesome a Lover, there's Hopes thou'lt make a more than ordinary quiet Husband. (p. 50)

The statement is partly the result of her affected manner and as such is an anticipation of Millamant's affectation of pettish acquiescence. But Belinda's remarks on courtship and marriage emphasise the status of their marriage as an inevitable device, a part of the comedy in which they find themselves performing:

Bellmour . . . Alas! Courtship to Marriage, is but as the Musick in the Play-
house, till the Curtain's drawn; but that once up, then opens the
Scene of Pleasure.
Belinda Oh, foh, – no: Rather, Courtship to Marriage, as a very witty
Prologue to a very dull Play. (p. 51)

The plot of the play is thus for them an irrelevance, an accident that is a necessary theatrical part but that is subordinate to the play as design, a dance of characters on and off and around the stage.

In casting *The Double-Dealer*, Congreve used many of the players who were so successful in *The Old Batchelour*. Of the eleven parts in *The Double-Dealer*, nine were played by actors who had appeared in *The Old Batchelour*. This is a far higher proportion than one would normally expect. Durfey's *The Marriage-Hater Match'd* uses seventeen actors of whom only eight reappear in *The Richmond Heiress*; only five of the actors in *The Wives Excuse* also acted in *The Maid's Last Prayer*. Congreve's consistency is surprising. Either Congreve cast in this way to indicate a similar attitude towards the characters or he is placing the cast inside a different structure, using some of the conventional background of the casting.

Congreve brought into the cast only two actors, Kynaston and Bowman. Bowman was usually cast as the rather pompous noble fop, roles like Lord Brainless in Durfey's *The Marriage-Hater Match'd* (1692), Sir Fopling Flutter in the revival in 1692 and Sir Nicholas Dainty in *The Volunteers* (1693). There had been no such part in *The Old Batchelour* but Bowman was the inevitable choice for Lord Froth. Bowman, placed in the company of Powell and Mrs Mountfort as Brisk and Lady Froth, provides an important clue to the play's design.

The characters of *The Double-Dealer* are arranged in a series of comparable triangles of adultery. At the top are the Touchwoods and Maskwell; next come the Plyants and Careless and finally the Froths and Brisk. Mellefont and Cynthia alone stand apart from this pattern. The triangles are closely parallel and the design of the play weaves them together. They constitute a hierarchical structure of dramatic form, from the evil and tragic-melodramatic mode at the top to the near-farce of the Froths. In each case, the husband is deluded by a simple device. The resolution of the entire play however is dependent on one of the husbands, Lord Touchwood, accidentally breaking the pattern and seeing his own mistake. The structure encourages the audience to connect different characters in a moral pattern. Brisk as a cuckolder is thus linked to Careless and Maskwell, Lady Froth to Lady Plyant and Lady Touchwood. Gosse commented, on the presence of Powell and Mrs Mountfort, that 'This particular combination, as well as Brisk's successful seduction, obviously gives more weight to the comic action than if the parts had been played by Mrs Bowman and Bowen.'[18] But the impact of their presence is far greater. Bellmour and Belinda had appeared successful and sympathetic when placed next to Vainlove. *The Old Batchelour* underplayed moral judgement – none of the opprobrium that is normally attached to a cuckolder in the 1690s is given to Bellmour. But *The Double-Dealer* is not a witty comedy. It is a highly moral comedy which explores a conflict, not between true wit and false wit (where the result had always been a foregone conclusion) but between good and evil, between a hero and heroine whose goodness makes them trusting and gullible and antagonists who are frequently indentified as monsters, villains and devils. Loveable and amusing though the fopperies of Brisk and the Froths are, Congreve makes it clear that their own little adulterous triangle leads directly towards treachery, incest and powerful evil. The fops' refusal to concern themselves with problems of morality, their choice of a frothy world of amorality is itself seen as a choice that permits evil. The audience which views their antics as inconsequential additions to the main plot fails to understand the singleness of the plot that Congreve emphasised in the dedication.

In such an intensely moral play, the analogy of fop-seducer and rake-seducer is likely to appear stronger. In fact, Brisk is less of a fop than a degraded rake-hero, as Powell's acting must have demonstrated. Powell is in this period so strongly associated with rake-hero roles that to cast him as Brisk is to bring Brisk and Careless (Verbruggen) close together. We are encouraged to ignore what Brisk says and instead to watch what he does. Unlike most fops, Brisk is successful in his seduction plot. Lady Froth as played by

Mrs Mountfort must have been more attractive than Lady Plyant (Mrs Leigh), who is seduced by the far more dashing figure of Careless. Further, Brisk's affair uses one of the rake-hero's greatest devices, the transposition of wooing into dancing (p. 53) which recalls Hippolita and Gerrard in Wycherley's *The Gentleman Dancing-Master*. While Gerrard is a rake made a fool by Hippolita, Brisk is a fool made a rake by the casting. As Gosse has shown, fools and villains do not come into contact until Act IV[19] but, while Gosse's analysis of the discreteness of the individual segments of the play is accurate, the compartmentalised groups of characters are deliberately transcended and undercut by the casting. The interconnections define some of the ways in which evil and folly combine.

Powell as Brisk is paralleled by Verbruggen as Careless. Verbruggen plays roughly the same type of secondary rake figure as Sharper, his part in *The Old Batchelour*, but Verbruggen was increasingly challenging Powell and Williams as Betterton's heir-apparent. Careless is, like Bellmour, a rake who enjoys his multiple affairs but, unlike Bellmour, he is kept apart from marriage. The seducer is clearly disqualified from marriage in the play. Love and adultery are incompatible, a complete reversal of the structures of *The Old Batchelour*. Careless's seduction of Lady Plyant is a rather pointless exercise. Lady Plyant is 'handsome, and knows it' (p. 5) but Mellefont does not actually advocate adultery – though he is close to it. Brisk, the foppish-rake, makes love to Lady Froth for his own self-esteem; Careless, the cynic-rake, makes love to Lady Plyant for his own amusement.

The third adulterer is the arch-villain Maskwell. Maskwell, as the rake who delights in his own brilliance, makes love to Lady Touchwood for his own self-advancement. In some respects, it is only a fairly short step from the manoeuvres and cunning of Horner to the actions of Maskwell. Maskwell's villainy is defined partly by his aims but also by the manner in which his actions are achieved. Horner at least pursues women for his own sexual satisfaction; for Maskwell, sex is, like marriage, a route to wealth and power. Even Horner manages to be sorry for Harcourt ('Poor *Harcourt* I am sorry thou hast mist her –'[20]) but Maskwell plots against Mellefont directly. Evil in this play has a tragic intensity; Maskwell, played by Betterton, mediates between the glory of successful cunning and the tragic villainy of, say, Shadwell's Don John. He is linked directly with the angel-devil ambiguity of Dorimant but with the balance tipped further towards the devil; he exercises on the audience a fascination

like Dorimant's or Iago's early in *Othello*, appealing to an enjoyment of cunning for its own sake that the play has to place, reject
and defeat both morally and theatrically.

Mrs Barry must have raised Lady Touchwood's rantings into
tragic passion. Imagine Mrs Barry handling speeches like the
following and the result is high Restoration tragedy:

Death, do you dally with my Passion? Insolent Devil! But have a care, –
provoke me not; For, by the Eternal Fire, you shall not scape my
Vengeance.  (p. 10)

The excess of this style is not comic but instead fractures the conventional limits of comic style, as Congreve plainly indicated in his
choice of motto, 'Interdum tamen, & vocem Comoedia tollit'.[21]
The tragic tone of Lady Touchwood is not in itself parodic; the
parody present in the play lies elsewhere. Lady Plyant's rhetoric, for
instance, her torrents of language, unconsciously mock Lady Touchwood and both Plyants produce quasi-tragic imprecations, especially
whenever their actions are influenced by a plot of Maskwell's:

*Lady Plyant*  Inhuman and Treacherous.
*Sir Paul*    Thou Serpent and first Tempter of Womankind. –  (p. 20)

For all this, it is the effect of the introduction of Kynaston into the
cast that is most striking. Betterton, Powell and Verbruggen constitute three variations on the theme of the rake-seducer. Mrs Barry,
Mrs Leigh and Mrs Mountfort are three versions of the promiscuous
woman. In each case the connection of the three players is unsur-
prising. But Kynaston is placed in the analogous position to Dogget
and Bowman. Throughout this period, Kynaston had an august
reputation for noble and dignified parts. Cibber's description reflects
this majestic manner perfectly, 'He had a piercing Eye, and in
Characters of heroick Life a quick imperious Vivacity in his Tone
of Voice . . . he had a fierce, Lion-like Majesty in his Port and Utter-
ance.'[22] Lord Touchwood, however, moves towards this majesty only
at the end of the play; Kynaston is displayed elsewhere as something
like a cuckold and a fool. Of seventy-three roles Kynaston is known
to have played from 1660 to 1700 – from Madam Epicoene as a boy
actor onwards – Lord Touchwood is the only cuckold he acted in
comedy.

Lord Touchwood is not therefore an ordinary cuckold. Neither
a foolish cit like Fondlewife and his predecessors nor a foolish lord

like Sir Davy Dunce in Otway's *The Soldier's Fortune* (1681) or Sir Thomas Credulous in Crowne's *The English Frier* (1690), he is something totally new, a cuckold with stature and dignity who believes the lies of the villain because of Maskwell's cunning, not his own stupidity. Congreve's warning to the reader about Mellefont applies equally well to Lord Touchwood: 'If this Man be deceived by the Treachery of the other; must he of necessity commence Fool immediately, only because the other has proved a Villain?' (A4b) Like Careless, Lord Touchwood 'never knew *Maskwell* guilty of any Villainy'. Before mocking Lord Touchwood's gullibility, we should remember Congreve's own advice: 'I would have 'em again look into the Character of *Maskwell*, before they accuse any Body of weakness for being deceiv'd by him. For upon the enquiry into this Objection, [I] find they have only mistaken Cunning in one Character, for Folly in another' (A4b).

The casting of Kynaston as Lord Touchwood should then eliminate any doubts we might entertain about the essential seriousness of the character. He is much more serious even than Chremes in Terence's *Heautontimorumenos*, referred to in the play's motto.

Again, as with Mrs Barry's rant, Lord Touchwood is mocked by the parallel with Sir Paul Plyant and Lord Froth. But the venom of the one character and the dignity of the other, as well as the serious form of the play's resolution, reinvests the two stock characters with new significance. Mrs Loveit, another role of Mrs Barry, becomes the much more dangerous and evil threat of Lady Touchwood. Lord Touchwood is like a Sir Jaspar Fidget who triumphs and defeats his adulterous wife and her lover. Lord Touchwood is as far from the conventional form as Kynaston's style of acting was from Dogget's as Sir Paul.

My concentration so far on the three triangles has, I hope, indicated how isolated Mellefont and Cynthia are in the play. Their terrified contemplation of the future stems in part from the examples of marriage that they see around them; as Cynthia wonders, 'I'm thinking, that tho' Marriage makes Man and Wife One Flesh, it leaves 'em still Two Fools . . . I have known Two Wits meet, and by the opposition of their Wits, render themselves as ridiculous as Fools' (p. 18). But they are also shown alone, unsure and vulnerable. Their intended marriage is threatened by something other than themselves. It had been one of the great achievements of Restoration comedy to suggest that marriage was not automatically a success once the blocking characters had been overcome. But *The Double-*

*Dealer* reverses this process. Mellefont can fail but still win. He does not have to prove himself but merely that the opposing characters are greater than he could hope to beat. The hero no longer has to be superhuman himself and also brilliantly clever. To justify his own failure and passivity, Mellefont has only to show that the others are 'heroic' in that way. Maskwell's rakish expertise is the source of Mellefont's success.

| | |
|---|---|
| *Cynthia* | Well, if the Devil should assist her, and your Plot miscarry. – |
| *Mellefont* | Ay, what am I to trust to then? |
| *Cynthia* | Why if you give me very clear demonstration that it was the Devil, I'll allow for irresistable odds.  (p. 44) |

Maskwell throughout the play is defined as 'villain/monster/ devil'. He is the 'irresistable odds', the rake-villain that the hero cannot conquer. Thus, though Williams and Bracegirdle, as Mellefont and Cynthia, are placed in a central serious role as they were in *The Old Batchelour*, the change in the structure of the play now isolates them from the entire company. It is no longer the curious psychology of a Vainlove that threatens to stop the wedding.

*The Double-Dealer* establishes an initial arrangement of characters that is drastically altered as the juxtapositions and parallels of the design become clear: a cuckold can be respected; a rake and a fop can become closely identified. These revaluations of the characters are achieved through an application of moral standards to the play's revelation of character. The emotional affective aspects of the play are offered to the audience as temptations, blandishments to dissuade them from the moral analysis of action and character. In the same way, folly is treated with Jonsonian severity: only to laugh at folly and not to condemn it is to acquiesce in its connection with evil. Folly, once accepted, enables evil to occur. The dedication emphasised the play's unity of action; a danger at one end of the chain, such as the foolishness of Lady Plyant, can lead to a disaster at the other, like the disinheriting of Mellefont.

Congreve is obsessively careful about the other unities as well. Again and again characters refer to the clock; they emphasise that the time of the action is 'from Five a Clock to Eight in the Evening' (a4b), extending almost exactly over the time of the performance. Tuke's *The Adventures of Five Hours* (1663) is similarly strict[23] but such stringency in the Unity of Time is rarely even approximated to elsewhere in the Restoration. This produces in the play an incredible claustrophobic intensity. To the audience it appears like a balancing-

trick: can the plot be fitted into three hours without seeming ludi-
crously over-compressed? can the unity of time prove the reality of
the play? The intention of the unity of action was to increase a play's
*vraisemblance* but this effect is possible only through its implicit
observation. Placed in a naturalistic frame of after-dinner events,
the over-emphasis on time becomes super-real. Time simply does
not function so prominently as a set of deadlines in the world of observed experience to which a play lays claim to providing an analogy.
As Anne Barton argues, 'The action acquires an hallucinatory
quality . . . Certainly, the clock which rules the comedy is not that
of a normal, or waking, world.'[24] The dream-world is more than
real; it belongs with an excessive naturalism, not a formalised
representation of it.

This tension of the real and the formal, analogous to that between
comedy and tragedy in the triangles of the roles, is also true of
Congreve's treatment of place. The scene is 'A Gallery in the Lord
*Touchwood*'s House' (a4b). The heading to the first scene adds 'with
Chambers adjoining' (p. 1), but the set is constant for all but one
scene, which takes place in a single adjoining chamber, Lady Touchwood's closet. Although we hear of other places, like the garden or
the dining-room, almost all we see is the gallery itself. The effect is
to emphasise place but to show it as an artificial limbo: it is real and
unreal at the same time. The single location also gives the play a
sense of claustrophobia. No previous Restoration comedy had
stayed so firmly in one place, had excluded the outside world so
completely. We cannot even be sure whether we are in London or
near St Alban's. Instead we are offered, not a view of 'the Town'
but an analysis of a structured group in a closed environment, almost
under laboratory conditions.

To put on stage a single place, to treat the theatrical space as susceptible to an unalterable *vraisemblable*, results in an inverse of the
expected result. The single place seems both real and theatrical.
It is matched by the play's emphasis on its own fictional world. The
play is introverted, rarely acknowledging the audience, even by a
sidelong glance. It has, for example, comparatively few asides.
Congreve uses the dedication to justify soliloquies in terms of a real
action rather than as a theatrical convention: 'We ought not to
imagine that this Man either talks to us, or to himself; he is only
thinking . . .' (A4a). Yet *The Double-Dealer* has a disproportionately
large number of soliloquies for a comedy and is curiously 'stagey'
in its use of them, placing them carefully at such emphatic stage

moments as Maskwell's self-revelation at the end of Act II or Melle-font's doubts at the end of Act IV.

The set has a further effect on the play. The pressures of location become so strong that it becomes either romantic or foolhardy to want to escape from the gallery. Mellefont's plan of elopement is a foredoomed ideal, based on the idea that the closed world can be avoided, can be escaped. He must instead wait until the flow of characters over the stage happens to produce the arbitrary oppor-tune combination necessary to destroy the plotters.

In the course of the play a tension grows between the movement and development of the plots and the movement of characters. Plots begin to seem over-complex and also irrelevant, present and absent at the same time, in exactly the same way that Congreve treats time and space. Anne Barton comments that 'Maskwell's schemes are far too intricate for the three hour space in which they unfold'.[25] But this intricacy is achieved partly by their planned irrelevancy. Maskwell's first plot that almost completely occupies the action of the first three acts, is, on his own admission, nothing more than a delaying tactic, a stop-gap:

*Lady Touchwood*  But I don't see what you can propose from such a tri-
          fling design . . .
*Maskwell*      I know it. – I don't depend upon it. – But it will prepare
          some thing else; and gain us leasure to lay a stronger
          Plot . . .   (p. 13)

Mellefont realises this as well – though of course he is wrong in his identification of the originator – 'yet this was but a shallow artifice, unworthy of my Matchiavellian Aunt: There must be more behind' (p. 23). The enigma lies in Congreve's choice of this 'shallow arti-fice', his insistence upon making the audience concentrate for so long upon 'the first flash, the priming of her Engine' (p. 23). The audience waits on Maskwell's leisure.

This is one of a number of theatrical gestures in the play. There is for example the scene in Lady Touchwood's closet. The discovery scene ('*SCENE* opening, shews Lady *Touchwood*'s Chamber' p. 59) has an intense theatricality; there is an excessive amount of hiding, locking of doors, play-acting (especially by Lady Touchwood), all of which connect with the basic style of Maskwell. Maskwell himself sees his plots as a kind of game in which he is actor and liar (the double sense of hypocrite), relishing his own performance.

The moral dimensions of the play are charted through the process of juxtaposition. Thus, for instance, Lord Touchwood, Sir Paul Plyant and Lord Froth all make their first appearance together, escorted by Brisk who has already appeared on stage. Act III is constructed around the three triangles in turn and in order, the Touchwoods (pp. 26–30), the Plyants (pp. 34–8) and the Froths (pp. 39–42), with Mellefont and Cynthia providing bridge-passages. The similar events are placed together, such as the gulling of Lord Touchwood next to the gulling of Sir Paul. When Maskwell arranges to be overheard by Lord Touchwood (p. 64), the moment parallels the overhearing planned just previously (p. 62) and anticipates its own reversal when Lord Touchwood and Cynthia accidentally over-hear Maskwell and Lady Touchwood (p. 73).

In *The Old Batchelour*, the action of the play depends on substitu-tion. In *The Double-Dealer*, Maskwell conspicuously uses substitution as his own device for the re-ordering of society. It is only to defend himself that Mellefont places Careless among the Plyants, sub-stituting Careless for himself; at the end of the play, Maskwell is finally beaten by Mellefont's substituting himself for Saygrace. Maskwell seeks throughout the play to replace and reverse the places occupied by Mellefont and himself: Maskwell will marry Cynthia and inherit the Touchwood estate; Mellefont will be thought to have seduced Lady Touchwood. Maskwell uses the pretence of this seduction as if it were fact, just as he uses telling the truth as a lie. It is still substitution.

This stage-managing by Maskwell extends throughout the play, including the discovery scene. Towards the end, he produces Mr Saygrace out of a chamber, conveniently at hand for the purpose. It is of course 'realistic' that the household should contain a chaplain and that Maskwell should have already suborned him but the manner of his appearance is part of a theatricality that can by this stage in the play be seen as specifically Maskwell's. Saygrace is more an intentionally arbitrary theatrical device than a means for incidental satire on chaplains. Through Saygrace the final attempt at substitu-tion is made.

There is then a contrast between juxtaposition (the method used by Congreve for the presentation of his view of the characters) and substitution (the method used by Maskwell to alter the truth). Maskwell eventually begins to fall because of an accident, Cynthia's meeting with Mellefont (p. 73), two isolated figures coming together at the wrong moment. The device is the final ambiguity of the play's manner. It is both natural that the two should meet by chance in the gallery that they have traversed often enough in the previous three hours, and yet it is clearly a theatrical device to resolve the problem of evil. To the audience it comes as a surprise. The solution to the play does not arise inevitably from the plot; instead it wholly denies the significance of plot. Once Maskwell has been defined as a 'devil', thereby releasing Mellefont from the need to triumph, the plot and the action of the play seem almost irrelevant.

Earlier in the play, Brisk and Lady Froth discussed her 'Heroick Poem' *The Sillibub*:

Lady Froth  . . . and my self; what d'e think I call my self?
Brisk       *Lactilla* may be, – 'gad I cannot tell.
Lady Froth  *Biddy*, that's all; just my own Name.
Brisk       *Biddy*! I'gad very pretty – Deuce take me if your Ladyship has
            not the Art of Surprizing the most Naturally in the World, –
            (p. 17)

Questioned further, Lady Froth proclaimed her deep knowledge of neo-classical orthodox criticism:

Brisk       I presume your Ladyship has read *Bossu*?
Lady Froth  O yes, and *Rapine*, and *Dacier* upon *Aristotle* and *Horace*.   (p. 17)

Lady Froth's learning is a commentary on the whole play's classical form. Her 'Surprizing' is as natural and as easy as the end of *The Double-Dealer* itself. The end of the play is not implicit in its observance of the unities; its accidents are too coincidental to be acceptable within the strict canons of neo-classical form. This is the final stage of the play's mocking abandonment of ordered, necessary plot. With evil only narrowly defeated there can be no triumphant wedding. The bizarre ending abruptly interrupts the play.

The emphatic realism of the observance of the unities produces a curious theatricality. As the drama of plot gives way to a drama of character, the theatricality points back to the world. The audience, surprised, has to reconcile its perceptions of the play with its knowledge of the society it claims to depict. Collier was not entirely wrong in his comments – he recognised that *The Double-Dealer* criticises society directly: 'There are but *Four* Ladys in this *Play*, and *Three* of the biggest of them are Whores. A Great Compliment to Quality to tell them there is not above a quarter of them Honest!'[26]

*Love for Love* was completed in 1694 and originally scheduled for production by the United company. After the secession of Betterton,

Congreve withdrew his play from the patentees and Betterton's company opened their first season with it in the hastily refitted Lincoln's Inn Fields Theatre on 30 April 1695. However, before the season opened, Joseph Williams and Susanna Mountfort left the secessionists after an argument about pay and status. In the prologue to *Love for Love*, 'Spoken at the opening of the New House', Congreve mentions the departure of these two back to Drury Lane:

> But since in *Paradise* frail Flesh gave way,
> And when but two were made, both went astray;
> Forbear your Wonder, and the Fault forgive,
> If in our larger Family we grieve
> One falling *Adam*, and one tempted *Eve*.                    (a2b)

The passage is one of the best indications in the period of how much the audience must have known about the theatrical personalities in the company. The prologue does not identify Adam and Eve and assumes that the audience will make the connection with Williams and Mrs Mountfort.

One effect of the secession and the change in the company acting *Love for Love* may have been a change in the final cast for the play. Taylor, in his biography of Congreve, suggested that Congreve had already cast Williams as Valentine and that Betterton took the part, even though he was originally intended to play Sir Sampson and was 'rather too old, short, and heavy to be Valentine'.[27] The suggestion is repeated as an established fact by Gareth Lloyd Evans:

[Congreve's] apparent lack of sensitivity about Betterton and Valentine is, of course, simply explained by the fact that Betterton was originally set down to play Sir Sampson ... The immaculate theorem of Congreve's sensitivity to creating the part for the actor is continued when we recall that Joseph Williams was originally set down to play Valentine ...[28]

But there is no firm evidence for such an intention and the idea does not even occur to E. L. Avery in his careful study of the play's stage history.[29] Nonetheless, as a conjecture, it still deserves careful consideration.

Had Williams stayed with the secessionists, he would have been the only young actor available to play roles like Valentine, since Powell had stayed at Drury Lane. The Lincoln's Inn Fields' company was extremely short of young male leading actors. Scandal was played by Smith who was brought out of retirement for the part. There was, of course, nothing essentially ridiculous about Betterton playing Valentine; he was a great success in the role and chose the part for his final farewell performance, at the age of seventy-four, in 1709. Though Taylor and Evans are concerned about the inelegance of Betterton's appearance, it had not prevented his having a great career as a young rake-lover, continuing to play such roles in new plays, Polidor in *The Married Beau* (1694), Bellair in *The Lover's Luck* (1696) and Bellamour in *The She Gallants* (1696), to pick three plays close in time to *Love for Love*. Sir Sampson was in fact played by Underhill. Aston complained that Underhill was disastrous in the part: 'he did great Injustice to Sir *Sampson Legend* . . . unless it had been true, that the Knight had been bred a Hog-driver'.[30] But while that record of failure might indicate a change of cast, Cibber was full of praise:

in the blunt Vivacity of Sir *Sampson* . . . he shew'd all that true perverse Spirit that is commonly seen in much Wit and Ill-nature. This Character is one of those few so well written, with so much Wit and Humour, that an Actor must be the grossest Dunce that does not appear with an unusual Life in it: But it will still shew as great a Proportion of Skill to come near *Underhill* in the acting it, which . . . I have not yet seen.[31]

Underhill had also played a domineering father in Durfey's *Love for Money* (1691) as Sir Rowland Rakehell, 'A covetous mercenary vicious swearing atheistical Old Fellow . . . who by cheating an Infant Orphan to whom he was Guardian, possessed an Estate of 3000l. a Year' ($\chi$1a). The title of Durfey's play is specifically recalled by Congreve's.

However successful Betterton and Underhill may have been as Valentine and Sir Sampson, casting Betterton as Valentine reverses the approach to Betterton that Congreve had taken and would take in casting his comedies. Like Heartwell, Maskwell and, eventually, Fainall, Sir Sampson makes the attributes of rakishness perverse and disconcerting. Sir Sampson sees himself as a lusty young man, a sexual athlete with a roving eye. It is precisely this self-deception that enables Angelica to trick him. Like the others, Sir Sampson is offered as an alternative to the comic hero, a darker and more malicious avatar of the libertine – even Heartwell rails furiously and viciously against the young. All four are obsessed with money as a means to love: Heartwell showers Silvia with money (p. 27); Maskwell pursues marriage for an inheritance and an estate; Fainall spends almost all the play chasing wealth. Sir Sampson's values are placed in opposition to Valentine's. Sir Sampson equates love with money: 'Odd,

Madam, I'll love you as long as I live; and leave you a good Jointure when I die' (p. 79), and Angelica picks up the concern with wealth and uses it as imagery to describe sex:

*Angelica* You'll spend your Estate before you come to it.
*Sir Sampson* No, no, only give you a Rent-roll of my Possessions – (p. 79)

Valentine begins the play with this view, believing that he can buy love ('love for money') but he comes to learn a moral code of generosity that leads to exchange ('love for love') and money as well. Betterton's other roles for Congreve are not compatible with such a development of character. Only Heartwell changes and then at the end of the play, a humours character knocked out of his humour. All four men are defeated and ridiculed; all but Heartwell leave before the end. All four can be seen to have indulged in a false use of reason, a false justification of their course of action; all four stand opposed to pure, sincere love and gentlemanly morality.

Even in looking at *The Old Batchelour* and *The Double-Dealer*, the audience must have seen that Congreve cast his plays in ways that drew out connections between them, that fixed actors in particular types of roles. It would seem probable then that the casting was disrupted by the secession and that Betterton had to be moved to another role. I am less sure that there was a part for Mrs Mountfort. Mrs Barry was definitely intended for Mrs Frail and, of course, no one but Anne Bracegirdle could have played Angelica. Mrs Mountfort may have been intended for Mrs Foresight. The part has some of the affectation and coquetry that characterises her roles at that time. But Congreve has begun to take a new attitude towards affectation. It is now a part of Angelica's character, used by her as a defence against the world. This looks forward to Millamant.

Foresight was played by Sandford, not here because of his tragic villain roles, but because of his new line in comedy, commensurate with his age, as crotchety foolish father. He played Sir Thomas Credulous in *The English Frier* (1690) and Sir Lawrence Limber in *The Marriage-Hater Match'd* (1692). He was physically well suited to the role of Foresight: Aston described him as 'Round-shoulder'd, Meagre-fac'd, Spindle-shank'd, Splay-footed, with a sour Countenance and long lean Arms'.[32]

In casting Mrs Barry as Mrs Frail, Congreve used her physical appearance as well. Aston pointed out that 'her Mouth op'ning most on the Right Side, which she strove to draw t'other Way',[33] and an anonymous *Satyr on the Players* implies that this distortion left her face in something of a grimace:

> Tho' Faces are distorted with meer Pain,
> So that wry mouth ne'r since come right again:[34]

Further, another satirist obscenely suggests that Mrs Barry drew attention to the grimace, rather than trying to cover it up:

> With mouth and cunt, though both awry before,
> Her cursed affectation makes 'em more.[35]

That affected wryness was ideal for the part, for instance in the scene of the discovery of her marriage to Tattle: 'O, Sister, the most unlucky Accident! . . . Ah Mr. *Tattle* and I, poor Mr. *Tattle* and I are – I can't speak it out.' (p. 87). But Mrs Barry was also notorious as a whore. *The Satyr on the Players* introduces her:

> There's one, Heav'n bless us! by her cursed Pride
> Thinks from the World her Brutish Lust to hide;
> . . .
> One that is Pox all o're; *Barry* her Name,
> That mercenary Prostituted Dame, . . .[36]

Robert Gould described her in *The Play-House, A Satyr* as

> A ten times cast off *Drab*, a Hackney Whore,
> . . .
> So Insolent! there never was a Dowd
> So very basely born, so very Proud:
> Yet Covetous; She'll Prostitute with any,
> Rather than wave the Getting of a Penny . . .[37]

Tom Brown said, in 1700, that 'Should you lie with her all Night, She would not know you next Morning, unless you had another five Pound at her Service'.[38] When Mrs Frail enters and announces 'Hey day! I shall get a fine Reputation, by coming to see Fellows in a Morning' (p. 14), the audience would recognise that that was precisely what Mrs Barry had done.

Yet for all the accuracy of innuendo there, it is Mrs Foresight whose actions come closest to Mrs Barry's reputation. Scandal, who sleeps with her in the night that passes between Act III and Act IV, questions her about it. She denies all memory at first but, under pressure admits:

*Mrs Foresight*  O yes, now I remember, you were very impertinent and impudent, – and would have come to Bed to me.

*Scandal*    And did not?
*Mrs Foresight* Did not? with that face can you ask the Question?
*Scandal*    This I have heard of before, but never believ'd. I have been
        told she had that admirable quality of forgetting to a man's
        face in the morning, that she had layn with him all night, and
        denying favours with more impudence, than she cou'd grant
        'em. – (p. 63)

This is precisely what Tom Brown was talking about, but it here
refers to Mrs Bowman, not Mrs Barry.

Congreve always cast Mrs Barry as a plotter. Even Laetitia con-
nives and schemes. Mrs Frail's attempts to get a rich husband, her
over-ingenious schemes, make her role the obvious one for Mrs
Barry. But just as Silvia in *The Old Batchelour* had had some of the
tragic intensity appropriate to Mrs Barry's acting under other circumstances, so here Mrs Bowman's role takes over certain of Mrs
Barry's personal characteristics. Mrs Bowman's reputation is pure,
so far as extant satires show. But the two actresses here merge,
through the specificity of the references to Mrs Barry, into a general
condemnation of false, secretive and promiscuous action.

*Love for Love* uses only two locations, Valentine's chamber (Acts I
and IV) and a room in Foresight's house (Acts II, III and V). Valentine's
chamber is no longer the place from which the rake sallies forth to
conquer the world. Instead it is a refuge from a world that is pursuing him for money. The same pattern had been used by Dryden as
early as *The Wild Gallant* (acted 1663) but now, thirty years later, the
device represents the rake in full retreat, not only from the pressures
of his creditors but also from himself. Valentine, unlike Loveby, has
to change dramatically and completely if he is to pass the test and win
Angelica. The libertine is now only a memory, proved true only by
his bills and his bastards. Even while Scandal indulges in rakish
promiscuity, he is juxtaposed with Tattle. Valentine's description of
Scandal's manner applies equally well to Tattle. The rake and the
fop are, like Brisk and Careless, increasingly indistinguishable:

*Angelica* Perswade your Friend, that it is all Affectation.
*Valentine* I shall receive no Benefit from the Opinion: For I know no
        effectual Difference between continued Affectation and Reality.
        (p. 35)

The entire play can be seen as being constructed around the exploration of that difference.

While the hero is vulnerable at home, he is even more so outside of it. Valentine goes to visit Angelica and she is out; he tries to persuade Sir Sampson and fails (though, as he says, it 'at least look'd well on my side' p. 27). Valentine's fall, his final rejection of the ethic by which he had lived, is as usual accomplished in the dupes' world. But that world itself has by then been shown to be more than foolish; it is also inverted, a clear case of the world upside-down, as even Foresight knows,

> When Housewifes all the House forsake,
> And leave good Man to Brew and Bake,
> Withouten Guile, then be it said,
> That House doth stond upon its Head ... (p. 19)

Old men try to be young rakes; women rule the men; the world is topsy-turvey.

The two sets thus provide their own polarity in the play, a theatrical structure of alternates that a play moving conventionally within the genre would seek to reconcile. But *Love for Love* in the end rejects both: the two contrasted worlds are equally unacceptable. It is not surprising, lacking any clear basis of place, that Valentine should not be sure what he ought to be and that Angelica should go through the play like a witty angel, mysterious and impossible to pin down.

But the alternating sets indicate a certain theatricality in the play. Throughout the play a tension is created in the adoption of a convention or device, as a means of hiding the self, of ignoring the truth. Later in the action Tattle and Frail are tricked into marriage by their over-eagerness but also, as it appears on stage, by their willingness to be theatrical and marry in disguise, assuming incorrectly that Valentine's madness and Angelica's compliance represent reality not theatrical affectation. The marriage springs from their own character but also, in its place in the sequence of the play, by their theatricality, their role-playing. Certainly in Mrs Frail's case, that is analogous to Mrs Barry's role-playing off-stage.

The clearest example of this excessive theatricality comes in Act IV. Structurally the scene of Valentine's feigned madness is placed in the corresponding position to the scene between Mellefont and Lady Touchwood played out for Lord Touchwood's benefit. Both are 'scenes' in a double sense, scenes in the play and also scenes acted out to other characters, hypocritical feigning. They are plays within plays, examples of the characters' willingness to take up a role for their own ends. Like the one in *The Double-Dealer*, this scene is emphasised as a scene by the use of the discovery:

*Jeremy* Mr. *Scandal* is with him, Sir; I'll knock at the Door.
　　　　[*Goes to the Scene, which opens and discovers* Valentine *upon a Couch
　　　　disorderly dress'd,* Scandal *by him.* (p. 58)

The discovery is, as I have argued earlier, particularly common in
tragedy. By 1695, it was also part of the increased use of the scenic
stage, the use of scenery as environment, as part of a fictional world,
that was combined with a move away from acting on the forestage.
This can be seen in *Love for Love* in Act II which opens on to '*A Room in
Foresight's House*' with Foresight and his servant discovered (p. 17).
In Act IV, the discovery of a tableau, particularly of someone lying
on a couch, is a direct invocation of the world of Restoration tragedy.
Thus Tate has Lear discovered 'a Sleep on a Couch'.[39] Valentine's
madness is a parody of the vatic mad scenes throughout Restoration
tragedy. The direct satire is coincidental, an indication of the parodic
status of the scene. The madman has no true place in contemporary
comedy. Significantly, the mad-scene in Durfey's *The Richmond Heiress*
(1693) had also had false madmen and used the pretended aberra-
tion as an excuse for satire. The use of the stage in *Love for Love* immediately indicates to the audience that the discovery is a transposition from another mode, from a serious drama. Valentine makes the
device work theatrically but against Angelica it is a complete failure.

The 'performance' shows the extent of the difference between
Mellefont and Valentine at this stage. Mellefont is the naïve victim
of the pretence; Valentine is the victim of his own ingenuity, as
Angelica wilfully misunderstands him. Valentine's failure is marked
by his own misjudgement over the type of 'play' he is in. Increasingly
frustrated by Angelica's actions, he demands abruptly that the disguise, the 'continued affectation' be abandoned even though he has
not indicated that he does love sincerely:

*Valentine* Nay faith, now let us understand one another, Hypocrisie apart, –
　　　　　The Comedy draws toward an end, and let us think of leaving
　　　　　acting, and be our selves; and since you have lov'd me, you must
　　　　　own I have at length deserv'd you shou'd confess it. (p. 72)

But a comedy does not end with the fourth act, nor can this one end
with Valentine still acting. It is the conscious theatricality of his
device that disqualifies him from success at this stage. Angelica's
reluctance to commit herself is confirmed by the way Valentine attempts to force an admission of love. Neither she nor the audience

can be sure exactly what type of rake Betterton is playing. They
cannot be sure that his conversion is genuine, that his love is sincere.

In Act v then, it is the turn of Angelica to use a trick, a stage-
managed manoeuvre, to put Valentine in the position from which he
must make the crucial decision. Although the play has questioned the
validity of the theatrical gesture, Angelica's device is justified both by
her own nature, accepted as virtuous by the audience, and by the
change of tone that accompanies the resolution. There is nothing else
in the play like the language Valentine uses for his generous gesture
of defeat:

*Scandal*   'S'death, you are not mad indeed, to ruine your self?
*Valentine*  I have been disappointed of my only Hope; and he that loses hope
       may part with any thing. I never valu'd Fortune, but as it was sub-
       servient to my Pleasure; and my only Pleasure was to please this
       Lady: I have made many vain Attempts, and find at last, that
       nothing but my Ruine can effect it: Which for that Reason, I will
       sign to – Give me the Paper.   (pp. 89–90)

The passage has an oddly flat quality. There is nothing extravagant
and heroic, nothing theatrical about the statement or the gesture.
Instead it convinces as a demonstration of sincerity and generosity
through a purity of tone which Restoration comedy had usually
managed without. Certainly the speech convinces Angelica absolutely. The contrast with the immediately preceding revelation of Tattle's
marriage to Mrs Frail is sufficient not only to show the audience how
to judge Valentine, but also to convince Scandal. Scandal moves
away from his alignment with Tattle-ish foppery and towards a belief
in sincerity.

The play as it unfolds clearly demonstrates Congreve's use of the
design to chart a changing evaluation of character. The audience
learns how to separate theatrical action from sincere action. The
stage intrigue is associated with affectation and excess – unless it is as
clear as Angelica's. Any excess of plotting now works against the
character. The audience must move from the premises of the casting
to an initial assessment of the relationship of actor to character.
Subsequently, they learn how to see that connection adjusted in the
course of the play. Congreve does not evidence distrust in the theatre
in attacking theatricality and associating it with foolishness. Rather,
he works through it, using it as a means of transcending the convention in order to reconnect the play with the audience's perception of
society. As Valentine learns that dramas have a fifth act, so *Love for
Love* moves through its own classicism of construction. Valentine's

generosity is proved by a repudiation of the intrigue that has brought on his disaster. He resolves the design and plot of the play by abandoning plotting.

On 12 March 1700 Lady Marow wrote to Arthur Kay, comparing two recent visits to the theatre:

I have been at a play 'The Island Princes' which is mighty fine. 'The way of the World', Congreve's new play, doth not answer expectation, there being no plot in it but many witty things to ridicule the Chocolate House, and the fantastical part of the world. [40]

Congreve answered the complaint against failure in the dedication:

That it succeeded on the Stage, was almost beyond my Expectation; for but little of it was prepar'd for that general Taste which seems now to be predominant in the Pallats of our Audience. (A3b)

He had anticipated the complaint about plot in a wry part of the prologue:

> Some Plot we think he has, and some new Thought;
> Some Humour too, no Farce; but that's a Fault. (a2a)

In fact, plot, design, and character intertwine and are unwillingly revealed moment by moment until the form is clear. The play's elegant surface hides an opacity of method that is part of its purpose. The audience has to work for its pleasure.

Most of the cast posed no obvious problem for the audience. Congreve used the patterns that he had established in previous plays and those of other contemporary comedies economically and clearly. Elinor Leigh, praised by Cibber for her 'droll way of dressing the pretty Foibles of superannuated Beauties',[41] was the obvious choice and inspiration for Lady Wishfort. Bowen's experience as Wittol leads to Witwoud. To cast Bowman as Petulant acted somewhat against his line; Petulant is a fool fiercer than those Bowman usually played, though he had played the fairly aggressive Shenkin in *The Richmond Heiress*.

It is with a part like Sir Wilfull Witwoud that Congreve's redrawing of the limits of the stock character, his request for a changing evaluation in the course of the play of an apparently simple figure, can be seen most clearly. Underhill first appears as usual as a boor, then as a drunk but always a fool. Yet through the generosity of Sir Wilfull's actions, Mirabell is able to say of him 'Sir *Wilfull* is my Friend; he has had compassion upon Lovers and generously engag'd a Volunteer in this Action, for our Service' (p. 87) and the audience immediately concurs. A fool, then, is not always a fool.

At her first appearance, brilliant and beautiful though she is, Millamant appears too affected, her view of the world too egocentric, for the audience whole-heartedly to approve. Perhaps she too is a fool. Expecting the radiant virtue of Anne Bracegirdle, the Restoration audience found a role closer to Mrs Mountfort's type, a heroine who appeared more like Belinda than Angelica. As she berates Witwoud for his excess of similes, she starts to make one herself: 'Dear Mr. *Witwoud*, truce with your Similitudes: For I am as sick of 'em –' (p. 26).

There had been two different groups of women in Congreve's comedies. Millamant is not only the last in Anne Bracegirdle's series of roles (Araminta, Cynthia, Angelica), but also the last of Mrs Mountfort's (Belinda, Lady Froth). Congreve now suggests that the two lines come together. Millamant uses her affectation as a defence against a world that the audience already knows from Act I to be complex and almost impenetrable. The heroine, like Cynthia, is no longer automatically granted a full perception of the deviousness of society. She must protect herself not only against the peril of a mistaken affection but also against the suppressed but violent evil that Fainall has begun to demonstrate to the audience. Mrs Mountfort was of course no longer available, but, in any case, Congreve's drama no longer needs her. His play's dialectic has gone beyond the conflicts of witty comedy. Instead he seeks to show the synthesis of true wit and virtue and the connection between false wit and evil. Millamant's affectation is shown to be a mask that she can separate from her essential personality. It is a social disguise, armour against society. Belinda and Araminta are combined in a heroine who is not only elusive and mysterious (Angelica), not merely witty but also the comic and social ethical ideal. Mrs Mountfort's absence leads directly towards the unification of the two types of heroine in the roles for Anne Bracegirdle, Angelica and Millamant.

The audience then must learn how to react to a character; Congreve, like no other dramatist since Wycherley, asks them fundamentally to alter their assessment of a character, their placing of him in a structure of relationships, a structure of morality. Just as they had to learn how to take Vainlove, so they learn about Millamant.

Betterton's previous roles for Congreve had not posed the same problem: it is quickly clear how we are supposed to take Heartwell, Maskwell or Sir Sampson. Even Valentine is not far from this type. But Fainall is different. From the perspective of the end of the play, the audience can see in Mirabell and Fainall a division of the rake-hero into two, good and evil. But the opening minutes of the play show the two men as similar and the later acts only gradually increase the moral distance between them. At the end of Act v, Fainall tries to run his wife through only a few speeches before Mirabell and Millamant dance happily into their future of love, trust and honesty. At the beginning the audience cannot be sure what Betterton is to be. Harriet Hawkins, in her excellent discussion of the play, comments, 'The original casting of the play may have contributed to the confusion between the two characters, since Betterton, who customairly played the hero, played Fainall.'[42] But Betterton was as likely, in Congreve at least, to be a villain or a fool or both. Even his recent success as Valentine only adds to the ambiguity.

The juxtaposition of Betterton with Verbruggen further clouds the issue. The Fainall–Mirabell conflict is a further stage in the theatrical conflict between Betterton and Verbruggen. Verbruggen oscillated between Rich's company and the secessionists for over two years from the division. He finally joined the secessionists only on 1 January 1697. Obviously he was Betterton's rival as the leading male actor in the company and the two frequently acted opposing parts in this period, (Sir John Brute and Constant in *The Provok'd Wife* (1697), Sanserre and Guillamour in Durfey's *The Intrigues at Versailles* (1697) and Beauclair and Wildlove in Mrs Pix's *The Innocent Mistress* (1697)). In Congreve's own *The Mourning Bride*, Almeria (Bracegirdle) is loved by and loves Osmyn (Betterton) who is loved by Zara (Mrs Barry) who is in turn loved by Manuel (Verbruggen). By the end, *The Way of the World* proves to have reversed the places of Verbruggen and Betterton in this pattern, placing Betterton as Fainall at the end of a chain that leads towards Verbruggen and Bracegirdle in the centre.

When confronted by the huge opening dialogue between the two men (pp. 1–8, with minor interruptions), the Restoration audience found it had conflicting experience to call on. It is almost as if the casting is wilfully bland and unhelpful. The audience finds itself in a world that is as confusing as the real one, a world that almost is the real one, where fragments of information give rise to premature judgements, where most of what we want to know is hidden but suggested. Like the audience of *Epicoene*, the audience at *The Way of the World* is divested of its privilege of omniscience. The more it watches the plot, the less it is sure. In the end the audience finds it has known less even than the fools. The play, like reality, poses itself as an enigma to evaluation and perception.

Like *The Double-Dealer*, *The Way of the World* observes the unities, though less strictly. The scene shifts from the Chocolate House to the park, before the final three acts all set at Lady Wishfort's house. The unity of time is observed exactly ('The Time equal to that of the Presentation', a2b) but not pressingly. The effect is of a drama that handles its formal limitations in a more relaxed fashion. While Maskwell's plots seem compressed, the movement of *The Way of the World* is leisurely. Nevertheless the audience does not know where that movement is heading. The audience is given barely enough information to piece it together. The famous passages that seem to alter the direction of the plot are veiled and mysterious, hints of another, hidden drama that for the most part we seem merely to overhear. When Mirabell hints to Mrs Fainall, 'When you are weary of him, you know your Remedy' (p. 24), the audience, uncomfortable because ignorant, is unsure what the 'Remedy' is. The passage joins others in suggesting a delicate problem with oblique and unascertainable solutions.

This mode can be seen in that first scene. For a play to open with two rakes talking is conventional. The rakes seem united later in the act, by contrast with, say, Witwoud. But the opening passage declares its tension without indicating which – if either – of the two is to be preferred. The tension is embodied, for example, in the metaphoric implications of the gambling, of playing against each other. Brian Corman has pointed to the disconcerting formality of the very first line, 'You are a fortunate Man, Mr. *Fainall*' (p. 1).[43] This is no play for Neds and Toms. There is also the strained dialogue with its hints of relationships with characters so far unseen and unknown:

Fainall   ... Yet you speak with an Indifference which seems to be affected; and confesses you are conscious of a Negligence.
Mirabell  You pursue the Argument with a distrust that seems to be un-affected, and confesses you are conscious of a Concern for which the Lady is more indebted to you, than your Wife.   (p. 4)

The careful use of 'seems' sets the vague tone exactly. The surrounding action is similarly ambivalent. As I have argued, Congreve suggests to his audience that, for the most part, plots and evil, or at least stupidity, have a natural attraction. Unsure yet how much of a hero Mirabell is, the audience is equally unsure how to react to the plot of marriage that he is hatching (pp. 4–5) and to its concealment from Fainall.

The tension is broken when Fainall and Mirabell unite against the common enemies, Sir Wilfull (p. 7), Witwoud and Petulant. The antagonism reappears with Witwoud's attempts to define himself as a truewit through maligning Petulant and finally through Mirabell's dissociation of himself and, by implication, the silent Fainall, from the rudeness and malice of Witwoud and Petulant (pp. 15–16). The clarity of this progression of characters onto the stage, the elegance of the movement of the audience's definitions and alignments of each, contrast with the veiled play already glimpsed. The separation of Mirabell from Witwoud is quickly and surely perceived, even if the audience is unsure how to treat the difference between Mirabell and Fainall. The pattern is Congreve's normal movement in the first act from wits to fools among the men.

So far I have defined two types of movement in the act, the veiled underplay and the conventional play with which it may prove to be in tension. There is a third type of presentation of information. The veiled hints at connections with characters unseen lead to a mode of over-definition:

*Mirabell* I have seen him [Sir Wilfull], he promises to be an extraordinary Person; I think you have the Honour to be related to him.

*Fainall* Yes: he is half Brother to this *Witwoud* by a former Wife, who was Sister to my Lady *Wishfort*, my Wife's Mother. If you marry *Millamant* you must call Cousins too. (pp. 6–7)

As Harriet Hawkins points out, Hédelin specifically warns against this kind of statement:[44] the first error in narration an author should guard against is 'when his Narration is obscure, and loaded with circumstances hard for the Audience to retain distinctly; such are *Genealogical* ones . . . or a great number of Names, with a Chain of actions embroyl'd one in another . . .'[45] Statements like Fainall's are bewildering. The pattern of family relationships is unnecessarily complex, over-determined and over-signified. The excess of clarity on this simple issue is in inverse proportion to its apparent significance. There seems no need for so complicated a family nor for the audience to be informed. The audience does want to know how to take Fainall and that information is not yet given. Congreve separates two types of procedure and juxtaposes each with the formal pattern of the play. There is a contrast between facts and impressions, between knowing what sort of part Betterton usually played and wondering what he is playing here, between knowing the formal links in the Wishfort family and wondering how the characters connect. The contrast is not only strikingly analogous to social patterns of perception, but also casts doubt on the nature of empirical observation, demanding instead an acceptance of the imprecision of perception unless susceptible to proof through a series of morally determining actions. In Congreve's earlier plays, the audience was distrustful of plotting; now it has to realign that distrust with the revealed character of the individual – the process already used for Angelica in *Love for Love*. Only at the end can it be sure that plots and moral virtue are compatible.

There is a further contrast between fixity and flux. Facts and knowledge are fixed in the play; increasingly, they are associated with the immutability of contracts and other legal documents.[46] But the movement of the action and the movement of the characters in the play suggest a fluidity, an inconstancy of judgement that is rapidly revealed as both desirable and necessary, if one is to perceive and cope with the way of the world. The play's flow, in conflict with its own orthodox form, embodies its own means of accepting reality.

The chocolate house is part of the men's public world, the source of wit and design as well as foolishness. The park is a place for formal public meeting and assignation. The formal lay-out of the park gives rise to the formal pattern of the second act. It opens with Mrs Fainall and Mrs Marwood in a dialogue emphasising the difficulty of recognising sincere statements, but the bulk of the act is concerned with the presentation of four couples, pairs of present and past lovers, a to-be-married couple and two newly-weds. The presentation of precise information as to the state of each couple serves to define exactly the contrast between Mirabell and Fainall. The gap between them is now defined as a moral distance. Millamant's entrance must be delayed because love between Mirabell and Millamant is not enough. The play first articulates a difference between Mirabell and Fainall according to their attitude to their affairs, past and present. Unlike Bellmour, Mirabell must have abandoned his promiscuity in order to earn from the audience the right to marry.

The anger and jealousy of Fainall and Mrs Marwood, the distrust and pretence that characterises their relationship is already implicit in the presentation of Mrs Marwood in the opening scene. Mrs Marwood and Mrs Fainall fence at each other, just as Fainall and

Mirabell had, but there is less doubt that Mrs Marwood's subtlety stems from a barely disguised aggression and viciousness. Alone with Fainall, Marwood's nature is plain. The adulterers are thus, through the fact of their relationship, shown as evil and immoral. The kindness and amicability of Mirabell and Mrs Fainall, the gentleness of the latter's reproaches, are indications of their essential goodness. Finally, with the entry of Millamant, the tension between plain statements, social masks and sincerity is fully opened out, brought together in her elusiveness, her beauty and her affectation. Mirabell seems by this stage to mark a developing ethical centre to the play. He is also apparently in control of the machinations of the drama, a successful plotter. Yet Millamant's wit escapes his control.

The three principal couples (Fainall/Marwood, Mrs Fainall/ Mirabell, Mirabell/Millamant) are placed into a formal relationship in Act II, a pattern of juxtaposition that should by now be familiar as Congreve's method. The Waitwell/Foible couple are linked to the practice of substitution that is offered as Mirabell's practice in the play. He had pretended to woo Lady Wishfort to gain access to Millamant; he had substituted Fainall for himself when Arabella Languish suspected that she was pregnant; he now substitutes Waitwell for his uncle. It begins to appear that Mirabell is playing the games of the world with an intensity that risks over-reaching. The tension between truth and suspicion, between sincerity and disguise, is already much stronger.

Mirabell's absence throughout Act III, as Fainall's throughout Act IV, reinforces the impression first given in Act II that the two are like buckets in a well, moral alternatives now not to be seen together until their antagonism can be resolved. Act III includes the discomfiture of Fainall through the discovery that he was a 'Cuckold in Embrio' (p. 49) and the defeat of Mrs Marwood through the wit of Millamant and her song (pp. 39–42). But while the mocking presentation of these two aligns them with the fools with whom the act is so densely peopled, at the same time they appear dangerous and threatening, capable of plotting in a way that the audience cannot be sure Mirabell will control.

Act IV revolves around wooing scenes: Sir Wilfull is forced to try to woo Millamant; Mirabell woos and contracts with her; 'Sir Rowland' woos and wins Lady Wishfort. While it has been easy to see how the stupidity of Sir Wilfull is articulated through the juxtaposition with Mirabell's wit and perception, critics have ignored the effect of 'Sir Rowland's' wooing as a commentary on Mirabell and

Millamant. The famous proviso scene, with its heavy emphasis on legal contract, is an attempt to define not a marriage but acceptable limits for Millamant's behaviour. Barring Mirabell's 'proviso' to 'get up in a morning as early as I please' (p. 57), all the discussion centres upon Millamant. The scene then is an attempt to limit some-one already defined as unconfinable ('Think of you! To think of a Whirlwind, tho' 'twere in a Whirlwind, were a Case of more steady Contemplation' p. 30). Mirabell and Millamant contract a marriage and article a relationship at a time when contracts, especially mar-riages, have seemed distinctly dangerous. Fainall's is a sham and so are Sir Rowland's designs on Lady Wishfort. Mirabell and Millamant may be taking care but the law they use is a sham, a social device to hide the truth rather than an embodiment of that truth. Mirabell tries to use legal forms to trap his whirlwind. When Waitwell starts to talk of contracts and the box of writings, the audience is clearly shown that law belongs to the world of untrustworthy knowledge, to that world where truth is almost always something other than it appears.

In a double sense, Mirabell's contract with Millamant is pre-mature. It is too early for them to resolve to marry when Fainall and Marwood are still undefeated and it is too soon for contracts when the power of the law seems distinctly shaky. There is a third sense too: it is too early for lovers to agree in the fourth act. The resolve is always vulnerable to the events of Act v. As in *The Double-Dealer* and *Love for Love*, the fourth act here depends on a piece of play-acting, a sham scene that fails for the hero. Though Waitwell ends Act IV without being discovered, the opening of Act v imme-diately shows the audience that the plot has failed. Mirabell, like his predecessors, is deceived and apparently defeated by the failure of his plot; like Valentine in particular, Mirabell appears to have mis-calculated the stage the play is in. The similarity of the 'Sir Rowland' scene to its predecessors emphasises the vulnerability of fourth act decisions arrived at so soon before. In the end, Mirabell's wooing has attempted to reach stability and fixity too soon.

The last act is full of the excess, the over-signification to which I have already pointed. There is of course the glorious excess of Lady Wishfort whose fantasies are wilder than ever, particularly in her dream of a pastoral idyll shared with Marwood (pp. 74–5). But the greatest excess comes in the manoeuvres of the plot. It is difficult enough to keep track of the state of play from the page, as Fainall's conditions swarm in; on stage it is virtually impossible. Like the genealogy of the Wishfort family, the plot is somehow in excess of its own needs. The law, the world of facts, is now invoked as a basis for the perversion of reality, as a justification of the excess of Fainall's demands. The audience's desire for resolution, its need to see the form of the play, to feel the move towards a satisfying end, is now in conflict with the fixity of law in which it had trusted in the proviso scene. The immutability of wills and testaments, the solidity of their existence is now the great disaster that threatens the play's happy ending. Mirabell's revelations of the truth of the relationship of Marwood and Fainall is accomplished by the sham of law, the oath sworn on the volume of poems, but it is not enough. What Mirabell must do to win is to defeat Fainall using the law (to beat him in the world's terms) and to win Millamant completely by coming to terms with her elusiveness. Mirabell has to combine the fixity of the past with the flux of the future, resolve the form of the play within the flow of the characters.

Much of the play's course has depended on the revelation of mystery, the elucidation of hints. The final mystery that is revealed is one whose existence the audience barely suspected. The writings in 'Sir Rowland's' black box are now revealed as the document of Mirabell's, one whose existence was known about and even witnessed by the fools, although they had forgotten:

> *Enter* Petulant *and* Witwoud.
> *Petulant* How now? what's the matter? who's hand's out?
> *Witwoud* Hey day! what are you all got together like Players at the end of the last Act?
> *Mirabell* You may remember Gentlemen, I once requested your hands as Witnesses to a certain Parchment. (p. 86)

Petulant sees the scene as a card-game. The scene is finally to resolve the tension between the players that had been shown at the opening of the play, '*Mirabell* and *Fainall* [Rising from Cards]' (p. 1). Witwoud reminds the audience that what it awaits is a formal conclusion to the design of the play, the resolution of the 'last Act'. Mirabell indicates that the source of the solution lies in the legal document.

The 'deed of Conveyance' is a trick. It is a legal document that antedates Fainall's demands, as Mirabell's affair with Mrs Fainall antedated her second marriage or as Waitwell's marriage would have antedated 'Sir Rowland's'. As such, it places the proviso scene in a new light, as a contract that antedates any planned wedding of Millamant and Sir Wilfull. Fainall has been outwitted by law and by

*'the way of the world*, Sir: Of the Widdows of the World' (p. 87), though
as the audience knows, it is Mirabell's device. At this moment, for
the very first time in the play, the audience is restored to its customary
position of full knowledge. The doubts and uncertainties that had
begun when Betterton and Verbruggen first appeared are finally
resolved. Mirabell has shown himself to be morally right as well as
socially adept. His success is then social but it is also a success at
game-playing ('who's hand's out?') and at dramatic resolution
('Players at the end of the last Act'). He plays his hidden card, uses
his theatrical trick at the moment which most fully justifies it.

But the trick in the deed of conveyance lies in its existence before
the play began. Even though its use at this stage is justified by its
place in the sequence of moral discrimination that is the design of
the play, yet it in fact renders redundant, irrelevant and excessive
almost all the plotting of the play. Lady Marow was near the truth:
the play has no plot because it does not need to have plot. The play's
premise, the existence of the deed, is an intentional perversion of
the necessitous pattern of motivation required by neo-classical
criticism. Even though the need for the use of the deed is only clear
at the end, Fainall has clearly been the central obstacle in the play.
But at the same time the deed is the way of the world. It points again
to the reality of society, guaranteed by the accumulated analogy
through the audience's perception of the events of the play. The
theatricality of the revelation of the conveyance is the guarantee of
its reality. The paradox is exactly that of the unities in *The Double-
Dealer*.

The pre-contract with Millamant must now be re-asserted.
Mirabell has proved his mastery of the law and the proviso scene
can stand. But the manner of the lovers' coming together is linked
to another major pattern of the play.

*Millamant*   Why do's not the man take me? wou'd you have me give myself
            to you over again.
*Mirabell*    Ay, and over and over again; for I wou'd have you as often as
            possibly I can. Well, heav'n grant I love you not too well, that's
            all my fear.   (*Kisses her hand.*)   (p. 88).

The final phrase has something of Millamant's affectation and the
whole speech comes to terms with Millamant's elusiveness. It points
to that fluidity and movement that stands against facts and the law.
Mirabell achieves a form of eternal present, a repetition of the
moment ('over and over again') that transcends time at the conclu-

sion of the play, the time of the drama and its three hours, just as it completes the flow of the drama, the movement of the play. The moment is echoed by the dance for which Mirabell's friend, Sir Wilfull, asks: 'Let us have a Dance in the mean time, that we who are not Lovers, may have some other employment, besides looking on' (p. 88).

The traditions of the comedy, the reliance on action as the essence of its form, are again overturned by Congreve. The tension of flow and form is decided. The play ends in the hardness of the world, but the mystery of the play has been resolved in accord with the audience's desire. The experience of watching the play has brought the various apparently irreconcilable strands together; the fragments of disrupted conventions are brought back into a harmony stronger than before. The performance, the experience of the flux in the theatre, in itself becomes the end of the text.

# Appendix A

# Restoration promptbooks

There appears to be some confusion over the number of Restoration promptbooks still extant. This list gives all the genuine promptbooks known to me.

| Author | Play | Form |
|--------|------|------|
| J. Dryden | *Tyrannic Love* | Q 1672 |
| E. Howard | *The Change of Crownes* | MS |
| J. Shirley | *The Ball* | Q 1639 |
| | *The Maides Revenge* | Q 1639 |
| | *The Sisters* | *Six New Playes*, 1653 |
| J. Wilson | *The Cheats* | MS |
| W. Cartwright | *The Ordinary* | *Works*, 1651 |
| | *The Lady Errant* | |
| J. Fletcher | *The Night-Walker* | Q 1640 |
| W. Shakespeare | *The Comedy of Errors* | F3 1663 |
| | *Hamlet* | |
| | *1 Henry IV* | |
| | *2 Henry IV* | |
| | *Henry VIII* | |
| | *King Lear* | |
| | *Macbeth* | |
| | *A Midsummer-Night's Dream* | |
| | *The Merry Wives of Windsor* | |
| | *Othello* | |
| | *Twelfth Night* | |
| | *The Winter's Tale* | |
| J. Wilson | *Belphegor* | MS |
| G. Etherege | *The Man of Mode* | Q 1676 |
| T. Heywood | *The Wise Woman of Hogsdon* | Q 1638 |
| W. Shakespeare | *The Comedy of Errors* | F1 1623 |
| | *A Midsummer-Night's Dream* | |
| S. Marmion | *A Fine Companion* | Q 1633 |
| W. Shakespeare | *Twelfth Night* | F2 1632 |
| J. Shirley | *The Wittie Faire One* | Q 1633 |
| W. Sampson | *The Vow Breaker* | Q 1636 |

Articles describing these promptbooks are included in the Bibliography. I would draw attention to the surprising number of promptbooks of plays by Shirley, indicating rather more popularity than he is generally assumed to have had.

| *Present location* | *Restoration company* |
| --- | --- |
| Folger | King's |
| Private | |
| Bodleian | |
| Sold At Sotheby's, 25 Nov. 1974 | |
| Folger | |
| Worcester College, Oxford | |
| Private | Duke's |
| | |
| Folger | Smock Alley, Dublin |
| | |
| Edinburgh | |
| Folger and Stratford | |
| Stratford | |
| Folger | |
| | |
| | |
| Edinburgh | |
| Folger | |
| | |
| | |
| | |
| Edinburgh | King's on tour or rebel actors in Edinburgh |
| Folger | Provincial touring company |
| Edinburgh | Provincial touring company or Nursery |
| | Provincial touring company or Nursery (unperformed) |
| British Museum | Unassignable |
| Folger | |
| Bodleian | |
| University of Melbourne | |

# Appendix B

# Casts for comedies 1691 to 1693

| | The Wives Excuse Dec. 1691 | The Marriage-Hater Match'd Jan. 1692 | Man of Mode[1] March–Dec. 1692 | The Volunteers Nov. 1692 |
|---|---|---|---|---|
| ACTORS | | | | |
| Betterton | Lovemore | | Dorimant | |
| Kynaston | Wellvile | | | |
| Bowman | Courtall | Ld Brainless | Sir Fopling | Dainty |
| Williams | Wilding | | | (absent) |
| Michael Leigh | Springame | | Y. Bellair | |
| Mountfort | Friendall | Freewit | | |
| Bright | Ruffle | Bias | Orange Woman | |
| Harris | Music Master | | | (absent) |
| Sandford | | Limber | | |
| Hodgson | | Darewell | Medley | Welford |
| Anthony Leigh | | Van Grin | O. Bellair | M-G Blunt |
| Dogget | | Solon* | | Hackwell Sr |
| Bowen | | Callow | Shoemaker | Kastril |
| Trefusis | | MacBuffle | | |
| Smeaton | | Thummum* | | |
| Cibber | | Splutter | | |
| Powell | | | Smirk | Hackwell Jr |
| Verbruggen | | | | Nickum |
| Freeman | | | | Dingboy |
| Pinkethman | | | | Stitchum* |
| Underhill | | | | |
| Haines | (absent) | | | |
| Lawson | | | | |
| ACTRESSES | | | | |
| Barry | Friendall | Subtle | Loveit | |
| Bracegirdle | Sightly | Phaebe | | Clara |
| Mountfort | Witwoud | (absent) | Harriet | Eugenia |
| Corey | Teazall | Bumfiddle | | (retires) |
| Richardson | Betty | | Pert | (retires) |
| Lascelles | | Berenice | Emilia | |
| Butler | | LaPupsey | Belinda | (retires) |
| Lawson | | Margery* | | |
| Knight | | | | Teresia |
| Rogers | | | | Winifred* |
| Elinor Leigh | | | Woodvil | Mrs Hackwell |
| Allinson | | | | |
| Perin | | | Busy | |
| Betterton | | | | |
| Rachel Leigh | | | | |
| Kent | | | | |
| Bowman | | | Townley | |

| The Maid's Last Prayer Feb. 1693 | The Old Batchelour March 1693 | The Richmond Heiress April 1693 | A Very Good Wife April 1693 | The Female Vertuoso's May 1693 |
|---|---|---|---|---|
| | Heartwell | | | |
| Gayman | | Shenkin | | Maggot Jingle |
| | Vainlove | Frederick | | |
| | | | Jeremy | |
| (murdered) | | | | |
| Ruff Rancounter | | Quibble Quere | Venture | Witless Sr |
| | | Guiacum | | |
| | | Hotspur | Wellborn | Meanwell |
| (dies) | | | | |
| Malepert | Fondlewife | Quickwit | | Witless Jr |
| Symphony | Wittol | Cunnington | Squeezewit | Trap |
| | | | Hickman | |
| | | | Aminadab | |
| Granger | Bellmour | Tom Romance | Courtwit | Clerimont |
| Garnish | Sharper | | Bonavent | |
| | | Sir Ch. Romance | | |
| Porter | | | | |
| Drydrubb | Setter | Stockjobb | | Sir Maur Meanwell |
| | Bluffe | | Sneaksby | Bully |
| | | | Crack** | |
| Malepert | Laetitia | Sophronia | | |
| Trickitt | Araminta | Fulvia | | Mariana |
| Susan Malepert | Belinda | (absent) | Annabella | Catchat |
| | | | Carroll | |
| | | Squeamish | Widow Lacy | Lovewitt |
| Maria | | | | Lucy |
| Siam | Lucy | Marmalet | Mrs Sneaksby | Lady Meanwell |
| Jano* | | | | |
| Christian[2] | | | | |
| Wishwell | | | | |
| Judy** | | | | |
| Florence | | | | |
| | Sylvia | Stockjobb | | |

1. The cast for *The Man of Mode* comes from a manuscript cast-list in a copy of the 1684 edition, now located at Harvard. It must fall into the period before Leigh's death in December but after the complaint in *The Lacedemonian Mercury* for 11 March 1692 that 'The Plain-Dealer and Sir Fopling Flutter rest untouch'd and unsought-for'. *Sir Fopling Flutter* is the subtitle of *The Man of Mode*. This is the only cast known for a revival of comedy in these two seasons and is therefore included here. The casting is exactly what one would expect: Leigh as the foolish old man, Bowman as the fop, Michael Leigh as the young man, etc. Casting Bright as the Orange-woman is precisely the sort of novelty that was common for revivals.

2. In the first edition, Christian is listed as being played by Mr Perin. Carey Perin was possibly still acting at this time, though he is not known to have played a new part since January 1685. By contrast, Anne Perin was just starting her career, playing servant roles (cf. her performance as Busy in *The Man of Mode*). There is no indication that Christian was a travesty role and I think it probable that the sex is a printer's error.

\* indicates a player's first recorded part


\*\* indicates a player's only recorded part

# Appendix C

# The casts of Congreve's comedies

| Actors | The Old Batchelour | The Double-Dealer | Love for Love | The Way of the World |
|---|---|---|---|---|
| Betterton | Heartwell | Maskwell | Valentine/ (Sir Sampson)* | Fainall |
| Powell | Bellmour | Brisk | – | – |
| Williams | Vainlove | Mellefont | (Valentine)* | – |
| Verbruggen | Sharper | Careless | – | Mirabell |
| Bowen | Wittol | | Jeremy | Witwoud |
| Haines | Bluffe | | – | – |
| Dogget | Fondlewife | Plyant | Ben | |
| Underhill | Setter | | Sir Sampson | Sir Wilfull |
| Kynaston | | Lord Touchwood | | |
| Bowman | | Froth | Tattle | Petulant |
| Smith | – | – | Scandal | – |
| Sandford | | | Foresight | |
| Trefusis | | | Trapland | |
| Freeman | | | Buckram | |
| Bright | | | | Waitwell |
| Actresses | | | | |
| Bracegirdle | Araminta | Cynthia | Angelica | Millamant |
| Mountfort | Belinda | Lady Froth | – | – |
| Barry | Laetitia | Lady Touchwood | Frail | Marwood |
| Bowman | Sylvia | | Foresight | Fainall |
| Leigh | Lucy | Lady Plyant | Nurse | Wishfort |
| Ayliff | – | – | Prue | |
| Lawson | | | Jenny | |
| Willis | – | – | – | Foible |
| Prince | – | – | – | Mincing |

– indicates a player not available
* see text

# Notes

*Preface*

1. Dryden, *Works* X 192–3.
2. F. Hédelin, Abbé d'Aubignac, *La Pratique du Théâtre* (Paris, 1657) translated as *The Whole Art of the Stage* (1684) I 44.
3. *Ibid.*
4. For an attempt to find another term, cf. R. D. Hume, *The Development of English Drama in the late Seventeenth Century* (Oxford, 1976) pp. 3–10.
5. Hédelin, *The Whole Art of the Stage* I 53.

*Chapter 1.   The text and the audience*

1. W. Shakespeare, *Hamlet*, ed. H. H. Furness (1877) p. v. My italics.
2. For full histories of the stage, see L. Hotson, *The Commonwealth and Restoration Stage* (Cambridge, Mass., 1928); A. Nicoll, *A History of Restoration Drama 1660 to 1700* (4th ed., revised, Cambridge, 1952); E. L. Avery *et al.*, eds., *The London Stage 1660–1800*, Part I 1660–1700 (Carbondale, 1965).
3. See J. Freehafer, 'The Formation of the London Patent Companies in 1660' *Theatre Notebook* 20.1965.6–30.
4. For a study of Restoration actresses, see J. H. Wilson, *All the King's Ladies* (Chicago, 1958).
5. For a history of the last years of the King's company see J. H. Wilson, *Mr Goodman the Player* (Pittsburgh, 1964).
6. See especially E. L. Avery, 'The Restoration Audience' *Philological Quarterly* 45.1966.54–61; H. Love, 'The Myth of the Restoration Audience' *Komos* 1.1967.49–56; A. S. Bear, 'Criticism and Social Change: The Case of Restoration Drama' *Komos* 2.1968.23–31; H. Love, 'Bear's Case Laid Open: Or, A Timely Warning to Literary Sociologists' *Komos* 2.1968.72–80.
7. See W. A. Armstrong, 'The Audience of the Elizabethan Private Theatres' *Review of English Studies* n.s. 10.1959.234–49.
8. BL MS Harley 6430, p. 21. Letter to Mr Harewell, 2 February 1668.
9. The Very Rev. Rowland Davies, *Journal*, ed. R. Caulfield (Camden Society, 1857) p. 24. Jephson became Dean of Kilmore in 1690.
10. Rev. J. Ward. *Diary*, ed. C. Severn (1839) p. 174.
11. Thomas, Earl of Ailesbury, *Memoirs* (1890) I 356.
12. Letter of 4 May 1665 in W. D. Cooper, ed., *Savile Correspondence* (1858) p. 4.

13. Letter of 26 December 1685 in Historical Manuscripts Commission 12th Report, Appendix, Pt 5, Rutland MSS, vol. II (1889) p. 99.

14. R. Hooke, *Diary 1672–1680*, ed. H. W. Robinson and W. Adams (1935) p. 206, 1 January 1676.

15. R. Hooke, *Diary 1672–1680*, p. 78. See also the entries for 3 July 1676 and 1 January 1677. See also the entry for 6 June 1689 in R. Gunther, *Early Science in Oxford* (1935) X 127.

16. Published plays remained fairly cheap throughout the period, apparently going up to one shilling around 1666: Anthony à Wood commented wryly, 'sermons they say were 12d a peice . . . and playes 6d a-peice; but now (and from the fire, 1666) playes are 12d a peice and sermons 6d'. (A. Clark, ed., *The Life and Times of Anthony Wood* (Oxford, 1891–1900) II 430). Between 1700 and 1704, the price went up to 1s 6d; see the prices given in *Bibliotheca Annua* between those years for the transition.

17. Letter of 6 July 1686 quoted in F. P. and M. M. Verney, *Memoirs of the Verney Family* (1892–9) IV 381.

18. O. Walker, *Of Education Especially of Young Gentlemen* (Oxford, 1673) p. 42.

19. W. Freke, *Select Essays Tending to the Universal Reformation of Learning* (1693) p. 224.

20. See e.g., T. Nourse, *A Discourse upon the Nature and Faculties of Man* (1697) p. 41 where plays are part of his model state, Italian.

21. F. Brokesby, *Of Education* (1701) p. 25.

22. *Ibid.* p. 112.

23. *Ibid.* p. 113.

24. *Ibid.* p. 114.

25. Pt I p. 94.

26. *Ibid.*

27. 5th edition, 1710, p. 69.

28. 'A DIALOGUE *between the same Persons and a Bishop, concerning* EDUCATION' in Edward Hyde, Earl of Clarendon, *A Collection of Several Tracts* (1727). The date of the dialogue is unknown but Clarendon died in 1674.

29. *Critical Works* I 294.

30. Quoted by L. Hook, 'James Brydges drops in at the Theater' *Huntington Library Quarterly* 8.1945.308.

31. *Critical Works* I 293.

32. *Ibid.*

33. The overlap is accounted for by visits to all three theatres on 7 January and an unnamed theatre on 11 April.

34. There is a slight difficulty here in that it is difficult to tell whether, when Pepys met people at the theatre, it was pre-arranged or by chance.

35. See the detailed accounts for 10–19 April 1668.

36. Gregory King, 'LCC Burns Journal' p. 250 (facsimile in P. Laslett, introduction, *The Earliest Classics: John Graunt and Gregory King* (1973)).

37. *Works* I 151.

38. *Apology* I 322. For a map showing this westward expansion of London, 1700–38, see J. Loftis, *Comedy and Society from Congreve to Fielding* (Stanford, 1959) p. 8.

39. Giovanni Torriano recommends the pit as 'the best place for to look upon

the Dukes, Earls, Barons, Knights and Gentlemen, with their Ladies in their Boxes . . . The inconvenience will be the Croud . . .' *Mescolanze Dolce di Varie Historiette* (1673) p. 126.

40. See G. J. Gray, 'The Diary of Jeffrey Boys of Gray's Inn, 1671' *Notes and Queries* 159.1930.456.

41. *Critical Works* I 294.

42. J. H. Smith, 'Shadwell, the Ladies, and the Change in Comedy' *Modern Philology* 46. 1948.22–33.

43. Quoted in Lady Newton, *The House of Lyme* (1917) p. 240.

44. Downes, p. 41.

45. This is based on Brunet's description of the *Dorset Garden* theatre, not Drury Lane, as having seven boxes with twenty people in each.

46. M. Summers, *The Restoration Theatre* (1934) p. 64.

47. See S. P. Zitner, 'The English Theatre Audience 1660–1700' (Ph.D. thesis, Duke University, 1955) pp. 71ff. Zitner estimates the maximum capacity of Dorset Garden at between 730 and 950 and Drury Lane as 1000 to 1200. E. A. Langhans, in 'Staging Practices in the Restoration Theatre 1660–82' (Ph.D. thesis, Yale University, 1955), estimates the capacities as Bridges Street up to 1500 (p. 51), Drury Lane *circa* 1500 (p. 162), Lincoln's Inn Fields 500? (p. 442) and Dorset Garden *circa* 1200 (p. 353). Langhans has to admit that Wren's 'Drury Lane' design (see below, plate 4, chapter 2) will only take 700 on his method of computation, even though he trusts it for so much other information.

48. P. Sawyer, 'The Seating Capacity and Maximum Receipts of Lincoln's Inn Fields Theatre' *Notes and Queries* 199.1954.290.

49. See BL Add MS 38607.

50. L. Hotson, *The Commonwealth and Restoration Stage* (Cambridge, Mass., 1928) pp. 288f.

51. See L. T.'s letter in *The Theatrical Inquisitor and Monthly Mirror*, July 1816 pp. 25–6.

52. *Ibid.* p. 25.

53. Gregory King 'Natural and Political Observations' p. 35 in P. Laslett, introd., *The Earliest Classics: John Graunt and Gregory King* (1973). For studies on King, see in particular P. E. Jones and A. V. Judges, 'London Population in the late Seventeenth Century' *Economic History Review* 6.1935.45–63 and D. V. Glass, 'Two Papers on Gregory King' in D. V. Glass and D. E. C. Eversley, eds., *Population in History* (1965) pp. 159–220.

54. G. King, 'LCC Burns Journal' p. 59.

55. D. V. Glass, ed., *London Inhabitants within the Walls 1695* (London Record Society, 1966) and his subsequent studies, e.g. 'Notes on the Demography of London at the End of the Seventeenth Century' *Daedalus* 97.1968.581–92 and 'Socio-economic Status and Occupations in the City of London at the end of the Seventeenth Century' in A. E. J. Hollaender and W. Kellaway, eds., *Studies in London History presented to Philip Edmund Jones* (1969) pp. 371–89.

56. A. Nicoll, *A History of Restoration Drama 1660–1700* (Cambridge, 1923) p. 8. The passage remained unchanged in the fourth revised edition (Cambridge, 1952) p. 8.

Chapter 2.   *Performance: theatres and scenery*

1. R. Barthes, *Essais Critiques* (Paris, 1964) pp. 61–2 (my translation).
2. See J. R. Northam, *Ibsen's Dramatic Method* (1953).
3. Barthes, *Essais Critiques*, p. 61.
4. G. Wickham, *Early English Stages 1300 to 1660*, vol. II part 2 (1972) p. 173.
5. F. A. Yates, *The Art of Memory* (1966) p. 359.
6. There are excellent records for this theatre. See Wickham, *Early English Stages*. II, pt 2, pp. 117–22; G. E. Bentley, *The Jacobean and Caroline Stage* (Oxford, 1941–68) VI 267–84; D. F. Rowan, 'The Cockpit-in-Court' in D. Galloway, ed., *The Elizabethan Theatre* (1969) pp. 89–102.
7. W. G. Keith first published the designs in 'John Webb and the Court Theatre of Charles II' *The Architectural Review* 57.1925.49–55 but he misdated them by thirty years.
8. *Inigo Jones on Palladio* (facsimile edition of Jones's copy, 1970), facing Palladio's title-page.
9. See Jones's design for Davenant's masque *Salmacida Spolia* without forestage, and his design for *Florimène* with forestage. The latter is more play than masque. BL MS Lansdowne 1171, fols. 3–4, 5–6 and 15–16.
10. J. Orrell, 'Inigo Jones at the Cockpit' *Shakespeare Survey* 30.1977.157–68.
11. See W. G. Keith, 'A Theatre Project by Inigo Jones' *Burlington Magazine* 31. 1917.61–70 and 105–11.
12. Inigo Jones's copy of Serlio (Venice, 1619) passed to John Webb who annotated it copiously (facsimile edition, Ridgewood, New Jersey, 1964).
13. B. Hewitt, ed., *The Renaissance Stage* (Coral Gables, 1958) p. 35.
14. Cf. D. C. Mullin, 'The Theatre Royal, Bridges Street: A Conjectural Restoration' *Educational Theatre Journal* 19.1967.17–29; E. A. Langhans, 'Pictorial Material on the Bridges Street and Drury Lane Theatres' *Theatre Survey* 7.1966. 80–100.
15. Conte Lorenzo Magalotti, *Travels of Cosmo the Third* (1821) p. 190.
16. There has even been a suggestion that the sketch represents the second Theatre Royal, built in 1672: see G. Barlow, 'Sir James Thornhill and the Theatre Royal, Drury Lane, 1705' in K. Richards and P. Thomson, eds., *The Eighteenth-Century English Stage* (1972) pp. 179–93. The claim is made on the similarity of Wren's sketchy proscenium arch with Thornhill's '1st Great flat Scene' but the measurements are faulty. Thornhill's design probably relates to a false proscenium, fitted along a shutter groove.
17. *The Diverting Post*, 7–14 April 1705.
18. Cf. the ground plan by Dumont in D. Nalbach, *The King's Theatre 1704– 1867* (1972) fig. 6.
19. *Apology* II p. 85.
20. See BL MS Lansdowne 1171, fols. 11–12.
21. The principal reconstructions based on the Wren section are R. Leacroft, 'Wren's Drury Lane' *The Architectural Review* 110.1951.43–6 and E. A. Langhans, 'Wren's Restoration Playhouse' *Theatre Notebook* 18.1964.91–100. Langhans claims strict adherence to Wren but refuses to allow the pit benches to be curved. Wren however clearly shades them so that they can follow the curvature of the front edge of the forestage, thus avoiding the most improbable form Langhans felt constrained to create.

22. Cf. the description by Brunet in 1676 and the engravings for Settle's *The Empress of Morocco* (1673). Langhans' attempt to build a model on this evidence is very dubious: E. A. Langhans, 'A Conjectural Reconstruction of the Dorset Garden Theatre' *Theatre Survey* 13.1972.74–93. See also J. R. Spring 'Platforms and Picture Frames: A Conjectural Reconstruction of the Duke of York's Theatre, Dorset Garden, 1669–1709' *Theatre Notebook* 31.1977.6–19.

23. *Apology* II 85.

24. *Ibid.*

25. R. Boyle, *Guzman* (1693) p. 35.

26. *Ibid.* p. 10.

27. Cf. the stage for *Salmacida Spolia* with four sets of wings at successive distances of 1 ft 6 ins, 3 ft 8 ins, 3 ft 10 ins, 3 ft 6 ins, 1 ft 8 ins from the proscenium to the back-shutters. BL MS Lansdowne 1171 fols. 3–4.

28. Thomas Shipman, in the Epilogue to *Henry the Third of France* (1678) mourning the burning of Bridges Street theatre, indicates that the shutters were painted in oils on wooden frames:

> The *Scenes*, compos'd of Oyl and porous Firr,
> Added to th' ruine of the *Theater*.
> And 'twas a judgement in the Poets Phrase,
> That *Plays and Playhouse* perisht by a blaze
> Caus'd by those *gaudy Scenes*, that spoil *good Plays*    (L3a)

29. Dryden, *The Rival Ladies* (1664) (*Works* VIII 108). Though props for a discovery could be set behind the opening shutters, props for the next forestage scene had to be carried on. In the following scene, Dryden demonstrates how to make a virtue of this necessity by having some of the play's exposition conveyed by two servants who are putting out chairs.

30. It is not uncommon for stage plans which are immensely accurate for the auditorium to be vague over the stage equipment: Dumont's plan for the Queen's Theatre shows no shutters at all!

31. Hewitt, *The Renaissance Stage* p. 208.

32. *Ibid.* p. 211. See also Sabbatini's design for a Hellfire, 'if there is behind the back shutter a space or inner stage which may be exposed', *ibid.* p. 126.

33. *Changeable Scenery* (1952) pp. 146ff.

34. This is the view adopted by J. H. Smith and D. MacMillan (Dryden, *Works* VIII 309). I am convinced that any attempt to adhere strictly to the Wren section is foredoomed.

35. A. Nicoll, *The Development of the Theatre* (5th ed., 1966) fig. 124.

36. *Ibid.* (1st ed., 1927) fig. 163.

37. *Ibid.* (1927) fig. 196. The illustration includes a back traverse curtain which certainly was a device in use after the Restoration, especially to conceal corpses in the fifth acts of tragedies, cf. e.g. Dryden's *The Duke of Guise* (1683) p. 75.

38. See Dr J. A. Worp, *Geschiedenis van den Amsterdamschen Schouwburg, 1496–1772* (Amsterdam, 1920) unnumbered illustrations.

39. *Apology* II 85.

40. *Ibid.*

41. Some plays did call for special wings. Nat Lee's *Theodosius* (1680) opens with a direction calling for a set in which 'The side Scenes shew the horrid

Tortures with which the *Roman* Tyrants persecuted the Church.' The requirements of operas were even more extravagant.

42. See the stage direction in *Mustapha*, 'The number on the Stage being now
twenty four' (p. 106).

43. It seems from the evidence of the plays that at this date only Bridges Street
had such equipment. Dryden makes typically elaborate use of it and all other
resources.

44. This is to be expected from the masques but see also the King's order for-
bidding spectators on the stage 'forasmuch as 'tis impossible to command
those vast Engines (which move the Scenes and Machines) and to order such
a number of Persons as must be employed in Works of that nature, if any but
such as belong thereunto, be suffer'd to press in amongst them'. Order of
26 Feb. 1673 in PRO. LC 7/3, see also *Calendar of State Papers Domestic Feb.-
Dec. 1685* 27 April 1685 pp. 138-9.

45. *Works* IX 74.

46. *Works* IX 78.

47. *Works* IX 83.

48. *Works* IX 86.

49. For other upstage torture scenes cf. e.g. T. Porter, *The Villain* (1662) '*Malig.*
discover'd pierc't with a stake', (p. 98); Crowne, *The Ambitious Statesman* (1679)
'The Scene drawn, the *Duke* is shew'd wrack't . . .' (p. 82); and the spectacular
scene in Settle's *The Empress of Morocco* (1673), matched by Dolle's engraving,
'Here the Scene opens, and *Crimalhaz* appears cast down on the Gaunches,
being hung on a Wall set with Spikes of Iron' (p. 70).

50. Sedley's play was used as an example by L. J. Martin in his important article
'From Forestage to Proscenium: A Study of Restoration Staging Techniques'
*Theatre Survey* 4.1963.3-28. But Martin unfortunately demonstrates how use of
a bad edition vitiates good work. For his discussion he used Pinto's edition
of Sedley (1928) and assumed that Pinto's editorial additions to the scene-
headings are original. Of the eighteen scene-headings, twelve are Pinto's;
some of the divisions into scenes do not exist and are not called for in the
original at all!

51. On the Restoration stage, the curtain was raised after the prologue and did
not drop again until after the epilogue, except in special circumstances.

52. This convention of using the scenic stage for songs in tragedy starts very early
in the period: see for example Shadwell, *The Royal Shepherdess* (1669) 'the
Shepherds and Shepherdesses are discovered . . .' and sing (p. 35).

53. This is of course one of the standard spectacular scenes. See Dryden, *Tyrannic
Love* (Bridges Street) Act V 'A Scene of a Paradise is discovered' (*Works* X 150).
The scenery for this production cost £335 10s. 0d. For the resultant lawsuit
see L. Hotson, *The Commonwealth and Restoration Stage* (Cambridge, Mass.,
1928) pp. 348-55.

54. Downes, p. 36.

55. Among hundreds of examples of the tableau state scene, cf. Dryden, *The Indian
Queen*, '*Zempoalla* appears seated upon a Throne . . .' (*Works* VIII 197) and
'*Zempoalla* appears seated upon her Slaves in Triumph . . .' (*Works* VIII 201).
Boyle frequently covers a tableau with the curtain, one of the few occasions
it was lowered in the middle of a play.

56. *Works* II 254.

57. *Works* II 167.

58. *Works* II 168.

59. Similar uses of the scenic area for sequences of fantasy and illusion can be seen in Otway's *The Atheist* (1684) and the Sforza scenes of Fane's *Love in the Dark* (1675), e.g. 'A *Scene* of *Paradise*, and Glorious Shows, with Musick. *Sforza* walking in it alone' (p. 41).

60. *Works* II 186. The same device is used to indicate the inside and outside of Sir Jolly's house later in the same Act (I 190).

61. These are especially common in comedy when the discovery is necessitated by use of props, e.g. Dilke, *The Lover's Luck*, where the actors are discovered 'rising from a Table with Bottles and Glasses' (p. 20). The discovery calls attention to the specific location, set as environment.

62. There is no good evidence that the lighting could be dimmed.

63. This accounts, for instance, for all three discoveries in *The Luckey Chance* (1687), both of them in *The Town Fopp* (1677), and three in each of *Sir Patient Fancy*, *The Younger Brother* (1696) and *The Second Part of the Rover* (1681).

64. See on the extent of this, J. Freehafer, 'Perspective Scenery and the Caroline Playhouses' *Theatre Notebook* 27.1973.98–113.

65. In his highly influential study, *Changeable Scenery* (1952) pp. 109f, Richard Southern argues that the stage directions in the text of *The Siege* refer equally to performances in 1656 at Rutland House and to those given in the years after the Restoration by Davenant's company at Lincoln's Inn Fields. Southern bases his case on the fact that the stage directions are not altered in the 1663 edition in spite of the additions made to Part I of the play when Part II was added to it after the Restoration. But Southern failed to use the bibliographical evidence, most of which was published by W. W. Greg, in *A Bibliography of English Printed Drama to the Restoration* (Oxford, 1939–59) II, item 763/827; also Ann-Mari Hedbäck in 'The Printing of *The Siege of Rhodes*' *Studia Neophilologica* 45. 1973. 68–79. There are four major states of *The Siege* up to the end of 1663. The first quarto was printed in 1656 (Greg 763 (aI)) twice reissued with different title pages, Greg 763 (aII) and the Dyce copy listed in Wing as D340). QI was reprinted in 1659 with sigs. A–D in page-for-page resettings but with EIb onwards reset to save space (Greg 763 (bI)). In 1663 this quarto (Q2) was reissued with the additional scenes added on three new half-sheets and one single leaf, and with four leaves replaced. The title page and prefatory material were also altered. This state (Greg 763 (bII)) with a phenomenally complex collation and some mad misnumbering of pages was used as the copy for Q3, also printed in 1663. In spite of Greg, the second part of the play was not printed at the same time as Q3 but instead as the running-titles show, was printed with the additions to Q2. The copy for the additions was *not* a playhouse manuscript and there is no evidence that the copy ever had any contact with the playhouse. It seems most likely that the copy was Davenant's own papers.

All this means that it is impossible to make assumptions about Restoration staging on the basis of the absence of certain apparently necessary scene changes in the Q2 re-issue and in Q3. None of the editions in 1663 or later provide any evidence of the staging of *The Siege* at Lincoln's Inn Fields. Hence, unnecessarily for the much larger stage at Lincoln's Inn Fields, the 1663 text keeps in the comment about including 'so much view of the Gardens and Hills about it, as the narrowness of the Room could allow the Scene' (1663, A3a), reflecting the tiny stage at Rutland House. When Southern comments that, in the first Entry, 'There now immediately enter Ianthe and her two women who are in Sicily ... *But no scene has been changed*! This 'prospect' of Rhodes in the distance serves to set both a scene inside Rhodes and a scene in Sicily' (*Changeable Scenery* p. 112) he is assuming that Q3 *is* an accurate reflection of Lincoln's Inn Fields staging practice, when there is absolutely no evidence for it.

66. Cf. the set in Shadwell's *Psyche* (1675) 'The Scene changes to the principal Street of the City, with vast numbers of People looking down from the tops of Houses, and out of the Windows and Balconies ...' (p. 37). In those scenes in which crowds 'pass over the stage', they do so within the scenic area, as background, as part of the stage picture, rather than on the forestage, cf. e.g. *The Plain-Dealer*, 'a crowd of lawyers, at the end of the Stage' or 'Several crossing the Stage' (pp. 37 and 55).

67. *Shakespeare at the Globe 1599–1609* (New York, 1962) pp. 64f.

68. Cf. *She Would If She Could* II.i and *The Man of Mode* III.iii.

69. *Shakespeare at the Globe*, p. 67.

70. Again the convention is the use of a scene showing the city from outside to back action inside the city.

71. See the indications made by Hand D in the manuscript for *The Change of Crownes*, ed. F. S. Boas (1949).

72. *Ibid.* p. 63.

73. *Ibid.* p. 56.

74. *Ibid.* p. 66 – the same set was needed for the opening scene of *Tyrannic Love*, two years later.

75. It was presumably therefore a stock set available for use. For details of the promptbook, see W. Cartwright. *The Plays and Poems* ed. G. B. Evans (Madison, 1951) pp. 258–62 and 799–806.

76. e.g. 'Enter *Don Fernando* and *Fabio*. As in the Room in the Inn' (p. 31).

77. See Dedication 'Upon my Perusal of *Guzman* in Manuscript' (a1a). I suspect that Tate, never one to pass up a chance of making money, found the manuscript gathering dust in the theatre and took the chance of publishing it.

78. See the specific locations in *Tryphon* and even in the unacted plays, *Herod* and *Saul*.

79. Used six times: I, III.iii, IV.i, IV.iv, IV.vii, V.i.

80. Used three times: II.iv, III.i, IV.viii.

81. '... your Chamber, in which we'll leave you' p. 23.

82. Folger MS 827.1. Smock Alley was very closely connected to the London theatres. This manuscript shows the precision with which doors were linked to particular offstage places; almost every entrance has the door specified.

83. The promptbook, which is in fragments, is described by G. Sorelius in 'The Smock Alley Prompt-Books of *1* and *2 Henry IV*' *Shakespeare Quarterly* 22.1971.111–28.

84. In any case, Etherege was probably involved in preparations for his trip to Constantinople. He was appointed secretary to the ambassador early in 1668

and, embarked, after delays, in August. Cf. T. H. Fujimura 'Etherege at Constantinople' *Publications of the Modern Language Association of America* 71.1956.-465–81.

85. D. Underwood, *Etherege and the Seventeenth-Century Comedy of Manners* (New Haven, 1957) p. 66.

86. As indication of the convention in retreat, Vanbrugh's *The Relapse* (1697) shows the fop's levée. This direct image of the inversion of power from wit to fop is backed up by Lord Foppington's adopting the cruel harshness heretofore the true libertine's prerogative (Compare his attitude to Young Fashion with Dorimant's treatment of Young Bellair as a potential cuckold in *The Man of Mode* ii. The effect is enhanced by the distancing of Young Fashion from the audience's sympathies and its concept of the real by having him played by Mrs Kent, a breeches role. For an earlier, tantalising fragment of parody, see the scene of Rochester's prose comedy which shows the fop waking (first printed in V. de S. Pinto, *The Enthusiast in Wit* (1962) pp. 111–12).

87. There seems almost to be a hierarchical structure over who could hide in wood-holes. No true gentleman ever does but for fools, see Snarl in Shadwell's *The Virtuoso* (p. 59).

88. Freeman wryly comments 'Faith, if it be as thou say'st, I cannot much / Blame the hardness of thy heart' (p. 9). The use of conditionals is vital to the play.

89. This is at the heart of the sympathy that the audience feels for Lady Cockwood, but it is not incompatible with a comedy in which the audience passes judgement. For the opposing view cf. J. Powell, 'George Etherege and the Form of a Comedy' in J. R. Brown and B. Harris, eds. *Restoration Theatre* (Stratford-upon-Avon Studies 6, 1965) 43–69. A letter by Etherege twenty years later shows that his fools were not to be thought of as despicable weaklings: 'They are to be pittied that fall under Mr Shadwell's lash. He lays on heavily. His fools want mettle ...' (Letter of 24 May 1688 in *Letters* ed. F. Bracher (Berkeley, 1974) p. 201).

90. Later in the play, Mrs Sentry matches play-time to real-time by such a reference: 'I knew they were to be / Found at the latter end of a Play' (p. 55). It being Act IV, it was also the latter end of Etherege's own play.

*Chapter 3.　Performance: actors and the cast*

1. See his writings on the Munich Artists' Theatre of 1908, G. Fuchs, *Revolution in the Theatre*, ed. C. C. Kuhn (Cornell, 1959).

2. See A. Righter, *Shakespeare and the Idea of the Play* (1962) for the native tradition and Jackson I. Cope, *The Theatre and the Dream* (Baltimore, 1973) for an attempt to link English Renaissance practice with Florentine neo-platonism.

3. Dryden, *Works* VIII p. 86.

4. J. Webster, *Works* ed. F. L. Lucas (1927) IV, 42.

5. Fuchs, *Revolution in the Theatre*, p. 64.

6. E. G. Craig, *Henry Irving* (1930) p. 32.

7. See also the very similar concepts in E. G. Craig, *The Theatre Advancing* (1921) pp. 204ff.

8. See the mother in *The Mother* and the heroine of *The Vision of Simone Marchand*, and also Craig's attitude towards Hamlet.

9. Fuchs, *Revolution in the Theatre*, p. 64.

10. N. W. Henshaw, 'Graphic Sources for a Modern approach to the Acting of Restoration Comedy' (Ph.D. thesis, University of Pittsburgh, 1967) p. 423. Dr Henshaw's thesis is a massive compilation of descriptions of social actions. A fragment appeared under the same title in *Educational Theatre Journal* 20.1968.155–70.

11. *Apology* I 142.

12. *The Actor* (1750) p. 187. Hill's book is an adaptation of P. R. de Sainte-Albine, *Le Comédien* (1747).

13. C. Gildon, *The Life of Mr Thomas Betterton* (1710) p. 80. There is no evidence that Betterton had anything to do with the rules of acting Gildon ascribes to him.

14. Hill, *The Actor*, p. 236. See the Jonsonian concept of the humour, especially in its Restoration manifestation, Shadwell's epilogue to *The Humorists* (1671), L4a–L4b.

15. Gildon, *The Life of Mr Thomas Betterton*, p. 236.

16. A. Aston, *A Brief Supplement to Colley Cibber, Esq*; in *Apology* II 307–8.

17. See J. H. Wilson, 'Rant, Cant, and Tone on the Restoration Stage' *Studies in Philology* 52.1955.592–8.

18. Prologue by Powell to *A Fatal Discovery* (1698), π3a.

19. Hill, *The Actor*, p. 125.

20. 'A Short Discourse of the English Stage' in R. Flecknoe, *Love's Kingdom* (1664) G6b–G7a.

21. *Ibid.* G6b.

22. Gildon, *The Life of Mr Thomas Betterton*, p. 40.

23. *ibid.* pp. 33–4.

24. Hill, *The Actor*, p. 93.

25. S. Foote, *The Roman and English Comedy Consider'd and Compar'd* (1747) pp. 38–9.

26. See E. R. Wasserman, "The Sympathetic Imagination in Eighteenth-Century Theories of Acting' *Journal of English and Germanic Philology* 46.1947.264–72.

27. 'The Character of an excellent Actor' *The Gentleman's Magazine* 13.1743.254. Cf. from the same article, 'I have an *Actor* in my Eye whose *greatest Merit* is, that he is *none*; whose Look, whose Voice, whose Action have nothing of the *Player*, but so much of the *Person* he represents, that he puts the *Playhouse* out of our Heads, and *is* actually to *us* and to *himself*, what *another Actor* would only *seem to be.*' (*Ibid.*)

28. J. Boswell, *Life of Johnson* ed. G. B. Hill, revised L. F. Powell (Oxford 1934–50) IV 244.

29. A theory of identification is argued for pre-Restoration acting by Bertram Joseph in *Elizabethan Acting* (revised edition, Oxford, 1964) pp. 1–7. Joseph's examples show only that the acting style tended towards a limited form of naturalism, so that comments about the actor being lost in the part tend to signify only that the acting was consistent and 'life-like'. In any case, most references to this deal with tragedy where the theory gained ground initially. The frequent comments on the actor as a protean creator point to a profound awareness of the significance of the actor as mediator and representer, not as a diminishing interruption between the audience and the character.

30. Hill, *The Actor*, p. 24. Ironically it was an adaptation of Hill's book back into French in 1769 that persuaded Diderot to write the *Paradoxe*.

31. *Characters*, ed. C. W. Daves, (Cleveland, 1970) p. 300.

32. *Ibid.* p. 301.

33. *Ibid.*

34. Downes, p. 29.

35. *Works* IX pp. 127–8. This play is particularly full of such precision. Sabina and Olinda (Elizabeth Davenport and Margaret Rutter) are distinguished by their different heights; Rebecca Marshall's dark hair is referred to.

36. *Works* II 311.

37. *Apology* II 302.

38. J. Wilson, *The Cheats*, ed. M. C. Nahm (Oxford, 1935) p. 195.

39. For a description of the only surviving Restoration example see E. A. Langhans, 'A Restoration Actor's Part' *Harvard Library Bulletin* 23.1975.180–5. For earlier examples see W. W. Greg, *Dramatic Documents from the Elizabethan Playhouse* (Oxford, 1931). Cue-scripts survived in English repertory theatre as late as the 1930s.

40. *Calendar of State Papers Domestic, 1664–5*, p. 139.

41. *Pinacotheca Bettertonaeana*, 24 August 1710, p. 22 Item 1.

42. *Apology* I 237.

43. Quoted by J. H. Wilson, 'The Marshall Sisters and Anne Quin' *Notes and Queries* 202. 1957. 106.

44. *Apology* I 189.

45. Once owned by W. W. Greg and described by him in *A Bibliography of the English Printed Drama to the Restoration* (Oxford, 1939–59) III 1268–9, now in BL, press mark C.131.c.14.

46. On Lenten performances in general, see P. H. Gray, Jr, 'Lenten Casts and the Nursery: Evidence for the Dating of Certain Restoration Plays' *Publications of the Modern Language Association of America* 53.1938.781–94.

47. Downes, p. 21.

48. *Apology* I 108.

49. Dedication to *The Invader of his Country* in *Critical Works* II 179.

50. E. Settle, *Fatal Love* (1680) A2b.

51. A. Behn, *The Second Part of the Rover* (1681) p. 85.

52. *Ibid.*

53. See Farquhar's preface to *The Inconstant*, (*Works* I 221) which capitalised on the success in its title.

54. Norris was by this time known as 'Jubilee Dicky' from his performance in this play.

55. See below, p. 90.

56. See for example Young Fashion in *The Relapse*, played by Mrs Kent. Mrs Mountfort may have played the role of Bayes in Villiers' *The Rehearsal* as early as the revival in 1687. Cibber describes how 'People were so fond of seeing her as a Man, that when the Part of *Bays* in the *Rehearsal* had for some time lain dormant, she was desired to take it up . . .' *Apology* I 167.

57. See *The Gentleman's Journal*, June 1694 p. 170: the second part 'doubtless must be thought as entertaining as the first; since in this hot season it could bring such a numerous Audience'.

58. *Critical Works* I 418.
59. *The Organization and Personnel of the Shakespearean Company* (Princeton, 1927).
60. See R. W. David's re-assessment of Baldwin in 'Shakespeare and the Players' in P. Alexander, ed., *Studies in Shakespeare* (1964) pp. 33-55.
61. See the roles given to Burbage in the casting charts, facing pp. 198 and 229.
62. Review of Baldwin, *Journal of English and Germanic Philology* 27.1928.562.
63. Dedication to *Sir Anthony Love* (1691) A2a.
64. Dedication to *The Fatal Marriage* (1694) A2b.
65. *Ibid.*
66. Preface, a1b.
67. Dedication, A1a.
68. Cf. R. Ames, *A Search after Wit* (1691), p. 12:
    > Yet is it no wonder when *Authors* want *Sense*,
    > The *Players* turn *Writers* in *their own defence*.
69. On the litigation see L. Hotson, *The Commonwealth and Restoration Stage* (Cambridge, Mass., 1928) pp. 274-6.
70. Preface, A2b-A3a.
71. pp. 47-54 and 58-62.
72. Dramatis Personae, A4b.
73. W. Redfield, *Letters from an Actor* (1967) p. 112.
74. As for example Betterton and Harris running the Duke's company after the death of Davenant, Betterton at Lincoln's Inn Fields after the 1695 secession, Hart at Drury Lane in the late 1670s etc. See also the praise of a particular actor's help, for example Dryden on Betterton's 'judicious' cutting of the over-long text of *Don Sebastian* for production, (Preface (1690), a1a).
75. Gildon, *The Life of Mr Thomas Betterton*, pp. 15-16.
76. Preface, A4a.
77. *Ibid.* A7a.
78. *Ibid.*
79. Downes, p. 28.
80. For the players' complaint see A. Nicoll, *A History of Restoration Drama* (4th ed., revised, Cambridge, 1952) p. 329 n 1 and J. M. Osborn, *John Dryden: Some Biographical Facts and Problems* (New York, 1940) pp. 184-91.
81. Osborn, *John Dryden*, pp. 184-91.
82. See the addition of Durfey's name to the company roster in May 1676, J. H. Wilson, 'Players' Lists in the Lord Chamberlain's *Registers' Theatre Notebook* 18. 1963. 27.
83. See the *Reflexions upon a late Pamphlet, intituled, A Narrative written by E. Settle* (1683), p. 2. Settle turned down £50 p.a. from the rival company.
84. Nicoll, *A History of Restoration Drama* (4th ed., 1952) pp. 381-2.
85. J. Dryden, *The Letters* ed. C. E. Ward (Durham, N.C., 1942) pp. 23-4.
86. i.e. Dogget, Sancho in *Love Triumphant*, called Solon from his performance in that role in Durfey's *The Marriage-Hater Match'd* (1692).
87. *Letters*, p. 54.
88. B. R. Schneider, Jr, 'The Coquette-Prude as an Actress's Line in Restoration Comedy during the time of Mrs Oldfield' *Theatre Notebook* 22.1968.143-56.
89. E.g. Millamant and Mrs Marwood in *The Way of the World*.
90. *Apology* II 306.

91. See R. H. Ross, Jr, 'Samuel Sandford: Villain from Necessity' *Publications of the Modern Language Association of America* 76.1961.367–72 for a useful analysis of his career.
92. *Apology* I 131.
93. *Apology* I 132–3.
94. E.g. Dominic in *The Spanish Friar* (1681), Teague in *The Lancashire Witches* (1682) and *The Amorous Bigotte* (1690), and the Abbé in *Sir Anthony Love* (1691).
95. See also L. Hook, *Mrs Elizabeth Barry and Mrs Anne Bracegirdle Actresses. Their Careers from 1672 to 1695, A Study in Influences* (New York, 1949).
96. B. Dobrée, *Restoration Comedy 1660–1720* (1924) p. 108.
97. R. D. Hume, 'Diversity and Development in Restoration Comedy 1660– 1679' *Eighteenth Century Studies* 5.1972.365–97.
98. *Diary*, 23 February 1663.
99. The description of a play by Henry Savile on 4 May 1665, even though he got the author wrong, is almost certainly of Howard's play. See J. R. Sutherland, 'The Date of James Howard's "All Mistaken, or the Mad Couple"' *Notes and Queries* 209.1964.339–40, and R. D. Hume, 'Dryden, James Howard and the Date of *All Mistaken' Philological Quarterly* 51.1972.422–9.
100. See W. van Lennep, 'Thomas Killigrew prepares his plays for production' in J. G. McManaway *et al.*, eds., *Joseph Quincy Adams Memorial Studies* (Washington, 1948) p. 805.
101. Pepys, 8 December 1666.
102. Probably on 14 February 1667.
103. See above p. 64.
104. See e.g. J. H. Wilson, *All the King's Ladies* (Chicago, 1958) p. 147.
105. 2 March 1667. Pepys also saw the play on 25 March, 24 May and 23 August that year.
106. Hart probably played the part from 1660 onwards but there is no recorded performance from March 1662 until 1667. The revival obviously capitalised on success.
107. Cf. the prologue to the revised play:

> And, much asham'd of what he was before,
> Has fairly play'd him at three Wenches more.
> (*Works* VIII 6.)

108. In spite of Nell's extra-theatrical activities, there is no reason why she should not have appeared in the play.
109. There is no cast-list in the printed text of 1668 but there was no one else in the company to play the parts.
110. *Diary*, 22 June 1668.
111. Betterton's illness at this time must have posed enormous problems for Davenant. Pepys first mentions the illness and Betterton's absence in October 1667 but his last certain performance is on 4 September. He did not return until July 1668, and when Pepys goes to Boyle's *Henry V* on 6 July, he is 'glad to see Betterton'.
112. *Works* I 286. On Farquhar and Collier see E. Rothstein, 'Farquhar's *Twin-Rivals* and the Reform of Comedy' *Publications of the Modern Language Association of America* 79.1964.33–41.

113. See W. S. Clark *The Early Irish Stage* (Oxford, 1955) pp. 207f for a list of Smock Alley actors.
114. *The Post-Boy* 14/16 November 1700 quoted by A. M. Taylor, 'Some New Light on William Bowen (1666–1718): Actor and Customs Officer' *Tulane Studies in English* 6.1956.35.
115. *The Post-Boy* 1/4 March 1701, quoted by Taylor, 'Some New Light on William Bowen' p. 35.
116. This is true in both directions. The two scenes of homosexual advances, by the Abbé in *Sir Anthony Love* and by Coupler in *The Relapse*, are rendered acceptable by being made to heroes played by women as breeches parts (Sir Anthony and Young Fashion).
117. *Apology* II 241.
118. *Ibid.* I 127.
119. *Ibid.* II 241.
120. *Ibid.* I 237.
121. *Ibid.* II 18.
122. *Ibid.* I 257.
123. *Memoirs of the Life of Robert Wilks, Esq.* (1732) pp. 9 and 23.
124. *Apology* I 135f.
125. *Memoirs of the Life of Robert Wilks* p. 30.
126. *Ibid.* p. 29.
127. See Jackson I. Cope, '*The Constant Couple*: Farquhar's Four-Plays-In-One' *ELH* 41.1974.488f.
128. There is a problem in this play over the casting of Cibber as the serious Lord Hardy. While in comedy, Cibber almost always played fops and fools, he did have pretensions to tragedy, where he had some success, 'had Nature given him Lungs Strenuous to his finisht Judgement' (Downes, p. 51). Steele was using this tragic ability to emphasise the serious nature of his play.
129. *Apology* II 244.
130. See above, p. 79.
131. *Apology* I 138.
132. *The Laureat* (1740) p. 35.
133. Cibber's adaptation had emphasised Richard's callousness not only by including the murder of Henry VI but also in the famous line 'Off with his head. So much for *Buckingham*.' (p. 45).
134. The refusal of loans by Richmore and Balderdash is much closer to Timon's rejection by his friends, than to anything in contemporary comedy. Shadwell's highly successful adaptation of *Timon*, first performed in 1678, was performed on 17 January 1701.

*Chapter 4.    Performance and the published text*

1. R. Williams, *Drama in Performance* (rev. ed., Harmondsworth, 1972), p. 174.
2. Williams too often confuses the two. He glosses the study of 'the written work in performance' (i.e., the bridge between writing and performance) as if it were a bridge between reading and performance: 'the dramatic structure of a work, which we may realize when we read it as literature, as this actually appears when the play is performed'. (*Drama in Performance*, p. 4.)

3. R. Williams, 'Base and Superstructure in Marxist Cultural Theory' *New Left Review* 82.1973.3–16.

4. On Dryden's involvement with proof-correcting, see F. Bowers 'Current Theories of Copy-Text, with an Illustration from Dryden' *Modern Philology* 48.1950.12–20.

5. For a brilliant study of these plays, see D. M. Bevington, *From 'Mankind' to Marlowe* (Cambridge, Mass. 1962).

6. *Ibid.* p. 6.

7. Cf. the announcement reported for *The Princelye pleasures of the Courte at Kenelworth* (1576), 'I have with much travayle and paine obtained the very true and perfect Copies, of all that were there presented & executed.' Cited in W. W. Greg, *A Bibliography of the English Printed Drama to the Restoration* (Oxford, 1939–59) III 1195–6.

8. See for example E. Sharpham, *The Fleer* (1607), with its epistle 'To the Reader and Hearer'.

9. For an example of the literary text *cut* for readers, see Jones' preface to *Tamburlaine* (1590), addressed to the readers. Jones hopes that the action will be as acceptable as it was delightful on stage but he has 'omitted and left out some fond and frivolous Iestures, digressing (and . . . far unmeet for the matter . . . to be mixtured in print with such matter of worth, it would proove a great disgrace to so honorable & stately a historie' (A2a–A2b). The comic passages were, of course, not necessarily by Marlowe.

10. See also R. Brome, *The Antipodes* (1640), L4b.

11. For example, Sogliardo's description of Puntarvolo, *Works* III 464f.

12. *Essays* I 75

13. *Works* III 426.

14. For Marston, see *The Malcontent* (1604), A4a; *The Wonder of Women* (1606), G3b; for Heywood, *The Rape of Lucrece* (1638), A2a; *The Iron Age, Part I* (1632), A4a.

15. *Calendar of State Papers Domestic, 1652–53*, p. 436.

16. L. B. Wright, 'The Reading of Plays during the Puritan Revolution' *Harvard Library Bulletin* 6.1934.107–8.

17. Although assigned lists are uncommon, unassigned lists appear in all three major folios, Jonson, Shakespeare, and Beaumont and Fletcher.

18. See Greg, *A Bibliography of the English Printed Drama to the Restoration* III 1261–93.

19. In *Apology* I xxv.

20. E. Howard, *The Usurper* (1664), A2a.

21. J. H. Wilson, *A Preface to Restoration Drama* (Cambridge, Mass., 1968), pp. 6–7.

22. See D. W. Sanville, 'Thomas D'Urfey's "Love for Money"' *Library Chronicle* 17.1950.71–7.

23. See Jonson's title-page for *The New Inn* 'As it was never acted, but most negligently play'd, by some, the Kings Servants. And more squeamishly beheld, and censured by others, the Kings Subjects' (*Works* VI 395).

24. Most of the necessary information is collected in J. Milhous and R. D. Hume, 'Dating Play Premières from Publication Data, 1660–1700' *Harvard Library Bulletin* 22. 1974.374–405. Publication was not necessarily the same thing as availability. Baker's *Tunbridge Wells* was probably first performed on 27 January 1703 and was published on 29 January. But the major London

booksellers did not buy and pool copies until nearly a month later on 22
February. Cf. N. Hodgson and C. Blagden, *The Notebook of Thomas Bennet and
Henry Clements* (Oxford, 1956) p. 121.

25. See J. G. McManaway, 'Songs and Masques in *The Tempest*' in *Theatre Miscellany* (Lutrell Society Reprints, 14; Oxford 1953) pp. 71–96. This practice
was parodied in Duffett's *The Mock-Tempest* (1674), See C. Haywood, '*The
Songs & Masque in the New Tempest*: An Incident in the Battle of the Two
Theatres, 1674' *Huntington Library Quarterly* 19.1955.39–56.

26. *Historia Histrionica* (1699) in *Apology* I xxv.

27. Quoted in F. P. and M. M. Verney, *Memoirs of the Verney Family* (1892–9) IV
227.

28. Here the change is marked between Downes, p. 8, and the 1671 quarto.

29. A production at York University in March 1976 reversed the effect by printing
her name in the programme, acted by 'Connie Farquhar'! Cf. for a similar
effect, Anthony Shaffer's *Sleuth* (1973), where non-existent characters were
listed in the theatre programme, complete with biographical details of their
equally non-existent actors.

30. (1710) A1b. (My italics.) The play was performed in 1670 but not published
until 1706, and under Betterton's name only in 1710.

31. See the details of *The Sicilian Usurper* version given in Tate's preface to his
*The History of King Richard the Second* (1681) $\chi$1b.

32. e.g. T. Durfey, *Don Quixote*, Part 2 (1694) A3a.

33. e.g. N. Tate, *Cuckolds Haven* (1685) A1a.

34. e.g. A. Behn, *The Widow Ranter* (1690) A2a.

35. See above for Aphra Behn on Angel's ad-libbing.

36. See J. W. Krutch, *Comedy and Conscience after the Restoration* (New York, 1924)
pp. 170–1.

37. See also, for Welsh, Scots and Irish examples, J. O. Bartley, *Teague, Shenkin
and Sawney* (Cork, 1954).

38. Similar notes exist in *The Princess* which was first printed in the 1664 Killigrew folio. See A. Wertheim, 'Production Notes for Three Plays by Thomas
Killigrew' *Theatre Survey* 10.1969.105–13.

39. *Ibid.* p. 106.

40. J. Wilson, *The Cheats*, ed. M. C. Nahm (Oxford, 1935), p. 123.

41. BL Add MS 27632, fol. 43.

42. Greg, *A Bibliography of the English Printed Drama to the Restoration* III 1313ff.
Oxinden (1608–70) bought most of his plays in the 1630s while he was kept
away from London theatres.

43. Cambridge University Library, uncatalogued Buxton MSS. The catalogue is
being edited by Mr. D. McKitterick who drew my attention to it.

44. A. C. Baugh, 'A Seventeenth Century Play-List' *Modern Language Review* 13.
1918. 401–11. Horne, a fellow of Oriel, became vicar of Headington in 1636;
again, plays and religion were not incompatible.

45. See T. N. S. Lennam 'Sir Edward Dering's Collection of Playbooks, 1619–
1624' *Shakespeare Quarterly* 16.1965.145–53.

46. S. Jayne and F. R. Johnson, eds., *The Lumley Library* (1956) p. 32.

47. R. H. MacDonald, ed., *The Library of Drummond of Hawthornden* (Edinburgh,
1971).

48. See J. L. Lievesay and R. B. Davis, 'A Cavalier's Library, 1643' *Studies in Bibliography* 6.1954.141–60.

49. H. R. Plomer 'A Cavalier's Library' *The Library* n.s. 5. 1904. 156–72. The entry 'For ballads & a play book o 3 6' (p. 161) marks the association of plays with low literature again. Cf. also the omission of plays in Donne's *The Courtier's Library* (ed. E. M. Simpson (1930), especially pp. 23–4).

50. G. W. Wheeler, ed., *Letters of Sir Thomas Bodley to Thomas James* (Oxford, 1926) p. 219.

51. *Ibid.* p. 222.

52. *The Character of a Town-Gallant* (1675) pp. 4–5.

53. G. J. Gray, 'The Diary of Jeffrey Boys of Gray's Inn, 1671' *Notes and Queries* 159. 1930. 455–6.

54. Sold with the library of Richard Wallop, 22 November 1697. This section is based on my study of over 100 sale catalogues in the period. References are by owner and date of sale, as in A. W. Pollard, *List of Catalogues of English Book Sales 1676–1900* (1915).

55. Sale of 9 May 1687, pp. 25 and 15.

56. See for example, Sir Godfrey Copley's library (Sprotborough Hall, sale at Sotheby's, 23–5 November 1925); John Hoyle, 14 November 1692 (five volumes of 10 plays each).

57. See for example, John Maitland, Duke of Lauderdale, sale of 27 May 1690 (48 plays); Arthur Annesley, 3rd Earl of Anglesey, sale of 25 October 1686 (23 plays); Sir Charles Scarburgh, 8 February 1695, (21); Richard Grahme, Viscount Preston, 9 November 1696 (32).

58. See for example, Pepys' library, vols. 1075 and 1604 bound as 'Loose Plays'.

59. Sale of 23 March 1703.

60. See for example, Ralph Hough, 1699; James Partridge 25 November and 16 December 1695; Edward Wray 20 June 1687; James Harrington 13 February 1695; William Cavendish, Duke of Newcastle 2 March 1719.

61. *Bibliotheca Smithiana* (1682) p. 275 Item 121. 15 May 1682.

62. The Library is known from the shelf-list in Trinity College, Cambridge and from R. De Villamil, *Newton the Man* (n.d.). Both sources include books dated after Newton's death. Newton also probably owned an edition of Dryden (1725), a bound-up set of Otway (1687) and a Shakespeare second folio (and also possibly a copy of Pope's Shakespeare). In addition three volumes of assorted plays by Lee, Banks, Otway, Dryden, and others may have been his. Cf. the sale of the Library of Mrs Anne Newton, including part of the collection of 'the great Sir Isaac Newton' (Leigh and Sotheby's, 22 March 1813).

63. J. Harrison and P. Laslett, *The Library of John Locke* (2nd ed., Oxford, 1971) p. 29.

64. See the absence from the Pepys library of *Adventures of Five Hours* (read 31 May 1663); *Indian Emperour* (bought 28 October 1667); *Secret Love* (bought 18 January 1668); *The Queen of Aragon* (bought 21 October 1668). He may of course have lost or lent them!

65. 8 January 1663; he was conspicuously less so on his second visit (17 January) but he blames it on himself ('I could discern it was not any fault in the play').

66. Cf. the emphasis, when he reads it, on *The Rival Ladies* as 'fine-writ' (18 July 1666).

67. E. Howard, *The Usurper* (1668) A2a.

68. J. Crowne, *Calisto* (1675), a1a. This attitude was commonly held to be Crowne's belief. In the satire *A Journal from Parnassus*, 'Crowne' claims 'I wou'd not for the World that any Play of mine should appear before such an Auditory in its Dishabilée, I mean without the Garniture of Scenes & Cloths, which are as essentially necessary to a Play as fine Teeth & fine Hands are to a Gentleman.' Apollo replies, 'you had spoken much more to the purpose if you had confess'd, that your Plays have succeeded much better upon the Stage than from the Press, which y$^e$ wiser sort suppose to proceed from their wanting the Garniture of Sense' (ed. H. Macdonald (1937) p. 17).

69. G. Langbaine, *An Account of the English Dramatick Poets* (1691) p. 202.

70. R. Flecknoe, *The Damoiselles a la Mode* (1667) A3b. Cf. *Erminia* A3a.

71. Sir Richard Steele, *Plays* ed. S. S. Kenny (Oxford, 1971) p. 299.

72. *Erminia* A3a.

73. See above p. 264 n. 9

74. F. Hédelin, *The Whole Art of the Stage* (1684) 1 p. 53.

75. *Ibid.*

76. *Ibid.* p. 54.

77. *The Usurper* A2a–A2b.

78. *Essays* II 46.

79. *Ibid.* I 278.

80. *Ibid.*

81. *Ibid.*

82. *Ibid.*

83. See H. J. Chaytor, *From Script to Print* (Cambridge, 1945).

84. *Essays* I 278.

85. *Ibid.* I 278 and II 46.

86. *Ibid.* I 278.

87. *Ibid.* II 45.

88. *Ibid.* II 46.

89. B. Beckerman, *Dynamics of Drama* (New York, 1970) p. 64.

90. L. B. Meyer, *Music, The Arts and Ideas* (Chicago, 1967) pp. 46–7.

91. *Ibid.* p. 53.

92. P. Edwards, 'The Danger not the Death: the Art of John Fletcher' in J. R. Brown and B. Harris, eds., *Jacobean Theatre* (Stratford-upon-Avon Studies 1, 1960) pp. 165–6.

93. 5 September 1667.

94. 18 February 1667.

95. J. C. Hodges, ed., *William Congreve: Letters and Documents* (1964) p. 60.

96. *Ibid.* p. 148.

97. *Works* (1710) I A3a–A3b.

98. *Ibid.* A2b.

99. *Short View*, p. 64.

100. N. Luttrell, *A Brief Historical Relation of State Affairs* (Oxford, 1857) IV 379.

101. See above, pp. 111–2.

102. Quoted by J. W. Krutch, *Comedy and Conscience*, pp. 174–5. The precise date of the case is not clear. On the legal pressures, see also A. Jackson, 'The Stage and the Authorities, 1700–14 (As Revealed in the Newspapers)' *Review of English Studies* 14.1938.53–62.

103. *Amendments*, p. 42.

104. See *A Letter to Mr. Congreve on his Pretended Amendments* (1698) p. 42 and *Animadversions on Mr. Congreve's late answer to Mr. Collier* (1698) pp. 43–4.

105. *Defence* (1698) pp. 46–7.

106. Translation by L. Echard *et al.*, *Terence's Comedies* (1694) p. 135.

107. Cf. Echard's treatment of the same point in relation to Terence when he attacks modern plays for the manner of delivery: 'only in our *Monologues* and *Asides*, our Actors have got a custom of looking so full upon the Spectators', L. Echard, *Plautus's Comedies* (1694), a8b.

108. 1710 changes to 'at' but 'out' is appropriate to Congreve's emphasis on solution.

109. H. Macdonald, *John Dryden: A Bibliography of Early Editions and of Drydeniana* (Oxford, 1939) p. 146.

110. See also bound-up neat sets advertised in the sale catalogues e.g. Sir Andrew Henley, sale in 1700 had 'Twelve plays by *Nath Lee*' and 'Seventeen plays all by Mrs *Behn*' (p. 42).

111. *Critical Works* I 324.

112. *Ibid.* I 322.

113. *Ibid.* I 324.

114. For Plautus, Venice 1472; Terence, Strassburg 1470; Aristophanes, Aldus' edition', 1498.

115. Jonson, *Works* IX 46f.

116. See for example T. Southland, *Love a la Mode* (1663).

117. *Essays* I 37.

118. *The Whole Art of the Stage* III p. 87.

119. *Ibid.* III pp. 87–8.

120. *Terence*, p. vi.

121. *Ibid.* e.g. pp. 306, 307, 319.

122. *Plautus* b2b.

123. *Terence*, p. xxii.

124. *Terence*, p. xii. Cf. Hédelin, *The Whole Art of the Stage* III p. 88 'one might have transpos'd any of their *Scenes*, without any injury to the *Play*'.

125. A3a. Cf. Echard's continual recommendation of the unities.

126. See below, chapter 7, for Congreve's manner of using the unities in these plays.

127. A. Gosse. 'The Omitted Scene in Congreve's *Love for Love*' *Modern Philology* 61. 1963.40–2.

128. *Ibid.* p. 40.

129. *The Whole Art of the Stage*, III p. 88.

130. Congreve again provides a correct *liaison* for this scene: Foresight now announces 'he's here already'.

131. The correction was made in Q2 (1706).

132. W. Congreve, *The Way of the World*, ed. J. Barnard (Edinburgh, 1972) p. 106.

133. Almost the only example is in *The Double-Dealer* where Sir Paul's 'She's a

passionate Woman' (p. 69) becomes 'You're a passionate Woman' (I 277) since Lady Touchwood has not left the stage.

134. The 1719 text is even worse with heavier punctuation (an obsessive use of exclamation marks) and centred speech-prefixes; a further stage on the road away from the theatre.

*Chapter 5.  Text and performance (1): the comedies, 1691 to 1693*

1. See S. S. Kenny, 'Theatrical Warfare 1695–1710' *Theatre Notebook* 27.1973.130–45; E. A. Langhans, 'Players and Playhouses 1695–1710 and their effect on English Comedy' *Theatre Annual* 29.1973.28–39; C. Winton, 'The London Stage Embattled: 1695–1710' *Tennessee Studies in Literature* 19.1974.9–19.

2. A. H. Scouten, 'Notes toward a History of Restoration Comedy' *Philological Quarterly* 45.1966.66.

3. See also *The London Stage*, Part I, pp. 398 and 411–12.

4. See *Apology* I 187.

5. W. Mountfort, *Plays* (1720) I K4a.

6. G. Powell, *The Treacherous Brothers* (1690) A3a.

7. *Plays* I K4a.

8. T. Durfey, *Collin's Walk through London and Westminster* (1690) pp. 145–6.

9. See A. S. Borgman, *The Life and Death of William Mountfort* (Cambridge, Mass., 1935) pp. 124–6.

10. *The Player's Tragedy*, p. 10.

11. Quoted by Borgman, *The Life and Death of William Mountfort*, p. 99.

12. *Apology* I 129.

13. *Ibid.* I 129–30.

14. Reprinted in W. J. Cameron, ed., *Poems on Affairs of State, Volume 5, 1688–1697* (1971) p. 371.

15. 'The Description of a Beau' in 'Collection of Choice Poems' BL MS Harley 7319, fol. 366a.

16. *Apology* I 129.

17. *Ibid.* I 129.

18. *Ibid.* I 129.

19. Lee's play was printed for the first time in 1689 and may therefore have been revived at that time.

20. The Reply of the Patentees, (1694), quoted from A. Nicoll, *A History of Restoration Drama, 1600–1700* (4th ed., revised, Cambridge, 1952) p. 376. Betterton was certainly not short of energy in the early years of the secession. I suspect he was disinclined to put himself out for the patentees.

21. T. Durfey, *The Intrigues at Versailles* (1697) A2b.

22. J. Dryden *The Letters* ed. C. E. Ward (Durham, North Carolina, 1942) p. 54.

23. N. Luttrell, *A Brief Historical Relation of State Affairs* (Oxford, 1857) II 435; see also Downes, p. 43.

24. E. Settle, *The Fairy Queen* (1692) π2b.

25. *Apology* I 187.

26. Cameron, ed., *Poems on Affairs of State*, V 371.

27. *Ibid.*
28. For detailed accounts of his death, see Borgman, *The Life and Death of William Mountfort*, pp. 123–69.
29. Reply of the Patentees, p. 378.
30. *Ibid.*
31. I have relineated the passage to recover Southerne's verse.
32. Reply of the Patentees (1694) p. 378.
33. Borgman, *The Life and Death of William Mountfort*, p. 171.
34. *Apology* I 166.
35. *Ibid.* II 313.
36. *Ibid.* I 67–9.
37. National Library of Ireland MS 13,226 (18).
38. C. Gildon, *The Lives and Characters of the English Dramatick Poets* (1699) p. 113.
39. The only plot for which there is no direct source is the title-plot, Annabella's cheating of the widow. Nicoll (*A History of Restoration Drama*, p. 261) suggested Middleton's *No Wit No Help Like a Woman's* but, though there are some similarities, neither that nor its Restoration adaptation by Aphra Behn as *The Counterfeit Bridegroom* (1677) provides the same sort of detailed source as exists for the rest of the play. It is possible of course that it is Powell's own invention but it is so Caroline in manner that I suspect it is plagiarised as well.
40. Southerne's method in *The Maid's Last Prayer* is so similar to *The Wives Excuse* that I shall only discuss the latter.
41. There has been some argument about this. W. J. Lawrence argued against a drop scene (*The Elizabethan Playhouse and Other studies* (1912) p. 175) but Summers accepted the idea (*The Restoration Theatre* (1934) p. 102). The scene is clearly both a discovery and played before a curtain ('The Curtain, drawn up, shews . . .' p. 5). For an extended discussion of the problem, see R. R. Thornton, '*The Wives Excuse' by Thomas Southerne: A Critical Edition* (Ph.D. thesis, Univ. of Pennsylvania, 1966), pp. cxiii–cxxii.
42. L. Echard, *Plautus's Comedies* (1694), p. 246.
43. E. G. Craig, *On The Art of the Theatre* (revised ed., 1956) p. 146.

*Chapter 6.  Text and performance (2): Wycherley's 'The Plain-Dealer'*

1. J. Dennis, *The Decay and Defects of Dramatick Poetry*, in *Critical Works* II 277.
2. M. P. Tilley, *A Dictionary of the Proverbs in England in the Sixteenth and Seventeenth Centuries* (Ann Arbor, 1950) P381. Apart from this proverb, the phrase was also in current use for a card game. Charles Cotton, in *The Compleat Gamester* (1674), comments 'He that deals hath the advantage of this Game; for if he turn up the Ace of Diamonds he cannot lose' (p. 142). There may be a connection with the struggle over the money and jewels in Wycherley's play. Certainly, Manly's disdain for wealth matches another proverb: 'Plain Dealing is a jewel but they that use it die beggars' (Tilley P382).
3. This is the famous story of the duchess calling out 'You, *Wycherley*, you are a Son of a Whore', best told by Dennis (*Critical Works* II 409).
4. I. Donaldson, *The World Upside-Down* (Oxford, 1970) p. 102.

5. There is the same play here on 'favour' as in the dedication to *Love in a Wood*.

6. W. Congreve, *The Double-Dealer* (1694), a2b.

7. G. Granville, 'A Character of Mr. Wycherley' in A. Boyer, *Letters of Wit, Politicks and Morality* (1701) p. 256.

8. Dennis, *Critical Works* II 411.

9. A. Pope, *The Correspondence* ed. G. Sherburn (Oxford, 1956) I 34.

10. M. Summers, ed., *The Works of William Wycherley* (1923) II 199, 201.

11. A. Pope, *The Correspondence*, p. 55.

12. *Ibid.* p. 80.

13. M. Montaigne, *Essays* translated J. Florio (1910) III 97.

14. *Ibid.* III 77.

15. Dedication, †2a. 'For sheer effrontery, nothing / Can beat a woman caught in the act; her very / Guilt adds fresh fire to her fury and indignation.' (Juvenal, *The Sixteen Satires*, trans. P. Green (Harmondsworth, 1967) p. 137).

16. Montaigne, *Essays* III 70.

17. *Ibid.* III 69.

18. Prefatory letter to Cotton's translation of Montaigne, *Essays* (2nd ed., 1693) I *3b.

19. Prefatory poem to Florio's translation, Montaigne, *Essays* I 13.

20. 'To a Vain, Young COURTIER; occasion'd by his speaking contemptibly of the PLAYERS'. *Works*, ed. Summers IV 241.

21. *Ibid.* pp. 241–2.

22. See J. H. Wilson, 'Biographical Notes on some Restoration Actresses' *Theatre Notebook* 18.1964.46.

23. See E. L. Avery, '*The Country Wife* in the Eighteenth Century' *Research Studies* 10.1942.146 and '*The Plain Dealer* in the Eighteenth Century' *Research Studies* 11.1943.240.

24. On Cartwright's early career, see E. Boswell, 'Young Mr Cartwright' *Modern Language Review* 24.1929.125–42.

25. *Critical Works* II 277.

26. J. H. Wilson, *All the King's Ladies* (Chicago, 1958) pp. 73f.

27. T. Davies, *Dramatic Miscellanies* (1784) III 262.

28. See Downes, p. 32; T. Thomas, *The Life of the Late Famous Comedian, Jo. Hayns* (1701) pp. 23–4; K. Cameron, 'Jo Haynes, *Infamis*' *Theatre Notebook* 24.1970.56–67.

29. In *Le Misanthrope*, of course, Philinte and Eliante are united at the end.

30. Quoted by H. P. Vincent, 'The Death of William Wycherley' *Harvard Studies and Notes in Philology and Literature* 15.1933.232.

31. P. G. Adams, 'What Happened in Olivia's Bedroom? or Ambiguity in *The Plain Dealer*' in T. A. Kirby and W. J. Olive, eds., *Essays in Honor of Esmond Linworth Marilla* (Baton Rouge, 1970) pp. 174–187.

32. For example Hughes' edition (1968).

33. Adams, 'What happened in Olivia's bedroom?' p. 187.

34. See for example N. Holland, *The First Modern Comedies* (Cambridge, Mass., 1959) chapter 10; R. Zimbardo, *Wycherley's Drama* (New Haven, 1965) pp. 142f.

35. See A. Righter, 'William Wycherley' in J. R. Brown and B. Harris, eds., *Restoration Theatre* (Stratford-upon-Avon Studies 6, 1965) 81–6; B. Dobrée, *Restoration Comedy 1660–1720* (1924) p. 88.

36. The reader has the additional information guaranteed by the feminine form of the name, given throughout, 'Fidelia'. The problem is therefore not as fundamentally impenetrable as the sex of Epicoene, where the fact of the stage's conventions is also the final, though unexpected, solution.

37. Pepys' Library, Magdalene College, Cambridge, MS 'Main Catalogue' p. 87.

*Chapter 7.    Text and performance (3): the comedies of Congreve*

1. W. Congreve, *Incognita* (1692) A6b.
2. M. Novak, *William Congreve* (New York, 1971) p. 24.
3. Cf. W. S. Clark, *The Early Irish Stage* (Oxford, 1955) p. 95; J. C. Hodges, *William Congreve the Man* (New York, 1941) pp. 26–8; Novak, *William Congreve*, p. 23.
4. Numbers refer to items in J. C. Hodges, ed., *The Library of William Congreve* (New York, 1955).
5. *The Complete Plays of William Congreve*, ed. H. Davis (Chicago, 1967) pp. 4–5.
6. J. Barnard, 'Passion, "Poetical Justice", and Dramatic Law in *The Double-Dealer* and *The Way of the World*' in B. Morris, ed., *William Congreve* (1972) p. 96.
7. See Southerne's notes on Congreve, BL MS Add 4221, fol. 341.
8. *The Way of the World*, A4b.
9. F. Hédelin, *The Whole Art of the Stage* (1684) III p. 6.
10. J. C. Hodges, ed., *William Congreve: Letters and Documents* (1964) pp. 212–13.
11. *The Double-Dealer*, A3a.
12. W. Congreve, *Works* ed. M. Summers (1923) I 16.
13. *Amendments of Mr Collier's False and Imperfect Citations* (1698) p. 15.
14. Jonson *Works* V 239.
15. T. Shadwell, *The Volunteers* (1693) p. 32.
16. G. Weales, 'The Shadow on Congreve's Surface' *Educational Theatre Journal* 19.1967.32.
17. *Apology* I 67–9.
18. A. C. Gosse, 'Plot and Character in Congreve's *Double-Dealer*' *Modern Language Quarterly* 29.1968.287.
19. Gosse, 'Plot and Character' pp. 281f.
20. W. Wycherley, *The Country Wife* (1675) p. 75.
21. 'Sometimes however even Comedy raises its voice' (Horace, *Ars Poetica* l.93).
22. *Apology* I 121.
23. See A. Gaw, 'Tuke's *Adventures of Five Hours* in Relation to the "Spanish Plot" and to John Dryden' in A. Gaw, ed., *Studies in English Drama* (Pennsylvania, 1917) pp. 54f.
24. Anne Barton, Introduction, *The Double-Dealer (1694)* (1973), π3b.
25. *Ibid.*
26. J. Collier, *A Short View of the Immorality and Profaneness of the English Stage* (1698), p. 12.
27. D. C. Taylor, *William Congreve* (Oxford, 1931) p. 64.
28. G. L. Evans, 'Congreve's Sense of Theatre' in B. Morris, ed., *William Congreve* (1972) p. 166.
29. E. L. Avery, *Congreve's Plays on the Eighteenth-Century Stage* (New York, 1951).

30. *Apology* II 307.

31. *Apology* I 155.

32. *Apology* II 306.

33. *Apology* II 302.

34. BL MS Harley 7319, reprinted in Downes p. 58.

35. J. H. Wilson, ed., *Court Satires of the Restoration* (Columbus, Ohio, 1976) p. 78.

36. Downes p. 58.

37. M. Summers, *The Restoration Theatre* (1934) pp. 311–12.

38. *Works* (1715) III 39.

39. N. Tate, *The History of King Lear* (1681) p. 51.

40. Historical Manuscripts Commission 15th Report, Appendix, Part I, Dartmouth MSS, vol III, (1896) p. 145.

41. *Apology* I 162.

42. H. Hawkins, *Likenesses of Truth in Elizabethan and Restoration Drama* (Oxford, 1972) p. 130n.

43. B. Corman, 'The *Way of the World* and Morally Serious Comedy' *University of Toronto Quarterly* 44.1975.200.

44. H. Hawkins, *Likenesses of Truth*, p. 117.

45. F. Hédelin, *The Whole Art of the Stage*, III p. 17.

46. On the pervasive use of legal language, see P. J. Hurley, 'Law and the Dramatic Rhetoric of *The Way of the World*' *South Atlantic Quarterly* 70.1971. 191–202.

# Select bibliography

This is no more than a list of some of the books and articles that I have found particularly useful in preparing this study. Any sins of omission are unintentional.

Adams, H. H., 'A Prompt Copy of Dryden's *Tyrannic Love'* *Studies in Bibliography* 4.1951–2.170–4.

Ames, R., *A Search After Wit* (1691).

*Animadversions on Mr Congreve's Late Answer to Mr Collier* (1698).

Archer, S. L., 'The Epistle Dedicatory in Restoration Drama' *Restoration and 18th Century Theatre Research* 10i.1971.6–13.

Archer, W., *Masks or Faces?* (1888).

Armstrong, W. A., 'The Audience of the Elizabethan Private Theatres' *Review of English Studies* n.s. 10.1959.234–49.

Avery, E. L., 'A Poem on the Dorset Garden Theatre' *Theatre Notebook* 18.1964. 121–4.

Avery, E. L., 'The Restoration Audience' *Philology Quarterly* 45.1966.54–61.

Avery, E. L. *et al,* (eds.), *The London Stage 1660–1800* (Carbondale, 1960–68).

Ayres, P. J., 'Production and Adaptation of William Sampson's *The Vow Breakers* (1636) in the Restoration' *Theatre Notebook* 27.1973.145–9.

Bachrach, A. G., 'The Great Chain of Acting' *Neophilologus* 33.1949.160–72.

Baldwin, T. W., *The Organization and Personnel of the Shakespearean Company* (Princeton, 1927).

Bear, A. S., 'Criticism and Social Change: the Case of Restoration Drama' *Komos* 2.1968.23–31.

Beckerman, B., *Shakespeare at the Globe 1599–1609* (New York, 1962).

Beckerman, B., *Dynamics of Drama* (New York, 1970).

Bedford, A., *The Evil and Danger of Stage Plays* (1706).

Behn, A., *Works* ed. M. Summers (1915).

Bentley, G. E., *The Profession of Dramatist in Shakespeare's Time, 1590–1642* (Princeton, 1971).

Betterton, T., (?) *The History of the English Stage* (1741).

Bevington, D. M., *From 'Mankind' to Marlowe* (Cambridge, Mass., 1962).

Blount, T., *Glossographia* (1656).

Booth, S., 'On the Value of *Hamlet*' in N. Rabkin, ed., *Reinterpretations of Elizabethan Drama* (Selected Papers from the English Institute, New York, 1969) pp. 137–76.

Borgman, A. S., *The Life and Death of William Mountfort* (Cambridge, Mass., 1935).

Boswell, E., 'Young Mr Cartwright' *Modern Language Review* 24.1929.125–42.

Boswell, E., *The Restoration Court Stage 1660–1702* (Cambridge, Mass., 1932).

Boyer, A., *Letters of Wit, Politicks and Morality* (1701).

Boyle, R., *Dramatic Works* ed. W. S. Clark, II (Cambridge, Mass., 1937).

Brauer, G. C., Jr., *The Education of a Gentleman* (New York, 1959).

Brett-James, N. G., *The Growth of Stuart London* (1935).

Brown, J. R., *Free Shakespeare* (1974).

Brown, J. R. and Harris, B. (eds.), *Restoration Theatre* (Stratford-upon-Avon Studies 6, 1965).

Brown, T., *Works* (1711–15).

Bulwer, J., *Chirologia* (1644).

Bulwer, J., *Chironomia* (1644).

Burner, S. A., 'A Provincial Strolling Company of the 1670s' *Theatre Notebook* 20.1966.74–8.

Cameron, K. M., 'Jo Haynes, *Infamis*' *Theatre Notebook* 24.1970.56–67.

Campbell, L. B., 'The Rise of a Theory of Stage Presentation in England during the Eighteenth Century' *Publications of the Modern Language Association of America* 32.1917.163–200.

Campbell, L. B., *Scenes and Machines on the English Stage during the Renaissance* (Cambridge, 1923).

Chadwick, W. R., *The Four Plays of William Wycherley* (The Hague, 1975).

Chetwood, W. R., *A General History of the Stage* (1749).

Cibber, C., *An Apology for the life of Mr Colley Cibber* ed. R. W. Lowe (1889).

Clark, W. S., *The Early Irish Stage* (Oxford, 1955).

Clark, W. S., 'Corpses, Concealments, and Curtains on the Restoration Stage' *Review of English Studies* 13.1937.438–48.

Collier, J., *A Short View of the Immorality and Profaneness of the English Stage* (1698).

Collier, J., *A Defence of the Short View* (1699).

Collier, J., *A Second Defence of the Short View* (1700).

*A Comparison Between the Two Stages* ed. S. B. Wells (Princeton, 1942).

Conaghan, J., 'A Prompt Copy of Etherege's *The Man of Mode*' *Library Review* 21.1968.387–8.

Congreve, W., *Works* ed. M. Summers (1923).

Cope, J. O., *The Theater and the Dream* (Baltimore, 1973).

Cope, J. I., 'The Constant Couple: Farquhar's Four-Plays-In-One' *ELH* 41.1974.477–93.

*The Country Gentleman's Vade Mecum* (1699).

Culler, J. D., *Structuralist Poetics* (1975).

Curll, E., *The Life of the Eminent Comedian Robert Wilks, Esq.* (1733).

Davies, T., *Dramatic Miscellanies* (1784).

Dennis, J., *Critical Works* ed. E. N. Hooker (Baltimore, 1939–43).

Donaldson, I., *The World Upside-Down* (Oxford, 1970).

Downer, A. S., 'Nature to Advantage Dressed: Eighteenth-Century Acting' *Publications of the Modern Language Association of America* 58.1943.1002–37.

Downes, J., *Roscius Anglicanus* ed. M. Summers (1928).

Dryden, J., *Letters* ed. C. E. Ward (Durham, North Carolina, 1942).

Dryden, J., *Works* ed. E. N. Hooker *et al.* (Berkeley, 1956– ).

Dryden, J., *Of Dramatic Poesy and Other Critical Essays* ed. G. Watson (1962).

Duvignaud, J., *L'Acteur: Esquisse d'une sociologie du comédien* (Paris, 1965).

Echard, L., *Plautus's Comedies, Rudens, Epidicus, Amphitryon Made English* (1694).

Echard, L., *et al. Terence's Comedies Made English* (1694).

Egerton, W., *Faithful Memoirs of the Life, Amours and Performances, of that justly celebrated, and most Eminent Actress of her Time, Mrs Anne Oldfield* (1731).

Etherege, Sir G., *Dramatic Works* ed. H. F. B. Brett-Smith (Oxford, 1927).

Etherege, Sir G., *Poems* ed. J. Thorpe (Princeton, 1963).

Etherege, Sir G., *Letters* ed. F. Bracher (Berkeley, 1974).

Evans, G. B., *Shakespearean Prompt-Books of the 17th Century* (Charlottesville, 1960–   ).

Evelyn, J., *Diary* ed. E. S. de Beer (Oxford, 1955).

Farquhar, G., *Works* ed. C. Stonehill (1930).

Fish, S. E., *Self-Consuming Artifacts* (Berkeley, 1972).

Flecknoe, R., *The Life of Tomaso the Wanderer* ed. G. Thorn-Drury (1925).

Freehafer, J., 'The Formation of the London Patent Companies in 1660' *Theatre Notebook* 20.1965.6–30.

Freehafer, J., 'Perspective Scenery and the Caroline Playhouses' *Theatre Notebook* 27.1973.98–113.

George, M. D., *London Life in the Eighteenth Century* (1925).

Gildon, C., *Lives and Characters of the English Dramatick Poets* (1699).

Gildon, C., *The Life of Mr Thomas Betterton* (1710).

Gosse, A. C., 'Dramatic Theory and Practice in the Comedies of William Congreve' (Ph.D. thesis, Columbia University, 1962).

Gray, P. H. Jr., 'Lenten Casts and the Nursery: Evidence for the Dating of Certain Restoration Plays' *Publications of the Modern Language Association of America* 53.1938.781–94.

Greg, Sir W. W., *A Bibliography of the English Printed Drama to the Restoration* (Oxford, 1939–59).

Hawkins, H., *Likenesses of Truth in Elizabethan and Restoration Drama* (Oxford, 1972).

Hédelin, F., *La Pratique du théâtre* (Paris, 1657).

Hédelin, F., *The Whole Art of the Stage* (1684).

Helbo, A. (ed.), *Sémiologie de la représentation* (Brussels, 1975).

Hewitt, B. (ed), *The Renaissance Stage: Documents of Serlio, Sabbatini and Furttenbach* (Coral Gables, 1958).

Highfill, P. H. Jr. *et al.* (eds.), *A Biographical Dictionary of Actors, Actresses, Musicians, Dancers, Managers, & Other Stage Personnel in London, 1660–1800* (Carbondale, 1973–   ).

Hill, 'Sir' John, *The Actor: A Treatise on the Art of Playing* (1750).

Hill, 'Sir' John, *The Actor* (new ed., 1755).

Hodges, J. C., *William Congreve the Man* (New York, 1941).

Hodges, J. C., 'The Composition of Congreve's First Play' *Publications of the Modern Language Association of America* 58.1943.1971–6.

Hodges, J. C., *The Library of William Congreve* (New York, 1955).

Hodges, J. C. (ed.), *William Congreve: Letters and Documents* (1964).

Hogendoorn, W., 'Reading on a Booke. Closet Drama and the Study of Theatre Arts' in *Essays on Drama and Theatre: Liber Amicorum Benjamin Hunningher* (Amsterdam, 1973) pp. 50–66.

Holland, N. N., *The First Modern Comedies* (Cambridge, Mass., 1959).

Hotson, L., *The Commonwealth and Restoration Stage* (Cambridge, Mass., 1928).

Hughes, L., *The Drama's Patrons* (Austin, 1971).

Hume, R. D., *The Development of English Drama in the late Seventeenth Century* (Oxford, 1976).

Ingarden, R., 'Les Fonctions du langage au théâtre' *Poétique* 8.1971.531–8.

Jackson, A., 'The Stage and the Authorities, 1700–1714 (As Revealed in the Newspapers)' *Review of English Studies* 14,1938.53–62.

Jackson, A. S., 'Restoration Scenery 1656–1680' *Restoration and 18th Century Theatre Research* 3ii.1964. 25–38.

Jonson, B., *Works*, ed. C. H. Herford and P. and E. Simpson (Oxford, 1925–52).

*A Journal from Parnassus* ed. H. Macdonald (1937).

Joseph, B. L., 'Stage Directions in a 17th Cent. Copy of Shirley' *Theatre Notebook* 3.1949.66–7.

Joseph, B. L., *Elizabethan Acting* (revised ed., Oxford, 1964).

Kenny, S. S., 'Theatrical Warfare, 1695–1710' *Theatre Notebook* 27.1973.130–45.

Kernodle, G. R., *From Art to Theatre* (Chicago, 1944).

Klaus, C. H., 'The Scenic Art of William Congreve: An Approach to Restoration Comedy' (Ph.D. thesis, Cornell University, 1966).

Krutch, J. W., *Comedy and Conscience after the Restoration* (New York, 1924).

Langbaine, G., *An Account of the English Dramatick Poets* (Oxford, 1691).

Langhans, E. A., 'Staging Practices in the Restoration Theatre 1660–1682' (Ph.D. thesis, Yale University, 1955).

Langhans, E. A., 'Wren's Restoration Playhouse' *Theatre Notebook* 18.1964.91–100.

Langhans, E. A., 'The Dorset Garden Theatre in Pictures' *Theatre Survey* 6.1965. 134–46.

Langhans, E. A., 'Pictorial Material on the Bridges Street and Drury Lane Theatres' *Theatre Survey* 7.1966.80–100.

Langhans, E. A., 'Restoration Manuscript Notes in Seventeenth Century Plays' *Restoration and 18th Century Theatre Research* 5i.1966.30–9 and 5ii.1966.2–17.

Langhans, E. A., 'The Vere Street and Lincoln's Inn Fields Theatres in Pictures' *Educational Theatre Journal* 20.1968.171–85.

Langhans, E. A., 'A Conjectural Reconstruction of the Dorset Garden Theatre' *Theatre Survey* 13.1972.74–93.

Langhans, E. A., 'Players and Playhouses, 1695–1710, and their effect on English Comedy' *Theatre Annual* 29.1973.28–39.

Langhans, E. A., 'New Restoration Manuscript Casts' *Theatre Notebook* 27.1973. 149–57.

Langhans, E. A., 'A Restoration Actor's Part' *Harvard Library Bulletin* 23.1975.180–5.

Leacroft, R., *The Development of the English Playhouse* (1973).

Lennep. W.van, 'Thomas Killigrew Prepares His Plays for Production' in J. M. McManaway *et al.*, eds., *Joseph Quincy Adams Memorial Studies* (Washington, 1948) pp. 803–8.

*A Letter to Mr. Congreve on his Pretended Amendments* (1698).

Loftis, J., *Comedy and Society from Congreve to Fielding* (Stanford, 1959).

Love, H. H. R., 'The Myth of the Restoration Audience' *Komos* 1.1967.49–56.

Love, H. H. R., 'Bear's Case Laid Open: Or, A Timely Warning to Literary Sociologists' *Komos* 2.1968.72–80.

Love, H. H. R., 'Dryden, Durfey, and the Standard of Comedy' *Studies in English Literature 1500–1900* 13.1973.422–36.

Lowe, R. W., *Thomas Betterton* (1891).

McKinnen, D. G., 'A Description of a Restoration Promptbook of Shirley's *The Ball' Restoration and 18th Century Theatre Research* 10i.1971.25–8.

Magalotti, Conte Lorenzo, *Travels of Cosmo the Third* (1821).

Mann, D., *A Concordance to the Plays of William Congreve* (Cornell, 1973).

Martin, L. J., 'From Forestage to Proscenium: A Study of Restoration Staging Techniques' *Theatre Survey* 4.1963.3–28.

Matlack, C. S., 'Parody and Burlesque of Heroic Ideals in Wycherley's Comedies: A Critical Reinterpretation of Contemporary Evidence' *Papers on Language and Literature* 8.1972.273–86.

*Memoirs of the Life of Robert Wilks, Esq.* (1732).

Meyer, L. B., *Emotion and Meaning in Music* (Chicago, 1956).

Milhous, J. A., 'Thomas Betterton at Lincoln's Inn Fields' (Ph.D. thesis, Cornell University, 1974).

Milhous, J. A., 'An Annotated Census of Thomas Betterton's Roles, 1659–1710' *Theatre Notebook* 29.1975.33–43 and 85–94.

Milhous, J. A. and Hume, R. D., 'Dating Play Premières from Publication Data 1660–1700' *Harvard Library Bulletin* 22.1974.374–405.

Morris, B. (ed.), *William Congreve* (1972).

Mullin, D. C., 'The Theatre Royal, Bridges Street: A Conjectural Restoration' *Educational Theatre Journal* 19.1967.17–29.

Mullin, D. C. and Koenig, B., 'Christopher Wren's Theatre Royal' *Theatre Notebook* 21.1967.180–7.

Nicoll, A., *The Development of the Theatre* (5th ed., revised, 1966).

Nicoll, A., *A History of Restoration Drama 1660 to 1700* (4th ed., revised, Cambridge, 1952).

Novak, M. E., *William Congreve* (New York, 1971).

Noyes, R. G., *Ben Jonson on the English Stage 1660–1776* (Cambridge, Mass., 1935).

Orgel, S. and Strong, R., *Inigo Jones: The Theatre of the Stuart Court* (1973).

Otway, T., *Works* ed. J. C. Ghosh (Oxford, 1932).

Pepys, S., *The Diary* ed. R. Latham and W. Matthews (1970–   ).

*The Players Turn'd Academicks* (1703).

*Poeta Infamis* (1692).

Pollard, A. W., *List of Catalogues of English Book Sales 1676–1900* (1915).

Righter, A., *Shakespeare and the Idea of the Play* (1692).

Rosenberg, M., *The Masks of King Lear* (Berkeley, 1972).

Rosenfeld, S. M., *A Short History of Scene Design in Great Britain* (Oxford, 1973).

Ross, R. H. Jr., 'Samuel Sandford: Villain from Necessity' *Publications of the Modern Language Association of America* 76.1961.367–72.

Rothstein, E., 'Farquhar's *Twin-Rivals* and the Reform of Comedy' *Publications of the Modern Language Association of America* 79.1964.33–41.

Scanlan, E. G., 'Reconstruction of the Duke's Playhouse in Lincoln's Inn Fields, 1661–1671' *Theatre Notebook* 10.1956.48–50.

Schneider, B. R. Jr., 'The Coquette-Prude as an Actress Line in Restoration Comedy during the time of Mrs Oldfield' *Theatre Notebook* 22.1968.143–56.

Sedley, Sir C., *Poetical and Dramatic Works* ed. V. de S. Pinto (1928).

Shaaber, M., 'A Letter from Mrs Barry' *Library Chronicle* 16.1950.46–9.

Shadwell, T., *Works* ed. M. Summers (1927).

Sheppard, F. W. (ed.), *The Theatre Royal, Drury Lane and The Royal Opera House, Covent Garden* (Survey of London, 35, 1970).

Sorelius, G., 'The Smock Alley Prompt-Books of *1* and *2 Henry IV*' *Shakespeare Quarterly* 22.1971.111–28.

Southern, R., *Changeable Scenery* (1952).

Sprague, A. C., 'Did Betterton Chant?' *Theatre Notebook* 1.1946.54–5.

Steele, R., *The Theatre* ed. J. Loftis (Oxford, 1962).

Steele, R., *Plays* ed. S. S. Kenny (Oxford, 1971).

Stevenson, A., 'The Case of the Decapitated Cast or *The Night-Walker* at Smock Alley' *Shakespeare Quarterly* 6.1955.275–96.

Summers, M., *The Restoration Theatre* (1934).

Summers, M., *The Playhouse of Pepys* (1935).

Summers, M., *Essays in Petto* ([1928]).

*Theatre Miscellany* (Luttrell Society Reprints 14, Oxford, 1953).

Thomas, T., *The Life of the Late Famous Comedian, Jo. Hayns* (1701).

Underwood, D., *Etherege and the Seventeenth-Century Comedy of Manners* (New Haven, 1957).

Vanbrugh, J., *Works* ed. B. Dobrée (1927).

Veinstein, A., *La Mise en scène théâtrale et sa condition esthétique* (2nd ed., Paris, 1968).

Velz, J. W., 'A Restoration Cast List for "Julius Caesar"' *Notes and Queries* 213.1968. 132–3.

Verney, F. P., and M. M., *Memoirs of the Verney Family* (1892–9).

Wells, S., *Literature and Drama* (1970).

Wertheim, A., 'Production Notes for Three Plays by Thomas Killigrew' *Theatre Survey* 10.1969.105–13.

Wharfinger, R., *The Courier's Tragedy* (1689).

Wickham, G., *Early English Stages 1300 to 1660* (1959– ).

Williams, A. and Novak, M., *Congreve Consider'd* (Los Angeles, 1971).

Williams, R., *Drama in Performance* (revised ed., Harmondsworth, 1972).

Wilson, C., *Memoirs of the Life, Writings and Amours of William Congreve, Esq.* (1730).

Wilson, J., *The Cheats* ed. M. C. Nahm (Oxford, 1935).

Wilson, J. H., 'Rant, Cant and Tone on the Restoration Stage' *Studies in Philology* 52.1955.592–8.

Wilson, J. H., 'The Marshall Sisters and Ann Quin' *Notes and Queries* 202.1957.104– 6.

Wilson, J. H., *All the King's Ladies* (Chicago, 1958).

Wilson, J. H., 'Players' Lists in the Lord Chamberlain's *Registers*' *Theatre Notebook* 18.1963.25–30.

Wilson, J. H., *Mr Goodman the Player* (Pittsburgh, 1964).

Wilson, J. H., 'Biographical Notes on some Restoration Actresses' *Theatre Notebook* 18.1964.43–7.

*Wit for Money* (1691).

Wright, J., *Country Conversations* (1694).

Wright, J., *Historia Histrionica* (1699).

Wright, L. B., 'The Reading of Plays during the Puritan Revolution' *Harvard Library Bulletin* 6. 1934.73–108.

Wycherley, W., *Works* ed. M. Summers (1924).

Zimansky, C. A., 'Editing Restoration Comedy: Vanbrugh and Others' in D. I. B. Smith, ed., *Editing Seventeenth Century Prose* (Toronto, 1972) pp. 95–122.

# Index

Angel, Edward, 63, 72
Armin, Robert, 70
Aston, Anthony, 79, 155, 226, 227

Baker, Thomas, *The Humours of the Age*, 91–2
Bancroft, John, *Edward III*, 141
Banks, John, *The Island Queens*, 107
Barnes, Barnabe, *The Divils Charter*, 103
Barry, Elizabeth, 4, 61, 64, 65, 66, 67, 71–2, 74, 76, 79, 117–8, 146, 149, 155, 158, 218, 227–9, 235
Behn, Aphra, 41–2, 132; *The Amorous Prince*, 115; *The Dutch Lover*, 72; *The Forced Marriage*, 115; *The Luckey Chance*, 109; *The Revenge*, 88; *The Rover*, 67–8, 78; *The Second Part of the Rover*, 67–8; *The Widow Ranter*, 88; *The Younger Brother*, 117
Belon, Peter, *The Mock Duellist*, 183
Bertie, Peregrine, 5
Betterton, Mary (Saunderson), 2, 67, 155, 161
Betterton, Thomas, x, xi, 2–4, 5, 59, 60, 65–7, 72–4, 76, 80–1, 88, 90, 98, 107–8, 142, 146–7, 155, 156, 158, 209–10, 217, 225–6, 234–5, 238, 261, *The Amorous Widow*, 80, 109, *The Prophetess*, 152
Blackfriars Theatre, 5, 21, 66
Blome, Richard, 8
Blount, Thomas, 26
Bludder, Sir Thomas, 115
Bodley, Sir Thomas, 115
Booth, Barton, 185
Bourne, Reuben, *The Contented Cuckold*, 139
Boutell, Elizabeth, 76, 77, 109, 170, 184–6, 191, 192, 199
Bowen, William, 69, 87, 89, 153, 158, 233
Bowman, John, 69, 149, 153–4, 158, 215, 218, 233
Bowman, Elizabeth, 216, 229
Boyle, Roger, Earl of Orrery, *Guzman*, 32, 47–8

Boys, Jeffrey, 15, 115
Bracegirdle, Anne, 4, 65, 69, 72, 73, 76, 78, 79, 142–3, 149–50, 152–60, 207, 220, 227, 234, 235
Brecht, Bertolt, 20, 55–6
Bridges Street, Theatre Royal, 2, 11, 26, 35, 36–8
Bright, George, 66, 88, 126–7, 153, 158, 246
Brokesby, Francis, 7
Brome, Richard, 159
Brown, Tom, 143, 228–9
Bruce, Thomas, Earl of Ailesbury, 5
Brydges, James, 10
Bullock, William, 88, 89–90
Bulwer, John, 60
Burbage, Richard, 61, 70–1
Butler, Charlotte, 76, 151
Butler, Samuel, 63
Buxton, John, 114

Carlell, Lodowick, *Heraclius*, 124
Carlisle, James, *The Fortune Hunters*, 145
Cartwright, William, (actor), 2, 181
Cartwright, William, (playwright), 45–6
Caryll, John, *Sir Salomon*, 47, 64, 81
Charlton, Mr, 181
Cibber, Colley, 4, 14, 28, 31, 35, 58–9, 65, 72, 79, 90–4, 144–5, 151–2, 160, 218, 226, 233, 260, 263; *Love Makes a Man*, 92; *Love's Last Shift*, 69; *Richard III*, 94; *Woman's Wit*, 73, 75
Cibber, Katherine, 73
Clarendon, Edward Hyde, Lord, 9
Clark, Thomas, 180–1
Cockpit-in-Court Theatre, 21–4, 26
Cockpit Theatre, 24
Collier, Jeremy, 4, 7, 86–7, 95–7, 111, 116, 126–7, 224
Congreve, William, 116, 125–137, 204–243; *Amendments*, 127; *The Double-Dealer*, 81, 97, 126–30, 134, 136, 215–24; *Incognita*, 204; *Judgement of Paris*, 205, *Love for Love*, 66, 80, 112, 128, 129–30, 134–5,

136, 224–33; *The Mourning Bride*, 10, 130, 235, *The Old Batchelour*, 81, 127, 135–6, 139, 155–7, 165, 204–5, 207–15; *Squire Trelooby*, 205; *The Way of the World*, 55, 57, 79, 81, 109, 110, 131, 134, 136–7, 233–43

Conway, Viscount, 115

Corey, Katherine, 2, 142, 150, 161, 189

Cotton, Charles, 270

*Country Gentleman's Vade Mecum, The*, 8, 14–15

Coventry, Sir William, 115

Craig, Edward Gordon, vi, 56, 169

Crowne, John, 75, 267; *Calisto*, 118; *City Politiques*, 112; *The Countrey Wit*, 80; *Darius, King of Persia*, 117–8; *The Destruction of Jerusalem*, 111; *The English Frier*, 88, 227; *The Married Beau*, 81, 226; *Sir Courtly Nice*, 144

Daniel, Samuel, 176

Davenant, Alexander, 4, 144

Davenant, Charles, 2

Davenant, Sir William, 1–2, 13, 26, 66, 82, 116, 131; *Salmacida Spolia*, 36; *The Siege of Rhodes*, 24, 28–9, 32, 36, 42–4, 256–7

Davies, The Very Rev. Rowland, 5

Davies, Thomas, 185

Dekker, Thomas, 8

Dennis, John, 9–10, 15, 67, 70, 170, 182–3; *A Plot and No Plot*, 89; *Liberty Asserted*, 132–3

Dering, Sir Edward, 114

Diderot, Denis, 63

Digby, George, *Elvira*, 46, 110

Dilke, Thomas, *The Lover's Luck*, 226, 256

Dogget, Thomas, 69, 73, 77, 111, 148, 155, 157–8, 160, 218–9

Dorset Garden Theatre, 3, 4, 14, 29, 34, 37, 38–40

Downes, John, 16, 40, 64, 66, 75

Drake, James, *The Sham-Lawyer*, 107

Drummond, William, 115

Drury Lane, Theatre Royal, 3, 4, 14, 16–7, 28, 29–35, 253

Dryden, John, x, 8, 14, 75–7, 110, 121–5, 131–2, 148, 173, 184; *Albion and Albanius*, 45; *All for Love*, 16–7; *Amphitryon*, 147; *Don Sebastian*, 145; *An Evening's Love*, 11, 85–6, 109; *The Indian Emperor*, 36–8, 108; *The Indian Queen*, 37, 255; *King Arthur*, 152; *Marriage A-la-Mode*, 13, 79, 82, 192, 208–9, 213; *Oedipus*, 204; *Of Dramatic Poesy*, 103, 133, 204; *The Rival Ladies*, 33, 84, 254; *Secret Love*, 84–5, 108; *Sir Martin Mar-all*, 85; *The Spanish Friar*, 121, 158; *The Tempest*, 85, 107, 116, 151; *Troilus and Cressida*, 66; *Tyrannic Love*, ix, 45, 109; *The Wild Gallant*, 55, 82, 85, 94, 177, 229

Durfey, Tom, 75, 141; *The Banditti*, 90; *The Commonwealth of Women*, 78; *Don Quixote*, 69, 126; *The Intrigues at Versailles*, 235; *Love for Money*, 60, 107, 151, 160, 226; *Madam Fickle*, 66; *The Marriage-Hater Match'd*, 139, 148–51, 155, 157, 162–3, 215, 227; *The Richmond Heiress*, 80, 139, 155, 157–9, 162–3, 215, 231, 233; *Squire Oldsapp*, 45; *The Virtuous Wife*, 90

Echard, Laurence, 133–4, 268

Edwards, Richard, *Damon and Pithias*, 101–2

Etherege, Sir George, 132; *Love in a Tub*, 80, 83, 85; *The Man of Mode*, 39–40, 50, 80, 126–7, 146–7, 208, 212, 215, 217, 246, 248; *She Would If She Could*, 12, 48–54, 82, 85, 86, 109, 207–8

Fairbank, Henry, 88

Fairbeard, Mr, 173,

Farquhar, George, 72; *The Beaux' Stratagem*, 112; *The Constant Couple*, 68, 80, 87, 90, 91; *A Discourse on Comedy*, 87–8; *The Inconstant*, 91, 95; *The Recruiting Officer*, 88, 98; *Sir Harry Wildair*, 68–9, 91, 95, 109; *The Twin Rivals*, 57, 86–98

*Female Wits, The*, 74

Flecknoe, Richard, 61, 119–20; *The Damoiselles a la Mode*, 74

Fletcher, John, and Francis Beaumont, 70–1, 104, 116, 132; *The Custom of the Country*, 15, 92; *A King and No King*, 123; *The Maid's Tragedy*, 12, 124; *Philaster*, 84; *Two Noble Kinsmen*, 105; *The Wild Goose Chase*, 84

Florio, John, 175

Foote, Samuel, 62

Freeman, John, 154

Freke, William, 7

Fuchs, Georg, 55–6

Furttenbach, 33

Gailhard, Jean, 7

Garrick, David, 62–3

Gildon, Charles, 59, 60, 62, 74, 117, 159

*Godly Queen Hester*, 101

Goodman, Cardell, 66, 67

Gould, Robert, 228

Granville, George, 173, *Heroick Love*, 111; *The She-Gallants*, 226

Griffin, Philip, 66, 181

Gwyn, Nell, ix, 2, 64, 76, 81–6, 91

Haines, Jo, 72, 76, 88, 156, 158, 160, 181, 187; *A Fatal Mistake*, 139

Halifax, Marquess of, 176

Harington, Sir John, 114

Harris, Henry, 2, 3, 12, 47, 108
Harris, Joseph, 72
Hart, Charles, xi, 2, 66, 67, 76, 78, 81–6,
  91, 170, 177–9, 182—6, 187, 191, 192,
  198, 202
Hédelin, François, Abbé d'Aubignac, ix–xi,
  120–1, 133–4, 204–5, 237
Heywood, Thomas, 104
Hidgen, Henry, *The Wary Widow*, 138–40,
  152, 162
Hill, 'Sir' John, 59–60, 62, 63
Hodgson, John, 152, 158, 160
Hook, Mrs, 87
Hooke, Robert, 6
Horace, 104, 119, 174, 191, 218
Horne, John, 114
Howard, Edward, 106, 118, 121, *The
  Change of Crownes*, 45
Howard, James, *All Mistaken*, 83–4,
  *The English Mounsieur*, 82–4
Howard, Sir Robert, 116, *The Committee*,
  89, *The Surprisal*, 84
Hughes, Margaret, 109
Husband, Benjamin, 87

Jevon, Thomas, 4, 80, 109
Johnson, Benjamin, 89
Johnson, Samuel, 63
Jones, Inigo, 21–6, 29
Jonson, Ben, 69, 104, 109, 114–6, 132, 133,
  *The Alchemist*, 164; *Catiline*, 187; *Epicoene*,
  81, 164, 208, *Every Man In His Humour*,
  157, *Every Man Out of His Humour*, 103–4,
  *Volpone*, 92
*Journal from Parnassus, A*, 267
Joyner, William, *The Roman Empress*, 185
Juvenal, 174, 175

Kent, Mrs, 69
Killigrew, Thomas, 1–3, 12, 82, 114;
  *Thomaso*, 67, 83
Killigrew, William, *The Siege of Urbin*, 83
King, Gregory, 12, 17
Knep, Elizabeth, 12, 181–2
Knight, Frances Maria, 69, 73, 180
Knight, Ursula, 180
Kynaston, Edward, 2, 66, 143, 147, 158,
  170, 182, 186, 189, 190, 218–19

Lacy, John, 2, 72; *The Dumb Lady*, 45;
  *The Old Troop*, 12–3, 112
*Ladies' Lamentation for their Adonis, The*, 144,
  152
Langbaine, Gerald, 119
Lee, Nathaniel, 72, 75, 132; *Gloriana*, 184;
  *The Princess of Cleve*, 81, 146–7; *The
  Rival Queens*, 16–7, 67, 80, 88, 184;
  *Theodosius*, 254–5
Legh, Richard, 15

Leigh, Anthony, 4, 76, 80, 112, 150, 153
Leigh, Elinor, 69, 80, 160, 217, 233
Leigh, Elizabeth, 72
Leigh, Michael, 159
Lincoln's Inn Fields Theatre, 2, 4, 5, 11, 13,
  16, 36, 48, 256–7
Locke, John, 6, 116
Lumley, Lord, 115
Luttrell, Narcissus, 126

Magalotti, Conte Lorenzo, 26
Marlowe, Christopher, *Tamburlaine the
  Great*, 120, 264
Marow, Lady, 233, 242
Marshall, Anne (Quin), 2, 65, 67
Marshall, Rebecca, 2, 66, 76, 84, 85, 170,
  182–5, 192, 260
Marston, John, 104, 105
Medbourne, Matthew, 72
Mills, John, 68
Mohun, Michael, 2, 66, 185
Molière, x, 40, 47, 160, 163, 186–7
Montaigne, Michel de, 175–6, 181, 193
Moor, Mrs, 88
Moseley, Humphrey, 105, 114
Mountfort, Susanna (Percival Verbruggen),
  4, 68, 69, 71, 76, 79, 91, 145–6, 152,
  155–6, 159, 161, 207–8, 213, 216–17,
  225, 227, 234, 260
Mountfort, William, 4, 65, 66, 67, 72, 90–1,
  143–6, 149, 150, 152, 153, 155, 156, 207;
  *Greenwich Park*, 140, 144–5

*Nero*, 184
Newton, Isaac, 6, 116, 266
Nokes, James, 2, 58, 63–4, 72, 75, 76, 80,
  90, 158
Norris, Henry, 68, 181, 260

Oldfield, Anne, 4
Oldmixon, John, *The Grove*, 118
Otway, Thomas, 72, 132, 204; *Alcibiades*,
  38–9; *The Atheist*, 64, 204; *Caius Marius*,
  66, 90; *Don Carlos*, 45; *The Souldier's
  Fortune*, 41, *Venice Preserv'd*, 41
Oxinden, Henry, 114

Palladio, 23, 24, 28
Peacham, Henry, 6
Pepys, Samuel, 2, 10–5, 17, 36, 47, 83, 84,
  85, 106, 108, 116–7, 124, 202–3
Percival, Susanna, *see* Mountfort, Susanna
Perin, Anne, 248
Perin, Carey, 66, 248
Perrin, Pierre, *Ariane*, 34
Pinkethman, William, 88
*Piso's Conspiracy*, 183
Pix, Mary, *The Deceiver Deceived*, 80;
  *The Innocent Mistress*, 235

Plautus, 131, 133–4
*Player's Tragedy, The,* 143–4
*Poeta Infamis,* 149
Pope, Alexander, 173
Porter, Thomas, *The Villain,* 45, 79, 255
Powell, George, 4, 60, 65, 66, 68, 72, 90, 140, 152, 153, 156, 158, 160–1, 169, 207–8, 216–17, *Brutus of Alba,* 45, 107; *A Very Good Wife,* 139, 159–60, 162
Preston, Thomas, *Cambises,* 101
Purcell, Henry, 69

Queen's Theatre, Haymarket, 14, 16, 28, 31
Quin, Anne, *see* Marshall, Anne

Ramesey, William, 8
Rapin, 204
Ravenscroft, Edward, *The Citizen Turn'd Gentleman,* 16, 40–1; *The Italian Husband,* 107
Rawlins, *Tom Essence* 45
Rhodes, Richard, *Flora's Vagaries,* 83, 84
Rich, Christopher, 4, 29, 31, 35, 75–6
Rochester, John Wilmot, Earl of, 174, 258
Rogers, Jane, 68–9, 91–2, 93, 95–6, 160
Rowe, Nocholas, 132; *The Biter,* 81
Rutland House, 24, 36, 43, 256–7
Rutter, Margaret, 2

Sackville, Thomas, *Gorboduc,* 102
Sandford, Samuel, 2, 66, 79–80, 94, 158, 227
Savile, Henry, 5
Schouwburg Theatre, 35
Sedley, Sir Charles, 13–4, 116; *The Mulberry Garden,* 12, 37–8, 85
Serlio, 24, 29
Settle, Elkanah, 67, 75; *The Ambitious Slave,* 72; *The Empress of Morocco,* 34, 255; *The Fairy Queen,* 45, 151–2
Shadwell, Thomas, 42, 47, 132, 203; *The Amorous Bigotte,* 151; *Bury Fair,* 58, 145, 147; *Epsom Wells,* 13, 80; *The Lancashire Witches,* 111; *The Libertine,* 81, 89, 204, 210; *Psyche,* 45, 107, 257; *The Squire of Alsatia,* 16, 19–20, 79, 80; *The Sullen Lovers,* 6, 86; *The Virtuoso,* 6, 80, 183; *The Volunteers,* 139, 141, 152–3, 164–5, 209, 215
Shakespeare, William, 44, 70–1, 104, 116, 132; *Hamlet,* 1, 66, 111; *I Henry IV,* 11, 48, 93, 108; *Julius Caesar,* 66; *King Lear,* 93; *The Tempest,* 71; *Twelfth Night,* 190, 201
Shaterall, Robert, 2
Shipman, Thomas, 254
Shirley, James, 159, 245
Slingsby, Lady, 66
Smith, Richard, 116

Smith, William, 3, 66, 67–8, 75, 225
Smock Alley Theatre, 48, 87, 204, 257
Smyth, John, *Win Her and Take Her,* 88
Southerne, Thomas, 205; *The Disappointment,* 204; *The Fatal Marriage,* 71–2; *The Maid's Last Prayer,* 139, 153–6, 160, 215; *Sir Anthony Love,* 71, 263; *The Wives Excuse,* 81, 113, 138–9, 141–8, 151, 154, 155, 156, 165–9, 215
Steele, Sir Richard, *The Conscious Lovers,* 120; *The Funeral,* 89–90, 91, 95
Swan Theatre, 21

Tate, Nahum, 47, 231, *Brutus of Alba,* 45; *Cuckolds Haven,* 72
Taylor, Joseph, 66, 70, 71
Teatro della Pergola, 35
Teatro Olimpico, 23, 24
Teatro S. Carlo, 35
Terence, 93, 116, 129–30, 131, 133–4
Theatre Royal, *see* Bridges Street; Drury Lane
Tonson, Jacob, 125, 126, 131, 132
Torriano, Giovanni, 251–2
Trefusis, Joseph, 66
Trenchfield, Caleb, 8
*Triumphs of Virtue, The,* 91
Trotter, Catharine, *The Revolution in Sweden,* 205
Tuke, Sir Samuel, *The Adventures of Five Hours,* 46, 82, 110, 113, 220

Underhill, Cave, 2, 59, 67, 69, 72, 78, 80, 81, 111, 153, 158, 160, 226, 233

Vanbrugh, Sir John, 28, 31, 132, 205; *The Provok'd Wife,* 81, 235; *The Relapse,* 69, 93, 112–13, 258, 263
Verbruggen, John, 4, 45, 66, 69, 73, 153–4, 160, 216–17, 235
Verbruggen, Susanna, *see* Mountfort, Susanna
Vere Street Theatre, 2
Verney, Edmund, 6
Villiers, Barbara, 172
Villiers, George, Duke of Buckingham, *The Chances,* 84; *The Rehearsal,* 74, 189, 209
Vincent, Samuel, 8–9

Wager, Lewis, *The Repentaunce of Marie Magdalene,* 102–3
Walker, Obadiah, 6–7
Wanley, Rev, Nathaniel, 5
Ward, John, 5
Weaver, Elizabeth, 65
Webb, John, 24–6, 44
Webster, John, 56; *The Duchess of Malfi,* 45, 70, 103, 105, 106–7
Wilks, Robert, 4, 66, 68, 80, 87, 90–2, 95–6

Willet, Deb, 11

Williams, Joseph, 142, 153, 154, 158, 161, 207, 220, 225

Wilson, John, *Belphegor*, 48; *The Cheats*, 64, 113

Wintersell, William, 2, 66

Wood, Anthony à, 251

Wren, Sir Christopher, 3, 6, 26–7, 29–35, 253

Wright, James, 105, 108,

Wright, Thomas, *The Female Vertuoso's*, 138–9, 160–1, 163–4

Wycherley, William, 116; *The Country Wife*, 49, 50, 144, 181, 184, 185, 193–5, 208; *The Gentleman Dancing-Master*, 63–4, 217; *Love in a Wood*, 172, 181, 182–4; *Miscellany Poems*, 174; *The Plain-Dealer*, 57, 79, 116, 170–203, 248